The Three Years

Emil Bock

The Three Years

The Life of Christ between
Baptism and Ascension

Floris Books

Translated by Alfred Heidenreich
Edited by Tony Jacobs-Brown

Originally published in German under the title
Die Drei Jahre by Verlag Urachhaus in 1946

First published in English in 1955
by The Christian Community Press, London
Fifth, revised edition published in 2005 by Floris Books

British Library CIP Data available

ISBN 0-86315-535-9

Produced in Poland
by Polskabook

Contents

Unless otherwise stated all quotations from the New Testament are from the translation by Jon Madsen (Floris Books 1994), which is closest to Emil Bock's own translation into German. Quotations from the Old Testament are from the Revised Standard Version.

Preface

Emil Bock was born on May 19, 1895, in Wuppertal-Barmen, Germany, in a strongly working-class, industrial environment. In October 1914 he was seriously wounded in Flanders and very nearly left for dead. Further active military service being impossible, he was able to begin studies in German language and literature and in theology, at Bonn and Berlin, lasting until 1921; in these he achieved brilliant academic distinction. But in 1916 he met Friedrich Rittelmeyer in Berlin and, in the following year, Rudolf Steiner. These meetings gave a new course to his life. He became convinced that there was no future for traditional Christianity unless the new understanding for spiritual realities to which Rudolf Steiner had opened the way was recognized and developed.

Emil Bock was thus among the group, consisting chiefly of very young men and women, who sought help in 1921 from Rudolf Steiner in order to inaugurate a movement for religious renewal. This event, and Emil Bock's part in it, have been described by Alfred Heidenreich in his book *Growing Point*. When the Christian Community was founded in September, 1922, Emil Bock became as a matter of course one of its leaders. After the death of Friedrich Rittelmeyer in 1938 he followed him in the central leadership.

In June 1941 the work of the Christian Community in Germany was forbidden by the Nazi government, its property confiscated, and many of its leaders imprisoned. Emil Bock was taken to a concentration camp at Welzheim, where his personality exercised a powerful influence. He was released in February 1942 and for the rest of the war maintained secret contacts with groups and personalities concerned with the Community. At Whitsun 1945 the public work of the Christian Community in Germany could be resumed under his leadership, and many new church buildings, with their distinctive forms, soon arose in the midst of the shattered cities. Emil Bock was now able to resume journeys to other countries in which the Christian Community had taken root, and to Palestine and Greece.

Under the Nazi rule, when particularly bitter attacks were made against the influence of the Old Testament, Emil Bock published three books showing how great and positive a significance can be found in the Old Testament for present-day Christianity: *Genesis, Moses and his Age*, and *Kings and Prophets*. These were followed by two books on the beginnings of Christianity: *Caesars and Apostles* and *The Childhood of Jesus*. After an interval of nine years, this book appeared in 1948, as the third in this series. It was followed by *The Apocalypse of St John*, and *Saint Paul*.

In 1950 Emil Bock published, in what he regarded as a provisional form, a new translation of the New Testament on which he had worked for many years, with commentaries and introductions. Many articles by him, often on the Bible or on the religious situation of the present day, appeared in the monthly journal which he edited, *Die Christengemeinschaft*.

He died in Stuttgart on December 6, 1959. Since his death have appeared, among other writings, a collection of biographical studies of *Rudolf Steiner*, and, in 1968, Emil Bock's *Letters*, edited by his daughter; these give a wonderful picture of the width of his human interests and his compassionate understanding.

In a period of human history during which to many 'soul' and 'spirit' have become meaningless words, and the needs of the human soul and spirit are often ruthlessly denied in practice, to encounter Emil Bock was to see the power of a soul devoted to spiritual realities demonstrated in vigorous and unfaltering physical action. When he spoke of the past, and particularly of Christian history, it was not just as an object of study; the listener was transported into something that is eternally living. And when he spoke of the future, it was not only in hope; Emil Bock knew that he would work for it, in the service of Christ, beyond this earthly death.

Adam Bittleston
1955

Foreword

Seven fateful years have passed since the last of the five books on the Old Testament and early Christianity* was published in 1939. And the fate we had to suffer also affected those works. In June 1941, the Christian Community in Germany was banned amid violent intervention. At the time all volumes of the series which could be found were taken away, together with the rest of our publications, and pulped together with the stocks held by the publisher. The books and papers which were removed from my apartment by the wagon load included the manuscript of several chapters of the next volume which should have appeared in late 1941. When I was released from concentration camp, I was able — in 1943 — to rewrite the lost sections and complete the missing parts. Nevertheless, since there was little time for such activities alongside the other work I had to do, I had to fall back in terms of the form of the book more than I would otherwise have done on a series of lectures which I delivered in the winter of 1939/40.

When the Christian Community was able to resume its work at Whitsun 1945, more than a year passed before it became possible to think about publishing new books again. Neither do the many tasks which currently have to be managed allow, in the foreseeable future, for the transformation of the sketchy material, jotted down during the period when the Christian Community was banned, into a more considered form which takes more recent developments into account. As a consequence, I am now faced with the question whether, at a time in which events are moving at such speed and the world is changing at such a fast pace, I can justify publishing work which was written some years ago. If I were able to start again today with this book, I would, of course, give greater weight to and indicate more openly the apocalyptic tension underlying current human destiny. If I nevertheless

---

* Three volumes on the Old Testament (1934–36: *Genesis; Moses; Kings and Prophets*), two volumes on early Christianity (1937 and 1939: *Caesars and Apostles; The Childhood of Jesus*).

respond to the urgent demand for the replacement of the literature on the gospels which was destroyed, then this can only be done in that I ask the reader to take into account the period when the text was created and its history — just as I must take it into account if the opportunity of reprinting the previous volumes should arise in the future.

But even in the current version of this book the reader will notice a certain resonance reflecting the destiny of our time. Just as in the earlier volumes — the books on the Old Testament appeared in the years from 1934 to 1936 — no word in this book is written without an awareness that the structuring and soul-filling ideals and impulses of a modern understanding of Christ must be set against the demonic feverishness and satanic superficiality of a civilization which has turned to chaos and is writhing in its death throes. In this sense my introduction relating to the history of ideas, 'Apollonius of Tyana and Jesus of Nazareth,' which I presented as a lecture in numerous cities in 1939 and 1940, was also experienced as a clear comment on the present time.

As far as the form is concerned, the present volume differs from the five previous ones to the extent that the continuous historical presentation has been replaced by individual reflections. The decision to return to the form used in the reflections on the gospels, as published in two series in 1925–27, is due both to the nature of the subject and to its basis in the lecture form mentioned earlier. Telling the 'Life of Christ' is only possible, strictly speaking, up to the events surrounding the baptism in Jordan (as I attempted to do in my last book, *The Childhood of Jesus*) because that is the period when we are dealing with a human biography. It is not altogether impossible to recount the three years between the baptism in Jordan and Golgotha in a similar way, but it assumes such ultimate maturity with regard to perception and formal matters that it all too easily becomes presumptuous to approach such a task. To penetrate to the historical and biographical facts of these three brief years, as unobtrusive and simple as they may have been, is the greatest and most difficult task in the struggle for a true understanding of the gospels and historical developments. Theologians of recent centuries did not perceive it like that. On the contrary, they believed that the external historical course of events was obvious and could, without further ado, form the starting point for everything else. As a consequence, numerous *Lives of Christ* were written. In reality, the first element to which we gain access in the gospels with regard to this divine and human biography is merely the imaginative layer, that is, a sequence of soul images which mainly reflect events within the soul and in the supersensory sphere. Hence I also began my reflections on the gospels by elaborating the imaginative element including the secret of its composition. And it was only through years of continuous further study that I was able gradually to penetrate the imaginative veil of images to reach the events which took place on the external physical plane at the time. The reflective form of this book entails a more expansive style, whereas a linear historical description would be significantly briefer and more concentrated. It does, however, allow us to approach the subject from many different angles. There really needs to be a far greater number of reflections; and so permit me to say that I made a specific selection from a significantly greater number of reflections simply to prevent the book from expanding too much.

Like the previous five volumes, the present book is also the fruit of the endeavour to apply the spiritual method of observation and wealth of knowledge newly disclosed by Rudolf Steiner to the study of the gospels and a comprehensive understanding of Christ. In 1935, just as the second volume on the Old Testament was in preparation, the Anthroposophical Society was banned in Germany. Nevertheless, I made reference to Rudolf Steiner and anthroposophy in the subsequent volumes where this was factually necessary. Now it is possible to make such references again in all transparency and in full. May this book contribute to the flowering of a new creative spirituality from the ruins of Europe, a spirituality which alone can provide support through future devastation and establish a new world.

Emil Bock
June 1946

CHAPTER ONE

Apollonius of Tyana and Jesus of Nazareth

The world of the gospels, like all that is Christ's, is quiet and gentle, like a grain of seed fallen into the earth. Without this quiet realm of the seed the noisy, power-hungry world would have no bread. In the catacombs, the first Christians felt themselves to be like grains of corn sown in stillness in comparison with the proud, noisy world of the Caesars which flaunted itself above those quiet underground corridors. They lived in the sure belief that the whole world would one day be changed through the power of this hidden seed.

It cannot be emphasized too much how utterly inconspicuous the events described in the gospels were in comparison with everything that stood in high repute at that time. In the history of humanity there is no greater contrast than that between Christ and Caesar. He who was really God-become-man walked the earth unseen and unnoticed. All the glitter of fame and power went to those who ruled the world from the thrones of the Caesars, and were worshipped almost as gods, when in reality they hardly succeeded in being human.

But there is another historical contrast which is still more illuminating than that of Christ and the Caesars. There lived at the time of Jesus of Nazareth someone who must be reckoned as one of the last of the great initiates of the ancient world, and who as a religious-prophetic genius so took everyone's breath away that his name — Apollonius of Tyana — was on everyone's lips. Compared with the world fame of this man, Jesus of Nazareth simply did not enter into the public consciousness of his time. No one knew him; most of those who could have known him missed the opportunity. On the other hand, there was hardly anyone who had not heard of Apollonius of Tyana. Today this is difficult to imagine. Nowadays everyone speaks of Jesus of

Nazareth without remembering how quietly his life went by, whereas the great initiate of that time is completely forgotten. Historians of our time cannot conceive that there could ever have been a man so head and shoulders above the usual stature of humanity, and therefore speak of him as though he were legendary.

Yet in Goethe's time he was not so forgotten as he is now; the historians could not just pass over him as they have since the middle of last century. Indeed, among the leading men of that day there is hardly one who was not drawn to make some effort to understand his being. Voltaire compared Apollonius with Jesus; perhaps because of this, Frederick the Great was encouraged to make a translation of the biography of Apollonius by Philostratus. He dedicated this work to Pope Clement XIV in 1774. Referring to the recent dissolution of the Jesuit order by the Pope, he called upon him to clear up the riddle of Apollonius and thereby to accomplish another great spiritual deed. Wieland tried, in his *Agathodaemon*, to rehabilitate Apollonius' reputation. He could do this, however, only by explaining away his miracles in terms of contemporary rationalism. Even Napoleon, when he was a lieutenant of Artillery, wrote an essay, now unfortunately lost, on Christ and Apollonius.

The miracles of Apollonius and the miracles in the gospels

It was the many astounding miracles attributed to Apollonius which, until a hundred years ago, aroused so much interest and so many puzzling questions among all who did not actually discredit his existence. If we are to believe the old accounts, news of these miracles spread Apollonius' fame, from his youth on, like wildfire through all civilized lands. Wherever he went, sick people came to him. All knew that he had great healing powers. He cured many who had baffled all medical skill. Innumerable blind, lame, those possessed of evil spirits and sick with plague, were loosed from their infirmities.

There are many similarities between the gospels and the early biographies of Apollonius. (The only complete *Life* preserved is by the Athenian Philostratus, of the third century.) For instance, there is a remarkable parallel story to that of the son of the widow at Nain. It was in the time of Nero, in Rome. Apollonius was in danger from the persecution of philosophers which broke out at the same time as the persecution of Christians. So he left the city. Just as he passed out of the gates, he was met by a funeral procession.

> A maiden had died on her wedding day. There seemed no doubt that she was dead. The bridegroom, lamenting, came behind the bier, and the whole of Rome mourned with him, for the girl came of a distinguished family. As Apollonius met the funeral procession he said, 'Set down the bier. I will dry your tears.' When he asked her name, they all thought he was going to deliver the usual funeral oration. However, he touched the corpse, spoke some incomprehensible words to her, and called her back to life. She lifted up her voice and spoke, and returned home to her father's house. (4. 45.)

The stories of the birth of Apollonius are similar to those in the gospels. As the mother neared the time of her delivery, an angel surrounded by a bright light appeared to her. She was afraid, and said, 'Who are you?' At first she received no answer. Then she asked who it would be to whom she should give birth, to which the angel answered, 'To me.' 'Who are you then?' the mother asked, and received the answer, 'I am Proteus, the Egyptian God.' Thus she beheld the being who had the power to change his form continually and who could slip into any shape. Certainly this atmosphere is utterly different from that of the opening of the Gospel of Luke, but there is no mistaking similarities with the appearance of the Archangel Gabriel to Mary in Nazareth.

The mother of Apollonius was near her time when she had a dream which bade her walk in the meadows and pick flowers; while her maids scattered over the meadow and occupied themselves with picking flowers, she lay down on the grass and fell asleep. Then swans came flying from every direction, surrounded her as she slept, and sang to her. A light breeze swept over the meadow. She awoke and bore her son. In the same instant a mighty flash of lightning struck down from heaven upon her and then returned at once into the sky before the eyes of the astonished beholders. From that moment, it is said, Apollonius was called a son of God.

Similar analogies can be drawn throughout the whole life-story of Apollonius. In his youth there is a scene set in the temple at Tarsus, where he astonishes the teachers with his wisdom, corresponding exactly to the story of the twelve-year-old Jesus in the Temple. When we later look at the travels of the man, we are reminded at once of those of Jesus. Apollonius, too, is surrounded by a close group of disciples, numbering, however, not twelve, but seven.

After the death of Apollonius, the similarities with the gospels continue. There are scenes which form a parallel to the Easter stories. For example, the followers of the dead master sit together, lost in talk on eternal life. They feel sure of life after death, through the philosophical art of thinking which they have learnt from their teacher. One guest, however, a young man who has come into their circle from a neighbouring temple city, is filled with doubts. Apollonius' disciples try in vain to pass on to him some of their absolute conviction. A few days later they are together again and talk on the same subject. While the doubting youth sleeps, the others draw geometrical figures on the ground. Suddenly he wakes and, springing up, shouts, 'I believe you.' The others ask in astonishment what has excited him so greatly and he replies, 'Do you not see Apollonius, who stands among us? Do you not hear the wonderful verses he speaks?' Now it is the turn of the others to doubt, until their guest writes out verses concerning the immortality of the soul which Apollonius, no more in the land of the living, dictates to him. In spite of the utterly different atmosphere, the similarity to the gospel narratives is unmistakable.

The comparison of Apollonius with Jesus roused violent discussions among the early Christians, especially in the days of the Church Fathers. Even Origen, without being too much disturbed by the problem, spoke of the great magician Apollonius, whom he knew of through a writing by Moeragenes, now lost. In his judgment of these matters he hardly differed from heathen writers like Apuleius who, when they were connected with the mysteries, referred to initiates and magicians as a matter of course. Two hundred years later, the Church Fathers Jerome and Augustine could not deny the miracles of Apollonius, but said they came from demonic forces, whereas the miracles of Jesus were performed through the power of God. They condemned Apollonius as a magician possessed by the devil. Eusebius, the writer of Church history at the time of Constantine the Great, took the same attitude.

Hierocles, in writing against Christianity, gives us an interesting glimpse of the conflicts between Christian theology and heathen philosophy. He was in about AD 300 the Roman Governor of a province in

Asia Minor. Under Diocletian he took an active and fanatical part in the persecution of Christians. His main theme is a comparison between Apollonius and Jesus of Nazareth. He writes: 'The Christians make a great thing out of their Jesus, claiming that he has given sight to a few blind people, and has healed a few who were sick.' In a polished, detached style he suggests that the few miracles of Jesus were of no importance compared with the manifold instances of extraordinary healings, raisings of the dead, and other miracles performed by Apollonius. Above all, Hierocles claims particular credit for the fact that non-Christians take 'a reasonable attitude towards outstanding men.' And he says, after he has recounted the deeds of Apollonius: 'Why do I mention these? Only to compare our exact, balanced opinion with the fancifulness of the Christians. For we do not imagine that such a miracle-worker is a god, but only one moved by the gods; while the Christians declare Jesus, because of his few unimportant miracles, to be a god.' Finally, he considers that the historical accounts of Apollonius can be shown to be incomparably better substantiated than those of Jesus of Nazareth. Hierocles' dignified superiority had probably a much greater influence at that time than the often angry diatribes of the Church Fathers.

From the Christian point of view, it showed a tragic misunderstanding of the mission of Christ to compare Jesus and Apollonius at all as miracle-workers. It did not lie in the intention or will of Christ to do miracles. On the contrary, the way he came as a man among men was at the opposite pole from any use of supernatural powers. That the healings of Jesus have been regarded as 'miracles' shows that the quite natural acceptance by the ancient world of healing through psychic powers has been forgotten. Apollonius, on the other hand, must really be considered a great worker of miracles. He travelled through the world as a self-avowed magician, proving his connection with supernatural powers by deeds which could not be attributed merely to human forces. If one could properly put the question which of the two, Jesus or Apollonius, did the most miracles, then without doubt the heathen philosopher is right — Apollonius would win the day. That Christ, in spite of the inwardness and stillness of his life, rises far above the last great initiate of the ancient world, does not rest on the outward influence which he had in his own time. When this is realized, there is no need to belittle the greatness of Apollonius in order to magnify the being of Jesus. A true 'Life of Jesus' in relation to his time will indeed be possible only when the injustice of recent historians has been made good, and the personality of Apollonius in all its historical importance is again brought to light.

Space and time in the life of Apollonius

Both in space and in time, the life of Apollonius of Tyana is more than 'life-size.' The first thing which becomes clear is the enormous geographical radius over which it spread. Apollonius was born at about the same time as Jesus of Nazareth in Tyana in the uplands of Asia Minor. Tyana lay as far north of the Cilician pass through the snow-capped Taurus mountains as Tarsus, the birthplace of Paul, lay south of it on the sea-shore. When he was only fourteen years old, Apollonius played an important role in the temples and mystery centres of Tarsus, where he caused a sensation among the Greek scholars. At that time the boy Paul, who may have been five or six years younger than Apollonius, was going to school in Tarsus. But there can be no certainty that their ways crossed, for Paul was instructed in less conspicuous places of learning.

Whatever Tarsus had to give, the young Apollonius soon learnt; he quickly outgrew his teachers. When he could learn no more from them, he went to other sources of wisdom. So we meet him in Aegea, a famous temple of the healing god, Aesculapius, on the shores of the Mediterranean, not far from Tarsus. Here he took part in the rites of initiation, and as a young priest of Aesculapius began to have enormous success in the art of medicine. His fame as teacher and healer was soon widespread. Great crowds of the sick flocked to Aegea for healing, solely because Apollonius was working there.

Then something happened which constrained Apollonius to check his impetuous climb to fame. His father died. The great riches which he inherited he gave away, and placed himself forthwith under the severe ascetic rule of the Pythagoreans. By his own choice he became a disciple of Pythagoras, and undertook a vow of silence for four years. At the same time he began his wanderings through the lands, following Pythagoras' example. A fascinating chapter in the life of Apollonius began. Twenty years old, he wandered in silence through the countries and towns of Asia Minor, where Paul the Apostle, as the ambassador of Christ, was to journey later on. His silence made him all the more a centre of interest wherever he appeared. People crowded to him for healing or for help. Silently he healed the sick by the laying on of hands. Without speaking, he effectively attacked the abuses he encountered in the cities. For instance, in one town where the inhabitants were suffering from hunger through the greed of profiteers he wrote a word or two on a tablet and put it up in the market place. The result was that corn flowed into the market and the town came to life again. The silent prophet, who was still a youth, wielded a unique authority and could with a gesture influence the social life of the people wherever he went.

When the time of his vow of silence was over, he travelled more widely still. First turning eastwards to the sources of human culture, he came through ancient Assyria and Babylon to India. Wherever he went, the temples and mystery centres were readily opened to him. The priests of all the gods recognized in him, notwithstanding his youth, a superior initiate. They allowed him to examine the arrangements of the temples and to put through any reforms he thought necessary. Everywhere men bowed before his knowledge and wisdom. In the words of Philostratus, 'When he arrived in a town, he invited the priests of the temple to meet him, spoke with them as a philosopher about the gods, and instructed them if they had departed from the ancient traditions.' As though it was his aim to gather together the remains of the wisdom and power which survived in the ancient holy places, he moved from country to country.

A conversation with the Assyrian, Damis, who in Nineveh offered his services as a guide through the empires of the East, throws a light on the sovereign faculties with which Apollonius travelled through foreign countries. Damis admired and honoured him and would have liked to spend the rest of his life in his company; and he told Apollonius, in order to win his favour, that he knew all the languages of the peoples along his route. Apollonius admitted him into the circle of his disciples, but indicated that he would not need an interpreter. 'I also, my friend, know the languages of all peoples, though I have never learnt them.' Damis stared at him with wondering admiration. 'Do not marvel that I understand all the languages of all men, for I understand all their silence, too.' (1.19.) To a modern mind this answer may seem meaningless. It can be understood only if one knows something of what an advanced clairvoyant consciousness could achieve, and will achieve again in the future. Apollonius was claiming to be able to read the thoughts in the souls of men before they were put into words. Only in this way, when he heard people speak, could he have penetrated through the outer sounds to the original common language of humanity, which underlies all the diverse languages of the world.

Apollonius came finally to India. There, on the 'Mountain of Wisdom,' lived the initiated Brahmin leaders. Later he described in soul-pictures the impression he gained of those who lived in the strictly guarded world of wisdom, high in the foothills of the Himalayas. 'I saw the Indian Brahmins, as they lived on earth and yet not on the earth, in the fortress and yet unfortified, without possessions and yet possessing all.' He related how he 'had seen them travelling along in the air, six feet above the earth, not so as to perform a miracle — for these men scorn the shows of fame — but so that they may please the godhead more by moving above the earth with the sun god.'

The Indian sages, headed by Jarchas, their kingly ruler, greeted Apollonius with lofty self-assurance, throwing open all their doors. 'Others ask strangers whence they come and why. The first sign of our wisdom is this — that you are not unknown to us.' Even Apollonius had reason to be astonished when the Brahmins, before he had spoken about it, told him his whole life-history up to the present, and his ancestry on both sides. When Jarchas encouraged him to put forward his requests and questions, saying, 'Now ask what you will; you are among men who know all,' Apollonius asked what the Brahmins thought of the central tenet of the Greek mysteries, that self-knowledge is the key to all world-knowledge. And he became convinced that the Greek wisdom in which he had been brought up was embraced in the Brahmin wisdom. Jarchas answered him, 'Just because we know ourselves, we know all. For none of us gains wisdom without first gaining self-knowledge.'

The story goes on to tell of Apollonius and Jarchas deep in repeated conversations, in which they disclosed to each other the treasures of their wisdom. So they came to speak of their earlier earth lives. Another time they discussed the elements of the earth. Jarchas taught Apollonius that there are not four elements, but five. Apollonius asked, 'What would the fifth be, apart from water, air, earth and fire?' 'The ether,' answered Jarchas, 'out of which the gods are born, for everything which breathes the air is mortal, but that which is of the ether is immortal and godlike.' So the great Greek sage and initiate found himself face to face with a greater, from whom he could learn.

After staying for several months on the 'mountain of the gods' with the Brahmins, Apollonius returned. He was now to make his real entry into the European world. He went first to Cyprus, where Paul came during this same period at the start of his missionary journeys. Apollonius went on to Ephesus, perhaps not long after Paul had stayed there. He debated in Athens with the same philosophers to whom Paul addressed his famous Areopagus speech. While in Athens, he was initiated into the Eleusinian mysteries. His route took him also to other centres of Greek life: Olympia, Sparta and Crete. Everywhere his path was marked by miracles. When he first came to Ephesus, he learnt that the town was threatened with a plague, and he advised the inhabitants how to avert the danger. They threw his good advice to the winds — and had to call him back to help them when they were attacked by the plague. At once, he returned from Smyrna to Ephesus, gathered the youth of the town in the same theatre where the gold-smith, Demetrius, had raised such an adverse tumult against Paul, and through a magic deed put a stop to the plague. He made the crowd stone a mysterious figure, which first they took for an old beggar, but later recognized as the evil spirit of the plague. Under the stones, the story relates, was found the body of a huge mad dog.

Presently Apollonius came to Rome, then the centre of Europe. On the throne of the Caesars sat Nero. Apollonius had already reached the age of sixty. It was then twenty years since one, unnoticed by the world, had been nailed to a cross in Palestine. There is no indication that Apollonius was aware of what had happened there. Even for him, whose inner sight could penetrate so far, this event was too remote and unimportant to make itself apparent. Here was a mystery to which his wisdom did not reach.

Apollonius almost succumbed to the persecution of philosophers, instigated by Nero after the burning of Rome, which caused the great-est sufferings and losses to the Christians. Paul was beheaded, and Peter crucified. Yet there is no hint of this in the biography of Apollonius. Even if Apollonius himself saw the importance of the fate of the martyrs, it obviously made no impression on people generally, while the destiny of Apollonius was played out on the open stage of public life.

The traveller who had once reached the furthest bounds of the East now turned westwards to Spain, where Paul is supposed to have gone during the last two years of his life. He came to the Pillars of Hercules, where the narrow seas between Africa and the rocks of Gibraltar were held to be the western frontier of the world. Then he turned southward, for he wished to make acquaintance with the non-European wisdom which, after that of the Brahmins, was considered to be the most advanced. He passed through Egypt and pressed southwards till he came to the sources of the Nile in the region where Ethiopia now is. There, he knew, dwelt a group of initiates similar to those of the community of Brahmins in the Himalayas. In the remote seclusion of the Ethiopian highlands he sought and found the Gymnosophists — naked ascetics, who through a certain nearness to the secret powers of nature cultivated their supersensory wisdom. They, too, accepted him into their inner circle and gave him access to their secrets and their rituals. But Apollonius was disappointed. The wisdom of the Gymnosophists was far behind that of the Brahmins. He soon recognized the decadence into which these last representatives of the Egypto-African school of initiation had fallen.

On his return from these great journeys Apollonius came to Rome for the second time. In the meantime he had reached the age of eighty. In many ways he had become another person since the day when, after his long Pythagorean silence, he took his path to the East. He had absorbed into himself the wisdom that can be acquired from the varied climates and continents of the earth.

He had no more need to travel, but set himself to put a spoke in the wheel of world history. His endeavour was to free humanity from the demonic power of the Caesars. And now, as thirty years before with Nero, the Emperor Domitian lay in wait to entrap him, recognizing him as an opponent and wishing to put him out of the way. But through his magic powers, Apollonius knew how to evade the grasp of his enemy. We meet him again in Ephesus, where he is quietly teaching, surrounded by his disciples. He lives to see and welcome Nerva on the throne of the Caesars. At the age of ninety-seven his rich life comes to an end. Though nearly a hundred years old, to the last he keeps the freshness of youth. No one notices his great age.

The all-embracing geographical span of Apollonius' life is aston-ishing. He crossed all the continents that were then known. In the whole of that world there were no mystery centres whose wisdom he failed to gather into his soul, and on every one of them he left his mark. By contrast, the geographical span of Jesus' life was inconspicuous. To invent journeys for him through the interior of Asia, all the way to India, is mere idle fancy. Within the narrowest compass (from the Dead Sea to the Lake of Gennesaret it is no more than sixty-five miles) the destiny of a man, in which was hidden the destiny of the gods, worked itself quietly out.

If we are to speak of geographical range in connection with early Christianity, it would be more fruitful to compare the life of Paul with that of Apollonius. In the circle of those around the Mystery of Golgotha, Paul was the only one who could be called a traveller. But the ground covered by Apollonius was so much greater; indeed in his wanderings Apollonius surpassed even Pythagoras who, five hundred years earlier, had travelled over the whole world, and whom Apollonius took as his teacher and example. (Among the lost books of Apollonius is a biography of Pythagoras.) In fact, there was no one in the ancient world who surpassed Apollonius in his travels. Nevertheless, the life spent in the quiet confines of Palestine is greater than the life of Apollonius. The great initiate was able to gather together all the wisdom which could come to man through experience of the most varied continents and climates of the earth. But in the other was embodied the spiritual power which came from macrocosmic realms of the universe, far outside the earth, and especially from the sphere of the sun.

In the length of his life, too, Apollonius surpassed the usual measure of man. It was a very special grace of destiny which allowed him, with the peerless endowments which he owed to his initiation, to reach almost his hundredth year. What an opportunity was given him to round off a rich life-work! His more than patriarchal age enabled him to span a whole epoch of history. As a contemporary of Augustus, Tiberius, Caligula, Nero, Vespasian and Domitian, he experienced the whole first stage of the rule of the Caesars. On the other hand, Jesus of Nazareth's life, seen from a human point of view, was already fin-ished just when his youth had ripened into manhood. We must count him, with John the Baptist, as one of those who come early to maturity. John reached thirty-one, Jesus thirty-three years of age. In contrast to Apollonius's fiery, personal wisdom, still youthful in old age, stands the mysterious light of another world which illuminates Jesus — a light we recognize among others who die in early maturity. But the mystery of the short life of Jesus is infinitely greater. In the bare three years between the baptism and Golgotha, the whole of eternity breaks in on the transcience of human evolution. Apollonius, as one of the last of the old initiates, could not, through labours spanning a whole century, save the course of temporal events from sinking even more deeply into futility. The swift outpouring of the divine sun-power in the soul of Jesus of Nazareth was able to arrest and heal this decay.

Among the closest disciples of Christ, however, there was one who could compare with Apollonius in length of life. The evangelist John lived nearly to a hundred. He was ninety-nine when he died in AD 100, as the ancient presbyter of Ephesus. At the last, with the congregation around him, he had only to say, 'Little children, love one another,' and from his words and his being there went forth such warmth and power that all those who were present felt changed in the depth of their souls.

This juxtaposition of John and Apollonius leads to a most interesting historical question. They are fundamentally different (although the polarity between Jesus and Apollonius is even more comprehensive), yet the two old men completed the last stages of their long lives in Ephesus, and, since they died within two or three years of each other, their paths must have crossed. Did they know of each other's existence? What did they think of each other? Did they even perhaps meet face to face? We shall see that by pursuing these questions we shall touch on the most enthralling connections in the destinies of the age.

Apollonius and politics

Apollonius of Tyana was conscious that he drew from sources beyond the visible world. Yet the wisdom which he possessed and which he extended through his many journeys was tied to the earth. Both its content and its colouring were largely conditioned through the nature and the psychological atmosphere of the different parts of the earth which he visited. It was therefore natural that he wished to have an influence on world affairs. Hence it becomes understandable that Apollonius was not content to sow a seed for the future. He was more concerned with having an influence on the immediate present and, though he always remained somewhat in the background, he aimed at a controlling influence on his contemporary civilization in the grand style. Thus he was not only successful as few others were, but he worked for his success with extraordinary astuteness and energy.

The profound difference between him and his contemporary in Palestine, who remained completely apart from the great world, becomes apparent if we observe the part which Apollonius played in the great political events of his time. Although historians of his day and of later periods have not seen it clearly, Apollonius achieved in the sphere of politics even greater miracles than he achieved as a healer. It is only because he managed his political influence with great wisdom that his activities are not so easy to trace. In discovering Apollonius at work with consistency and boldness within the political conditions of his time, we gain a rare glimpse behind the scenes of history in the second half of the first Christian century.

When Apollonius came to Rome for the first time, the life of the capital was completely ruled by the madness of Nero. The Emperor's right hand was Tigellinus, the head of the Roman police — that monster of cruelty who could never adequately satisfy his desire to drown in blood all who had spiritual interests. It was Tigellinus who, at the slightest hint of his lord, threw into prison the members of the schools of philosophy, or the Christians who refused to conform to the worship of Caesar. From prison it was only a short way to the circus and the lions.

At the court of Nero Apollonius had a friend who held a high office and who was secretly his disciple. His name was Telesinus. Telesinus smoothed the path for him when Apollonius endeavoured to protect the philosophical ideals of moderation, humanity and wisdom against arbitrary oppression. He succeeded in working with effect in the temples and schools of philosophy in Rome. Through acts of healing and prophecies he eventually gained access to Tigellinus himself. It was inevitable that Tigellinus should ask him what he thought about Nero. Apollonius had the courage to criticize with complete frankness the

madness of the Caesar and to control by his superior power the angry
Tigellinus, although he realized what extreme risk he was running.
Perhaps this was the only occasion on which anyone dared to face the
bloodthirsty henchman of Nero. But Apollonius recognized that the
time was not yet ripe for direct political action, and he evaded his enemies by going to Spain.

In Spain, he pulls his strings in an indirect manner. He mixes with
the Roman legions and uses every opportunity to make propaganda
against Nero's megalomania. He knows many stories and anecdotes
which he needs only to tell in order to ridicule the antics of Nero. His
aim is clear. He thinks that the army should get rid of the monster
under whose oppression humanity is suffering. In actual fact, after
Nero had been driven to suicide, the legions proclaimed successively
the three soldier emperors, Galba, Otto and Vitellius. These three war-
lords were of course unable to replace the madness of Nero by the
humane spirit for which Apollonius was working. For this reason their
time was short. But the firm hold of the Ceasarean power was so
shaken that it might have been possible to plant a new seed into the
troubled field of international politics. It is at least a legitimate question whether the change was not brought about through the co-
operation of Apollonius who, under Nero, openly sponsored a
rebellion by the army.

During the interlude of the three military emperors a general
comes gradually to the fore who looks like being able to take into his
own hands the imperial power and wield it in a more humane fashion.
This is Vespasian. But he hesitates, and appears to avoid taking the
decisive step. Now a very interesting scene takes place. Vespasian and
his son Titus are in command of the Roman legions which besiege
Jerusalem in the Jewish war. It is AD 69. The heroism of the defenders
has brought the Roman onslaught to a stop, and Vespasian uses his
time for other purposes. He summons Apollonius into his camp, and
the two engage in political conversation. Apollonius encourages the
commander to seize the imperial power. He tries to persuade him to
let himself be proclaimed Caesar.

Then another dramatic scene follows. While the legions under
Titus continue the siege, Vespasian goes to Alexandria, and Apollonius
accompanies him. As if by chance, an enormous multitude of people
gathers at the theatre to honour the general. Vespasian, without fully

realizing what is happening, is placed on a throne-like seat which has been prepared for him. It is obvious that an invisible stage-manager is at work. Then an event occurs which reduces everybody to astonished silence. A group of sick people is brought in. They have sought healing in the temple of Serapis, but the priests have told them to go to Vespasian and ask him to put his hands on them. Vespasian is a cynic, and too much inclined to a materialistic outlook to believe in divine healing. However, in the end he accedes to the request and, behold, before the eyes of the spellbound multitude the sick are healed. Tremendous enthusiasm takes hold of the assembly, and Vespasian is proclaimed Emperor.

A whole series of Roman writers has described this scene. It is recorded by Dio Cassius, Suetonius and Tacitus, although the presence of Apollonius is not mentioned. Obviously, even at the time it was not quite clear who managed the scene from the background, and who sent the sick people from the temple to Vespasian. But it is more than likely that it was not only a supposition, but the true solution of the riddle when Philostratus says that it was Apollonius who organized everything. It was also he who, through his own healing powers, brought about the miracle of Vespasian. He had no hesitation in using such theatrical means if a decisive influence on the supreme leadership of the Roman Empire was at stake. He had faith in Vespasian, and hoped that he would be strong enough to unite power with humaneness. At that time Vespasian must in fact have been open to the influence of Apollonius, for he took great pains to secure him as a permanent councillor. But Apollonius refused. In his place, Josephus, who as we know from his *History of the Jewish War* regarded Vespasian as the promised Messiah, became court philosopher. Perhaps Apollonius foresaw what would happen later: Vespasian disappointed his hopes, and went the way of Nero. Apollonius challenged him with frankness and energy, particularly on account of his cruel oppression of Greece. In a letter he wrote to him, 'Thou fanciest thyself to be greater than Xerxes, and yet thou art less than Nero.'

Titus, Vespasian's son, who became co-regent, was also full of admiration for Apollonius, and tried to win him as companion and adviser. For a time, Apollonius was willing to give him advice, but from a distance. Later he gave him one of his disciples, Demetrius, as councillor. It may well be that he realized that Titus too would not fulfil expectations and would be incapable of philosophic government. For even he was not entirely free from the Ceasarean mania. Vespasian and Titus have left a vast monument of their megalomania in the Coliseum, the biggest of all the blood-soaked circuses of Imperial Rome, which they built in the place of an artificial lake in one of Nero's parks. Having destroyed the Temple in Jerusalem, they built the Coliseum as a kind of substitute.

Domitian, who followed Vespasian and Titus on the imperial throne, relapsed completely into Caesar-madness. Now Apollonius, who was already eighty years old, felt a definite call to oppose the tyranny more openly. The period of his life which now begins is a drama in itself. Philostratus, who wrote the biography of Apollonius in the time of Origen, begins his report of this period with a sentence which reads like a motto: 'Despotic governments are the test of philosophers,' and he indicates it as the aim of his report to show 'how the Tyrant did not conquer the Philosopher, but the Philosopher the Tyrant' (7.1). To describe in general the attitude of Apollonius, Philostratus says: 'His behaviour under the government of Nero was only a prelude. He did not challenge him in person, he only encouraged the avenger, frightened Tigellinus, and so undermined the tyranny ... Under Domitian, he appealed with success in the Senate to masculine virtue and resolve against the tyrants, so uniting the intelligentsia; he visited the people and taught the teachers that tyranny is not everlasting, but mortal through the fear which it creates' (7.4).

Then Apollonius dropped all restraint. Wherever he went he made speeches calling for open opposition. Perhaps it was due to him that a conspiracy was formed in Rome with the aim to remove Domitian and to replace him by Nerva, who was already of advanced age and a philosopher in outlook. The conspiracy was discovered and Nerva exiled to an island. Apollonius was not afraid to speak up for him, and to visit him in his exile. He could not have shown more openly his share in the schemes directed against Domitian. He began now to include prophecies of the end of Domitian in the public speeches which he made wherever he went.

Thus his activities could not be hidden, and a member of the Stoics, Euphrates, betrayed him to Caesar. Euphrates was the Judas in the life of Apollonius, who was now summoned to Rome by Domitian.

Apollonius' friends, convinced that this meant his destruction, tried to hold him back, but Apollonius went on his way. To his friends he said that he was going on a secret mission.

One can perhaps see the hand of destiny in the fact that Apollonius reached Rome by the same route by which, twenty years earlier, the apostle Paul had been carried as a prisoner. Like Paul, he interrupted the journey at Syracuse. Like Paul, he landed at Puteoli in the Bay of Naples, and walked northward along the Appian Way until he reached the lion's den.

Even now Apollonius had a friend at court, by name Aelian, and one who, like Tigellinus at the time of Nero, was chief of police. Aelian considered himself as 'the keeper of a horrible tyranny,' and endeavoured to soften the cruelty of Domitian wherever possible. He had given Domitian a certain picture of Apollonius before his arrival, and he also prepared Apollonius for what was in store for him by informing him beforehand of the charges laid against him.

A meeting took place between Apollonius and Domitian. Domitian, adorned with a green wreath, received him in the court of the Temple of Adonis, as if he were himself the god Adonis condescending to listen to a human being. He desired to see him privately. All this shows that the great initiate puzzled him. Some deep instinct within him sensed the greatness and importance of his visitor. Thus he uttered no angry word. As a god, he desired to converse with the prophet. But soon the conversation turned to Nerva. Domitian demanded to hear in what relation Apollonius stood to the conspirators. Apollonius courageously defended the loyalty of Nerva, although every word he said was a reproach to Domitian. The Emperor grew angry and, only because in another part of his soul he was deeply impressed by Apollonius, did he order a regular trial. But he commanded Apollonius to be thrown into prison, and to have his long white beard and hair cut off.

The day before the trial Apollonius was released. But at the moment when he entered the rostrum to speak in his own defence, he received a hint that his destruction had been decided on. At that moment something incomprehensible occurred. Apollonius flashed the words at Caesar, 'You cannot kill me,' and then he vanished from the astonished and terrified assembly without anybody seeing him go through the door. What had happened? We must assume that

Apollonius used magic means which are denied in our enlightened Europe, but which are well known among the fakirs of India.

From that moment Domitian lived in terror. After some time Apollonius appeared in Ephesus, nearly a hundred years old, and devoted to the quiet teaching of philosophy. Suddenly, in AD 96, a strange event occurred. Apollonius was teaching in the garden of his school, walking up and down under the trees. The pupils were listening, spellbound by his mature wisdom. Suddenly, Philostratus reports,

> he stopped in his speech, as if his tongue were paralysed by shock. He endeavoured to continue, but very haltingly, like one whose mind moves somewhere far away. In the end he grew completely silent, looked down to the earth, and, stepping two or three steps forward, shouted 'Throw the Tyrant down! Throw him down!' This he said as if he had the event before his own eyes. All were terror-stricken. Apollonius stopped, as if waiting for the final turn of events. Then he said 'Be of good cheer, ye people of Ephesus, for the Tyrant has been killed today. But, by the Goddess Athene, if I say today I mean now, at this moment, when I stopped in silence.' And he continued while everybody listened to him in awe, 'I am not surprised that there are some who refuse to believe what at this moment not even the city of Rome knows, but behold, Rome receives the news. The news is spreading. Thousands know it by now. They rise up in joy. Now they are twice, now three times as many. Now the whole town knows it. Soon a messenger will arrive here too. Postpone your sacrifice until he arrives. I will go and pray to the gods on account of what I have seen' (8.6).

For a few days the disciples of Apollonius were in doubt and uncertainty, but soon messengers arrived who reported the assassination of the tyrant, and who confirmed exactly the day and the hour in which Apollonius saw in his vision what happened in Rome.

The scene in the colonnades of the school of philosophy at Ephesus is one of the most dramatic moments of that period. In classic style it showed once more the magic power of the ancient clairvoyant faculties. It made clear, too, how much the great initiate of the ancient world was connected with the conspiracy which desired to remove the imperial tyranny. It was the culmination of Apollonius' intervention in the field of world politics. Nerva, the philosopher and friend of the initiate, ascended the imperial throne. His character was a safeguard against the demons of megalomania. And although we are without documentary evidence, we may conclude from the further development of Roman history that Nerva, in co-operation with Apollonius, took measures to prevent the recurrence of tyrannical dictatorship.

Here we touch on the solution of one of the biggest problems posed by the history of the Roman Caesars. One can divide the successive Caesars into three groups. The first group runs from Augustus to Domitian. While Augustus, who first introduced the religious worship of Caesar, was still a man of relatively disciplined character and mental clarity, his successors, starting with Tiberius, drifted more and more into a Luciferic recklessness and megalomania, which was the source of unheard-of acts of cruelty and tyranny. In his lectures *Building Stones for an Understanding of the Mystery of Golgotha*, Rudolf Steiner has described that the deification of the Roman Emperors involved the misuse of mysterious rites of initiation through which the Emperors forced their way to a contact with supersensory forces which, however, they were unable to control. Mental derangement was the consequence. This is how such diabolical conditions appeared on the surface of society, while the quiet sphere of spiritual seed lay hidden in the catacombs of the Christians.

The death of Domitian is an important turning-point in Roman history. With Nerva begins the second group of Caesars which is quite different from the first. For a time, the Ceasarean madness disappears. From Nerva to Marcus Aurelius personalities of moral standing and wide education occupy the imperial throne. Although under Trajan and Hadrian the earlier demonic fire threatens to break through at times, the general line of harmony is preserved. The persecution of Christians and of the schools of philosophy is almost completely suspended. But after the death of the philosopher-emperor Marcus Aurelius, the dam bursts. The old madness rears its head. Commodus, the son of Marcus Aurelius, begins the third group of Caesars. In figures such as Commodus and Caracalla the demonic possession of the first group seems even to have been surpassed.

When, one day, historians begin to take seriously again the personality and the life of Apollonius of Tyana, they will realize what caused the intervening epoch of humane government. The political

importance of Apollonius is not confined to the fact that with his coop-
eration Domitian was replaced by Nerva. It was through him that from
AD 96 to 180 — nearly a century — the history of the Roman emperors
shows a more humane character. To what was his success due? At the
accession of Nerva, a principle was introduced which all succeeding
Caesars down to Marcus Aurelius maintained. It is no mistake to suppose that Nerva changed the law of succession at the advice of
Apollonius. The principle of adoption was introduced, according to
which the ruling emperor was prevented from nominating one of his
own offspring as successor, but was obliged to designate by adoption
a man who was suitable and worthy on account of his moral qualities
and philosophical character. Trajan, Hadrian, Antoninus Pius and
Marcus Aurelius owe their elevation to the imperial throne to this law
of adoption. However, Marcus Aurelius could not resist the temptation
to make his own son the successor, and at once the flood of demonic
possession was let loose again. The persecution of Christians under
Caracalla and Diocletian was only one symptom of the tragic relapse,
until finally Constantine the Great made Christianity the established
religion of the Empire.

Apollonius and St John

The activities of Apollonius of Tyana were not without significance for
early Christianity. By helping to still the storm on the ocean of politics
for nearly a century, he mitigated the cruel opposition which the
Christians had to face. At one point his activities affected immediately
and concretely the destiny of early Christianity. This is the point where
the world of John the Evangelist meets with that of Apollonius.

The patriarchal presbyter of Ephesus was taken prisoner and carried to Rome under the same Domitian whom Apollonius opposed.
Before the gates of the city he was subjected to the most cruel tortures.
Since, however, he remained steadfast in spite of his advanced age,
and since the henchmen of Domitian saw that they could not really
touch him, he was exiled by the Emperor's command to the island of
Patmos. The fruit and the blessing of this exile has come to us in the
Revelation to John. Thus we owe the Apocalypse, the book which we
should estimate most highly as an inward guide to our apocalyptic
age, ultimately to the oppression exercised by Domitian. After the

assassination of Domitian in AD 96, the aged St John was released from his exile and allowed to return to Ephesus where, in the last few years of his life, he wrote the Gospel of John. Thus we owe, in a sense, the Book of Revelation to Domitian, and the Gospel of John to Apollonius of Tyana who, without knowing it, through his share in the assassination of Domitian brought it about that St John was able to return from Patmos to Ephesus.

After this important turning point in Roman history, Apollonius lived approximately another year. During this time, he lived and worked at the same place with John, who survived him by three years. Considering the effect which the political activities of Apollonius had on the life and work of John, it seems safe to assume that the two sages met each other during the year which they spent together at Ephesus. If this should be so, we may wonder whether, on this occasion, perhaps the first glimmer of an understanding of the mystery of Christ passed through the soul of the last Greek sage and initiate.

In a mysterious manner which shows also how much interest in these personalities existed among the occult circles at the time of Goethe, the co-existence of Apollonius and John appears in Schiller's novel *Geisterseher*. Referring to an Armenian who poses as a great magician, but is later unmasked, the novel says, 'Some people even think he is a departed soul who is allowed to walk twenty-three hours a day among the living. In the last hour, however, his soul must return to the underworld to suffer his punishment. Many take him also to be the famous Apollonius of Tyana, and others even to be John the beloved disciple, of whom it is said that he is to tarry until the last Judgment.'

Unlike Apollonius, Jesus did not enter into world affairs; yet, quiet and unassuming, he was in fact the centre of human history, the incarnation of God. He took no part in politics. He did not go out of his way to challenge Pilate or Herod. He possessed the spiritual greatness which enabled him to tell those who showed him the coin stamped with the head of Caesar, 'Render unto Caesar what is Caesar's, and unto God what is God's.' He stood above the level of the play of political forces. He fulfilled the civic duties which the social conditions and political circumstances of the time demanded. Although the government of the world was not in the hands of human beings, but in the power of demons, he felt no call to organize external opposition and counteraction. Had he done so, he would have given more honour to the political powers than they deserved. He stood above the powers of this world so far as to let himself be crucified. Here a veritable gulf is fixed between the world of Apollonius and the world of Jesus.

Apollonius was the great magician and initiate. In this capacity he had tremendous success, both through teaching and healing, and through the part which he played in world affairs. In contrast, it was not the will of Jesus of Nazareth to be anything but a human being, because only so could he be *a brother of every man*. For this reason he refused to be a worker of miracles in the fashion of Apollonius. The initiate and adept, the last superman grounded in the ancient super-sensory forces, stood in contrast to the true human being. This explains why Apollonius meant so much in contemporary opinion, while Jesus of Nazareth remained undiscovered. On the stage of world history the success was with Apollonius. Those who extolled Apollonius as against Jesus failed to realize that Apollonius was great and successful because he wanted to be so. But Jesus emptied himself of all other possibilities, and took on the form of a servant. In his plain humanity he was God-become-Man. The two figures face each other like past and future. Apollonius is the last superb example of those who were great in the past from divine magical sources. In the simple figure of Jesus of Nazareth a new heavenly impulse enters humanity. In him ripens the new impulse which will lead the whole world to new life out of decay and death.

From this it is not difficult to learn a lesson for Christian living in our time. The urge for success in Apollonius aims at everything *big*. The patient expectation of the future in Christ who, with divine non-interference, allows the political demons of his time to have their way, aims at the *whole*. In the last analysis even the greatest success in the outside world as Apollonius achieved it is like water in the sand. After he had succeeded in removing the tyrants from the imperial throne, it took barely a hundred years for them to return. Even the greatest external successes in the world prove themselves to be little in the end. The significance of the life of Jesus did not consist in any external change or reformation of the world, but the world received a seed of new life. The seed of a new world, which has been sown through death and resurrection into the field of humanity and the whole earthly cosmos, is above all space and time. It does not require a vast spatial and temporal radius like that of the life of Apollonius. He who unites himself with the power of Christ can be sure of sharing in an impulse which aims at the whole; and he can draw from this fact the courage to seek and to find his path in the strong, quiet humility which is the way of a grain of corn.

CHAPTER TWO

The Beginning of Christ's Ministry:
the Baptism – the Temptation – Miracles

Criticism and belief in miracles

For many centuries Christendom has forgotten who Christ is. Already
by the time of Constantine the Great, when Christianity was declared
the state religion, a conflict had begun amongst theologians as to
whether the nature of Christ was divine or human. Since that time
many Christians have based their faith in the divinity of Christ only
upon the so-called miracles of Jesus. Finally, however, this faith too has
been shaken.

For the last two centuries there have been two distinct camps
among the leaders of Christianity. On the one side are those who
'believe in miracles' and on the other those who dispute whether they
actually occurred, regarding them either as pious legends by means of
which the early Christian communities sought to glorify Christ, or else
explaining them rationalistically or symbolically. The denial of miracles has been constantly on the increase. Towards the end of the eighteenth century, Christ's walking on the water, for example, was
explained as his standing on a floating plank unseen by the disciples,
or the miracle of Cana as a transformation of the water of the Jewish
religion into the wine of Christianity. Sometimes both these miracles
were regarded as legends. The critics came to regard the belief in miracles as a superstition, while believers came to regard the critics as
unbelievers. The cleft between these two camps goes deeper than is
usually realized.

One can well understand the anxiety of those who still cling to the
old way of belief, and who regard every kind of negative approach as
unbelief, for to lose part of the gospel is really to lose the whole. It is

no wonder that intellectual criticism is regarded as irreligious and as 'unbelief.' On the other hand it would be blindness to deny the justification and necessity of critical and intellectual proof. It was and still is a necessary stage in the progress of the human spirit that humanity should feel a greater obligation to study the laws of nature than the biblical miracles. Modern man cannot but refuse to have his religion measured by his belief in miracles, even if he has to pay for his freedom of thought with the loss of the gospel. Just as the denial of miracles by modern criticism is rightly regarded as 'unbelief,' so is the completely uncritical belief in miracles rightly regarded as 'superstition.' The way to a recovery of the gospel, and with it of the whole Christian outlook, leads between Scylla and Charybdis, between unbelief and superstition. The reason for the conflict between the two views lies in the modern materialism of both. In solving the problem there is therefore no question of 'either ... or.'

We shall only be able to find the meaning and truth of the so-called miracles if we break the spell of materialism and try earnestly and honestly to arrive at the conception of *actual spiritual events,* conceiving, for instance, Christ's walking on the water as an event experienced by the seeing *souls* of the disciples. Then wonders will cease to be *wonders* in the common usage of the word, that is, as miracles. They will become a window through which we behold a far higher world, to perceive which is infinitely more wonderful than to believe in miracles at the cost of thought. To use an expression from Friedrich Rittelmeyer's book on Jesus, 'the so-called miracles of Jesus are not a breaking of natural laws, but rather a breaking through of higher laws of existence.' The old belief in miracles has barred the way to a true view of Christ's nature quite as much as has critical unbelief. The way will be open once more when the gospels become a window for the higher sphere which is revealed through the scenes of the life of Jesus. In place of the many single miracles the central miracle in the destiny of humanity appears: the miracle of Christ's incarnation, the miracle of Christ himself.

The classical contradiction of the customary belief in Christ's miracles is contained in the gospel itself, that is, in the account of the threefold temptation in the wilderness. To see in Christ a wonder-worker or magician, of the type of an Apollonius of Tyana, would in reality be a belittling of his nature. If, in the accepted meaning of the term, he had worked wonders, then he would finally have succumbed to the temp-tation which he withstood during the forty days in the wilderness. What indeed did the tempting powers demand of him but to use his divine powers magically: first in their effect upon the surrounding world of matter (turning stones into bread); then in their influence on men's souls (to make himself Lord of the World), and thirdly in their effect on his own person (casting himself down from the pinnacle of the Temple)? To work miracles was not part of the nature or intention of Christ. His greatness lay in the fact that he did no miracles, although he beyond all others could have done them. He was determined to tread the path of becoming human to its end: only thereby could he become the brother of all humanity and their saviour. A second classi-cal contradiction of the belief in the miracles of Jesus lies in the description of the intention of Christ given by Paul in the Second Chapter of the Epistle to the Philippians: 'Be imbued with the same state of mind which also filled Christ Jesus himself. For although he was of divine nature and form, he chose not to lay claim for himself to be equal to God. Rather, he emptied himself in offering and took on the form of a servant. In human form he took on body, and he showed himself in the form of a man throughout his whole life. Humbly and selflessly he submitted to the laws of earth-existence, even to the expe-rience of death, the death on the cross.' (Phil.2:5–8.)

It never seems to have dawned on the theologians that the story of the temptation shakes the belief in Jesus as a miracle worker. The believers in miracles were not interested in finding something in the gospel which refutes their view. The story of the temptation was dis-solved by the modern critics into an abstraction, like the miracles themselves. It was reserved for a poet to push open the great door which leads to a true understanding of the Christ by bringing together the story of the temptation with the miracles. Dostoevsky does this in the 'Legend of the Grand Inquisitor' in his novel *The Brothers Karama-zov*, which relates:

> In Seville at the time of the Inquisition once more a hundred
> heretics had been burnt at the stake. Christ appears, walking
> through the streets in earthly human form. Out of pity for poor
> suffering humanity he has descended once more, if only for a
> short time, to earth. The people intuitively recognize him and
> flock towards him. He heals the sick and blesses the suffering.

Along comes the Grand Inquisitor, a cold and ancient man of ninety years. The people having learnt obedience stand on one side. At a sign from the old man Christ is seized and cast into prison. Here the Grand Inquisitor faces him with the words: 'Is it Thou? Thou? Answer not. Keep silence! Besides, Thou hast no right to add one single word to what Thou hast already said of old. Why then art Thou come to hinder us? For Thou art come to hinder us and Thou knowest that.'

And now the old man unfolds before the silent figure of the Christ his grand-inquisitorial thoughts. 'It is good that Thy work has passed over to us. We reckon more with the weakness and baseness of human nature than Thou dost. Thou didst will to give men freedom, the most disastrous gift in the world. We know that man does not desire freedom but to obey and be a slave. Thou didst reject the challenge of the wise and dread Spirit of the Wilderness when he counselled Thee, "Turn these stones into bread." But we know that it is bread and not spirit that men desire. We see that Thou didst start a fatal error when Thou didst not follow the spirit that spoke with Thee. So we will follow him and not Thee and thereby we shall become better administrators of thy work than Thou thyself. And if for the sake of the bread of heaven thousands shall follow Thee, what is to become of the millions and tens of thousands of millions of creatures who will not have the strength to forgo the earthly bread for the sake of the heavenly? Or doest Thou care only for the tens of thousands of the great and strong ...? Thou didst reject the temptation to do wonders for the sake of Thine idea of freedom. Thou didst hope that men, following Thee, would cling to God and not ask for a miracle. But Thou didst not know that when man rejects miracles he rejects God too; for man seeks not so much God as the miraculous. And as man cannot bear to be without the miraculous he will create new miracles of his own for himself, and will worship deeds of sorcery and witchcraft. Thou didst not come down from the cross when they shouted to Thee, mocking and reviling Thee, "Come down from the Cross and we will believe that Thou art He." Thou didst not come down, for again Thou wouldst not enslave man by a miracle and didst crave faith given freely without a miracle. Thou didst crave for free love and not the base raptures of the slave before the might that has over-awed him for ever. But Thou didst think too highly of men therein for they are slaves of course, though rebellious by nature ... That is our mystery! It's long — eight centuries since we have been on *his* side and not on thine ... Just eight centuries ago we took from him what Thou didst reject with scorn, that last gift he offered Thee, showing Thee all the kingdoms of the earth. We took from him Rome and the sword of Caesar. Why didst Thou reject that gift? Hadst Thou accepted that last counsel of the mighty spirit, Thou wouldst have accomplished all that man seeks on earth ...'

Here Dostoevsky touches on the essential problem of the nature of Christ and of historical Christianity. The Grand Inquisitor passes through all ages of Christian evolution, here more subtly, there more obviously. He wishes to proclaim to men a Christ who will accommodate himself to human weakness. Therefore he puts in the place of Christ who resisted the threefold temptation, one who does wonders in the realm of the senses. He mixes materialism into the concepts of the gospel and especially of the miracles, and merely distorts the picture of Christ himself. The many supposed wonders conceal the central wonder of the Christ-being.

The baptism

The *incarnation of Christ* is the one great central miracle. Through it the downward trend of human evolution received a fresh upward impulse, though this was at first hidden. This great central wonder extended throughout the three years of the actual life of Christ and was fulfilled in the death and resurrection of the Mystery of Golgotha. A dramatic event of the highest spiritual significance proclaimed its dawn, although nothing of it was visible to earthly eyes. The evangelists point to this decisive event when in their account of the baptism of Jesus they say the heavens were opened, and the image of the Holy Spirit revealed itself to inner sight, while to inner hearing there resounded in love the voice of the godhead.

The first thirty years of the life of Jesus are a human biography, though within them providence has woven in magnificent threads and patterns the epitome of the whole history of humanity up to that time. The three short years between the baptism and the Mystery of Golgotha are more than a human biography. They depict the entrance into human existence of the highest being. They contain the progressive miracle of the incarnation of the Christ in the man, Jesus of Nazareth, and so what took place spiritually at the baptism was the actual birth into the physical world of Christ. This was known or at least clearly felt in the early Christian centuries, when the Christmas festival was not kept on December 25, the birthday of Jesus, but on January 6, the day of the baptism in the Jordan. This mystery is indicated in the Psalm where in the moment when the heavens are opened the Father God utters his will of love, 'You are my son, today I have begotten you' (Psalm 2:7). In the first three gospels the clear wording of this text in the Psalms is slightly altered, as though a veil were drawn over the mystery. In the two other passages of the New Testament where it is quoted, in the Acts of the Apostles and twice in the Epistle to the Hebrews it is used in an unveiled form as the words accompanying the birth at the baptism in the Jordan (Acts 13:33, Heb.1:5, 5:5).

When our knowledge can embrace again the true nature of the human being and his incarnation, we shall understand too what happened at the baptism in the Jordan, and what the nature of Christ is as God-become-Man. Our age has more and more lost sight of the human being as a spiritual and supersensory being, but must regain it. The author acknowledges the work of Rudolf Steiner as of the greatest possible help in this endeavour.*

Man's true nature is neither his visible physical body, nor his soul which in thinking, feeling and will reveals itself through the body. Paul could still distinguish the bodily, psychic and *spirit* man. In his essential nature man is a being of spirit, an ego, incarnating in various enveloping sheaths. The lowest and densest of these is the physical body. Interpenetrating this, as mediator between body and soul, is the etheric or life-body. The soul is likewise only a sheath in which man dwells; in Steiner's anthroposophy it is called the astral, or soul

---

* The spiritual world-conception which Rudolf Steiner developed, with its own exact method as an expansion of natural science, is described as anthroposophy or 'knowledge of the nature of the human being,' because it starts with a description of man as a spiritual, supersensory being. In addition to what is indicated briefly here of the various members of man's nature, see the fundamental books of Rudolf Steiner.

body. Within these three bodies the ego lives, which is the real human being.

The whole significance of the life of Jesus between his birth and the baptism lay in the preparation of the purest and maturest human sheaths, so that when the time was fulfilled the Christ-being should be able to enter them. Up to the baptism and especially during his twelfth to thirtieth years, the ripest and most all-embracing ego that ever existed within humanity lived in the physical body, the life-body and the soul-body of Jesus of Nazareth. He was the fulfilment of humanity so far as this could be reached by earthly man, and so he merited the title *Son of Man*. But even this fulfilment could only lead within the soul of Jesus to a concentrated awareness of the whole tragedy of humanity's spiritual impoverishment, and with it the deep longing for divine help. Jesus did more than share the general Messianic expectation of his time: distressed and shaken by the failure of even the purest and ripest of human powers in that age of dying soul-forces, his vision must have reached the glorious light of the Christ-being, who in his descent to earth had arrived at the portal of incarnation.

He must at the same time have realized that it would be false to hope for spontaneous divine help. Only through the sacrifice of the highest human soul could the divine sacrifice be made possible, and the door opened whereby Christ could find entrance to humanity. It was this great self-sacrifice which filled the soul of Jesus as he made his way to John the Baptist. His exalted human ego made way for the divine ego of Christ. It went the way that human souls go in death, and into the sheaths of his body and soul which had been purified and spiritualized by him the ego of Christ entered, as the heavens opened and there sounded the voice of God. The Son of God had become one with the Son of Man.

When Christian theologians began to discuss in abstract terms the divine and human nature of Christ as early as AD 325, at the Council of Nicaea, there were still some thinkers who could talk positively and discriminatingly, through spiritual vision, of the connection between the human and divine nature of Christ Jesus after the baptism. But even at that time such positive statements, which allowed the mystery of the incarnation of Christ to penetrate once more the ever-deepening fog, shocked and frightened people. It was not willingly admitted that only in this way could the living knowledge of Christ, so active in the first three Christian centuries, be saved. Those who came forward with such positive descriptions were therefore condemned as heretics. One of the most prominent among these was Apollinaris of Laodicea. Following the ancient wisdom of the threefold nature of man, reflected also in Paul's epistles, he explained that the sheaths of body and soul, *sarx* and *psychê*, were human, but that in these sheaths not a human spirit, *nous*, but the divine *logos* dwelt.

Those who became the pupils of John the Baptist and were baptized by him underwent a great transformation. The baptism itself, however, was only the conclusion of a development which had taken place in the soul through intensive spiritual training. John's flaming words lived in his pupils for many weeks, and so their hearts and minds received a twofold knowledge. They became aware of all the weaknesses and imperfection of their human nature through relentless self-knowledge, and thereby realized the imminent danger of the death of souls, which was threatening humanity more and more. On the other hand, the Baptist's prophecy of the Messiah kindled the spark of a great hope in their hearts. Through his words his hearers may often have felt that the heavens which were bringing them the Messiah were already close at hand. Their longing for personal healing grew into a prophetic knowledge of salvation for humanity, and in the final act of baptism this preparatory knowledge was brought to glorious fulfilment. In baptism the candidate was submerged in the waters of the Jordan until the connection between body, soul and spirit was loosened, as happens in death. Through the previous preparation the soul and spirit were not so closely connected with the body as usual. In baptism the disciple beheld for a few moments the vast tableau usually experienced in the first days after death, so making a new beginning and receiving strength for his further life. In near death experiences people today have often had a similar experience to that of John's baptism. Such people have often described how at the gate of death they saw the whole of their past life before them in a mighty tableau. Past errors manifest themselves in the human soul, together with hints of future destiny. Those who were baptized in the Jordan experienced this tableau to the highest degree of intensity. Their own sins and those of humanity appeared accusingly before them in menacing blackness. But at the same time the soul, freed from the body, beheld the glory of the approaching Christ.

In John's baptism we have one of the last echoes of ancient initiation rites. At that time they could be performed because man's bodily nature was still elastic and porous enough to allow his soul and spirit to continue again a balanced life within the body, in spite of having passed through a partial death. Human bodies have long since become so friable and brittle in their inmost structure that today John's baptism would no longer be possible without causing severe injury to health and balance of mind.

When Jesus came to John he encountered in the immediate neighbourhood many of those who had been transformed through the Baptist's spiritual training and the final act of baptism. And now he too bowed to the effect of the Baptist's flaming words, and was baptized. It was outwardly a quiet and peaceful scene, as he submitted in all humility and was submerged beneath the waters of Jordan. Inwardly, however, occurred the cosmic drama of a new beginning which excelled in importance everything that had previously happened on earth. Indeed, a man deeply prepared was raised in soul and spirit to experience an immense tableau, reflecting the past and anticipating the future. But this time, instead of the human ego with its purified and exalted soul returning to the body, the ego forsook the earth, and the soul, as a pure sacrificial vessel offered to heaven, received into itself a superhuman, divine being. In returning to the body, it bore with it and brought to embodiment the ego of Christ, the Messiah so longingly awaited by humanity. The saying used later by Paul, 'Not I, but Christ in me' was realized in this silent soul-act of Jesus. Jesus became bearer of the Christ: *Christophorus*. The miracle of the incarnation of God began.

It is clear that what happened at this moment could only have been a beginning. The heavenly content was too great and overpowering for the earthly vessel into which it was poured. It required three years' wrestling with destiny before the divine ego of Christ could accomplish its incarnation completely within the soul and very veins of the man Jesus. The hour of death on the hill of Golgotha was at the same time the culmination of the incarnation into the earthly body, and a passing over into a new form of existence. In every breath, every word, every deed of these three years the vast cosmic ego worked more firmly into its narrow human dwelling. The miracle of the incarnation lasted from the baptism to the death on the cross, because it was the continuous sacrificial deed of a God who, for the salvation of humanity, humbled himself and took upon himself the form of a servant and became obedient unto human death.

The nature of the earthly body into which the Christ-being entered was more than small and narrow in relation to the cosmic greatness which must now possess it. Although the sheaths of the physical, etheric and astral body were indwelt and prepared by the most mature and pure of men, they were nevertheless part of all earth existence, which through the Fall has come under the spell of weakness and imperfection. Christ's cosmic power of creation breaks into the earthly human body. The cosmic streams of life that pulse through him break into human strength, the majestic soul breaks into the being of the human soul. In the three earthly elements of body, life and soul Christ encounters the powers which have estranged man from his divine origin and brought him under the curse of mortality. This is the core of the threefold temptation which took visible shape as he withdrew into loneliness directly after 'the baptism. The decision to withdraw from human contact and seek loneliness in the desert of Judea must have been taken as a result of the first experience which Jesus had after being filled with the spirit, and after the great transformation had come over him. As he encountered in his own physical human body the powers of hardening and bondage to earth, he also felt that he could transform the corruptible into the incorruptible. He felt too that with the streams of life which poured forth from him he could conquer the force of gravity as well as the full power of death itself. When he encountered in the soul the flickering deceptive phantom lights and sensual desires which lead humanity into error, he felt at the same time that with the sunlike power of purpose which was his, he only needed to appear before people in order to rescue and lead them in his own direction. He may even have felt alarmed at the hitherto undreamed of possibilities which were suddenly placed at his disposal. It can have been no part of his purpose to exercise the superior power of his divinity over humanity. A bewildering tempest of wonders would have overpowered men without enabling them to receive freedom and the seed of an organic transformation. Only by himself draining the cup of human existence to its dregs, by penetrating the human being to its last fibres with the new force, could he embody within earth-existence the germ of a future salvation through which man might become divine, and the earth become *sun*. When the gospels say that Jesus was led 'by the Spirit' into the wilderness, they hint that, through what in the very first stages after the baptism proceeded from his transformed nature, he was led to recognize the true significance of his earthly task. In his condition he must begin to work among people. He must even withdraw from them in order not to overpower them, so that he might accomplish first a minimum of that inner sacrificial act by which alone he could achieve the balance between the divine content and the human vessel. As yet the heavenly wine foamed too powerfully over the rim of the earthly vessel.

The temptation

Christ's greatness lay in the fact that he renounced all the divine glory and superhuman greatness that properly belonged to him and descended into the same depths in which other men must find their way. The classical saying in the Epistle to the Hebrews that Jesus was tempted as other men does not refer to any weakness that attached itself to his nature, but to the fundamental purpose and intention of the incarnation. 'For we do not have a High Priest who cannot suffer our weaknesses with us. He made himself like us and endured the same temptations in everything, only he remained free of sin.' (Heb.4:15). That Christ was faced with the threefold temptation in the wilderness was not because he was weak like other men, but because he had willed to take upon himself the weakness of human nature, as well as all the rest of human destiny. Yet in the temptation of Jesus deeper laws may be read which fundamentally underlie all temptation to which man is subject.

This threefold temptation did not come to Christ from without but rose up from within. Modern man who has lost the capacity to reckon with supersensory experiences and their inner laws supposes that the Devil approaches Jesus Christ from without. At the same time, of course, he scorns the ancient naive belief in demons as fantastic and superstitious.

It is characteristic of the landscape where Jesus goes for forty days that external nature is completely withdrawn. On the steep slopes of the wilderness of Judea, bearing as they do the stamp of death, the outer world ceases to exercise any influence on man, and he is thrown back entirely on his own inner being. So also is the temptation of Jesus to be understood: within his soul, forces are stirred which at once reveal themselves as something foreign, and finally show in clear visionary form the powers that oppose humanity.

The most important key to the story of the temptation is its immediate link with the baptism. The temptation occurs not in a moment of weakness, but in the new condition of blessing and power. It is not the humanity of Jesus that invites the tempter, but the divinity of Christ which has so newly entered into earth-existence. Before the baptism such a temptation would have been impossible. During the preceding thirty years not only a morally exalted man, but the maturest and purest individuality of the whole of humanity had walked the earth. But when within the soul of Jesus the mystery of the divine indwelling begins, and the human being becomes the bearer of the incarnate God, the temptation occurs. We might at first sight have supposed that nothing could have lifted man so far above all wavering or temptation as the indwelling of the divine within his soul. But it is precisely the greatness and the celestial quality of the Christ-ego appearing on earth that invites the storm of temptation.

After the baptismal transformation possibilities presented themselves in the soul of Jesus which were not previously there, but also which had never existed on earth. The vision of what he could accomplish if he used these possibilities without reserve became the content of the temptation. He could of course turn stones into bread, protect himself from harm in casting himself from the pinnacle of the Temple into the depths, and become Lord of the world. But he would thereby depart from the purpose and will that led him to incarnation on earth from the divine heights. He stood at the crossroads. Not for a moment was he in doubt that the possibilities presented to him by the opposing powers would mean a wrong use of the divine powers within him. The right and God-willed use of these powers could only be in self-resignation, to transplant them wholly within humanity, bringing them into the very veins and fibres of human nature, incarnating them deeply, and as far as possible completely, thereby implanting them in humanity as the seed of the future. Because the meaning and purpose of his own destiny stood clearly before the soul of Christ Jesus, he also saw clearly the divine purpose of human existence in general, that is, to incarnate heaven in earth and the spiritual within earthly matter.

In human life the nature of temptation is always the urge to use inward powers in a wrong way. If we fall into temptation, this is by no means only due to our own weakness. On the contrary, it may be that without really noticing it we have reached a turning point in our life, where something from another world seeks to influence us, and only our own incapacity rightly to receive and hold this blessing leads us astray. All aberrations into which we can fall, all crimes which we can commit, are nothing more than perverted possibilities of growth. The sins of men are more than mere lapses. Moral aberrations have world significance, for behind every vice is hidden a virtue gone wrong. In every high moment of our destiny we must learn to 'go into the stillness.' The gospel shows us the great archetype and model in Jesus Christ as he entered into quietness after the great transformation of the baptism. Here he can absorb and bring under the direction of the divine spirit what has so overpoweringly entered his being.

If in future religious life is to bear fruit, entering into the stillness will become more and more necessary. All genuine Christian experiences should be approximations to the mystery of the indwelling Christ which Paul has expressed: 'Not I, but Christ in me.' Thus religious experience will contain elements analogous to Christ's baptism. If the blessing of divine forces which enter the human soul is to bear fruit for life, then these forces must, through being consciously cultivated in inner quiet and stillness, find their way to deeper levels of man's being. For the sacramental Christianity of the future, not only the preparation for a worthy reception of the sacrament will be important, but also the taking in and allowing to echo on of the divine gift received. The oft-repeated words of blessing 'Christ in you' in the Act of Consecration of Man (the communion service of the Christian Community) in place of the Latin *Dominus vobiscum,* kindle in souls rightly prepared the spark of 'Christ in us.' But if the necessary inner activity does not follow on the initial preparation, it can happen that the very divine force of which men have partaken slips down and is transformed into the impulse of temptation towards sensual desire. To the tasks we already have to fulfil in the outer world we must through conscious effort add the task which gives our human existence its meaning: we must incarnate the divine in the human being and the spiritual in earthly matter.

The forty days in the wilderness

Although it is a risky undertaking, we can, on the basis of what has so far been said, try to form ideas of what transpired in the life of Christ during that first decisive period after the baptism, as though it were part of a human biography. During the forty days of withdrawal into loneliness Jesus was absorbed into a powerful and active meditation. The first result of the cosmic exaltation of his consciousness retreated to a certain distance, became remote, as it were. All the same, the meditation and self-recollection must have had as its content also the tableau of the previous thirty years. And this must have led to an appropriation of that thirty years' experience by the higher ego which now dwelt within Jesus.

What of the eighteen 'silent years,' the time between the account of the twelve-year-old Jesus in the Temple and the baptism? If we accept Rudolf Steiner's description given in lectures which have been published under the title *The Fifth Gospel,* Jesus of Nazareth as he grew up was led into connections with the three most important spiritual currents that existed at that time within humanity. Each of the three contacts lasted for about six years. As humanity at that time was at the lowest ebb of its spiritual life, this experience can have been nothing but a threefold disillusionment, first with Judaism, then with paganism and finally with the order of the Essenes, which at that time was the most important representative of ascetic occultism.

First in the memory-tableau of the forty days there appeared the time in which Jesus, up to his eighteenth year, had been able to gain the most intimate insight into the sphere of the Old Testament. After the doctors and teachers of the Law in Jerusalem had observed at the Passover feast the surpassing ability and wisdom of the boy, they can hardly have failed to try and draw him into their theological school in order to secure in him a great teacher. Earnestly however as he sought to reach the spiritual source from which the Jewish community still drew, he only met a religious culture which had already become rigid. Its theology, in spite of all its intricacies, was only a cold head-knowledge. Jesus found himself surrounded by a world of religious intellectualism which was not only in itself lifeless, but which inevitably killed whatever was living. Herein lies his first great disillusionment. The religion of the Law of his fathers offered men death instead of life, stones instead of bread. At this moment the memory-picture attained immediate actuality. The cold Spirit of Cleverness, which the young Jesus must have learnt to know in its practical aspects, took on form and came before the eyes of his soul as an actual entity. Jesus sees Ahriman, the dark spirit of soullessness. As the picture came into focus it became at the same time a prophetic vision, not only of his own future, but of the whole of humanity. Jesus knew that the same cold, merely clever spirit, whose breath he first learnt to know in Judaism, would at some time in the future lead humanity to the most astonishing discoveries, which would however become a growing menace, leading to the loss or death of the soul. Ahriman will inaugurate an age of purely external observation of nature, and the more he deludes humanity into believing that only in this way will they get bread to eat, so much the more will he in reality give them stones instead of bread. In our age of technical organization and mechanization we can understand from personal experience what a vista of the future the first memory-picture yielded. The death-bringing curse of Ahriman is being fulfilled all around us today.

The spectral vision must have aroused in Jesus a new consciousness of humanity's peculiar task, and a decision to fight for the impulse of the future. He knew that he could drive Ahriman from the field if he so wished. Out of his divine fullness of power he could give humanity that which otherwise Ahriman, in the course of the coming millennia, would give them, but at the price of all warmth and activity of soul. He could give it to them without their being driven into a terrible emptiness. He could anticipate all the discoveries and inventions of the human intellect by performing the miracle of turning stones into bread. But at the moment in which it became clear to him that he could do this it became equally clear to him that he could never wish to do so. Though he could use magic, he had not come to be a magician, but to become man and to take on himself the destiny which everyone has to bear. He had come to bring to the world a new seed of inward life. In the ground of the human being he had to plant the seed of a spiritual force which would one day be capable of working even into man's physical body and of reconstructing it, although it might require thousands of years before the seed matured. Even though during these millennia the Ahrimanic forces might celebrate numberless triumphs, it would still be more important that the human ego should awaken to freedom through the patient inward growth of that force, than that dead stones should be turned into living bread by divine intervention, without the co-operation or effort by which these human egos should mature. In the possibility of magic which rose up before his soul Jesus recognized the temptation of Ahriman who, from the sphere of the physical body, encountered the divine ego which had entered him. In that he was able to see through the Ahrimanic temptation, the decision to become man which he had made from eternity gained here on earth its full clarity and determination. He did not magically strike the Ahrimanic powers out of the way, but allowed them to go their way. Yet in future times when Ahriman celebrates his greatest triumphs, the seed which Christ planted in earthly soil, through his quietly becoming man, will have become the strength that can form in man the counter-force to the powers of death.

In the memory-picture there followed now the second period between his twelfth and thirtieth years. At that time, following his calling as a carpenter, Jesus had to travel through the countries of Syria and Phoenicia on the northern border of his home in Galilee. In this pagan neighbourhood he found the inner decadence into which the pre-Christian religion had fallen. In the temples, which had once been centres for the presence of gods among men, he saw human beings longing for what they had lost. He saw them flocking to the altars, seeking heavenly aid, but there were no longer any priests who could summon the gods to earthly altars. Humanity seemed to him as sheep without a shepherd. The altars were not merely empty, however: in the place of the ancient gods, demons ruled among men. The degeneration of spiritual leadership had brought humanity into the danger of falling a prey to whole hosts of demonic beings. This was the second great disillusionment of his life. In Rome also at that time, through the recently established worship of the Caesar, a storm of Ceasarean madness was raging. Jesus saw there not a spirit of cold shrewdness, but a being of unbridled passion. All these moving and disturbing impressions, which he had received between his eighteenth and twenty-fourth years, came again before the soul of Jesus in the loneliness of the desert, and once more the memory-picture became reality. The glittering spirit of Lucifer appeared proudly before him, gloating over the almost unlimited dominion he had obtained over the souls of men. Once again through this encounter an impulse was set free within the soul of Jesus. Through the radiance of divine glory which now filled him, he could attract to himself the hosts of those who longed for true leadership. He could snatch them away from triumphant Lucifer and arouse in them the fire of divine enthusiasm. But the moment he recognized that if he so willed he could sweep Lucifer from the field and place himself as leader at the head of all humanity, something that only he could decide became quite clear to him: he had not come to rule, but to serve. It would be nothing but a great act of mass hypnotism were he to quench the thirst of men for leadership through the divine power of his personality. He who makes use of hypnotism commands, even when he appears to help. In the possibility of such leadership Jesus saw a temptation of Lucifer himself, when he led him to the summit of the mountain and offered to lay the whole world at his feet. At this moment the great cosmic impulse of love, which Christ had brought to earth, came to full self-consciousness within his human soul. The way is clear now. It will lead to the quiet room on Mount Zion, where Jesus washed the disciples' feet before he gave them bread and wine.

The years immediately preceding the baptism appeared also in the meditative memory-picture. Coming from Nazareth, which was originally a colony of the Essenes, Jesus was continually surrounded by leaders of this order. After his experience of Judaism and paganism he was finally prepared to penetrate the spirituality cultivated in the remote cloisters of the Essenes. He saw the amazing results achieved there by their ascetic training. Here he encountered a last living branch of occultism. The strict fasting and devotional practices of the Essenes had led to a marvellous power of self-control. Amongst them Jesus found not only clairvoyants but some who, like the Indian fakirs, were able to master the forces of gravity within their own bodies. But from the first moment he recognized the onesidedness and fundamental error on which the occultism of the Essenes was based. He could not fail to realize such a training was only possible when men isolated themselves completely, leaving the rest of the world to itself. Self-perfection was sought at the cost of everything that bound them to earth. Jesus experienced this isolation deeply, and felt it as a wrong against humanity. The spirituality of the Essenes seemed to Jesus like a theft from thirsting humanity through the egoism of soul and spirit which prevailed there. This completed the measure of painful disillusion, as Jesus sought what still remained on earth of spiritual forces. He found the Essene occultism to be the result of a complicated co-operation between Lucifer and Ahriman. This appeared again before him now when his consciousness was so infinitely heightened. At that moment he felt that, if he so willed, he too could do all that the Indian fakir or the Essene occultist had achieved. He could, from his own divine power, sow the seeds of a new occultism. He could, for example, cast himself down from the pinnacle of the Temple without injury, but how far that would have been from the purpose of his love towards suffering humanity! For him to have taken one step along the path of fakirism would have been a misuse and a tempting of the highest divine forces in the cosmos. Out of the seed that Christ sowed, there will grow in the future a new mastery of man over his life and body. But this mastery will be healthy only when it is exercised in the midst of everyday life, where men bear one another's burdens. This third temptation which sprang from the level of the life-forces, and which brought home most clearly to Jesus the peculiar position in which he stood, finally strengthened in him the will to drain the cup of being human to its dregs.

The clarity of mind and the governing motive, which in the forty days of loneliness were won and confirmed, remained as a standard during the brief three years of Christ's life. Everything that the gospels relate as the deeds of Christ must be judged by the threefold temptation which he withstood. Here alone can we find the key to the so-called 'miracles' of Jesus.

The story of the temptation is the conclusive refutation of every external and materialistic interpretation of the deeds of Christ. If in the feeding of the Five Thousand and the Four Thousand Christ had brought about a physical increase of bread, using magical forces to make much out of little, then he would afterwards have succumbed to the temptation in which the Ahrimanic powers demanded that he should turn stones into bread. He could have used magical forces, but he chose to empty himself of them. He did not wish to be a magician but a saviour. Instead of a renewal of magic, he sowed the seeds of a spiritualization of humanity. If we relate the account of the feeding of the multitude to the story of the temptation of Jesus, we see clearly that in the miraculous feeding there is a supersensory, inner process which, within the realm of soul, is at least as great a reality as the use of magical forces upon the physical plane would have been. If the acts of healing and raising of the dead by Jesus were actually 'miracles,' if they had depended on a sensational interference with the souls and destinies of other men, this would have meant the subsequent triumph of Lucifer who desired that Jesus should make himself from the height of the mountain ruler of the souls of all humanity. By bringing together the stories of healing and the account of the temptation the historic truth will be confirmed to which we have already been led in considering the biography of Apollonius of Tyana: psychic treatment of the sick was at that time a quite usual and organic proceeding. In those days many more were healed spiritually than by physical medicaments, and for Christ it was a most natural expression of his own great love for men when he laid his hands on the sick. There is no question here of hypnotic suggestion — this was foreign to his nature. Not the capacity for suggestion, but the power of a love that serves, was strengthened in humanity by the Christ. If in the night after the feeding of the multitude Christ had walked on the Sea of Galilee (the Lake of Gennesaret) with his physical body, this would have meant that he would have followed the promptings of the demonic powers which had shown him how to cast himself down from the pinnacle of the Temple without injury. The walking on the water and the story of the temptation together confirm that there is a real supersensory event and that what the disciples experienced by night on the Sea of Galilee was a spiritual encounter. Christ rejected *fakirism* completely. It could play no part in his life. Instead he sowed in man the seeds of *obedience* and of *patience*.

Parallels in the Gospel of John

The more clearly we grasp the supreme importance of the story of the temptation for an understanding of the life and nature of Christ, the more we are impelled to ask why the Gospel of John contains no corresponding description. In the Fourth Gospel, not even a hint is given of the content of the forty days after the baptism as described by the first three evangelists. It is true that the cleansing of the Temple which the Gospel of John places quite near the beginning has sometimes been taken as a parallel to the temptation. There we see Jesus, as also in the wilderness, in victorious conflict with the spirit of negation and the spirit of opposition. Nevertheless, the scene in the Temple is quite opposite to the scene in the wilderness. The conditions prevailing in Jerusalem were in absolute contrast to anything like remoteness from humanity. Both city and Temple were crowded with great masses of people, for it was at the Passover festival that Jesus overthrew the tables and used the scourge of cords. Thousands of pilgrims coming together from all over the Roman world could witness the judicial majesty in the countenance and bearing of Jesus. Which then is the correct description — that of the first three evangelists, which shows how Jesus was withdrawn from men, or that of the Fourth Gospel which describes him in their very midst?

This perplexing contradiction can lead to a deeper knowledge of the life of Jesus if we keep our minds open for a comprehensive view of all four gospels. Here, better than anywhere else, we can learn the art of a complete *synopsis*, a term which is normally, and rather superficially, applied to the first three gospels only, because of the obvious parallels in the events recorded by Matthew, Mark and Luke, and their general agreement. For a real understanding of the New Testament all four gospels must be described and understood synoptically. In this comprehensive way of reading *the* gospel in the four gospels we shall find, beyond the obvious, a wealth of what is less clearly expressed, but which can lead to further and deeper mysteries. The mysterious condition in which Christ Jesus found himself after the baptism is revealed in the gospels only through the silent speech of gesture and composition. What light does a complete synopsis of the four gospels throw on the beginning of Christ's activity?

The first three gospels, after the account of the baptism, speak of the forty days in the wilderness. Then they show us how Jesus comes into the open, and in his Galilean home begins to proclaim his mission. But it is not yet in the strict sense *his* message, for he uses the same words with which John the Baptist first appeared before men, 'Change your hearts and minds. The realms of the heavens have come close' (Matt.4:17, Mark 1:15). At first sight, we might suppose that this happened at the end of the forty days. Not for nothing, however, do all three gospels add a date. They say that Jesus came into the open after Herod Antipas and Herodias had cast John the Baptist into prison. That dramatic event, however, occurred in fact some time after the Passover, when four or five months had already elapsed after the baptism. After the forty days of the temptation, and before the public appearance of Jesus, more time had elapsed than is usually supposed. During this time, up to the feast of the Passover, there is room for a further forty days. And since, as we shall see later, the first appearance of Jesus occurs at the Jewish Pentecost, the period over which the first three gospels draw a veil includes even those later forty days which will be of such significance in the third year after the resurrection.

In the early chapters of the Gospel of John there is a frankness of description which must strike us as quite astonishing in view of the ideas we have tried to form of the particular conditions prevailing at the beginning of Christ's ministry. John seems to be quite free of the reticence of the other evangelists, who either keep silence about the first period, or speak in mythical hieroglyphics of the story of the temptation. St John describes what happened after the baptism much more openly. Jesus comes to John the Baptist, and in connection with this meeting finds Peter, Andrew, Philip and Nathanael. Then the scene changes, and Jesus goes from Judea to Galilee. There we see him with his mother and disciples and guests at the marriage at Cana. Once more the scene is changed. As the feast of the Passover draws near, Jesus proceeds to Jerusalem to keep the feast within the sacred precincts of the Temple, together with the other pilgrims who flock from all over the world. There follows the cleansing of the Temple. Continuing, as it were, the dramatic Passover events, comes the mysterious conversation between Jesus and Nicodemus at night. Then he turns back towards Galilee and passes through Samaria where, at the ancient well of Jacob, he talks with the Samaritan woman.

If John's Gospel omits the withdrawal of Jesus after the baptism, where then does the first appearance of Jesus, which the first three gospels so expressly emphasize, belong? Do the three events of the marriage at Cana, the cleansing of the Temple and the conversation with Nicodemus come before or after this point of time? Not only is the reticence of Christ lacking in the first three events, the reticence and restraint which are so essential a part of the story of the temptation, but, on the contrary, an overpowering influence seems to stream forth from the figure of Jesus. The astonishing thing is that Jesus does greater wonders at the beginning than he does later.

The gospel itself answers the question by giving a date. The marriage at Cana, the cleansing of the Temple and the conversation with

Nicodemus belong to the time before the beginning of Christ's activity. We are told that after his conversation with Nicodemus Jesus and his disciples stayed and worked in Judea. All this activity remained within the sphere of John the Baptist's work and influence. The gospel mentions specifically that John himself was still teaching and baptizing when, in the circle which began to form round Jesus, John's way of baptizing was adopted. As if it were desired to build a bridge for that synoptic view of the four gospels which is just here so important, John's Gospel, with the same precision as the other three, connects this point of time with the imprisonment of the Baptist. 'John had not yet been imprisoned' (John 3:24). Matthew, Mark and Luke speak of the work of Jesus in so far as this begins *after* the imprisonment. John is able to speak of an activity that took place *before* this point of time. Although the activity of the circle around Jesus was at first nothing more than an extension of the Baptist's work, the question of the relation between John and Jesus had already begun to exercise the minds of the people. The disciples of John question their master, and John gives the answer in the human, yet cosmic terms of the bridegroom and the friend of the bridegroom, ending with the key words, 'He must increase, but I must decrease.'

The result of this collective view of the gospels is certainly startling. The first three evangelists have shown the time between the baptism and the imprisonment of John as a time of great mystery. If they do break silence in giving the story of the temptation, they nevertheless remain true to this silence through the mythical manner of their description. John's Gospel allows us to look into that space of time which shrouds so great a mystery. Yet this is certainly not done without expecting that we shall treat with special reverence and caution what is here revealed. The marriage at Cana, the cleansing of the Temple, and the conversation with Nicodemus cannot be read in one breath with the other scenes in the gospel. Only if we feel the mysterious intensity of that early stage within the being of the Christ, and experience at the same time the mingled restraint and the will for sacrifice, can we hope to understand what is here related. As the threefold temptation was the content of the first forty days, so we gain here an intuitive insight into the content of the second and third forty days.

The marriage at Cana, the cleansing of the Temple and the conversation with Nicodemus

The three scenes of the temptation, which occurred supersensibly within the soul of Jesus, correspond to three events which took place apparently quite apart from any such time of loneliness and isolation. They took place externally, in the midst of the world of men, and yet, because of a continued will for restraint, they remained in reality within a sacred and protective aura. Obviously, the threefold events of the marriage at Cana, the cleansing of the Temple, and the conversation with Nicodemus cannot be understood simply as parallels to the threefold temptation. Nevertheless, the same essential mystery of the early stages of the incarnation of the Christ-being pulsates in them. And strange as it may sound, we must use what we have learned from the story of the temptation as a key for an understanding of these three scenes.

Jesus sets foot on the fertile slopes of his home country, Galilee, as one transformed, where he is among the guests at the wedding at Cana. No longer did the human ego of Jesus dwell within his soul, but the cosmic sun-ego of the Christ-being. The baptism and the forty days of loneliness had taken place in the most typical Judean environment, where the Jordan empties itself into the Dead Sea, and among the awful rocky heights of the desert of Judea. To pass from the spell of this strange, dead landscape and return to the lovely and living regions of his home country must have wrung from the soul of Jesus a great human sigh of relief. But this sigh became the revelation of a new self-discovery by the Christ who was entering into incarnation. At that season, the glory of spring was poured out over the paradise of Galilee, and Cana, in the very midst of this flower-strewn landscape, was like a focal point of the enchantment of spring. It was just at this time of year that the secret of Galilee was revealed. The earthly nature of Galilee recalls the ancient condition of our earth when it was still united with the sun, and a revelation of the richest beauty comes with the breath of spring. Through the yearly spring shines something of that planetary spring which the earth once passed through in its cosmic course. The Christ-being who had descended to earth from the spiritual heights of the sun-sphere had first found himself in a human body at the place where the earthly landscape is a picture of the cosmic descent — the Fall. Now, in Galilee, he looked through human eyes on an earthly world which reflected the life-bearing sun-sphere, the source of creation in light itself.

Not only for the human soul of Jesus, but also for the new self-consciousness of the Christ-being, it was an earthly home-coming when the scene of the life of Jesus changed from the mount of temptation to Cana in Galilee. The consciousness of Jesus finds itself surrounded on earth by a revelation of heaven. The Christ-consciousness which became human, whose aim it is that the earth shall again become a sun, finds on earth this trace of the ancient sun-existence as a prophetic picture of the new sun of the future. In this sense the spring in Galilee mirrors the transformation that has taken place in Christ Jesus. Although it is only a human wedding that is being celebrated, a super-earthly spring shines on this gathering.

It was a sun-miracle that was accomplished when the guests at the feast drank and tasted wine, although fresh spring water had been poured into the pitchers from which they were served. It is the sun which every year changes the water of the grape into wine. In the depths of their souls, only half awake, the guests experienced echoes of a primal past, when the transforming power of the sun penetrated the earth much more powerfully. With this, they also felt premonitions of a distant future in which the new sun, radiating from human beings themselves, would be able to work transformingly within the kingdom of nature. The fact of this miracle at Cana shows us that in those early days it was not possible completely to restrain the influence which flowed from the divine forces of Christ. It was not in accord with the purpose of Christ Jesus that this should happen. He even said, 'Mine hour is not yet come.' The will to hold himself back ruled his entire soul; yet those around him experienced the streaming forth of his being right into physical substance. That which lived in him could not be hid.

Rudolf Steiner has indicated that the changing of water into wine, which the Gospel of John describes as the first of the seven signs, is not only to be traced back to Christ, but grows out of a mystery that operated between the soul of Jesus and his mother. The way in which Jesus answers his mother points to this mystery. It is not only a misunderstanding, but a complete misrepresentation to translate the words as 'Woman, what have I to do with thee?' The Greek words, *ti emoi kai soi* are not a rude rebuff. As a formula from the mysteries they point emphatically to a positive connection, and can be translated, 'Pay heed, O woman, to the power which flows between me and you' (John 2:4). The same formula occurs again in the gospels. Luke relates how Jesus at the beginning of his ministry, in the synagogue at Capernaum, was addressed in these words by the demon who troubled the souls of those who were possessed, *ti hêmin kai soi* 'What is it that binds us to you?' (Luke 4:34). The demons speak like this because they are already aware of the superior spiritual power that is making itself felt in their sphere.

The co-operation that was possible between the soul of Jesus and his mother at the marriage at Cana is a visible fruit of this great moment of his life, and reveals much. Mary, as well as Jesus, has passed through a significant transformation. According to the *Fifth Gospel,* an exalted spiritual power entered into the soul of Mary when Jesus had a parting conversation with his mother before going to John the Baptist at the Jordan. Through this she was able to share in the crisis of his soul. The painful shock he had experienced between his twelfth and thirtieth years through the discovery of the utter depths of emptiness into which humanity had fallen, and, on his mother's side, the growing premonition of her son's destiny and his stupendous task, had unlocked Mary's soul. Through the spiritual being who since then had lived in her, she had become the bearer of the virgin Mother-soul of the world. At the marriage of Cana she saw her son once more. But how changed he was! His countenance no longer reflected, as it had done during that farewell conversation, the whole misery of humanity, for now the divine ego had entered the soul of Jesus. The maternal World-Soul in Mary feels this. Two exalted heavenly beings find each other again on earth. Jesus still holds back. He says to Mary, 'Mine hour is not yet come.' It is true that he had entered into incarnation when the heavens opened and the voice of God said, 'This is my beloved Son,' but his birth on earth is not yet complete. He maintains around himself a cosmic maternal sheath from which he will not step until his ministry among people is due to begin. Nevertheless, in this hour of meeting, there operated between these two transformed beings something that might be described as the divine octave of the human Mother-Son relationship. By the radiant light of the being that ensouled her, Mary recognized intuitively in her completely changed son the power of the sun-being, the Christ. This it is that brought about the miracle of Cana. That which passed to and fro between Jesus and Mary, in this hour of their re-encounter, gave a particular colouring and natural power to the radiance that could no longer be hidden, and which streamed forth from the Christ. The water in the pots was changed, for those who partook, into the costliest wine, as the noblest gift of the sun to the earth.

The Passover feast is now drawing near. Although having returned so recently to the Galilean home from Judea, Jesus now turns his steps as a pilgrim towards Jerusalem, as other pious people are doing. Moving among the festive crowd that throngs the holy city, he goes to the Temple. He has no other purpose than reverently and simply to keep the Passover feast with everyone else. He does not wish to work. His hour is not yet come. He cannot, however, help *being* what he is. And now his entry into the Temple is a homecoming in a different sense from his return to Galilee. God enters the house of the Godhead. It is his first visit to the Temple since the twelve-year-old boy answered his parents with the words, 'Do you not know that I must be in my Father's house?' (Luke 2:49) So Jesus cannot remain indifferent in face of the obvious alienation and covetousness around him. A holy anger surges within him, which is more than mere human indignation. He does not break his self-imposed restraint. There is no necessity for this. No more than his presence is needed. Such flaming majesty radiates from his soul that those around him cannot protect themselves from it. The tables of the money-changers are overturned. Panic seizes the crowd. A magic power drives them out of the Temple. Something happens which has not happened since the days of Moses and Elijah. The mere presence of such a man, who of course is more than a man, brings about in all those around him a common visionary experience, as though the godhead himself were punishing the people in anger. Once, the presence of Moses let loose the ten plagues upon the Egyptians. The prayer of the prophet Elijah on Mount Carmel brought down the fire of heaven upon the priests of Baal. And now the people are spellbound as they perceive a figure who picks up a rope from the floor and swings it like a scourge over the heads of the fleeing crowd. In reality, Jesus stands in the Temple without stirring, but his presence is experienced as the judgment of God.

Waves of excitement surge through those who stay in Jerusalem for this Passover feast. It is part of the after-effects of the scene in the Temple that on one of the nights following the feast, Nicodemus, one of the highest Jewish leaders, comes to Jesus. This nocturnal conversation between Jesus and Nicodemus embodies no less of a *miracle* than the one which occurred at the marriage of Cana or during the feast. It was Rudolf Steiner who first explained what lies hidden in the statement that Nicodemus came to Jesus *by night*. This has commonly been taken to mean that Nicodemus had not the courage to come to Jesus by day, and so came under the cover of night. It is the Gospel of John, however, that tells us how Joseph of Arimathea was a disciple of Jesus, 'but kept it secret for fear of the Jews' (19:35). In relating that Nicodemus came to Jesus by night, the gospel would have given a similar explanation had this applied. In fact, wherever this episode is mentioned, the same terse formula is used: 'Nicodemus ... who had first come to Jesus in the realm of night' (19: 39). The point is that this is not a bodily encounter between Jesus and Nicodemus, but a supersensory spiritual meeting. The use of the word *night* indicates that the souls of Jesus and Nicodemus meet while free of the body, as souls always are in sleep. In this case, however, the night-condition is not one of sleep. It is rather a meeting between two individualities who maintain full consciousness and converse together. Thus the conversation is raised from the ordinary human level to the occult; it is a conference between two *Masters*. Thus it is that Jesus and Nicodemus both address one another as *Master*, and in this connection both use the word, 'we.' Nicodemus speaks in the name of the initiation of ancient times, and Jesus also says, '*We* speak of that we do know and bear witness of what *we* have seen.' This conversation between Masters must be understood as a real spiritual meeting between two men who recognize each other as initiates and are able to meet in this way. Even now Christ does not break through his self-imposed restraint. We are not told that Jesus comes to Nicodemus, but that Nicodemus comes to Jesus. The inner initiative springs from the scene in the Temple at the Passover feast. The influence proceeding from Jesus at that time causes Nicodemus to recognize in him an initiate and Master. And now the Jewish initiate of the Pharisees cannot rest. He is drawn to the other, who is greater than he, finds himself fully accepted, and is honoured by spiritual instruction from the Christ-being, before Jesus has begun to teach his disciples. In this conversation with Nicodemus, as well as in the marriage at Cana and the cleansing of the Temple, we see possibilities at work which are above the level and the law of ordinary human existence. We see Jesus able, as a matter of course, to participate in the faculty of the ancient initiates for acting and conversing independently of the physical body.

Finally, we have to recognize that the three scenes related in John's Gospel about the first period after the baptism, taken together in their threefoldness, correspond in a certain way to the threefold temptation of which the first three gospels speak. Involuntary impulses stream out from Christ Jesus which echo the magical possibilities suggested to him by the powers of opposition during the forty days. Our awareness of these parallels can gradually deepen our relationship to the Fourth Gospel. We feel the amazing breadth of view and candour which pervade it, and feel bound to read it with ever-increasing wonder and reverence.

The turning of water into wine at Cana seems at first sight to be related to the Ahrimanic temptation to turn stones into bread. But when we penetrate more deeply into the mysteries of the soul at work in the marriage at Cana, we shall see that the temptation is overcome. Through the great self-surrender and will-to-incarnation of the Christ, the possibility of interfering magically in the outer world is transformed into an inner impulse of spiritualization. But everything is still so new that the sunlike radiance streaming out among men becomes a revelation. It awakens for all time an idea of the divine cosmic greatness of Christ, and illuminates, as a distant goal, a wonderful mastery of the human spirit over earthly matter.

In the same way, the cleansing of the Temple belongs to the realm of the Luciferic temptation which leads Jesus on to the mountain and offers to make him Lord of the world. But now, at the Passover feast, for a moment it was shown what immense power over the souls of men he possessed. It was manifest in a negative form, inasmuch as the people were frightened by the divine austerity that was in him, and were put to flight. But it could also have shown itself positively. With their longing for true leadership, it would have needed very little effort on Christ's part to have brought about an immense mass-movement. But the further path of Christ will show how his power of leadership is completely transformed and fused into love. Jesus renounces absolutely all that men usually regard as success, and goes about quietly and unostentatiously. Only when he lays his hands on the sick does he allow a glimpse of the masterly power of which he would also have been capable to flow through his healing love. The radiance of his being, which was felt at that first Passover feast, was a human manifestation of divine wrath. But divine wrath is nothing else than the other side of divine love. Christ came into the world to bring about again the active power of God's love. He wishes only to serve, never to rule.

Although it is not at first obvious, the conversation by night with Nicodemus is reminiscent of the temptation in which Lucifer and Ahriman united and approached Christ with the suggestion that he should cast himself down from the pinnacle of the Temple. Had Jesus so wished, he could have appeared spiritually to men before the resurrection. Through breath-taking appearances, he could have convinced men of his absolute spiritual power. But this was no part of his will. All that belongs to magical occultism and fakirism was foreign to his purpose. After what Nicodemus had seen of Jesus at the Passover feast, he supposed him to be an initiated adept. But the conversation by night led him to feel intuitively that the full power Christ had over his own bodily and soul nature was of different origin. And when at the third Passover feast, on the hill of Golgotha, he came forward once more, with Joseph of Arimathea, in order to anoint the body taken down from the cross, he would fain transform his own adeptship to Christ's purpose.

The hints of the threefold temptation within the three Johannine scenes set a seal upon the superiority of the Christ over the demands of the opposing forces. While John's Gospel allows us a glimpse into the special phase at the beginning of the three years, which is otherwise so reverently veiled, it allows us at the same time to take part in the living progress of the transformation through which the divine incarnates and is changed within the human. In this is expressed the great confidence which John's Gospel has in people. The moment of the actual appearance of Christ is not postponed and then emphasized as it is in the other gospels. Nothing need be hidden, since Christ himself is intent on the veiling of his own being. He is incorporating the divine in himself within the veils of earthly incarnation. We shall relate ourselves intimately to the secret of the incarnation, from the baptism onwards if, following the Johannine presentation, we observe how at the opening of the three years the divine glory, unable to be altogether veiled, breaks forth powerfully from the human form. How the Christ-being lives more and more into the human element, and renounces the glory of miracles, will form the content of the three years. The *miracles* decrease the nearer the life of Jesus approaches Golgotha. Among all Christ's deeds on earth, what happened at the marriage of Cana can, more than any other, be described as a miracle. In the sense of the old belief in miracles, the greatest one happened at the beginning. But in reality, the greatest is the death on the cross, for here we have the climax of divine renunciation, and here the one great miracle of Christ's becoming Man is consummated.

CHAPTER THREE

The Call of the Disciples

The way of discipleship

In times when human interest is generally extrovert, man's inner life
calls for conscious and persistent cultivation. He who knows and follows an inner path will not break down if blows of fate strike him
unexpectedly, forcing him perhaps to relinquish a way of life which he
has grown to love, and to adapt himself to new and strange conditions.
Christianity offers such a path. Rightly understood, Christianity is
simply the path of discipleship of Christ. *The Imitation of Christ* by
Thomas à Kempis, expresses the meaning of Christianity, and the
gospels, above all, are a great picture-book of the stations of this spiritual path. If we leave aside theological abstractions and merely moral
interpretations we shall discover the soul-sphere of the gospels as a
world of its own. A wonderful panorama opens up by which in turn
spiritual bearings may be taken, just as on earth bearings can be taken
by mountain peaks. For the disciples every word and every deed of
Jesus which they are allowed to witness, whether it be addressed to
them or to the people, represents a station on the path of their souls.
Providence itself directs the steps and stages by which they set out to
walk with Christ.

The experiences of the disciples are at once inner and outer stations. They follow the paths of their souls as representatives of humanity of the future, although they are not conscious of this until he whom
they follow is no longer in earthly, bodily form among them. An
inward reconstruction of the scenes in the gospel is necessary if we are
to understand the transformation which took place each time in the
souls of the disciples, and which all humanity must go through. The
more clearly the course of this archetypal story is seen the more natu-

ral it is that our own souls should feel themselves reflected in the figures of the disciples, and receive the incentive to work for spiritual transformations which at times correspond to the experience of the disciples. Thus the gospel is a picture-book of discipleship, wherein we can try to read the picture-writing and decipher what it tells of the first steps of the path.

Matthew and Mark: homelessness

The gospels give different accounts of the call of the disciples. They seem to contradict one another and, indeed, the more so, the more one studies them in detail. Three scenes of the call of the disciples are pictured. First by St Matthew and St Mark, secondly by St Luke, and thirdly in the Gospel of John.

From the picture drawn by the first two gospels a special idea can be formed of Jesus' first meeting with the disciples, the beginning of the path of discipleship. It is a picture of deep spiritual fraternity, of clear unsurpassed harmony. The whole wonder of Galilean sunshine irradiates it. Only two fishing boats near the shore break the blue surface of the lake. The nearer boat lies a little way from the land; the two fishermen in it are casting their net, and so have put out into open water. To these two brothers Jesus addresses his call first: 'Follow me.' The two men leave their nets, row the boat in, and henceforth accompany him on his way. Going further, he calls to the men in the other boat, again two brothers; they are mending their nets, close inshore. They, too, respond to his call immediately. And Jesus continues his quiet way accompanied by the two pairs of brothers, Peter and Andrew, and the sons of Zebedee, James and John. At first, all that happens is that these four men leave the idyllic setting of the Sea of Galilee, and the contemplative fisherman's life, to share in the simple human fellowship of Jesus in his wanderings.

In its simplicity, this scene is clearly archetypal. It is a parable of Jesus — not spoken, but acted. To gain as much as possible of its inner pictorial value one must feel the quality of the scenery. This spot on the shore of the 'lake of lakes' where the call took place stands out among all other landscapes because of its sun-filled spiritual beauty. In other countries there are landscapes of more spectacular splendour, as perhaps in the Alps, or among the rocky islands of the Gulf of Naples, or in the primeval fertility of the South Sea Archipelago; but here on the northwest bank of the Lake of Gennesaret is a landscape of unsurpassable enchantment.

The name of Bethsaida, the town near which Jesus called the two pairs of brothers to follow him, means 'the House of Fish.' Where Peter, Andrew, James and John are fishing their work exemplifies something of the spirituality of the place. Today, when the town of Bethsaida has long since fallen into ruin without trace, the site is called Tabgha. This is an Arabic name, derived from the Greek word *Heptapegon*, meaning 'Seven Springs.' Indeed, near the paradisal little settlement which has grown up here many streams rise in the nearby hills surrounding the lake and flow into its blue waters. Five may be counted immediately. The striking thing about them is that all these springs and brooks have, from time immemorial, been clearly distinguished from one another by their fragrance. The various kinds of mineral compounds give the waters of each spring an entirely distinct taste and smell. One is strongly sulphurous, others are salty or sweet — each one different from the rest. It is as if they carry in proportions which are not accidental the quintessence of the earth, and especially of Galilee, into the waters of the lake. Looking down from the hills to the water when the lake is glassy and still — a fairly rare occasion — one can see at the mouth of the delta a great milky bow spreading far out into the cobalt blue. This is formed by great shoals of fish which are attracted by the taste and smell peculiar to the water here; it thus becomes an ideal place for the casting of nets. Here the life and work of the fisherman becomes a parable. The earthly waves reflect the ocean of the spiritual world from which at birth the soul descends to the shore of bodily existence, and into which it dips again at night, when in sleep it is freed from the body. The profusion of fish in the lake reflects the profusion of heavenly gifts which still surround little children, and by which man is refreshed and strengthened each night in sleep. The fisherman's work is carried on where land and sea meet; from the standpoint of the soul, it leads along the borderline between this world and the world beyond. So the life of the fisherman is more strongly interwoven with the feeling-element of soul and consciousness than is the life of men who work on dry land.

The wealth of fish in the waters of Bethsaida emphasizes, however, only one side of the miracle. The atmosphere is filled with something which can hardly be described, for it is not of this world. It springs from the peculiar interplay of the strong, cool air coming from the lake, with the substantial warmth of the surrounding atmosphere. For the Sea of Galilee lies more than 600 feet below sea-level. Particularly around Bethsaida, an extraordinary balance is preserved between stimulating coolness and soft, caressing warmth. The meadows bright with flowers on the hillsides, the silent eucalyptus woods where the level shore runs inland, even the little tropical gardens on the terraces of the hostel which stands there today — all these diffuse an unobtrusive stillness. And the feeling of well-being gained here cannot easily be surpassed, although the landscape itself is not imposing.

Here one feels, more clearly than anywhere else in the Holy Land, at a focal point in the process of cosmic growth. The miracle of Galilee is present in its fullness, echoing those primeval ages when the planet earth was permeated much more directly by the substance and influence of the sun. In spite of the steppe-like country, the result of centuries of forest-clearing, there can yet be sensed something of the special spiritual nearness of the sun. And there is not only, in general, the breath of spiritual sunshine, but all who come here feel deeply impressed as though, returning from a long absence, they remember their place of origin. The reason is that here by the lake the world before birth is especially clearly reflected. There is still a deep memory of that sphere in every human being. Borne by the rays of the spiritual sun, the influence of the world before birth makes itself felt and awakens memories extending far beyond life on earth. The path of the disciples begins in a landscape deeply affected by the nearness of the etheric sun, and therefore bears within it the peace of God that comes with feeling most inwardly at home.

Looking ahead, one can imagine where the path of discipleship will lead at the end of the three short years of the life of Christ. Only then, through the resulting contrast, will the miracle of the beginning become really clear. The landscape of Judea, where three years later the cross of Golgotha is to stand, is diametrically opposed to this. Judea, with the desert of Judah and the Dead Sea, is an inferno compared to Galilee. It is a petrified landscape, almost like that of the moon, where the earth is robbed of its vitality, a victim of cosmic mineralization. Something more than old age has laid hold of it. The path of the disciples begins at the pole of life; it ends in the landscape of death. It comprises the great cosmic polarity which is concentrated in the Holy Land, because here the earth preserves genuine remains both of its sun-existence and of its moon-condition. The way of discipleship does not lead to material happiness; it corresponds to an expulsion from paradise; it leads from a paradise to a hell.

Bethsaida, the House of Fish, was the home of many of the Twelve. Philip, too, came from here. Finally, the call to follow reached Matthew, the customs officer, in the same place. He was stationed here, where the ancient road between Babylon and Egypt runs along the lakeside. No one in the world could have had a more home-like home than these men. The quality of an original, archetypal homeliness is spread out over the place. But the path of the disciples leads from home to homelessness. By following Christ's call, the disciples were uprooted. They would not have been able to find Christ had they not been able to leave the cosmic beauty of their home. The renunciation which leads them to homelessness belongs to the beginning of their spiritual path. The first two gospels stress the necessary detachment. It is expressly emphasized that the second pair of brothers left not only their boat and nets, but also their father. Giving up home life involves also detachment from blood-ties.

The step from home to homelessness must be taken in some way or other by everyone. As a child man has his home always with him, whether he remains in the place of his birth or not: the aura of the world before birth clings to him. This disappears as he grows older. When an adult sighs for his lost childhood, he really wishes to have again that aura which surrounded him as a baby. But this homelessness is essential for his own salvation; it is the condition of maturity. Because modern man no longer attaches any spiritual value to the God-willed homelessness of adult life he falls into a vacuum. He loses the art of growing old; spiritual emptiness threatens his maturity. Here, religious re-orientation is necessary. This will bring with it the power to experience rightly every stage of life with its own religious content. The inner beauty of age is different from the external beauty of childhood. It is not so obvious, and only appears when strength is consciously gathered to master the homelessness. Only he who practises a positive resignation and relies on spiritual sources can remain young, even in old age. It is part of the foolishness of this materialistic age to think that one can keep young by purely natural means.

Knowledge of the spiritual path of the soul involves above all recognition of homelessness as the necessary starting-point of all spiritual growth.

The call of the disciples at the Sea of Galilee gives instruction to the last detail on this essential first step of the spiritual path. In order to follow Christ, the two pairs of brothers have to leave their boats and go ashore. This is a picture of the first step to the spirit: the way from the sea to the land. Falling asleep each night is like putting out from dry land into the open sea. Dry land is the material world of the day-mind. The sea is the land of soul and spirit, entered into during sleep. Waking up is like returning to dry land. What gives the scene its symbolic significance is that in the case of the fishermen the external and internal events are synchronized; the external event is at the same time an imaginative picture wherein, throughout the ages, he who treads the spiritual path may see reflected the beginning of his own conversion.

The step of the fishermen of Bethsaida from the sea to the land has even more significance. People who grew up on the shore of Galilee and who, because of their work as fishermen, constantly lived on this mysterious frontier-line between earth and water, were bound to be different from, for instance, people born and bred in Judea. Travellers in Palestine during the last century, especially the gifted Frenchman, Ernest Renan, have recorded that they met many people round about the Lake of Gennesaret who possessed second sight; who had the old dreamlike, clairvoyant consciousness. The paradisal world of Bethsaida kept alive the old clairvoyant faculties which had been lost. It took these people slightly out of themselves, producing a kind of prophetic experience. It is important to realize that the first disciples still shared in the ancient heritage of clairvoyance, and had not yet reached the nadir of spiritual consciousness which was characteristic of the inhabitants of Judea, and is still more so of people today. In districts where fishing is the main occupation, as for instance the Frisian Islands or the Hebrides, there are still the remains of an atavistic clairvoyance which either fades rapidly, or passes over into the seeing of ghosts. Nearness to water enhances the power of divination. Where land and water touch, the soul meets the spiritual world more easily.

What, then, is the meaning of this picture of the four men leaving the lake and their boats and coming ashore? The spiritual process indicated by the external event is the awakening from the dreamlike clairvoyant condition, the casting off of the nature-given link with the supersensory. The disciples have to take leave not only of their home, but also of the consciousness of heaven which has grown from the elemental forces of their native land. A world of dreams and pictures is exchanged for objective earthly consciousness. The nets filled with fish are a picture of the symbolic dreams and visions given to the soul which sets forth on the sea of dreams. With their fishing-boats and nets the disciples leave behind a whole world, but in so doing they find the world of him whom they will henceforth follow.

Luke: the vision of apostleship

The Gospel of Luke has no direct parallel to the scene of the call of the disciples in the first two gospels. It shows Jesus of Nazareth hard at work, without saying first how the group of disciples was formed. Instead, it describes at a rather later stage, in chapter 5, a scene which can ultimately be recognized as parallel to the call of the disciples. Important motifs from the scene of the call in the first two gospels can be discovered in individual details.

Jesus is on the shore of the Sea of Galilee surrounded by the crowd. Many come to him, desiring to hear him. As they become too many, 'he saw two boats on the beach; the fishermen had got out and were washing their nets. And he stepped into one of the boats which belonged to Simon, and asked him to row a little distance out from the shore. And he sat down and spoke to the crowd from the boat and taught them.' (Luke 5:2f). Thus Jesus turns the fishing boat into a pulpit from which to speak to the multitude. The gospel continues: 'Then he stopped speaking and said to Simon, "Put out into the deep and let down your nets there for a catch." Simon answered, "Master, we worked all night and caught nothing; but because you say so I will cast the nets".' Peter follows the instruction of Jesus and so many fish are caught that the nets nearly break. The two fishermen have to call their partners in the other boat in order to bring the catch to land. 'When Simon Peter saw this, he fell on his knees before Jesus and said, "Lord, depart from me, I am a sinful man".' The gospel expressly emphasizes what is taking place in the souls of the men directly concerned. '... great alarm had overwhelmed him and also the others who were with him, because of the catch of fish which they had made. James and John, the sons of

Zebedee, who were partners with Simon, had the same experience. And Jesus said to Simon, "Do not be afraid, from now on you will be a fisher of living men".' And the fishermen of the Lake of Gennesaret determinedly set out on the path of discipleship. 'And they brought the boats to land, left everything and followed him' (Luke 5:9–11).

It is this last sentence whereby Luke's account of the miraculous draught of fishes may be recognized as a parallel to the other scenes of the call. Also the words addressed to Peter about becoming a fisher of men link this story with the corresponding scene in the first two gospels; in the gospels of Matthew and Mark, Christ speaks these words to Peter and Andrew, the first-called pair of brothers. True, the scene in Luke's Gospel cannot be accepted as the very first meeting between Jesus and the four fishermen of Bethsaida, like the parallel scene in the first two gospels, for in Luke's Gospel the healing of Peter's mother-in-law precedes the miraculous draught of fishes, in which Peter plays the main part. Thus Luke draws attention to a call addressed to Peter and the other fishermen of Bethsaida which seems to come later than what is related in the first two gospels, and to present a new stage.

St Luke's scene belongs to a part of the gospel which can be understood only when it is seen as an imaginative rendering of events of the soul, rather than as a description of external events. The beginning of the story has indeed a very definite physical setting. The picture of Jesus speaking to the people from the pulpit of the fishing boat is one of the most vivid and impressive given of his life. Yet the second half of the narrative, describing the actual experience of the disciples, leads right into the imaginative world of the soul. And surprisingly the step which the disciples first had to take is here reversed. The main point is no longer the disciples forsaking the sea for land. Rather, at the word of Jesus, they forsake the land and set out on the lake. If we take this description as the imaginative expression of a spiritual process, in St Luke's sequence the call of the disciples is linked with the impulse to strive boldly upwards and out from the earthly, physical plane to the sphere of the spirit. Clearly the step which the first two gospels place at the beginning — the step leading from the old dreamlike spirituality into the sober, objective consciousness of the physical plane — is here already presupposed. The quintessence of that to which the disciples are to be led on their path is seen here in a great imaginative picture. They will share in a new, more conscious way, the riches of the spiritual worlds. The soul-picture representing the necessary parting from the old spirituality is replaced by one containing the impulse to the new spirituality. The secret of discipleship is twofold: to stand firmly with both feet on the ground, yet to strive to find the spiritual in the earthly and to press out into the wide open sea of spiritual consciousness.

Starting from the first point of the scene, with its distinctly physical and historical setting, an idea may be formed of the external, biographical process which underlies the second, pictorial happening — the miraculous draught of fishes. Jesus spoke to the people. He had, moreover, as if accidentally, taken up a position which offered his listeners a wide, inspiring view. They saw him sitting in the boat, with the dark blue lake as a background and the boundless blue sky above. The mountains on the far side of the lake appeared only as a shimmering red line between the two shades of blue. A picture was formed which awakened feelings in the depths of the hearers' souls as if they confronted the spirit-world itself, thrown open in its breadth and depth. The disciples also listened with the assembled multitude, in the atmosphere of their native country. While Jesus used their boat as a pulpit, he was drawing them to himself, actively and intensively. For the first time they shared fully in that deep stirring of the spirit which fills the earthly environment with a super-earthly mood. It may have been simple parables which Jesus spoke from the pulpit of the boat, but they opened wide doors to the deeper feelings of his hearers. Now Jesus stopped speaking, and the powerful after-effect of his words burned in the souls of the disciples. They lived through a great enhancement of the impression which remains always in sensitive men when they have passed through a powerful experience. If this no longer happens with modern people, it is only because we have become barbarians in the way we deal with such experiences, and no longer possess the inner calm and receptivity to await what is released in the soul afterwards. We dash from one impression to another, and pass over the most important things, the answering echoes and reflections which appear on a deeper level of the soul. The after-effect of having heard Jesus speak against that natural heavenly background produced in the souls of the disciples so potent a vision that it appeared as something more real than their external, tangible surroundings. The inner truth of the picture-experience into which they were drawn is confirmed by the fact that they all experienced it alike. In a prophetic image they were shown how rich will be their harvest if they follow the spiritual impulses which lay in the words of Jesus.

If nowadays people were not estranged from their own nature, they might constantly have similar experiences. If, in the daytime, a man has experienced something impressive, whether religious, artistic or humanly stirring, and if his soul has been sufficiently trained to allow the echo of the experience to resound within it, then in one of the following nights it will certainly take in a wonderful draught of fishes as a result. The soul, freed from the body in sleep, will be able to bring back those spiritual treasures to which the original experience had given access. It is part of the tragedy of modern humanity that even after tremendous experiences nothing new follows, because the soul is governed by the great illusion that existence finishes in the foreground of life.

Hence the call of the disciples in Luke's Gospel by no means merely presents a teaching concerning the beginning of the path of discipleship. It shows that after the disciples have taken the step from the lake to the land, they are given a glimpse of the end of the path on which they have entered. They are granted strength for all the renunciations and sacrifices which they will now have to make, when they recognize: 'If we follow the path of discipleship, we shall become rich in a new way; we shall be in a position to take an infinitely more valuable catch than we have ever been able to do in our fisherman's life.' The words that Christ speaks to Peter in Luke's Gospel, 'From now on you you will be a fisher of living men,' give the disciples the key to the great vision which still perplexes them. The apostolic task lies open before them. They see in this picture the great community which will one day result from their missionary work as disciples of Christ. It is a Pentecostal vision which rises before the souls of Peter and the other fishermen of Bethsaida.

The countryside of John the Baptist

If the two scenes of the call of the disciples in the first three gospels have important correspondences, in spite of their differences, the description of the call of the first disciples in John's Gospel strikes an entirely different note. The Fourth Gospel tells of the call at the very beginning. Jesus has come to John the Baptist, and has been baptized by him in the River Jordan. It was not solely a meeting between Jesus and John, for John was surrounded by a group of disciples. John calls the attention of some of the disciples to him who, silently and unobtrusively, has joined the group receiving baptism. John is deep in conversation with two of his disciples. Then he sees Jesus passing, and says to the two who are with him, 'Behold the Lamb of God!' This indication may have awakened in them, perhaps, no clear knowledge as yet, but a strong presentiment which constrains them to follow, as in a dream, him to whom the Baptist has pointed. Jesus, noticing that the two are following him, turns round and looking at them says, 'What are you seeking?' John's two disciples ask the counter-question coming perhaps from the dream-depth of their soul: 'Where do you live?' And now Jesus bids them come with him: 'Come and see.' The gospel records that they remained with him the whole day. One of the two was Andrew, Simon Peter's brother. In a state of inspiration, he must tell his brother what he has discovered. So Simon also comes to Jesus, who names him Peter, the rock, in acknowledgment of the elemental forces he has recognized in his nature. More of the Baptist's disciples join those who recognize the supernatural character of Jesus.

Nothing could be more unlike the description of the call of the disciples given in the first three gospels. To begin with, the landscape here is completely different from that of the Sea of Galilee. These encounters take place in Judea itself, not just in Jerusalem, where the typical Judean characteristics are moderated, but in a place where the subearthly, infernal character of the landscape is most powerful — deep down at the foot of the wilderness of Judah near where the Jordan enters the Dead Sea. The sea of death breathes its poison over a country in which nothing can thrive. The deadly brine of the Dead Sea penetrates even up the river. As the deepest point of the earth's surface, the Dead Sea is framed by magnificently fissured mountains, whose moonlike character is mysteriously enhanced in the short hours of sunrise and sunset when the air assumes unearthly colours. Nothing brings out more clearly the contrast between the two Palestinian lakes than the fact that no fish can live in the Dead Sea whereas the Lake of Gennesaret is blessed with a wealth of fish. Even at the place of John's baptisms, the Jordan can no longer harbour fish. Here — where the

Jordan, already weary with the loss of its vitality, enters the region of death, framed by cosmic pictures of the deepest fall of creation and of man's fall into sin — here John the Baptist raised his voice, and directed his burning prophetic summons like a flame of fire, calling humanity to a change of heart.

It is significant that the site of the baptism in Jordan is known by a name which, as the designation of another place, was to play a part later in the gospel. The place of baptism is called Bethany,* and has therefore the same name as the little town on the eastern slope of the Mount of Olives near Jerusalem, where the wilderness of Judah begins. Bethany means 'The House of Poverty.' Low-lying Bethany, which John the Baptist made the scene of his activities, gives cosmic expression to this name; it shows the state of impoverishment into which the whole of the planet earth must come if it merely follows the course of natural development, which is a continual wasting and los-ing of its heavenly dowry. The Bethany near the summit of the Mount of Olives, where Lazarus is to become the disciple John, is a more human 'House of Poverty,' lying at the edge of the spectacular descent where the steep waste of the wilderness falls away.

As the theology of the last hundred years has generally discounted the historical value of the Gospel of John, and has regarded the synop-tic gospels as the only serviceable record of the life of Jesus, a compar-ison of the contrasting scenes of the call of the disciples is one of the points where a certain change of valuation becomes necessary. The Gospel of John narrates the historical course of events so concretely that it becomes difficult to understand how theology has failed to rec-ognize this. We must discover the Gospel of John anew and realize the historical value of its every detail. It appears in quite a new light if attention is focused on its factual descriptions. On the other hand, we grasp the quality of the synoptic gospels more adequately if we recog-nize their stories as imaginative renderings of what took place in the souls of the disciples. Here, everything is filled with a symbolism which reveals the gospel as a picture-book for the spiritual path. If then the Gospel of John is read as a biographical and historical record, the question arises as to where in fact Jesus did first meet the disciples. What is the answer? Did he meet them in Judea or in Galilee?

---

* Bethany is the name contained in the best and earliest manuscripts. *Bethabara,* as the Authorised Version reads, is a later version.

The sequence in the calling of the disciples

Passing on from the geographical contrast, a consideration of the temporal distinction which the gospels bring out with great precision leads to a most surprising answer. In the gospels of Matthew and Mark, the scene on the shore of the Sea of Galilee is introduced by the sentence: 'When Jesus became aware that John had fallen into the hands of his enemies, he went to Galilee' (Matt.4:12; Mark 1:14.) These gospels therefore refer to a later point in time than does the Gospel of John, where the reference to John the Baptist being cast into prison does not occur until 3:24, while the call of the disciples is contained in the latter part of chapter 1. There is nearly half a year between the baptism of Jesus and the arrest of the Baptist, and so also between the two calls of the disciples. The first of these, the Judean call, is definitely associated in the Gospel of John with the baptism. Much must have happened in this interval.

The gospels of Matthew, Mark and Luke relate nothing of all that lies between the baptism in the Jordan and the arrest of John the Baptist except the enigmatic scene of the temptation in the wilderness of Judah. In this account, Jesus does not call the fishermen of Bethsaida until after the arrest of John the Baptist. On the other hand, the Gospel of John admits us into the secret of the interval which the synoptic gospels veil with silence. Not only is the meeting and call of the disciples described in direct association with the baptism of Jesus, but it is followed by the scene in which, at the time of the preparation for the Passover, Jesus goes as guest to the marriage in Cana of Galilee, together with his disciples and his mother. Then comes the dramatic scene of the cleansing of the Temple, which took place at the Passover. The conversation by night between Jesus and Nicodemus follows as an echo of this first 'Easter' drama. This is still within that period of which the other gospels are silent. For in the Gospel of John, after the conversation with Nicodemus, it is written: 'After this Jesus and his disciples came to the land of Judea. There he stayed with them and baptized. John also baptized; he was at Aenon near Salim, because there was much water there.' (John 3:22f). And the gospel adds expressly: 'John had not yet been imprisoned' (3:24). The prophetic activity of John the Baptist again becomes apparent as he tells his disciples of the bridegroom and the friend of the bridegroom and he cries, 'He must increase, but I must decrease.'

The scenes shown by St John as the content of this otherwise veiled interval lead beyond the Passover of that year in which the baptisms in the Jordan had earlier taken place. Hence the call of the disciples in Galilee described by the other gospels must have been preceded by many scenes in which the disciples took part, such as the marriage in Cana; on the other hand, the call of the disciples in Judea, described by St John, occurred even before the temptation of Jesus. This is an astonishing example of the apparent contradictions of the gospels. The scene by the Sea of Galilee which has been understood as the first meeting between Jesus and his disciples, proves to be an event which took place very much later than the first meeting of Jesus with the Galilean men in John the Baptist's circle. The call of the disciples in Judea is in the beginning of the year. The Galilean scene, by contrast, is in the season of Pentecost in the same year. This leads to a completely new understanding of the scene on the shore of the lake. It now becomes necessary to approach this scene anew.

There must be a gap between the two scenes. At some point, Jesus must have dismissed the disciples who had followed him at the Baptist's word, and they must have returned to their homes and their fishing in Galilee. The initial experience associated with the meeting in the Baptist's circle had to fade, and perhaps indeed to sink deep into the unconscious. When Jesus walked along the shore and called the fishermen from their boats to follow him, they had not only been long known to him, but he was also known to them. This is not expressed in words; the gospels make it clear through the silent language of their composition, which gives access to a comprehensive synoptic view of the various presentations. Profound biographical secrets on which the gospel lays a seal are thus revealed.

The two pairs of brothers whom Jesus calls from their fishing boats are by this time no longer what they appear to be — simple Bethsaida fishermen. They had already been through decisive experiences, even when John the Baptist first drew their attention to Jesus, for his fiery message had called them from the peace of their homes into the homelessness of the landscape around the Dead Sea. But there was more than this. Peter, Andrew, Philip and the others, had received the baptism of John before Jesus was baptized in the Jordan. Their souls had already been transformed by that which took place when body and soul were loosened through immersion in the river, when the soul, freed from the body, awoke to the great vision experienced at the boundary between life and death, Then it went on to perceive the imminent coming of the promised Messiah. It was as converted men that the disciples were directed to that other who was present in their midst, still and silent.

The first meeting of the disciples with Jesus of Nazareth in the circle of the Baptist was, then, like a grain of corn falling on prepared virgin soil. The consciousness of the disciples was fundamentally opened up in a way quite different from anything they could have experienced in the paradisal atmosphere of their Galilean home. It was raised above everything earthly. Although they were treading the hard ground of the low-lying desert valley of the Jordan, their souls were hovering between heaven and earth. To a much higher degree, however, was the spiritual condition of Jesus himself affected by the baptism: with him it was not as with the disciples — that his own ego found itself again in a changed, expanded and heightened soul-space. The human ego of Jesus had passed out of his body altogether. In constant self-surrender, it had made real the spiritual mystery expressed later by St Paul, 'Not I, but Christ in me.' It had made a space for the divine ego, which had just reached the portal of incarnation in its descent for the salvation of humanity. The divine Christ ego had entered the soul of Jesus of Nazareth, expanded and heightened by the baptism, bringing with it the sunlike strength which the devout of ancient days had worshipped as the spirit of the sun. The experiences of the disciples, and especially of Jesus, which followed the baptism are not to be measured in terms of everyday life. Seen from the earthly angle of observation, Jesus and his disciples might have appeared as though walking in a dream. In reality, however, the vast providential processes and events of the turning-point of all earthly history were passing through the soul of Jesus, and in a lesser degree through the souls of the disciples. Of course, their consciousness was not fully contained within normal earthly confines, and it becomes understandable why the first three gospels shroud the long space of time between the baptism and the arrest of John the Baptist in a veil of secrecy, only to break their silence to record the three stages of the temptation, which are purely spiritual experiences. If the Gospel of John passes over in silence a considerably shorter period, that is, from the baptism to the Passover festival, and describes then the marriage of Cana, the purification of the Temple and the nocturnal conversation with Nicodemus, it presupposes a maturity of feeling which can take fully into account the special conditions under which these acts and events took place.

In the meantime many things happened. Eventually, after the Passover of that year — perhaps indeed, on one of the days before the ancient festival of Pentecost — Jesus came walking along the shore of the Sea of Galilee and summoned the fishermen to follow him. The scene on the lakeside, which at first seemed to be only an imaginative picture of inward steps and resolutions, proves to be now of unsuspected biographical importance. It is not a beginning that takes place here; many and great things have preceded it. But because a quite definite stage of spiritual maturity has now been reached, it is nevertheless a wonderfully fresh new start, granted and prepared by destiny for the fishermen of Galilee.

The more clearly the calendar of that wonderful spring is revealed, the clearer appear the different stages expressed in the scenes on the lakeside. If, at the time of the call related by the first two gospels the feast of Pentecost was near, then the miraculous draught of fishes described by St Luke is really the pentecostal event of this first year. For the first time 'the day of Pentecost was fully come.' It is now possible to see the canonical laws and harmonies in the life of Christ: the events of the third year, culminating in Golgotha, have their exact correspondence in the preceding years. The marriage in Cana corresponds to the institution of the Lord's Supper. The Resurrection has its preparatory stage in the cleansing of the Temple, placed by John's Gospel at the Passover festival of the first year. The teaching of the Risen Christ during the forty days between Easter and the Ascension is a fulfilment of the conversation by night with Nicodemus after the Passover of the first year. In the same way the pentecostal experience of the disciples in the third year when through the flame of the Holy Spirit their souls awoke to the vision of their apostolic mission, was foreshadowed in the pentecostal call in Galilee, particularly as described by St Luke.

According to Rudolf Steiner, the experience of the disciples at the 'real' Pentecost in Jerusalem consisted in this — that they suddenly awoke to what they had actually been through. They had walked for three years with Christ, and yet had not been fully conscious of their unique privilege. They experienced overwhelming remorse when they realized that they had 'slept' most of the time they had walked the land with Christ. And this great awakening gave them the impulse to go forward into the world as apostles.

A first instalment of such an awakening must have come to the disciples on the lakeside, as Jesus called them to follow him. Their experiences with John the Baptist, the vision of the *status nascendi* of the incarnating god, had at first been like a dream. Now they began to wake up. Scales fell from their eyes as Jesus said to them: 'Follow me.' They began to tread the path of discipleship now in reality, and to grasp the mystery of the glory of light, previously seen as in a dream. When Jesus said to them: 'I will make you fishers of men,' the vision of apostleship began to shine.

St John implies that already, between the two calls, the disciples shared at times in the life of Christ. After their eyes had first been opened for Christ, as a direct result of the baptism, a considerable time of separation followed. Jesus spent forty days in the wilderness, and afterwards did not return to John the Baptist. He pursued his quiet wanderings in Galilee, perhaps even continuing his former handicraft. In the meantime, those of the Baptist's disciples who had been able to absorb some idea of the greatness of the being of Christ, had now returned to Galilee. Thus Jesus and these disciples met again. They were invited together as guests to the marriage in Cana. It is not without significance that the Gospel of John here picks up the thread that was dropped after Jesus had met the disciples in the group around the Baptist. The little town of Cana in Galilee was, according to the last chapter of St John's Gospel, where Nathanael lived, the last one to be called at the first call. Perhaps it was Nathanael who brought about the meeting between Jesus and the disciples at the marriage in Cana. The Gospel links the disciples' experience in Cana with the first impressions imparted to them in the Baptist's circle: 'He made manifest the radiating power of his being' (John 2:11). It was still part of the wondrous *status nascendi* when Jesus said to his mother 'My own hour (the hour of his open manifestation) has not yet come.'

But not only in Galilee could the disciples renew their acquaintance with Christ. When they went to Jerusalem for the Passover they could perceive there, in the vicinity of the ancient Temple, the supersensory power of the Christ. As witnesses of the cleansing of the Temple, they received into their souls a seed which germinated two years later, when they understood the enigmatic words of Christ about the destruction and rebuilding of the Temple as referring to his own resurrection. After the Passover, both Jesus and the disciples worked for a time in the neighbourhood after the fashion of John the Baptist. The Baptist was still the great forerunner, and Jesus and the disciples prepared those who came to them for his baptism. Some of the disciples also performed this baptism. It has been said that Jesus too baptized. In fact, however, he remained in the background, only serving. His hour was still not yet come. During this time, the Baptist, as if already feeling the nearness of his great sacrifice, once more directed the disciples to Christ: 'He must increase, but I must decrease.' Eventually they journeyed with Jesus back to Galilee and on the way, at Jacob's well in Samaria, they took part in the episode of the Samaritan woman. Presumably each then returned to his daily work: the disciples to their occupation as fishermen, and Jesus to his lonely wanderings through Galilee.

With the arrest of John the Baptist, however, everything suddenly changed. It was a summons of destiny; for now that the voice crying in the wilderness was hushed, it became very clear that humanity was a flock without its shepherd. Now it was time for Jesus to emerge from his obscurity, and the disciples were ready to stand by him and to begin their apostolic mission. The first Pentecost comes round, and the disciples receive the grace of their first commission.

But it is still more surprising that the Gospel of John, before passing over a period of two or three months, reveals events immediately following the baptism. The call of the disciples in John's Gospel is wrapped in the very deepest mystery. The great transformations of soul which not only in Jesus but also in the disciples broke the bounds of ordinary human experience, have only just taken place. We witness the most significant illustration of a *status nascendi* in human history. The chemist speaks of a *status nascendi* when various chemicals are about to combine. The process begins with a flaring and boiling up of forces, followed by a more quiet mutual interpenetration. In the soul and spirit of Jesus of Nazareth the greatest *status nascendi* occurs that ever was or will be possible on earth. Divine element and human element meet in order to unite and interpenetrate entirely. The process begins with a tempestuous flashing up of the divine cosmic spark within the human being. With this in mind we may ask what happened when John the Baptist pointed two of his disciples to Christ. Their response is far more than an external one. With somnambulistic precision John's disciples use a comprehensive symbol for distant past and far future. The words exchanged apply only apparently to the earthly situation. They are of quite different dimensions. When Jesus asks 'What are you seeking?' their uplifted and almost disembodied souls must feel themselves addressed in the very depths of their being, from which they have sought their way through the ages. The answer 'Rabbi, where do you live?' comes from these depths and asks after the nature of him who, so infinitely transformed, is present among them. The Greek text alone makes it clear that they ask by no means only after the home of Jesus. At the site of the baptism in Jordan this question would be meaningless anyway. The Greek sentence *pou meneis* contains a basic Johannine word. The verbal form *menein* is usually translated as 'abide.' In order to feel the tone of this word in the Gospel of John we need only remember the sentences in chapter 15. 'Abide in me and I in you. As the branch cannot bear fruit by itself unless it is given life by the vine, neither can you unless you stay united with me. I AM the vine, you are the branches. He who remains united with me and I in him, he bears much fruit, for apart from me you can do nothing ... If you abide in me and my words live on in you, pray for that which you also *will*, and it shall come about for you.' (John 15:4–7).

The noun occurs at the beginning of chapter 14: 'In my Father's house there are many dwellings.' It is clear that *monê* ('mansions' or 'dwellings') means more than an earthly home. It is the sphere of soul and spirit which appertained to an immortal entelechy. And so, in the question addressed to Christ by the two of John's disciples it seems as if the earth is wondering about the divine being who, by the greatest miracle in world history, is suddenly present in earthly existence. Jesus answers, 'Come and see.' And the gospel says that the two disciples stayed with him the whole day. The disciples received their first intimate teaching, but this was not given in words. They were received, through unfathomable faith, into the sphere of the Christ-being, who was about to pass through the momentous mystery of the *status nascendi*. Transformed, they were overshadowed by the presence of the greatest of all transformations, and for a whole day were drawn into the fire in which God became man and man became God.

The meeting between Jesus and Nathanael is the conclusion of the calling of the disciples in the Fourth Gospel. At the end, Jesus says to Nathanael: 'You will see heaven opened, and the angels of God ascending and descending above the Son of Man' (John 2:51). The boldness of these words spoken by Jesus at the very beginning of his fellowship with the disciples might almost frighten us. But these words express no more than what the disciples would experience in this first superhuman stage of their path with Christ: while they are allowed to gaze upon the Christ-being, their wondering souls perceive more than the human figure in whose company they are. This human figure is surrounded by an aura soaring far into the heights of heaven. He who in their midst is descending more and more deeply into human incarnation, is the Lord and the Heart of all the hierarchies, whose retinue includes every sphere in the domain of the angels of God.

The calendar of the first spring

When the Christ-being entered the soul and body of Jesus of Nazareth, heavenly wine was poured into an earthly vessel, and the heavenly wine had at first to froth up and brim over. It required a patient emptying of self on the part of the Christ-being to condense the fullness of the divine cosmic power into the narrow dwelling of the human body. In the story of the temptation, the first three gospels show imaginatively how Christ achieved that great self-renunciation. The forty days during which Christ was in the loneliness of the desert must have begun comparatively soon after the baptism. In this case the call of the disciples according to the Gospel of John falls into the short period which Jesus spent in the circle of John the Baptist, after his baptism and before his withdrawal into solitude. Perhaps the powerful influence which he exercised in those days on the dreaming souls of the men of Galilee was one of the reasons which led Christ to withdraw for a time. When St Matthew and St Mark show Christ beginning his activities only after the arrest of John the Baptist, this may be an indication that only then was the process of incarnation, dependent on the divine self-emptying, so fully achieved that he could appear before men without overwhelming them.

The meeting of the disciples with Christ, in the circle of John the Baptist, appeared to them like a vast dream beyond their power of apprehension. Their being allowed to behold his glory planted in their hearts the most momentous seed for the future. At first they were unable to relate it to the material, earthly plane. It must have seemed to them that all this had happened while their souls were in another world, as before birth or during sleep. They felt themselves further advanced in their earthly consciousness as disciples of the Baptist. The meeting with Jesus granted to them through the suggestion of John the Baptist, remained more as a great dream than as anything which had brought them into a new relationship on the human plane. All that had first to fade away. As Jesus was seeking solitude, he even dismissed the disciples, who had completed their time with the Baptist, so that they now reverted to their life as fishermen in Galilee. Destiny left them time for the seed sown into the ground of their being to grow towards the light.

Events preceding the calling of the disciples

The scenes at the sea of Galilee relating to the calling of the disciples at Whitsun were preceded not only by the calling of the disciples in Judea and the events told in the first three and a half chapters of the Gospel of John. The preparation of the disciples in terms of their destiny for the actual period of their discipleship goes back much further. We can assume with regard to at least some of the men from Galilee that they already knew Jesus when they encountered him in the circles of John the Baptist. Rudolf Steiner's descriptions in his lectures on the so-called *Fifth Gospel* about the events in the life of Jesus between the age of twelve and thirty allow us to see something of the roots from which the tree of the disciples was later to grow.

The young Jesus of Nazareth, particularly between the ages of eighteen and twenty-four, wandered a great deal through his Galilean homeland and the neighbouring lands. He did so in pursuit of his carpentry trade which he had learned and taken over from his father Joseph. All the people whose homes he entered were left with deep, indelible impressions of his being. It was less what he said than the infinitely pure power of love which streamed from his heart, remaining in the depressed souls as a brilliant light. In the years in which he no longer visited them, the people whom he had attended thought back frequently to the beneficial and positive effect of his being. Often when they sat together at night and spoke about him in joint recollection, they felt as if his brightly shining figure was joining them in their dim rooms. Thus the years passed. The time of the baptism in Jordan approached. After the forty days spent alone in the desert, Jesus for a time continued to travel through the hamlets and villages of Galilee as before. After the great transformation which had taken place in his being, the whole world had been transformed for him. He was even more silent than previously because the speech spoken around him no longer appeared to be the real expression of what was happening in people and in the world. But when he entered the houses of such people who had known him previously and who had remembered him in the interim with such great love and gratitude, they often perceived with great wonder the change in his being through their feeling. They experienced a new power radiating out from him. In his presence they felt brought into harmony and made healthy down into their physical bodies. 'Previously they had experienced his love, goodness and mildness, but now he radiated a great miraculous power. Whereas previously they felt comforted, now they felt healed.' Many of those who experienced these things joined his travels in the course of time. They may have formed a part of the extended circle of disciples to which the Gospel of Luke refers. But undoubtedly some of the closer circle of the twelve became disciples in this period between the calling of the disciples in Judea and Galilee. Perhaps there were some among them who had not previously been disciples of John the Baptist. 'Travelling through the lands ... in this way, it turned out that those who experienced most deeply how Jesus of Nazareth had been transformed became his disciples and followed him. He took with him people from various hostelries who followed him. ... In this way a group of such disciples came together.'

Relationships of destiny

Where Christ in his farewell discourses to the disciples says: 'I AM the vine, you are the branches,' he adds these deeply enigmatic words: 'You did not chose me, but I have chosen you' (John 15:16). Here he is indicating the archetypal relationship at work both between himself and the disciples and between the disciples themselves. The miracle of finding one another not only happens in many different ways here in the context of the present life on earth; close connections between the disciples are renewed here also from previous lives.

In his lectures on the *Gospel of St Mark,* Rudolf Steiner explains that the twelve disciples embodied the twelve main figures from the Books of the Maccabees: the five sons of the priest Mattathias, who placed themselves at the head of their people one-and-a-half centuries before Christ in the heroic liberation struggle against the Seleucid tyrants, and the seven sons of the widow who suffered martyrs' deaths at the same time (2Macc.7). In calling the twelve disciples, Jesus is not making an arbitrary selection, although all the different types of human being are completely represented. The wisdom of providence had already made such an objective selection in previous lives on earth, thus preparing the group through which Christ can gather representatives of the whole of humankind around him. The words of Christ that they did not choose him but he chose them reveals a profound secret. It lets us see that as the master of destiny and providence he steered from time immemorial from the sun regions of the spiritual world the path of development of these twelve human individuals, before descending to earth to become man. When the group of twelve formed, people met once again who already belonged together from many previous lives on earth and who most recently had been the exponents of the historical moment at the time of the Maccabees as the two groups of brothers. At the same time it was also a rediscovery of the Christ-being in whose surroundings they had prepared their next incarnations in the past while they were in the spiritual world between death and a new birth. The great sun magnet, who had brought them together again and again from ancient times, now brought them together on earth as the group of twelve apostles.

An important step lies between the incarnation of the twelve at the time of the Maccabees and their present life on earth. In the surroundings of Jesus old destinies are not only renewed but they are also transformed. As the two groups of seven and five brothers they represented the ripe fruit which had blossomed on the tree of the old blood relationships. Now they can form the core of the new community element. In the group of the twelve disciples a free spiritual relationship replaces the old blood relationships. By calling them, Christ did not call unprepared people. Out of a profound love of the divine they had themselves undertaken preparatory steps and transformed their being when Christ called on them to follow him. This can be seen most clearly in those who had followed the powerful prophetic call of John the Baptist into the desert at the Dead Sea. But those of the twelve, too, who had not previously been disciples of John had undergone the purifying fire of testing destiny. In this way they had all made their contribution to enable Christ to renew the calling which had existed from ancient times. Right from the beginning it was spiritual impulses which founded the community among them. As the group of disciples they became the first family based on the spirit in the new humanity.

Blood and spiritual relationships in the group of disciples

If we believe the Catholic popular traditions and the accounts of Catherine Emmerich, for example, all the disciples were closely related and were mostly brothers. There is a penchant in these traditions to hold on to the old blood connections at the cost of the spiritual community which was established at that time in its archetypal form. At most, there is in the background a subconscious reminiscence of ther incarnation at the time of the Maccabees. The watershed between the ages is very small and precise. What was still justified and, indeed, of archetypal correctness before the time of Christ had already lost its validity in the group of the disciples.

There are, nevertheless, a series of close blood relationships among the twelve. The Gospel of Matthew (similar to the Gospel of Mark) lends support to the backward looking principle through its unconcerned imaginative style, being the most backward looking of the gospels. When the disciples are called, the first to become followers of Christ, according to the report in Matthew, are two pairs of brothers: Peter and Andrew, James and John. The solution cannot simply consist of understanding the sibling relationship as being meant merely imaginatively, that is as an image for inner relationships. Things are more complicated than that. Peter and Andrew really are physical brothers. Through them the old principle of the relationship between the five Maccabee brothers extends as an echo into the group of disciples. Here we are to be given to understand that there are transitional stages: spiritual relationships do not exclude blood relationships. The former can be real and fruitful despite a blood relationship which may also exist. But it is an interesting feature that the presence of this pair of brothers in the group of twelve also signals an archetypal rejection of the old social laws: Andrew is the older of the two brothers, yet it is Peter who will later be given the office of taking on the leadership. The devaluation of the rights of the first-born which we see throughout the Old Testament is continued here.

The sons of Zebedee are also physical brothers. And if the composition of the group of twelve were simply the one assumed by the imaginatively stylized gospels, we would indeed here encounter a puzzling accumulation of old blood relationships. But John, the brother of James, is not really one of the twelve. He is only keeping a place open for Lazarus. The entry of Lazarus-John, for whom the one son of Zebedee makes way, shows in a truly dramatic way the replacement of the old blood relationships through new, sharply individualized spiritual connections. If we only possessed the three imaginative gospels, the powerful presence of the actual new principle would remain covered by the old principle. The truth only becomes evident if the Gospel of John is added. It is part of the universal nature of the group of twelve that physical connections also extend into it untouched in one particular situation. Where this appears to be repeated in a second instance, precisely the opposite is the case.

There appears to have been a third pair of brothers among the twelve: James the younger is consistently described as the son of Alphaeus. But the Gospel of Mark also describes Levi, who is otherwise called Matthew (also in Mark), as a son of Alphaeus. It therefore appears as if James the younger and Matthew were brothers. That would lead to a similar process as between the Zebedee brother John and Lazarus. For James, the son of Alphaeus, is only a placeholder for James, the brother of the Lord, who, however, only joins the group of twelve after Easter.

But once the actual James has appeared, the problem of blood or spiritual community occurs in an apparently much more intense form. Now even a very close relation of Jesus himself appears to belong to the group of disciples: 'the brother of the Lord.' Once again the sibling relationship presents an image which hides the truth for as long as the mysteries surrounding the special destinies associated with the events on Golgotha are left out of consideration. Jesus and James are not blood relations. James was the physical brother of the solomonic Jesus. Jesus in terms of his body is Lukan. From her first marriage, his step-mother brought James as the eldest of her children to the carpenter and his son. We have here a family relationship which is not just blood relationship but which, as the result of the feelings of antipathy and hate, places the greatest obstacles in the path of the development of a spiritual relationship. And it is indeed the case that up to the time of his Easter experience, James' attitude is an antagonistic one rather than one of a disciple. A kind of analogy exists with St Paul's destiny.

The precise synopsis of the gospels, which takes finer nuances into account, confirms our results. Thus in the catalogues of the apostles Matthew and Mark expressly mention John as the brother of James. Luke simply says: James and John. He leaves it open that someone other than the physical brother might be referred to by the name of John and in this respect forms a bridge to the Gospel of John.

Chapter Four

Stages of Incarnation

Space and time in the life of Jesus

It is hardly more than a hundred and fifty years since men set themselves the task of investigating and describing the life of Jesus in terms of a human biography. The impulse to do this started in the Age of Reason, when the last instinctive feeling for the supersensory began to die out. Before that, and especially at the time of primitive Christianity, the dim awareness and reverence for the divine Christ-being still had far too much vitality for anyone to venture an approach to the gospel with the standards applied to the lives of great men.

With the failure to recognize the Christ-being went also a failure to understand the gospels. Although the dogma of 'inspiration' still affected rationalistic theology, the feeling that the gospels represented an expression of supersensory perceptions at different levels died out, and with it died also an appreciation for the significant differences in style between the different gospels. There resulted a confusion which had very serious consequences. In the attempts to piece together the external course of the life of Jesus, preference came to be given to the first three gospels as historical sources, while the Gospel of John, which was looked upon as mainly philosophical, was declared historically unfruitful and unreliable. But in fact it is just the first three gospels which, coming from pictures of imaginative knowledge, place physical and supersensory, outward and inner events indiscriminately side by side, whereas the Gospel of John, which derives from exact inspiration, penetrates the veil of imaginative pictures to the concrete historical events.

The impulse to work out in detail the life of Jesus was in itself a good and necessary one. In spite of the rationalistic bias with which virtually all descriptions of the life of Jesus have hitherto been tinged, this phase of research has its value. For the will of the Christ-being to incarnate and become man was fulfilled on the level of hard physical reality. The life of Jesus is also the biography of a man. But it must not be overlooked that it is only so through Christ's will to self-renunciation. Thus from beginning to end the indispensable key to this life is that it is at the same time a *divine* biography, a history of earth *and* heaven.

The first and foremost mistake to be overcome is the idea that the biographical facts are easy to find in the gospels. What we first meet, especially in the synoptic gospels, is composed of soul-pictures of spiritual patterns and relationships. This affords a dim idea of what happened in the inner places of men's souls. To come to the external biographical fact can only be the final fruit of a long familiarity with the gospels. It goes without saying that this cannot be attained until the concrete historic character of the Gospel of John is rediscovered in all its supreme value.

The importance of the Fourth Gospel becomes evident directly one tries to get a clear outline of the events between the baptism in the Jordan and the Mystery of Golgotha. The first three gospels alone present a magnificent general story, but not an account of the various journeys nor of the duration and order of events. Only by taking the Gospel of John into account can concrete movement come into the picture, and only so can one arrive at a tangible chronology of the life of Jesus.

The four evangelists have very different ways of representing the movement of Jesus' life between the two contrasting archetypal landscapes of Galilee and Judea. Matthew and Mark condense their versions in such a way as to suppose only one move from Galilee to Judea. The structure is of the simplest: both these two gospels are divided into a Galilean half and a Judean half. To begin with, the friendly sunny world of Galilee is the continuous scene of the life of Jesus, as if it had really been so without any break. The change in mood and atmosphere which takes place with the journey to Jerusalem is at the same time the introduction to the events of the Passion and of Golgotha. The story of Good Friday and Easter make up the entire second half of both these gospels. If we have eyes to see it, the cosmic polarity of the two landscapes is brought out with great force in the structure of the first two gospels, each taken as a whole.

St Luke shows the same geographical polarity; but his gospel is divided into three parts. Between the Galilean and Judean sections a large middle part describes in detail the transition from Galilee to Judea. This, however, does not mean that Samaria, which lies between Galilee and Judea, must necessarily be taken as the setting of the middle part. It is rather that the large middle section of the gospel is independent of geographical conditions. The journey which Jesus makes with his disciples from Galilee to Judea is here at the same time the 'great path': the inner road that Christians have to travel is projected into space. Higher criticism was groping for this secret when it observed that St Luke makes use of a 'travel plan' for the composition of the middle section of his gospel.

It is true that at the beginning two events are mentioned by Matthew, Mark and Luke which take place in Judea — the baptism and the temptation. But the simplicity of the structure as a whole is so great that this short prelude cannot disturb it. Even less is it disturbed when at the end of the Gospel of Matthew for a brief moment the Galilee-motif lights up in the Judean framework, and on the summit of the mountain in Galilee the Risen One appears to the disciples. Here the Galilee-motif is wholly imaginative. The disciples felt transported to Galilee without going there bodily.

The scenic pattern underlying the first three gospels is enriched by what we might call the prologue of the first two chapters of St Matthew and St Luke, which describe the childhood of Jesus. St Matthew introduces his Galilean section with a special Judean prologue, which gives two glimpses of humanity beyond Palestine. The great kingdoms of the East are brought in by the pilgrimage of the three magi. The country of the ancient holy temples on the banks of the Nile beyond Judea appears through the flight into Egypt. But the prologue leads to Galilee in the end when it says distinctly that, after their return from Egypt, Joseph and his family lived not in Bethlehem but in Nazareth.

In the Lucan prologue the lively interchange between the landscapes of Galilee and Judea begins with the announcement to Zacharias of the birth of John, which takes place in Jerusalem, in Judea. Then, in Nazareth in Galilee, the archangel announces the birth of Jesus to Mary. Back to Judea, and Mary visits Elizabeth. In Judea John is born. And again from Nazareth in Galilee Mary and Joseph go for the census to Bethlehem in Judea, where Jesus is born. Once more the pendulum swings back to the peace of Galilee, where Jesus spends his childhood. Finally, when he is twelve years old, there is one more move to Judea, on which a shadow already falls of that solemn journey to Jerusalem which he will undertake twenty-one years later.

The living interchange between Galilee and Judea governs the whole structure of the Fourth Gospel. When the cosmic dimensions of the version of the creation given in the prologue condense to earthly scenery, the setting is at once the lunar landscape of Judea. The figure of John the Baptist emerges, and the baptism of Jesus which John accomplishes in the Jordan's depths near the Dead Sea is not dismissed in a few words as in the first three gospels. St John not only has the courage to dwell on this scenery of the cosmic Fall: his gospel also reveals the mysterious event which is directly connected with the baptism. The veil of the mystery is lifted, and Jesus meets his disciples for the first time, long before he calls them at Whitsuntide in Galilee as described in the first three gospels. The whole of the long opening chapter is set in the depths of this Judean landscape. Then, in Galilee, in the most magical spring of this landscape of archetypal springtime, the miracle of Cana takes place. But soon, with the swing of the pendulum, Jesus goes to Jerusalem in Judea for the festival of Passover. This part of John's Gospel could also be called a prologue, for it deals with the time which preceded Jesus' active entry into public life. Nevertheless, nothing is mentioned of the long preliminary stay in Galilee which is suggested by the other gospels. The solemnity that will dominate the last entry, when the event of Golgotha lies ahead, already casts a cloud over this first of all the journeys to Jerusalem since the baptism in Jordan. In Jerusalem the storm of the purification of the Temple breaks. In the course of its after-effects Nicodemus meets Jesus by night. As if to evoke a mood in complete contrast to that of the first three gospels, the Gospel of John describes Jesus as still remaining for a while in the Judean countryside. Once more he is drawn back into the sphere of John the Baptist, before he begins to work in his own name. Once more the heroic figure of John the Baptist appears in the background of the forbidding landscape, now saying of Jesus, 'He must increase, I must decrease.'

At last, by way of Samaria, Jesus returns to Galilee. At Jacob's Well at midday, he talks with the woman of Samaria. Then, in Capernaum in Galilee the centurion who in Cana had asked Jesus for help, finds his son healed. But almost immediately the scene changes back again to Judea. In Jerusalem the sick man at the pool of Bethesda is healed. Again the coming crisis is foreshadowed; Jesus meets his adversaries with the sword of the Word. Only on one further occasion are we permitted to breathe the air and the wonder of Galilee. The last scene in Galilee is at Sea of Galilee, on the occasion of the feeding of the five thousand, and of Christ's walking on the waters. But the shadow of Judea seems to fall even here. In arguments with adversaries who even here wish to hamper his activity, Jesus utters the saying about the bread of life.

This brings to an end the part played by Galilee in John's Gospel. From now on Judea is exclusively the stage of events. In all, it is only short parts of the second and fourth chapters and the sixth chapter which take place in Galilee. St John not only describes from the outset the constant interchange between the two landscapes, but he gives preference to the harsher land of Judea. The balance of the two landscapes expressed in the first three gospels is completely upset. Judea dominates everything. This alone shows that John's Gospel gives the life of Jesus a firmer and more consistent basis on the hard ground of physical reality than do the other gospels. Only at the end, in the last Easter chapter, which is really only an appendix, does the scene return to Galilee. But here, as in the Easter story of Matthew's Gospel, Galilee is only a landscape of the soul. The disciples see and experience the lake with the Risen One while their physical bodies remain in Jerusalem.

The first three gospels give no idea of how much time elapsed between the baptism and the crucifixion. Taking these gospels alone, one could come to the conclusion that there was only one year between these two events; in fact many theologians, owing to a one-sided appraisal of the first three gospels, have held this view. A truer evaluation of St John's Gospel as a biographical document, however, leads quite clearly to the secret of the three years. The journeys between Galilee and Judea reach three times the point when 'the Jewish Passover was at hand [*en de engus to pascha tôn Ioudaiôn*].' This is said for the first time after the Marriage at Cana before the Paschal journey to Jerusalem (John 2:13); the second time before the feeding of the five thousand (John 6:4); the third time before the Raising of

Lazarus (John 11:55). The threefold repetition of the Passover formula first presents a basis for Christ's biography, and it is significant that out of the four it is St John who builds this foundation. Thus the chronology accords with early Christian tradition.

In our time, however, it is right to seek the true duration of the life of Jesus behind the veil of feeling which has hitherto hidden the truth as if in a cloud of light. In fact, Jesus' life does not last a full three years after the baptism. If on the twenty-fifth of December in the year 30 the first three decades in the life of Jesus as described by St Luke were completed, and at the beginning of the year 31 the baptism took place, then, according to the three Passover festivals, there remains a period of only a little more than two years up to the time of Golgotha. At the third Passover, in the spring of the year 33, the Mystery of Golgotha was accomplished. However, with a qualitative feeling for time, it is nevertheless justifiable to speak of three years. This has a parallel in the traditional reference to 'the three days' between the death and the resurrection of Christ. There are not three full days between the hour of death on Good Friday and the early hour of Easter morning. For a superficial view the interval is only a day and a half. Qualitatively speaking, however, it is three days. Friday, the day of Venus; the Sabbath, Saturn's day; and finally the sun's day — all three are included in the important interval between death and resurrection. This is a key to the secret of the three years. Superficially speaking it was a startlingly short time during which the incarnate God walked our earth; but what seems such a short time was nevertheless sufficient to introduce into this earthly life the full breath of eternity.

The Jesus-consciousness and the Christ-consciousness

Quite simple biographical facts emerge from the 'imaginative layer' of the synoptics. Even after Jesus turned with conscious intention to public life (which according to the first three gospels happened at the season of Pentecost in the year 31, when John the Baptist had been thrown into prison) the picture given is only of simple journeyings. The task of the Christ is not to do anything specific. He only needs to be there. The fact that he is there, living among men, is in itself the fulfilment of his mission, and the beginning of a new stage of evolution for humanity. The importance of a mere 'presence' can sometimes be observed in a small circle of human beings. The most silent member of a group may by his mere presence be of the utmost consequence to all the others; far more enlightenment, encouragement and help may come from him than from those who are more outwardly active.

Christ journeys quietly through the countryside, surrounded by his disciples, sharing people's experiences, and above all the burdens and sorrows which have caused the spark of longing for salvation to glow in their souls. Through this devoted participation in life and suffering the humanity of Christ is perfected. But his is more than human devotion. It is God's participating in all human destiny. It is not surprising that the intensity of this experience closed Jesus' mouth rather than opened it. Silently he went his way, so that his being often presented a baffling enigma to the disciples. Strindberg, in his play *The Dream* allows the daughter of a god, 'Indra's Daughter,' to step down to earth from the divine realm because she longs to participate in the destiny and experience of men. Again and again, at the sight of human suffering, her heart is wrung with pain and she cries, 'Alas, poor men!' There is however a trace of arrogance in these words. They show that the daughter of the god has only apparently taken on human form, and that she does not identify herself completely with humanity. Whole worlds separate the inner attitude here expressed from that of Jesus. The human need that he makes his own can only render him more and more silent. He feels called upon to speak chiefly when he meets selfishness and vulgarity instead of reverence and devotion. There live in Jesus in unbroken strength the original ideals and impulses which humanity brought with it from its divine origin. To begin with he may have remained silent even in his encounters with evil. There was no need to express himself in words. The majesty of his being, as it shone forth in the purification of the Temple at that first Passover festival, was eloquent enough without words.

At times the quiet traveller breaks his silence. It may be to answer a question put to him either by the disciples, or by people he meets on his way. Often, too, he steps out of his quiet reserve to extend a helping hand, especially when he meets a sick man who, discerning who it is that passes by, asks his help. Each time that Jesus speaks or acts on such an occasion it is as if his being were suddenly changed. His hearers experience a warm and all-embracing love, such as can scarcely emanate from one who is only man. This is even more marked when his speech or action evokes the hatred of those who, out of a traditional obstinacy or from personal ambition, suspect a threat to the paltry content of their own lives. The spirit flashes up in Jesus' dealings with his adversaries. It may only be for a brief moment that his reserve is thus broken. When it does happen, the Christ-consciousness is revealed through the human Jesus-consciousness. To speak of the alternation between the consciousness of Jesus and that of Christ is really only to grope after a mystery. All the same, without this, one cannot understand the true biographical element in the life of Jesus. The disciples must have undergone constant trials of their souls through this alternation. Again and again there were moments when their Messianic expectations were stimulated and encouraged by what radiated from Jesus. But then the periods of silence returned, periods which would often last for days, and despair would overcome them, especially as many awaited in suspense the appearance of a Messiah who would exercise a powerful influence in the material world of affairs.

Jesus had no organized programme of teaching and healing. When he taught or when he healed the sick, it was simply the natural and unpremeditated consequence of sharing in the life of the men he met on his silent journeys. The instruction and training which he gave to his disciples was the only thing that he carried through with increasingly clear method and consistency. But here, too, he only needed to go over again with them what had been said in conversation with the other people, or to speak about the destiny of those to whom help had been given. But this instruction was carried on only during part of the two to two-and-a-half years. It began first with his call to them on the shores of the Sea of Galilee at Pentecost in the year 31. Then, in the late summer of the same year, after the death of John the Baptist, he sent them out two by two, so making them entirely dependent upon themselves for a long period. It was not until just before Passover in the year 32 that he gathered them around him again. From then on, the special privilege of the disciples lasted only a single year.

Laws of incarnation

Through centuries the mystery of the incarnation has been the object of devout study and meditation. Earlier ages often approached it together with the mystery of the crucifixion. In Bach's *Mass in B Minor* the link is expressed by the striking harmonization of the two choral phrases *et incarnatus est,* and *et crucifixus est.* Also in Anton Bruckner's *Mass in F Minor, incarnatus* and *crucifixus* are built up from the same thematic material.

But for modern humanity the approach to the understanding of the incarnation leads through a fresh understanding of man's own nature, and of human life generally, in terms of 'in-carnation.' Much of the confusion and decadence of our time is due to the fact that we have forgotten what the human being is. What we are able to see of one another is only a vehicle. Man himself, the content of the vehicle, is invisible. Each of us is the incarnation of a supersensory being. We are distinguished from the animals by the fact that the soul, which is their highest member, is for us only the vessel in which our spiritual ego-being dwells. Incarnation is a continuous living process. One cannot say that man is already fully incarnated as soon as he is born; he is not even fully incarnated when his body stops growing and reaches maturity. Herein lies the secret of human life, with all its different stages, that the spiritual content masters the body and soul progressively, and the invisible being of man descends more and more deeply into incarnation.

If people had a living feeling for incarnation, they would know that a child enters a new phase of life as early as its third year. The first three years of childhood differ fundamentally from the whole of later life. They form an intermediate stage which leads from the life before birth into the process of incarnation. In this first stage the human being has of course a body, but he does not yet live in it — he only feels his way slowly into it. Not only in his being, but in his consciousness, the ego of the little child lives far above the body, borne by angels as before birth. If we look back on our childhood, we come at about the third year to a wall behind which our memory is not able to penetrate. Consciousness during the first three years belongs more to the angels than to the human being, which is why we remember nothing of it as we grow older.

The process of incarnation which goes on throughout one's whole life is divided into seven-year rhythms. These stages are at first obvious, the change of teeth marking the end of the first seven years, and puberty the end of the second seven years. From the age of twenty-one onwards the several stages are no longer so clearly recognizable because they are more inward. The normal course of incarnation goes on through nine times seven years. The fifth period of seven years is the middle of life. Up to this point, man's development leads to deeper and deeper embodiment, and from now onwards it gradually extricates him from the all-too-deep and firm union with the physical body. The higher 'members' of man's being which incarnate from now onwards make it necessary that a slow process of loosening should take place at the same time. The middle of life is a kind of zero point between the downward urge and the re-ascent. The tragedy of modern man, especially if he is intellectually educated, lies in the fact that he has great difficulties in overcoming the zero point.

Man develops through the first four seven-year stages quite naturally, and reaches the end of the fifth period, the middle of life, without any personal effort. But further development requires an inner force which the person of today mostly fails to develop, and to which contemporary cultural life offers no stimulus or help. Thus it comes about that behind the curtain of convention very many people, especially professional men, remain at the point that they reached at the age of twenty-eight. They become older physically, but not more inwardly mature, and they try to find a way of escape in the routine and the habits of everyday life, without admitting to themselves that they have become inwardly stale. The challenge of middle age will be met only if people find the strength to go through an inner death and resurrection. From then onwards the natural man dies, and the first sign that the force for a new development is growing is that he now gains the capacity to live as if he were already dead. Only so can he look forward to wise old age, and not to an empty shell of existence. Then at the end of life there can be a bridge between the life on earth and the existence free of the body after death. It is this which renders extreme old age and the time just before death so sacred.

With these stages in mind, a view of the life of Jesus leads to rich prospects of enlightenment. A human life was once lived which at the age of thirty flowed into the great miracle of the incarnation of Christ. For three years, until the age of thirty-three, Jesus was the true *Christophorus*, the true Christ-bearer. He bore the Christ in himself. His body and his soul were the sheaths of the divine ego, which had come down to earth to become man. Here we have the most exalted archetype of a life sanctified from heaven. The divine spiritual seed was once and for all implanted in human existence, in that period of life in which man finds his further path aright only if a new inner force grows in his soul. The future of humanity is assured if human beings on reaching the middle period of their lives between the ages of thirty and thirty-three find an inner connection with the being of Christ, and thereby overcome their own zero point. What took place in these three years in the life of Jesus of Nazareth can be reflected in the corresponding years of the life of every person who unite themselves with Christ.

A further helpful secret becomes clear if, instead of looking at the age of the man Jesus, we think of the earthly age of the Christ-being himself. For Jesus, the time between the baptism in the Jordan and the crucifixion constituted the middle period of life, the thirtieth to thirty-third years. For the Christ-being, it was the first three years. One could call the three years of Christ the divine octave of the three years at the beginning of every human life, which are still so closely connected with the angels. A cosmic impulse of re-animation enters into humanity with these three short years. When Christ said, 'Unless ye become as little children ye cannot enter the kingdom of heaven,' he put before us the aim of working *consciously* again in the sphere in which the child lives during its first three years. He could present this challenge because he bore within himself this realm in its real cosmic character, and carried it into ageing humanity during the three years of his human existence. For each individual, the three Christ-years bear the source of the power which carries him through the natural dying and becoming of middle life. For humanity as a whole they contain the elixir of youth and the medicine which heals every form of ageing and hardening of the soul.

The great stages

In those three years there were focused all the stages of human development which are normally spread over a whole lifetime. For this reason every word that Jesus utters, every deed he performs, is not only the sign of an advancing higher ego-being; it expresses also the particular stage through which he is passing. Be it in silence or in speech, in suffering or in action, nothing can happen which does not mark a further step in the incarnation of the ego of God in the being of man.

Every event has its given moment. None would be possible in just that way at any other moment. For example, the order in which the gospels narrate the healing acts of Jesus could not be otherwise than it is. Everything rests upon the foundation of what went before. Not only does every act of healing presuppose those that preceded it, but whatever makes up the content of Jesus' life happens against the background of some crucial events, which mark a new stage, and are the result of a new level which the Christ-being has reached on his path of incarnation. The healing of the lunatic boy at the foot of the mount of transfiguration was possible only as a result of what had taken place on the summit. Again, one cannot imagine the Raising of Lazarus at any other moment than when it actually happened. Lazarus could not have been called back to life had not the force ripened in Christ Jesus which was to enable him a few days later himself to overcome death. The death and resurrection of Lazarus have to be understood by their nearness to the death and resurrection of Christ.

In the life of Jesus all merely general talk of development is out of place. A sense for concrete, succeeding stages is required. Then the incarnation of Christ will be perceived *as a process,* and from the discovery of its different stages a new conception of development in general will result, which we feel compelled in the end to apply to our own lives. We realize that mechanical regularity and repetition, the mere clinging to pedestrian habits, is the biggest obstacle in our own progress. Each age, indeed every single year and even each day of life attains its own quality and fulfilment only when we see it in relation to the whole of our life, and appreciate it as a stage on the way. In this way, a study of the life of Christ can have a most stimulating effect on our own life, and the science of Christ will link up with the science of man.

The first of the crucial events in the progressive incarnation of Christ in Jesus was the baptism in the Jordan. Outwardly, nothing special happened. But for supersensory perception the flame of the spirit flashed from earth to Heaven. The self-surrender of the ego of Jesus made way for the divine Christ-ego, which entered into incarnation in place of the human ego. The heavens opened; the broken link between heaven and earth was forged anew. Those whose souls could see the flash experienced its immense power toned down to the tender image of the dove.

For over a year the life of Jesus followed its course quietly, for the most part, both before John's imprisonment and after his death, in conscious reserve or withdrawal. Then the fire of the Christ-ego breaks through afresh. The second stage in becoming man is accomplished: the Christ-ego permeates the soul- or astral-body. It is before Passover of the year 32. The disciples, who have just been reunited after having travelled through the country for a while two by two, experience the healing force of the astral body of Jesus, now filled with the Christ, as extending prophetically over the whole of humanity. In the picture of the feeding of the five thousand the future of their apostolic mission stands before them. They see that to them is entrusted the spiritual nourishment which humanity is to receive into the far distant future as food and drink. The basket, from which they can give the bread of life without its becoming empty, is there because now a human astral-body has been permeated with spirit by Christ.

In the night that follows, the disciples are able to see directly the new stage of existence which the Christ-being has now attained. They see Christ walking on the stormy waves of the lake. Christ's walking on the sea reveals the second main stage of incarnation. This experience of the disciples is not a sensational physical phenomenon: it is not the physical form of Christ that meets them on the sea. It is the astral-body of Jesus, completely filled by the Christ-ego which now has such an intensity that it can reveal itself to the disciples as if it were a constituent part of the sense world. The human soul-nature, glowing and tranquil in the fire of the spirit, reveals its fullness of power: the storm of the elements is stilled.

The third theophanic event marking a stage is the transfiguration on Mount Tabor. Even the three most trusted disciples, Peter, James and John, could not have seen the Christ in this glowing, sunlike form at any other moment than when he showed himself to them on the summit of the holy mountain. It was their tremendous privilege to witness a crucial point in the maturing of the Christ-being. A further sphere of the human organism, the life or etheric body of Jesus of Nazareth was pervaded through and through by the fire of the sun-spirit.

There is a special secret connected with Christ's permeation of human life-forces; otherwise it would not have been only the three trusted disciples who were allowed to witness the transfiguration.

What came to fulfilment then was at the same time the incipience of a future event. The transfiguration of Christ foreshadows his resurrection. The body in which later the Risen One will reveal himself to his disciples is the etheric body, now filled by the spirit. But after the crucifixion this body will at the same time be filled with the quintessence of the physical body, permeated by Christ, and will thereby have an intensity which enables it to work right into the physical sphere. Then the whole circle of the disciples will be able to behold the Christ.

The fourth stage will be reached when the ego of Christ presses fully through the human physical body of Jesus. This in the end is *incarnation* in the strict sense of the word. Literally, incarnation means 'becoming flesh.' When the Bible says 'flesh,' it means the physical body. Of course the Christ-ego had been dwelling in the physical body ever since the baptism, but he was only able to take the final and most advanced step into complete possession of it at the end of the three years. Providence disposed that an external entry was to reflect the hidden entry of the Christ-ego into the physical body. So the entry of Jesus into Jerusalem becomes the theophanic picture of this last stage of incarnation. The city of Jerusalem seems to be the quintessence of all that is physical. Not for nothing is it in the centre of Judea, whose landscape is the expression of the physical and mineral world, whereas Galilee, where the transfiguration took place, is a picture of the etheric world. Looked at superficially, Jesus' riding into the city upon an ass was nothing remarkable; but the ecstatic cries of *Hosanna* from the crowd are the echo of the spiritual event with which it is associated. Once more the old clairvoyance is aroused, and the people see the form of Jesus surrounded by an aura of spiritual fire. In human terms, this is the manifestation of the final resolve which burns in his soul. It reveals the new and last stage of incarnation just attained. And yet the entry into Jerusalem is only the beginning of this last fulfilment. Ultimate possession and permeation of the physical body is achieved only in the hour of Golgotha. As the process of incarnation is completed the physical life comes to an end. Incarnation turns into excarnation. The fire of the Christ-ego has burnt to ashes the sheaths in which it has lived for three years. It is a profoundly moving truth, to which Rudolf Steiner once drew attention, that the life of Christ would have come to an end then even if he had not been nailed to the cross.

The connection between the third and fourth stages is shown by mysterious symbols. When the disciples beheld the transfigured form of Christ upon Mount Tabor, they perceived at his left and at his right Moses and Elijah. They sensed dimly the universally human significance of the event and felt stirred in their will-forces. They saw themselves called to a role which, however, they could not yet clearly understand. Thus, when a little later James and John say to Jesus, 'Grant that we may find our place at your side ... one on your right, the other on your left,' (Mark 10:37), a kind of after-effect of the appearance on Mount Tabor makes itself felt. But they do not know what they ask. When the fourth stage is accomplished a new triad will appear. This time Christ will be flanked by two crosses, one on each side of him. Here is a solemn lesson for us. He who desires to share in the gracious effects of the incarnation of Christ cannot be at his right or at his left hand on the mount of transfiguration unless he is also ready to take his place on Golgotha and to accompany him through death.

Of the four crucial events on the path of incarnation the first and the last belong to Judea, and the two intervening ones to Galilee. The special conditions of the Christ-being, first after the baptism and at the end before the death on Golgotha, correspond to the character of Judea. Both at the beginning and at the end we may imagine the form of Christ as sheathed in a flashing aura of overwhelming light. The *status nascendi* after the baptism has its counterpart in the *status moriendi* of the Passion. At the beginning the energy of the divinity becoming human is perceptible; at the end humanity becoming divine is revealed with fiery power. The *status nascendi* was the cause of the conscious reserve of the Christ-being. The intensity of the *status moriendi,* however, comes about because the Christ has now become wholly man. By taking possession of the depths of the human will he assumes the majesty required for decisive battle with all the powers of opposition.

The crisis

The importance of the entry into Jerusalem as incarnational stage is fundamental. The intensity of Christ's will, at the attainment of the fourth stage of incarnation, sheds fresh light upon the passion and death of Christ. What might appear to be merely passive suffering and what has given rise to the widespread, popular picture of the 'Man of

Sorrows' is in fact the most heroic deed ever performed on earth. Various events surrounding Palm Sunday emphasize this; the fact alone that the entry of Jesus into the city is repeated daily during Holy Week underlines the importance of this stage. Jesus was staying not in Jerusalem but in Bethany, in the house of Lazarus. Thus the entry which on Palm Sunday had been accompanied by the ecstasy of the people was repeated in the quiet of each morning, as if the process of the final descent into the depths of the physical body had to be strengthened again and again. After the night of Maundy Thursday — the first night that Jesus passed not in Bethany but together with the disciples in the house of the Last Supper and in the Garden of Gethsemane — once more, for the last time, he made a special entry into the city. But this time the scene of ecstatic jubilation of the crowd had changed to one of distressing ignominy. Arrested in Gethsemane, he was led in chains towards Jerusalem.

The understanding of the incarnation as a process in stages throws a new light on two events which follow Palm Sunday, the cursing of the fig tree and the second purification of the Temple. Details of these stories are discussed in Chapter Ten, where the whole sequence of the days of Holy Week is dealt with. Here we are concerned with the place which these events occupy in the incarnational process.

St John's Gospel speaks of a purification of the Temple at the first Passover, not long after the baptism. The synoptics report a purification as following the entry into Jerusalem. On each occasion the majesty of the being of Christ is such that all human degradation feels itself unmasked. Nevertheless the two purifications are not the same. They are rather revelations of those two exceptional and diametrically opposed conditions which represent the beginning and the end of Christ's incarnation. At the beginning, when Jesus is still holding himself in conscious reserve, the stormy effect comes solely from the being of Christ. There is no need for Jesus to do anything particular. The Christ-being has not yet entered fully into incarnation, He is only just preparing to become human. Simply the presence of Jesus has the effect that the divine judgment of Christ comes to people's consciousness in terrifying and dramatic soul pictures. On the second occasion the Christ-ego is on the point of draining the cup of incarnation to its dregs, as it is described at Gethsemane. Now that the act of becoming man is almost accomplished, the Christ as man can perform a

conscious deed of battle. Within the picture of the great Temple built
of stone lives the picture of the smaller human temple. Man's physical
body is indeed, as St Paul says, also a temple of God. The incarnation
of Christ in the human body of Jesus of Nazareth was at the same time
a Temple purification which he accomplished in order to implant the
seed of healing into man's body. This inner purification is twice
reflected outwardly, once when the Christ-ego has just entered incarnation, and again when he has penetrated the bodily nature to its very
foundations.

Similarly, the apparent contradiction between the reference to the
fig tree in the thirteenth chapter of St Luke, and that on the day after
the entry into Jerusalem, resolves itself. The passage reads:

> Once, a man had planted a fig tree in his vineyard. And when
> he came looking for fruit, he found none. Then he said to the
> gardener of the vineyard, 'Look, for three years now I have
> been coming, and have looked in vain for fruit on this fig tree.
> Cut it down; why should it go on using up the earth?' But the
> gardener answered, 'Sir, leave it for just one more year. I will
> dig the earth all around it and give it some manure. If it then
> bears fruit, well and good; if not, you can cut it down.'
> (Luke 13:6–9).

How different is the mood of this parable from the severity with
which Jesus cursed the fig-tree! But for those who watch the gradual
course of Christ's becoming man the contradiction is not insoluble.
Between the time that Jesus gives the parable of the fig-tree and his
entry into Jerusalem there is still a year to go — just the amount of time
that the vine-dresser begs for the fig-tree. By the time of the entry into
Jerusalem this time is over, and the final uselessness of the forces of the
fig-tree (which symbolize the ancient powers of instinctive clairvoyance, as described later, pp. 240f) justifies the stern attitude which
Jesus adopts.

Three Easters

Through our tentative groping for the pattern of Christ's part in the life
of Jesus, the qualitative differentiation between the three years comes
gradually to light. Three springtimes lie between the baptism and the
crucifixion. Round each of these new beginnings of the year's cycle we

find gathered, with significant changes from year to year, an archetypal series of events. The events of the third year represent fulfilment; those of the two preceding years, preparation.

Thus two other 'Easter' festivals preceded the Easter festival proper. The festival of the first year happened in the period of reserve and of the divine *status nascendi*. The Temple was cleansed, as described by St John. Christ uttered the bold paradox which the disciples only two years later, in the light of the Resurrection, understood as an Easter prophecy: 'Destroy this temple and in three days I will build it up again.' The Easter event of the second year takes place in the seclusion of the night, when the disciples see Christ walking on the waves of the lake. Having descended fully into the human soul, the divine ego of Christ comes to a triumphant pause; the fully spiritualized astral-body of Jesus at length outgrows the laws to which the physical body is subject. In this astral body, in majesty and in peace which calms the storms, Christ shows himself to the souls of his disciples. The Easter event proper, in the third spring, lies beyond the hour of Golgotha and shows that the history of Christ does not end with the death of the physical man, but moves into a new stage of existence. By the fire of his will, which in the raising of Lazarus had already shown its power over death, the victory of Easter is won.

In each of the three years the Easter event is preceded by a transubstantiation. The Marriage at Cana and the feeding of the five thousand in the preceding years correspond to the Last Supper on Maundy Thursday. The turning of water into wine is still as it were a natural process, but of a higher kind. The cosmic sun-ego of Christ has entered the earthly sphere, and overflows the vessel of incarnation before contracting fully into the ego of a man. Just as the external sun brings about the transformations of ripening and concentration among plants and forces of the earth, so the Christ-ego, radiating into his environment, moves in the direction of the transformation which he himself undergoes in the course of his incarnation. The sunny landscape of Galilee, in the brilliance of springtime, allows the sunlike transformation to manifest itself in festal clarity.

The pre-Easter event of the second year also takes place in Galilee, at Bethsaida, on the shore of the Sea of Galilee, but this time no material substance is the bearer of transformation. The increase of bread comes before the souls of those involved as an imaginative picture, enabling them to experience the fullness of a soul wholly permeated by Christ. It is the quiet middle period in the three years, the time in which the cosmic love of Christ reveals itself in the form of human generosity and goodness. A prophetic picture reveals to the disciples that from them is to go forth a priestly influence which will be the instrument of Christ's all-embracing love for humanity.

In the third year, as fulfilment draws near, a transmutation takes place at the Last Supper. It arises entirely out of inner devotion, but nevertheless takes hold of the substances of bread and wine. The inner process runs its course in the opposite direction from that of the Marriage at Cana. Then the ego of Christ was entering into incarnation and revealing himself as the divine being becoming human. Now this divine being has grown fully into the physical body, and in self-sacrifice begins to free himself from the body again and to grow beyond it. This, however, is no limitless outpouring of himself. The Christ, who has become completely human, moves into a larger body, and thereby becomes divine again. He prepares the new and greater stage of his incarnation, which will reveal the meaning of death and resurrection, because through it the whole earth will become the body of Christ. Bread and wine become body and blood of Christ because in them the earth begins to become sun. Now the miracle of transubstantiation has reached even the hard soil of Judea; and, instead of being in the peace of Galilee, the sanctuary of the Last Supper is in the midst of the hatred of enemies bent on destruction.

There are even in the two preceding years correspondences to the forty days of the final year in which the Risen One instructs the circle of his disciples. At the first Easter festival, Nicodemus was granted his nocturnal conversation with Jesus. In the supersensory teaching with which Jesus answers the questions of Nicodemus the authority speaks which he had brought with him from heaven. The teaching of the Risen One in the forty days after Easter comes from the victory that the Christ had won by having become human. For the middle year the corresponding teaching is found in the seventh chapter of St John. It is shifted, however, from the period after Passover to Michaelmas, and thereby shares in a measure in the grandeur of the approaching final act of the drama, instead of in the quiet mildness of the middle year. Although physically Jesus has remained in Galilee, he appears at the Feast of Tabernacles in Jerusalem. The usual translations make it seem as if Jesus, after he had just said to his brethren that he did not wish to go to Jerusalem, changed his mind and made the journey after all, only 'not publicly but secretly.' But the Greek expression *en kryptô* (Latin, *in occulto*) means 'in an occult manner' — free from the body. Jesus is present in Jerusalem in such a spiritually intense way that the people think they see and hear him in the flesh. Those who wish to arrest him are not able to lay hands on him. Jesus teaches in the Temple and finally utters the words which express the mood of the middle year: 'Whoever fills himself with my power through faith, from his body shall flow streams of life-bearing water' (John 7:38).

Christ and the angels

The picture of the stages of the life of Jesus, as a process of the heavenly becoming earthly, takes on warmth and colour when the theme of Christ and the angels is followed in the gospels. In the modern conception of the world there is no place for angels. Only when the mood of Christmas, with its childhood memories, comes over the are people of today momentarily inclined to believe in angels without calling themselves to account for their inconsistency. Then it may perhaps occur to them that angels are mentioned repeatedly in the gospel. But they may also discover that it records angelic manifestations as occurring only to souls which are ready for supersensory perception. Otherwise the gospels reveal little of the life of the hierarchies.

By far the greater number of angelic interventions in the life of Jesus lie outside the period between the baptism and Golgotha. The scenes with angels are grouped round the pole of Christmas in the fullness of light; they appear at the pole of Easter in a quieter, more hidden fashion. The Christmas events, at the beginning of the thirty years of human biography which prepare for the Christ-life proper, have a complicated retinue of angels. Angels of annunciation appear to the fathers of both John and the Jesus of Matthew's Gospel, as well as to the mother of the child in St Luke. The heralding host of angels also appears to the shepherds in the fields at Bethlehem. At first only a single angelic being appears to the shepherds, as in the case of the earlier annunciations, but then all the angelic hierarchies gather round the 'angel of the Lord.' An exultant festival of light accompanies the birth of the little child in the manger.

In the early Easter morning, the grave on Golgotha, like the crib in Bethlehem, is surrounded by the light of angelic manifestations. The Christ-being who hovers over the newly born little body in which he will one day live, and the Christ-being who wrests the form of resurrection from the entombed body in which he has lived for three years, is not alone. The whole hierarchical circle which surrounds him is brought into the earthly sphere. But the happiness that prevailed around the child gives way at Easter to solemn maturity. And as soon as they have drawn back the curtain, the gospels at once close it again. Again, it is to souls specially prepared that the angels appear. Like another annunciation the vision of the women at the tomb forms no more than a prelude to the mystery of Easter; the angels announce and prepare the disciples for the actual experience of the Resurrection. The four evangelists have different names for the angel-beings and seem to point to different hierarchies. But a study of the various expressions, 'the angel of the Lord' (Matthew), 'the young man' (Mark), 'the two men' (Luke), 'the two angels' (John), will show that each time the reference is to a different experience, representing a further development both in time and in space. Each time the women have moved a step deeper into the tomb.

Only on one further occasion do angels appear: at the Ascension, when their figures are described as 'two men.' The male adult character of the hierarchical manifestation is thereby expressed. When the form of the Risen One has vanished from the sight of the disciples, rising into the clouds, they see the two men in white garments, and receive from them instruction as to the future progress of the revelation of Christ.

Within the three years of Christ the gospels give only very guarded and sparing glimpses of the angel spheres surrounding the Christ. It confirms our observations of the stages of Christ's becoming man, that the angels are mentioned only at the beginning and at the end of the three years of Christ, as if it were intended thereby to draw attention to these two special conditions.

Christ is surrounded by angels after the baptism. The Christ-ego which has just entered the earthly body undergoes the threefold temptation. When the demons are conquered the first two gospels simply say that 'angels came to him and served him' (Matt.4:11; Mark 1:13). What is referred to here, however, is not happening for the first time.

From the moment when the heavens open above the Jordan, the choir of ministering angels is there. It forms part of the divine aura proper to the Christ in *status nascendi*. Pictorial tradition, which finds no direct refutation in the gospels, has always shown ministering angels at the moment of the baptism. Angels holding Christ's garments while John plunges him into the waters are to be seen in all early Christian paintings of the scene of the baptism. This is an imaginative expression of the fact that the Christ-being now exchanges the heavenly aura of the angels in which he has lived till now, for the vehicle of the human body. John's Gospel hints at the hierarchical surrounding of Christ at the outset of the three years, through the bold saying of Jesus to Nathanael immediately after the baptism, 'Yes, I say to you all: You will see heaven opened, and the angels of God ascending and descending above the Son of Man.' (John 1:51). What is said there as a promise for the future is at the same time a description of what John the Baptist and a few of his disciples, now entering on their path as pupils of Christ, have already experienced. At the baptism a birth of a higher order occurred. Thus the presence of angels in the mystery of Epiphany is a confirmation, more intensive than extensive, of the manifestation of the angels at Christmas.

The sentence referring to the angels at the end of the temptation has an exact parallel in the scene at Gethsemane, at the end of the three years. The threefold meeting of Christ with the powers of opposition in the solitude of the Judean desert corresponds to the lonely wrestling with death in the Garden of Gethsemane during the night before Good Friday. Once more Christ passes through a singular condition. But what shines around him now is no longer the glory of the God becoming man. After having drained to the dregs the cup of human existence, he burns in the fire of the man becoming God. The sacrificial outpouring of his being had begun in the room of the Last Supper on Mount Zion, when he washed the feet of his disciples and gave himself to them in bread and wine. Now the power of death approaches him, abandoned by even the most faithful of his followers, to snatch him away before his time, thus seeking to draw the free-willed act of dying under its own dark spell. By resisting and struggling with death, Christ consummated his full occupation and permeation of the physical body. At this moment the angels were around him. 'Then an angel from heaven appeared to him and gave him strength' (Luke 22:43).

Luke, the physician, who makes use of the technical expression *agony* for the death-struggle of Christ, thereby describing exactly the process of entry into the physical body, reveals also the angelic presence around the being of Christ. Matthew's Gospel hints at this same mystery only as a reflection of a saying of Christ. Jesus said to Peter who raises his sword against the officers, 'Do you think I could not ask my Father for help? He could send me at once more than twelve legions of angels' (Matt.26:53). In fact, heaven had sent angels to his assistance, but they did not fight against men on his behalf. They only strengthened him in his struggle against death. Instead of the avenging angel, who since the days of Egypt was abroad on this night of the Passover, ministering angels were near Christ.

Even the angelic presence in Gethsemane was not something that happened then for the first time. An angel drew near as soon as the last stage of incarnation had been reached. John's Gospel, which because it is silent about the transfiguration on the mountain, combines the miracle of the transfiguration with the entry into Jerusalem, gives a hint of this. As Jesus entered the city, the gospel says, 'Then a voice sounded from heaven: "I have revealed it, and I will reveal it anew." The crowd standing by and listening said, "It thundered." Others said, "An angel spoke to him".' (John 12:28f.) The manifestation associated with the entry into Jerusalem made itself felt on all levels of existence. The earth joined in by raising the voice of thunder which all the people heard. To those who were capable of seeing beyond the world of senses the angelic aura of Christ was revealed.

This angelic aura also manifested itself, though mysteriously veiled, midway on his path to becoming man. When Moses and Elijah became visible to the right and left of the sunlike form of Christ on the mount of transfiguration, for the first time the spiritual design became apparent which later showed itself to the women on Easter morning and to the disciples on the mount of the Ascension when the two men in white garments appeared. The figures of Moses and Elijah formed the pattern of a transparent screen, through which at Easter the archangelic spirit-form became visible. Thus the hierarchies of angels were silently present when for the first time that light of the spiritualized life-body was kindled which later became the light-body of the Risen One.

Finally, the theme of Christ and the angels can become a key to the great process of Christ's incarnation far beyond the stages of the three years. As the words of Christ acquire more and more apocalyptic power, we hear him speak prophetically of his relationship to the angels. When he speaks of the Second Coming he speaks at the same time of a new manifestation of the angelic kingdoms. 'When the Son of Man comes, illumined by the light of revelation, surrounded by all angels, then he will ascend the throne of the kingdom of his revelation' (Matt.25:31; 16:27; 24:30.) The angelic beings will again be present at the Christmas of the future, although in the new revelation there is a continuation not so much of the childlike mood of Christmas as of the solemnity of Easter. The significance of the Second Coming of Christ as a stage beyond the Resurrection lies in the fact that the supersensory world as a whole will be perceived again together with the form of Christ. The angels are no longer isolated supersensory phenomena; they represent the totality of that world. The manifestations of angels during the life of Jesus were the remnants of the ancient faculty of clairvoyance which was dying out at that time. Between the two events lies the period of human history which has been void of spiritual vision. After two thousand years of blindness, the seed which was then sown in the earth and in humanity must grow up as the new spirit-consciousness, capable of conscious, disciplined supersensory perception. Then will Christ be able to manifest himself as the sun-centre of the angelic spheres.

Stages of John and stages of Peter

The gospels contain a number of sequences which do not automatically coincide with the stages of incarnation of Christ as we have sought to present them. A classic example of this is the series of seven miracles in the first half of the Gospel of John:

1. Transformation of water into wine
2. Healing of the nobleman's son
3. The healing of the sick at the pool of Bethesda
4. Feeding the five thousand
5. Walking on water
6. Healing of the man born blind
7. Awakening of Lazarus.

That this sequence with its corresponding references in the other gospels, above all in Matthew, does not coincide with the stages of Christ becoming man set out by us is due to the fact that it refers less to the Christ biography itself than primarily designating the stations on the path of the soul typically undertaken by the various disciples. The seven miracles in John are a projection in outer events of the path which Lazarus-John, the 'disciple whom Jesus loved,' had to undertake. This path still comes closest to the development passed through by Christ become man. But if, for example, we consider the correspondence of the seven miracles of John in the Gospel of Matthew, we see a strongly divergent metamorphosis: here we see the stations of the soul of Peter which is characteristically different from the path of John, not to mention from Christ's incarnation. It is here that we can understand how it is above all in the first three gospels that an imaginative veil of images is woven in front of the mystery of the actual life of Christ, and that it is not a simple thing to penetrate to a real view of the 'Life of Christ.'

In the first three gospels we find Christ saying: 'But no other sign will be granted it except the sign of the prophet Jonah' (for instance in Matt.16:4). This saying has rightly always been perceived as a prediction of the death and resurrection of Christ. But the awakening of Lazarus is also a fulfilment of this prediction. We can therefore also take this last of the seven miracles in John as the 'sign of Jonah' and the previous six stages leading up to it as its preparation. That the death and resurrection of Christ is preceded by the death and awakening of Lazarus shows the closeness of the stages in John to the stages of Christ. In fact the awakening of Lazarus represents the introductory stage of the entry into Jerusalem in the progression of the incarnation of Christ as we have described it here, coming to fulfilment in Gethsemane and Golgotha. It is characteristic of Peter the man that he cannot penetrate as far as the sign of Jonah on his inner path. The seventh stage is missing. Hence we only find correspondences to the first six miracles of the Gospel of John in the Gospel of Matthew.

The miracle of the first stage, the transformation of water into wine at the marriage of Cana, is an outer projection of the *spirit becoming ego*. Wine is different from water in that it contains not only general cosmic streams, but forces related to the ego which strengthen the ego. The correspondence between the path of John and the path of Christ at this level lies in the entry of the Christ-being into the human ego sphere, which occurred at the baptism in Jordan, being revealed at a more advanced stage at the marriage in Cana. A certain correspondence to the marriage of Cana can be recognized in the Gospel of Matthew in the Sermon on the Mount, in that the latter leads over from the general spirituality of the Old Testament law into Christian spirituality associated with the ego and free personal decision-making powers. If abstract allegorical interpretations of the gospels sometimes say that the meaning of the marriage of Cana is that the water of Jewish religion has been transformed into the wine of Christian religion, then an indication has inadvertently been given that the stage of the Sermon on the Mount is the same as the miracle of Cana. The similarity to the first stage in John is clearly evident particularly in the words: 'You have heard that the elders were told ... but *I* tell you...'. Christ says the words 'but *I* tell you' not just on his own behalf, but on behalf of every human ego. The stage of law is replaced by the stage of egohood and freedom.

The correspondences in Matthew to the healings reported by John at the second and third stages can be found without difficulty. The healing of the nobleman's son is also reported, although with characteristic differences, in the first three gospels. The healing at the pool of Bethesda corresponds in terms of its stage to the healing of the man taken with palsy. This is told in particularly vivid imagery in the first gospels in that it is expressly located in the interior of the house: because the crowds make it impossible to reach Christ, the people bringing the man suffering from palsy take the roof off the house and lower the stretcher down through the roof to where Jesus is speaking to the crowd. If the miracle of the second stage consists of achieving the *balance between the inner and outer human being,* the 'healing in the house' represents the stage at which the *inwardness of soul which has become personal is harmonized* and strengthened. In the end, the healing of the man suffering from palsy only represents the physical effect of Jesus saying to him: 'Your sins are taken from you.' The healing of the sick man at the pool of Bethesda also takes place from within through his own inward forces being strengthened and encouraged by Christ.

The content of the fourth and fifth stage is the same in the Gospel of John and the first gospels. (Indeed, the feeding of the five thousand is the event in which all four gospels correspond most closely.) Here the congruence of the stations of the disciples with the stages of the incarnation of Christ are most obvious. The feeding miracle as the centre of the seven stages in John represents the step from the personal to the supra-personal. The miracle of community building is revealed to the watching souls of the disciples as a joyful future perspective. They learn for themselves and for the people among whom they are to fulfil their apostolic mission to *live out of the spirit*. That they can find and dispense the higher nourishment is due to the fact that the Christ ego on its way to becoming human has now fully penetrated the space of the human soul body. Henceforth humanity will have soul characteristics filled with Christ which is the source of all true community.

The walking on the water adds the power of *standing in the spirit*. In describing how Peter wants to go to meet Christ on the water, the Gospel of Matthew shows how the path of the disciples and the path of Christ touch at this point.

The healing of the man born blind as the content of the sixth stage is the outer reflection of the inner process which we can describe as *acquiring vision in the spirit*. Peter achieves a reflection of this stage in his confession of Christ at Caesarea Philippi. Jesus has asked the question whom people and whom the disciples consider him to be. Spontaneously the words breaks out of Peter's soul: 'You are the Christ, the Son of the living God' (Matt.16:16). In saying: 'Blessed are you Simon, son of Jonah, you have not received this revelation from the world of the senses but from the world of my Father in the heavens,' (Matt.16:17) he confirms that Peter's avowal has flowed from spiritual vision, even if it is only momentary. The power of Christ's question opens Peter's inner eye, and the true figure of Christ, as will be revealed later to him in the transfiguration on the mountain, is shown in a soul awakening in a momentary flash. (That Peter is called 'son of Jonah' shows that here he gains the part in the 'sign of Jonah' of which he is capable. It is no coincidence that Christ's words about the 'sign of Jonah' are spoken a short time previously in the same chapter.) The Gospel of Mark confirms the equivalence of the confession of Peter and the healing of the man born blind in that it tells the story of the healing of the blind man, which takes place at the Sea of Galilee, between the feeding of the five thousand and the scene at Caesarea Philippi.

Directly following the avowal of Peter, Jesus begins to instruct the disciples in the secret of his forthcoming passage through death and resurrection. The seventh completed stage is heralded here. Here Peter fails. The revelation of the suffering of Christ makes him angrily burst out: Do not allow this to happen to you! And Christ, who just a few moments before could tell him that the light and power for his confession had come from good spiritual powers, now has to tell him that his angry words originate in the whisperings of Satan. Instead of going with Christ through death and resurrection like Lazarus-John, Peter sinks into the dulled darkness of the denial of Christ. His confession of Christ indicates his closeness to Christ. But immediately afterwards his proximity to Judas is tragically revealed.

The seven stages of John are also reflected in the seven sacraments:

Cana (Sermon on the Mount)	*Ego development*	*Christening*
Nobleman's son	*Balance of exterior and interior*	*Confirmation*
Bethesda (palsy sufferer)	*Inner strength (forgiveness of sins)*	*Confession*
Feeding of the five thousand	*Living in the spirit*	*Communion*
Walking on water	*Standing in the spirit*	*Marriage*
Blind man (Peter's avowal)	*Becoming seeing in the spirit*	*Ordination*
Awakening of Lazarus	*Rebirth in the spirit*	*Anointing*

The comparison between the stages of John and Peter throws light on important secrets of Christian history. The avowal at Caesarea Philippi means that Peter has reached the stage at which he is ordained to the priesthood. Christ answers him with the words about giving him the keys to the kingdom of heaven and says: 'You are Peter, the Rock. On this rock I will build my congregation.' (Matt.16:18) The Christian priesthood for the first great stage of Christian development is not assigned to John, who penetrated as far as full Christ initiation, but to Peter who, as the *rock*, does indeed possess the load-bearing elemental powers of earth-bound human nature, but who can only reach an unfinished stage on the path to Christ. The reason why he flags at the threshold of the seventh stage is because he was not fully able to take the key step from the third to the fourth stage. With him, the whole of Petrine historical Christianity became stuck under the spell of the three lowest stages. Expressed in imaginative terms, we might describe the first stage as the step 'from the sea to land.' The step 'into the interior of the house' follows in the second and third stages. But the fourth and, above all, the fifth stage assumes that the step 'from the house to the shore of the sea' can be undertaken once again. The third stage, which takes place 'in the house,' is the stage of personal Christianity. At the fourth stage the supra-personal, community building element is added as indicated in the mystery of the feeding of the five thousand, the sacrament of bread and wine. Although the sacrament of bread and wine has been entrusted to Petrine historical Christianity, its actual meaning will only become fully effective when the sun of the Christianity of John has risen. Until such time the miracle of the fourth stage will be diminished and held under the influence of the third stage. The reception of communion will be related more to the personal salvation of the individual than to objective community building. Similarly all the sacraments corresponding to the miracles in John from the fourth to the seventh stage will remain under the influence of the third stage. The striving for personal salvation dominates everything but is only justified at the third stage. If it fails to grow beyond itself in sufficient measure, it blocks the path of John. Only when the Petrine period is replaced by the time of John is the human fulfilment of all the stages contained in the Gospel of John possible. The sign of Jonah will then be open to every person.

CHAPTER FIVE

Christ the Teacher

Christology

Christianity is no new teaching. The German philosopher Schelling, in his lectures at the University of Berlin on the philosophy of mytholgy and revelation expressed the elementary truth when he said, 'The real content of Christianity is simply and solely the *person* of Christ. Christ is not the teacher, as he is usually made out to be. He is not the founder of Christianity, he is its *content.*' For Christians, naturally, Christ is the source of the highest wisdom, as well as of the highest love and strength. But if Christianity had come into the world only as a new teaching, it would in the last resort be merely of human origin. It is distinguished from all other religions by being an event, a deed; for it has its origin solely in the fact that once upon a time a being belonging not to the human plane, but to the highest realms of the gods, walked the earth and brought into the world a force of the highest cosmic rank.

The assumption that the teachings of Jesus are the essence of Christianity could very easily arise in these latter intellectualistic centuries owing to the large amount of space taken up in the gospels by his sayings and discourses. The work of understanding these sayings and discourses and the so-called teachings they embody, in the light of the knowledge that the being of Christ himself is the content of Christianity, is something which still remains to be done. All true Christian teaching is Christology, as it was in earlier times when it drew on the old instinctive wisdom before this wisdom gradually stiffened into dogma. In the future it will be so again, renewed in the light of an unfettered knowledge, in proportion as thinking reaches beyond the sphere of sense-perception to the realities of the spiritual. But if the content of Christian doctrine is always the Christ-being himself, the secret of Christ must be found through the sayings and discourses of Jesus. What has hitherto been understood as the 'teaching of Jesus' is at bottom always a self-bestowal of the Christ-being as well.

Looked at superficially, the gospels direct attention mainly to two kinds of activity of Christ, his teachings and his healings. It is of the greatest importance to recognize that both these can be understood entirely out of the humanity of Jesus, and not to begin with as the manifestation of the divine Christ-being. The story of the twelve-year-old Jesus in the Temple shows that in Jesus, long before the Christ-ego entered into him at the baptism, a great teacher of humanity had arisen. A stream of surpassing wisdom would have issued from Jesus of Nazareth, even if he had not in his thirtieth year become the bearer of the Christ. From the moment when the three years of the actual life of Christ began, all the teachings of Jesus become more than the highest human wisdom; every word of Jesus is a revelation of the divine essence of the Christ living behind it.

The same can be said of the healings described in the gospels, which will be discussed in the next chapter. The apocryphal gospels suggest the truth in their untiring efforts to describe the miracles of healing performed by the child Jesus. Jesus of Nazareth would have become a great healer of men even without the transformation which he underwent at the baptism. The name *Jesus* means the 'healer.' And it cannot be emphasized often enough that it would be wrong to base belief in the divinity of Christ on his healing activities.

By elaborating the two origins of the being of Jesus, who was to prepare for the incarnation of Christ, the gospels of Matthew and Luke lead first to an understanding of both the teaching and the healing of Jesus on the human level. In the teachings, the wisdom of the Jesus whose origin is described by Matthew is placed at the disposal of the Christ-being. In the healings, the Christ is able to make use of the harmonizing health-giving forces of the Jesus whose origin is described in the Gospel of Luke.

But behind the voice of the Christ-being, the power of the *Logos*, the cosmic Word, is heard sounding through the sayings and teaching of Jesus after the baptism. To perceive the word of Christ in the word of Jesus is one of the ways in which the fact that the gospels are 'The Word of God' will again become true personal experience. No single word of Jesus is spoken just with the purpose of introducing new knowledge into the world; it is the living seed of a new world. In every utterance, as well as in every gesture and every deed, Jesus manifests the divine being that we call the Christ. The voice of Christ can be heard when Jesus speaks, and into each of his utterances, even when it appears to deal with quite other matters, is shed the mystery of the self-bestowal of Christ.

Theological problems

By concentrating attention on the teaching of Jesus, modern Protestant theology has lost sight of the Christ, and found itself faced with a series of insoluble problems and contradictions. It has come to a parting of the ways, where the gospel will either be completely lost, or will have to be rediscovered. One of its problems was the unmistakable difference of style which theologians thought they could detect, not only between the several gospels in general, but especially between the sayings of Jesus which the gospels record. There seemed to be an unbridgeable gulf in particular between the way in which Jesus speaks in the first three gospels, and the stamp of his words and sentences in the Gospel of John. Wholly absorbed in the human foreground of the events of the gospel, theologians found it difficult to understand that even this man could have spoken in two such very different styles. They believed that to understand how Jesus had really spoken they had to make a choice between the two styles. Finally they came to the conclusion that only the first three gospels contained the true words of Jesus, while the Fourth Gospel reproduced what Jesus had said at John's own discretion and in John's own language. It is, of course, undeniable that in the sayings of Jesus in the first three gospels there is a completely different tone from those of John's Gospel, with its finer distinctions of expression.

We cannot simply bypass these contradictions and problems. But if one approaches the four gospels as a whole, in the effort to perceive through the word of Jesus the speech of Christ and the voice of the Logos, the apparent contradictions will themselves become sources of deeper knowledge and experience. The words of Jesus in the several gospels are a more or less translucent medium for the manifestation of the being of Christ. The Word, the primal Word of all being and existence, the highest spiritual Word-being himself, rings out from the four directions of space. And the significance of John's Gospel, the key to which has long been lost by Protestant theology, is that in it the voice of Christ sounds most directly through the human speech. It is Matthew who best hears and imparts the words as teaching; John gives them most directly as the self-bestowal of the Christ-being.

Another problem for modern theology arises through its preoccupation with the composition of the words of Jesus as summarized, for example, by Matthew. Believing that the purpose of the gospels was to give a straightforward report of what took place on the strength of memory and tradition, readers felt obliged to ask whether Jesus really said this or that in a particular context. For example, it is inconceivable from the point of view of biography that the Sermon on the Mount should have been spoken just as it is given in the Gospel of Matthew. Therefore scholars became more and more inclined to ascribe to the evangelists arbitrary principles of composition of their own, according to which they were thought to have arranged the sayings and the life of Jesus. It was inevitable that as a result of such views, and in particular through discounting the biographical accuracy of the Gospel of John, the whole should be finally undermined.

But once more the threatened loss can be turned into unexpected gain. In future we shall see the Christ-being manifested through the words and deeds of Jesus, even more directly than elsewhere, just in those passages where the composition of the gospels is most baffling. It is as if a strong magnet were brought close to a heap of scattered iron filings. As the filings are attracted towards the magnet, they fall at once into a pattern which enables one to learn something of the nature of the magnet as well as of the form of the iron filings. It will then be possible to understand why the principle of composition works most powerfully and most logically in the Gospel of Matthew. John's Gospel, illumined right down to the biographical details by the real presence of Christ, does not need the medium of composition to the same extent. The Gospel of Matthew, on the contrary, concentrates attention primarily on the human foreground of Christ. Nevertheless its purpose also is not to give a merely historical report. It, too, derives from supersensory vision. And at the points in the life of Jesus which mark turning-points in the destiny of Christ, the Christ-being works in from the background as a strong invisible magnet and brings about special formations in the composition.

The framework of the parables

One useful result of the theologians' exclusive concentration upon the human teaching of Jesus is that special attention was given to the parables. The parables of Jesus do in fact present a living idea of the way in which he may have spoken and answered questions during his quiet journeys. Outwardly these scenes were probably homely and unassuming; the throng of listeners will have consisted of scarcely more than a hundred people. All the same, in the parables addressed to the people the words of Christ reached their greatest depth and nearness to humanity. But Jesus retained the parable form even when going beyond the simple teaching of the people, be it for the intimate instruction of his disciples, or by using them as a sword in conflict with his enemies.

But although it is easiest to recognize in the parables the human aspect of Christ's utterances, we shall misunderstand them entirely, even in that sense, if his words are not read in the light of the Christ in them. True parables are spoken only when the heavens are open. He who knows only thoughts, and nothing of the realities and beings of a higher world, reaches at best abstract allegories, not authentic parables. And so Protestant theology of the last century, which knew little of the being of Christ, could not really understand the parables of Jesus, although it drew attention to them with the joy of discovery. For a time the work of Adolf Jülicher, *Die Gleichnisreden Jesu* (the parables of Jesus) was regarded in Germany as epoch-making. Jülicher rejects the allegorical interpretation of the parables which he takes to have been universal in earlier theology. He considers that it is not in accordance with the character of Jesus, or of the gospel, to work out a series of thoughts corresponding to all the details in a parable. He sees in each parable the illustration of a great idea, the discovery of which is its salient point. Compared with this fundamental idea, the details seem to him unimportant. He even expects to find discrepancies in the details. He repeatedly comes to the conclusion that many parables express precisely the same meaning. For instance, he classes the parable of the hidden treasure and the parable of the pearl of great price together as a pair.

> The two parables illustrate one and the same thought, that as every man willingly and joyfully surrenders all the smaller

things, all he possesses, for the sake of great wealth, so must man renounce all else for the sake of the kingdom of heaven. In this pair of parables Jesus gives a drastic illustration-intended not chiefly as an attack on Jewish expectations, but as a stimulus to his own disciples — of the full joy of complete sacrifice, the inestimable value of the Kingdom of Heaven.

This kind of interpretation is no more capable than the allegorical of penetrating to the true nature of the parable. The allegorical conception tries to deduce a number of thoughts from the picture; Jülicher's conception confines itself to one fundamental thought. The pictures remain arbitrary. The implication is that Jesus wished to inculcate the same idea over and over again.

It is only when the parables of the gospel are read under an open heaven — that is within the range of a conception which is aware of a real supersensory world — that their meaning and their divine necessity become apparent down to the last detail. An explanation in terms of thought becomes superfluous and inappropriate. One learns to 'remain in pictures,' instead of pondering abstract thoughts that dissolve the picture. The picture is not the illustration of a thought, but the expression of a supersensory reality. 'Everything transitory is only a parable.' He who knows the supersensory reality can interpret the script of transitory existence which gives information about the realm of the spirit. But in all the parables of Jesus the core is always the Christ-being. Even when at first they seem only to reveal the laws of the universal spiritual life, the parables are ultimately self-bestowals of the Christ. This becomes quite clear if we consider the sequence of the pictures and their composition in the several gospels.

In order to develop a feeling for the Christological content of the parables of Jesus, it is best to start with the Gospel of Mark. This gospel has only four parables. Three of them belong together and come at the beginning of Christ's activity. Their background is the fertile land of Galilee. The fourth belongs to the last solemn act of the drama. It is thrown in the face of Jesus' enemies in Judea, in Jerusalem. The three parables in chapter 4:

> *the sower,*
> *the seed growing secretly,*
> *the grain of mustard seed,*

all hinge on the secret of the seed. They call attention, very appropriately for Mark's Gospel, to the spiritual in its embryonic condition. They show primary spiritual forces which are only just germinating. Their Christological meaning is evident, while they also bring to our notice laws which underlie all true spirituality. Through the incarnation of Christ a heavenly seed is sown in the depths of the earth. The paradisal land of Galilee, itself a parable, where the force of creation seems not yet to be completely dead, affords the first premonition of the new creation now implanted in the whole of earth-existence. Particularly the parable of the young seed growing in secret, which is especially characteristic of Mark's Gospel, is filled with the mood of the cosmic Christ-Impulse and gives a great hope for the earth.

The Judean parable, *the wicked husbandmen,* at the beginning of the twelfth chapter is more a reckoning with the past tendencies of humanity than a foreshadowing of the future. The lord of the vineyard constantly sent messengers to the vineyard to receive its fruits from the husbandmen. But these men forgot that what they were regarding as their own property in fact they held only in trust, and they handled the messengers roughly and killed them. At last the lord of the vineyard sent his own son; but the husbandmen killed him too. Then this stern parable goes on to prophesy events immediately ahead. The Christ tells his enemies to their face how they are going to treat him. But he foretells too the collapse of their world as a result. With terrifying clarity this parable of Jesus merges into a self-bestowal of the Christ.

The composition of the parables in Mark's Gospel is simple in design, but fundamental. The first two parables of the seed take place in the field in which corn is growing for 'daily bread.' The scene of the last one is set in the vineyard, where wine is trodden from the grapes. By leading from bread to wine, the parables of St Mark manifest the polarity of earthly substances — those earthly substances which Christ calls his body and blood when, later, he tells the disciples how he will unite himself with everything earthly in his great sacrifice.

Parables on the way

This also gives a fine clue to the parables of St Luke, the richest in parables of all the gospels. The parables according to St Luke have a beginning and an end in common with those of St Mark. At the beginning there is the parable of the sower, at the end that of the wicked husbandmen. Thus the parables in St Luke are similarly enclosed within the polarity of bread and wine.

But a glance at the structure of Luke's Gospel as a whole shows that the parables of the sower and of the wicked husbandmen are not simply the beginning and the end of a continuous series. They are like two pointers between which the real parables in St Luke unfold. Luke's Gospel is divided into three parts. It does not simply contrast the Galilean and the Judean parts of Christ's life in a great duality, as do Matthew and Mark. This gospel also begins in Galilee and leads to Judea, but its larger middle part is occupied with the great journey (see Chapter 4). In Luke Jesus and his disciples are shown 'on the way' from Galilee to Judea. Most of the many parables fall within this middle part of the gospel. Only the first and the last do not take place on the way. Jesus gives the parable of the sower in Galilee, before he starts on his momentous journey. He utters the parable of the wicked husbandmen after he has reached the place of decision.

One section of the parables in Luke has touched the heart of Christendom very deeply. Parables such as that of the good Samaritan, of the lost sheep, of the prodigal son are the culminating point of the gospel's inner teaching. They reveal the deepest secrets of love. Since, with the exception of the parables given in Galilee and Judea, all the rest are given in the course of the 'great journey,' they all form part of the instruction that Christ gives for the inner path of the soul, and represent stages on that path. There are two series of these parables: one has *love* for its theme. From these parables springs the mood of devotion, so characteristic of this gospel. The other series, interwoven with this, has *prayer* for its theme. The parables which concern instruction about prayer represent a quiet in-drawing of breath. Those which tell of the secrets of the capacity for love represent a breathing out. Only he who breathes in by meditation and prayer is able to breathe out his inmost being in love.

The very first parable on the way reveals the secret of unselfish love. It shows how the Samaritan of alien blood has more love for the man who has fallen among thieves than have the priest and the Levite, who might be expected by reason of their callings to practise human love. The first parable about prayer, that of the importunate friend, is led up to in various ways. In the preceding chapters Luke's Gospel has shown Jesus himself in prayer, on six occasions. Prayer is always the preliminary condition of a special manifestation of Christ. Luke shows Jesus praying at the baptism, when the heavens open (3:21), after the healing of the leper (5:16), before the choosing of the twelve apostles (6:12), before the confession of Peter (9:18), and before the transfiguration (9:28). And finally, after Jesus had started upon the journey from Galilee, the gospel again says that he withdrew to pray (11:1). When he rejoins the disciples, they say to him, 'Lord, teach us to pray, as John also taught his disciples.' With this the real instruction by the wayside is introduced. Jesus gives the Lord's Prayer to his disciples, and follows it with the parable of the importunate friend, which is an encouragement to overcome inner reluctance for prayer and to develop perseverance in meditative effort. The Greek word *anaideia* (11:8), which the Authorised Version renders as *importunity*, means just this stripping off of inner reluctance and inhibition. Thus the instruction on meditation which the disciples receive on the great journey emerges from the experience which they themselves have had of Christ's own prayer.

Between the parables of the good Samaritan and the Importunate Friend, as a further preparation for the instruction on prayer, comes the scene in the house of Mary and Martha, while Jesus is staying there. Martha, in her loving domesticity, is a variation of the note which came to expression in another way in the figure of the good Samaritan. But Mary, in her quiet absorption in the words of Christ, indicates the inner source from which alone the capacity for love receives sincerity and constancy. Thus the picture of the two sisters is the first link in the chain of the parables of love and prayer. The series which begins with the parable of the good Samaritan goes on with the parable of the rich man (12), the fig-tree (13), the leaven (13), the great supper (14), the lost sheep (15), the prodigal son (15), the rich man and Lazarus (16), the Pharisee and the publican (18). After the parable of the importunate friend come the further series of the parables on prayer: the watchful servants (12), the grain of mustard seed (13), the order at table (14), the building of the tower (14), the lost piece of silver (15), the unjust steward (16), the importunate widow (18), and the ten pounds (19).

Galilee
1. The sower

On the Way

Love	*Prayer*
2. The good Samaritan	3. The importunate friend
4. The rich man	5. The watchful servants
6. The fig-tree	7. The grain of mustard seed
8. The leaven	9. The order at table
10. The great supper	11. The building of the tower
12. The lost sheep	13. The lost piece of silver
14. The prodigal son	15. The unjust steward
16. The rich man and Lazarus	17. The importunate widow
18. The Pharisee and the publican	19. The ten pounds

Judea
20. The wicked husbandmen

The law of breathing in and out, which governs the two series, gives vitality and clarity to the course of the parables in St Luke. Now an important distinction can be made within the group of the three parables in chapter 15, the parable of the lost sheep, the parable of the lost piece of silver and the parable of the prodigal son. Hitherto these parables have been treated as variations of the same fundamental thought. But this has given rise to a difficult problem. The love which prompts the shepherd to abandon the ninety-nine sheep to seek the one lost is as pure as the love of the father which flows out more abundantly towards the returned prodigal than towards the other son who has never strayed. But the attitude of the woman who searches the house untiringly in order to find the piece of silver she has lost is different. The lost piece of money cannot attract the same feeling of love as does the lost sheep or the prodigal son. If, by classing the three parables together as a unity, one assumes that the same feeling is involved, one might seem to foster an attachment to material possessions, even a worship of money. The difficulty is solved as soon as one sees that this rhythm of breathing in and out also applies to this group of three parables. Placed between the two parables of love, that of the lost piece of silver refers to the meditative work upon one's soul. It is the task of the most personal exertion in meditation to search for that coin which is a picture for the ego-core of one's own being, and without which the human soul is lost.

The harsh parable of the unjust steward also becomes understandable now, as a parable of the laws of meditation. Only he who has the courage to practise the holy egotism which is necessary for an unswerving cultivation of the meditative life can be truly selfless and loving. If one were to take the unjust steward as a model of conduct, one would get inevitably involved in selfishness and injustice. But if the same determination and skill used in everyday affairs is applied to secure periods of withdrawal from life in the service of life, one will reach the inner realms and the strengthening forces with which one can take one's place in life with greater love and spirituality.

The last of the parables on the way is that of the ten pounds. Of all parables this one can do the greatest harm if applied directly to daily life. Indeed, one cannot help saying that through a wrong understanding and application of one of the most important parables, Christian teaching has for many centuries conduced to the weakening rather than the strengthening of souls. The indiscriminate use made of the parables in Matthew of the hidden treasure and the pearl of great price, as well as of the parables in Luke of the unjust steward, and of the ten pounds or talents, recorded both by Matthew and by Luke, have greatly contributed to religious egotism and to the cloaking of earthly greed in the guise of religion. Through the parable of the ten pounds, all forms of usury as well as of 'good Christian business' may seem justified. It is, however, not without reason that this parable is placed at the end of the journey recorded by St Luke. It is the culmination of the teaching about prayer. In imaginative language it points to that spiritual organ of humanity which cannot be used unless it is awakened and strengthened through prayer and meditation. Today the organs for seeking God are not only not trained, but are generally forgotten. Theologians of every description have even set up a theory which is in rank contradiction to the parable of the talents, declaring it wrong to work at one's own soul, and claiming that one should leave all inner experience entirely to divine grace.

Rightly understood the parables of the Gospel of Luke become readily translucent for the self-bestowal of the Christ-being which lives in them. In the parables of love the divine love is made known which is the being of Christ himself. In them is manifested that higher force which works also in the healings of Jesus. The evangelist Luke was a physician and therefore had a special call to describe Christ as the Healer. But more important, he was open to the cosmic healing force of love which flowed even more warmly and with greater strength through the parables of love which he recorded, than through the healings of the sick.

The series of parables about prayer is also full of the self-bestowal of Christ. The soul engaged in prayer breathes in the substance of the Christ-being himself. Only thus can a soul, actively engaged in 'breathing out' in the normal course of daily work, be a vehicle of cosmic love, of the soul-substance of Christ.

At one point in the parables of prayer the self-bestowal of Christ appears with special clarity. Where the Second Coming is referred to, in the parables of the watchful servants and of the ten pounds, Christ is speaking clearly of himself. He is the lord who has entrusted his house to his servants and who will take account of their guardianship. He is the king who leaves his pounds behind with his servants while he takes over another kingdom, but who on his return will recognize as loyal only those who have understood how to increase the property entrusted to them.

The parables and the 'I am' sayings

John's Gospel contains no parables. This is one of the reasons why theologians have thought that John placed his own arbitrary stamp upon the teachings of Jesus. Here is a difficult problem which is solved only by the recognition that what Christ says in the Fourth Gospel is on an altogether different level from that of the other three. In fact the parables have their Johannine parallels. They are the seven *I am* sayings of Christ. It was one of the important discoveries of Friedrich Rittelmeyer to point this out for the first time and to lay stress upon it.*

---

* See Rittelmeyer, *Meditation.*

1. I am the bread of life
2. I am the light of the world
3. I am the door
4. I am the good shepherd
5. I am the resurrection and the life
6. I am the way, the truth and the life
7. I am the true vine

In these seven sayings all the veils are drawn aside from the self-revelation and self-bestowal of Christ which in the parables is only implied. The *I am* sayings are direct illustrations of Christ himself. Indeed, they can be applied also in a general human sense. They hold good for the true higher ego, in whatever human being it may light up. Then the exact meaning could also be conveyed in an impersonal paraphrase like 'The ego is the bread of life' and so on. But this general application can be found in the *I am* sayings only because, since the incarnation of Christ, the mystery of indwelling is generally established. If a man is really the bearer of his true higher ego, then the Christ is in him, and he can apply the *I am* sayings to himself, because they are true of Christ in him.

The seven *I am* sayings throw light on the composition of the parables in Mark and Luke as a whole. The sayings stand clearly and openly between bread and wine. In the series of parables beginning with the sower and ending with the husbandmen, the significant move from bread to wine can be discovered indirectly. But in the *I am* sayings, which openly begin with bread and end with the vine, the order is fully disclosed.

It is interesting to note that just as in the Gospel of Luke 'the Way' is unfolded between the two parables which enclose it, similarly between the 'I am the bread' and the 'I am the vine' stands that other *I am* saying, 'I am the way.' And in the Gospel of Mark the reference to the candle set in a candlestick (4:21–22) following upon Mark's first parable of the sower, can be taken as an adumbration of the *I am* saying of the 'Light' following the first one of the 'Bread.'

Besides the seven fundamental pillars of the *I am* sayings, there are seven more passages in St John's Gospel in which the sign of Christ in the *I am* is evident, not with the pictorial character of the parables, but still quite clearly (4:26; 6:20; 8:18; 8:23; 8:58; 8:19; 18:5–8). These other

I am sayings form a significant pattern. The three middle ones, all in Chapter 8, are words of challenge addressed to Christ's adversaries. 'I [AM he who] bears witness to myself, and the Father who sent me also testifies to me' (8:18) 'You come from below, I AM from above. You belong to this world which perishes, but I do not come from this world.' (8:23) 'Before Abraham was born, I existed as the I AM' (8:58). These three sayings addressed to his adversaries are framed by others addressed to the disciples in moments of particularly intimate experience. At the walking on the water, Christ comforts the frightened disciples with the words, 'I AM, have no fear!' (6:20). At the washing of the feet, he says, in reference to his death, 'I say this to you now, before it happens, so that when it takes place you may know with certainty that it is I' (13:19) The framework of the whole series consists of two *I am* sayings at the beginning and at the end; they are addressed to strangers but in their starkness they reflect the special condition in which the Christ found himself after the baptism, and again immediately before his death. On each occasion a superhuman courage breaks through. Christ openly gives the Samaritan woman at Jacob's Well to understand that he is the Messiah. The woman says, 'I know that the Messiah is to come whom we call the Christ.' And Jesus answers her, 'I AM he, speaking to you' (4:26). While at the beginning, in the *status nascendi,* Christ speaks an *I am* to a stranger, at the end the *I am* sounds forth three times out of the fiery intensity which the Christ-being attained at the final stage of his descent into physical corporality (18:5–8). Thus Christ makes himself known to the officers in Gethsemane. As he speaks they fall to the ground under the power of this mightiest manifestation of an *I am* on earth.

There is no clearer proof that throughout St John's Gospel the voice of Christ himself sounds through the word of Jesus, than the twice-times-seven *I am* sayings, which flash forth through the gospel like sparks and flames.

Parables for the people, for the disciples and the adversaries

The Gospel of Matthew is almost as rich in parables as Luke's Gospel. Here too the parables of the sower and of the wicked husbandmen are recorded. But here the parable of the wicked husbandmen does not close the series, but stands third from the end. This is because there is

an altogether different structure in Matthew's Gospel, where everything is crystallized to the last detail, as though it were subject to the
laws of the mineral kingdom. This rigid principle of form determines
the architecture of the gospel as a whole, and also the interrelationship
of the sayings and discourses of Jesus recorded in it.

The Gospel of Matthew contains twice times seven parables. The
first seven are closely compressed into chapter 13. The second seven
are spread out over almost the whole of the latter part of the gospel,
from the eighteenth to the twenty-fifth chapter. The first group consists
of the following parables:

1 The sower
2 The tares
3 The grain of mustard seed
4 The leaven
5 The hidden treasure
6 The pearl of great price
7 The net of fishes

The first four parables are akin in mood as well as content to the
three parables in St Mark which give pictures of the organic growth of
spiritual forces, and in particular of the Word of Christ in Man. Then a
different element enters in. The parables of the hidden treasure and of
the pearl of great price could only have been so often made the subject
of sermons because the problems in them were ignored. For the attitude
of the man in the parable of the hidden treasure is surely very shock-
ing. When he discovers the gold, he covers it again with earth, and
when he buys the field, he refrains from telling the owner his true
motive. The owner lets the field go for a price far less than he could
probably have got for the treasure hid in it. Superficially speaking,
there is plain deceit here. And even when the thought of the heavenly
kingdom lifts the souls who hear the parable a little above the earthly,
it is inevitable that the attitude usually attributed to the treasure-seeker
should impart a touch of egotism to their souls. It is the same with the
parable of the pearl of great price which, unless taken with the necessary discernment, may produce an egotistic aversion from the duties of
life and an exclusive interest in the salvation of one's own soul.

Here again, composition is all-important. The first four parables are given in quite a different situation from the last three. *They are parables for the people.* Jesus gives them on leaving the house for the lakeside, and speaks to the people from the pulpit of the fishing boat. This is also the one place in the whole of the gospel where the step from blood-relationship to the new spiritual relationship is clearly made. Just before giving these parables Jesus describes his disciples as his true kinsmen. The feeding of the five thousand will shortly celebrate the new relationship. The step from the house to the open shore of the lake is a reflection in miniature of the great inner stage which has just been reached. After the four parables for the people, Jesus goes back into the house and here, after having expounded the popular parables to the disciples, he gives them the last three parables, which begin with those of the hidden treasure and of the pearl of great price. These, the *parables for the disciples,* are an intimate teaching which, unlike the popular instruction on the lakeside, is not by any means to be taken without preparation. The content of the three parables to the disciples shows how inwardly, within the house, the step from land to sea is made anew. The treasure is found buried in a field, the pearl at the bottom of the sea, and the full net is already drawn in on the opposite shore.

It is important to note that the three parables for the disciples begin on a level at which the overcoming of egotism is taken for granted. The events described can then no longer be taken in a purely earthly sense, and their meaning misconstrued. They are from the outset imaginative pictures of inner processes.

After death, the earth upon which the soul looks down appears like a field. If the earthly life that has just come to an end had served the divine purpose for humanity, then a bounty of gold shines out of the darkness of the earthly field. The sight of this awakens in the soul the longing to live again upon the earth, and to be able there to take up again the struggle for the spirit. From this angle it is clear that the parable is really intended to express an inner consent to the earth and its tasks. The usual egotistic interpretation of the parable is a complete reversal of the true meaning. In the further progress of its life after death, the soul plunges deep into the world of the soul. It finds pearls in its depths only as far as it has endured pain and suffering on earth. Even the material pearl is a fruit of suffering, produced by the oyster when injured by a foreign body. Desire to possess the precious pearl therefore means final assent to the burden that life on earth has brought about, and the admission that suffering is the force in our destiny that really brings us forward. Lastly, the soul comes in its development after death to the shore of the real spirit land. Here it is only mature enough for the stern sifting and separation of its future potentialities if its longing for the hidden treasure and for the pearl of great price has become a dominant force.

The three parables to the disciples are of course not applicable only to the life after death. They are valid for all true effort which in its search for the spirit has already lifted itself above the earthly level. By giving them these parables Christ treats the disciples as souls who have already entered and advanced on the path of spiritual development. The sharp cleavage between the parables to the people and the parables to the disciples in the first seven parables of St Matthew, teaches a distinction that has to be applied throughout the gospel. Everything that Jesus says to the disciples is to be understood differently from what he says to the people. And it will be observed that by far the greater number of the sayings and discourses of Jesus belong to the more intimate instruction of the disciples.

The second group of seven parables in the Gospel of Matthew consists of the following:

1. The unmerciful servant
2. The labourers in the vineyard
3. The two sons in the vineyard
4. The wicked husbandmen
5. The marriage of the king's son
6. The ten virgins
7. The talents

This series contains parables to the people. The instruction of the disciples is carried further, but with a break in the middle of the series. Between two pairs of parables to the disciples three parables are directed at the enemies in the last momentous spiritual struggle; they are thrown out as a challenge to those who, later, will nail Christ to the cross.

This second series of seven parables has a multiple framework. To begin with, they are enclosed between the first and the last prophecies of the Passion, all of which are therefore bound up with these parables. The second framework hangs on the secret of the Second Coming (16:27;

25:31–33). In Matthew's Gospel, too, the theme of the Second Coming of Christ rings out with increasing force within the series of parables. This interweaving of the parables with the prophecies of the Passion and the Second Coming makes it clear that they relate to the path humanity has to follow between the first and second coming of Christ.

Two pictures form a third framework to these seven parables: the shepherd with the lost sheep and the shepherd who is at the same time king and separates the sheep from the goats. These two pictures, not unlike parables, are closely related. They stand like instructive figure-heads at the entrance and exit of a path that leads on to the heights of a temple. At the beginning we meet the shepherd who restores the lost sheep to his flock (Matt.18:11–14); at the end the shepherd who has become king decides to divide his flock and turn away the goats (Matt.25:32f). Between these two pictures there lies the time of testing through which the human ego has to pass between the first and second coming. The picture of the lost sheep points to the tragic necessity by which the human being in whom the ego is just dawning has to cut himself off from the shelter of the flock. The shepherd's love, however, restores unity among the ego-men who belong to him. Finally the community of ego-men is no longer under the guidance of the loving shepherd, but of the king from whose being the spirit of egohood shines forth in majesty. In his presence, a separation of spirits inevitably takes place.

In the parables in Matthew's Gospel the secret of the self-bestowal of Christ does not at first appear as openly as in the parables of Mark and Luke, and certainly not so clearly as in the *I am* sayings of John's Gospel. The rocklike structure of the first gospel is not transparent in the same way. But the apocalyptic revelation of the secret towards the end of the second series of seven parables is all the more dramatic.

Taken as a whole, the two series of parables also link bread and wine. The first group of seven opens with three parables on the seed. The second series contains three parables of the vineyard (the second to the fourth). We are led out of the kingdom of cosmic growth, in which the mood of bread prevails, into the realm of ego-development, which leads through error and guilt and stands under the sign of the vine, in that it necessitates the drinking of the cup of trial and suffering. Here, too, behind the sequence of parables we divine him who is the meaning of all development in humanity, and who alone is able to call the bread his body and the wine his blood.

The last of the three parables of the vineyard is the parable about the wicked husbandmen who finally kill the son of the owner of the vineyard. In this parable Christ speaks directly of himself. At the same time the prophecies of his Second Coming reach their climax; and the last two parables resolve into this theme. The parables of the ten virgins and of the talents are themselves parables of the Second Coming. When the new revelation of Christ dawns, only he who has paid attention to the cultivation of the inner soul-light (the parable of the Ten Virgins) and to the development of the organ of spiritual vision (the parable of the Talents), will be able to witness it.

By passing through the middle region of strife, represented by the three parables to the opponents, the teaching of Jesus reaches apocalyptic power. Thus ultimately in the final picture of the separation of the sheep from the goats, Christ speaks of himself in a way that echoes the Johannine *I am* sayings, and in the boldness of his claim even goes beyond them. 'Yes, I say to you, what you did for the least of my brothers, that you did for me ... what you neglected to do for the least of my brothers, you failed to do for me' (25:40, 45). Thus the parables in St Matthew merge fully into apocalyptic Christology.

The Sermon on the Mount and the Apocalypse on the Mount

It is in accordance with the architectural structure of the Gospel of Matthew that the sayings of Jesus are gathered into two collections: *the Sermon on the Mount* at the beginning of the three years (Chapters 5–7) and of the *Apocalypse on the Mount of Olives* immediately before the last act of the drama (Chapters 24, 25). In St Luke these two collections are broken up. In the long middle portion of his gospel, many sayings which St Matthew assembles in the two synopses are woven one by one into the teaching on the path.

The first step to an understanding of the Sermon on the Mount and of the Apocalypse on the Mount of Olives is to apply the precise distinctions which the structure of the parables in St Matthew has shown. The Sermon on the Mount, in particular, has been almost always misunderstood hitherto, because people have not noticed that it constitutes the first intimate instruction of the disciples. It is not addressed to the people, and to try to envisage it as Jesus' 'system of ethics' can lead only to fatal mistakes. The disciples are not given the Sermon on the Mount as privileged individuals on a special inner path; they are being prepared for their priestly service to humanity. The Sermon on the Mount is a list of golden rules for the priesthood. As in the case of the three last parables in Chapter 13, one must remember that the Sermon presupposes a level of understanding above ordinary human consciousness. Thus the famous saying, "If someone wants to fight with you and take your coat, let him have your cloak also,' is not intended simply as a universal rule of conduct; it means rather that he alone is a priestly individual who tries not only to satisfy people's needs, but gives himself, in everything that he says and does, placing at the disposal of the seeker the mantle of his own soul. Nevertheless, the Sermon on the Mount stands in an important relationship to the people; to humanity in general. This is the meaning of its opening sentence, 'When he saw the crowd of people, he went up on the mountain. Then he sat down, and his disciples came to him.' (Matt.5:1f). The sight of the people like a flock without a shepherd is what caused Jesus to begin the instruction of the disciples. By leading them along the path of priesthood he prepares the time when the flock will again have shepherds. The people do not hear the instruction, but have a deep feeling that something is happening which concerns them. And so at the end of the Sermon on the Mount, the gospel can say, 'When Jesus had completed this teaching, great excitement arose among the people, for he taught as one in whom the creating powers themselves are at work; not in the usual style of the scribes' (8:28f).

More recent critical theology may well be right in holding that the sayings of the Sermon on the Mount were not given to the disciples all at once. It is more probable that single sayings or groups of sayings were given in instruction spread over longer periods of time. However, it would be wrong to think that the evangelist Matthew chose the concentrated catechismal form of the sayings arbitrarily. The Sermon on the Mount was doubtless given as a compact whole to the supersensory perception out of which Matthew's Gospel flowed.

This is a most important example of how two layers of perception work into one another in the consciousness of the evangelists. The first layer is directed towards the details of what took place around Jesus. The second layer is directed towards Christ himself. And he works here as the magnet that draws the separate sayings together into a pattern.

In an attempt to understand this, we imagine appearing before the soul of Matthew a picture of the moment when Christ, moved by the sight of humanity without a leader, begins his special instruction to the disciples. A holy tempest sweeps through the soul of the Christ-being. Once more his full divinity lights up in a state comparable to that in which he found himself immediately after the baptism. But this blaze of primal spiritual power in the being of Christ is not seen unveiled by the evangelist. It remains in the background. It is only indirectly perceived as it draws together into one mighty tableau the scattered fullness of the 'sermon.' The concentrated totality of the Sermon on the Mount arouses a picture, as if the experience on Mount Sinai were renewed and transformed. Upon the Mount of the Ten Commandments God spoke out of the powers of nature to Moses, who thereby became the founder and leader of an important branch of humanity. Upon the Mount of the Sermon Christ speaks with primal spiritual power to the first men of the new priesthood.

The Apocalypse on the Mount of Olives is similarly to be understood. Here, too, the summit of the mountain upon which Christ instructs his disciples indicates an inner culmination in the development of his being. As the Sermon on the Mount arises from a renewal of the *status nascendi,* the Apocalypse on the Mount of Olives comes from the *status moriendi;* it reveals the resolve that culminates on Golgotha. The Christ-being has fought his way down so far into incarnation that he can now begin to pass through it into activity outside the physical body. Now it is no longer divinity entering human incarnation, but heightened humanity, glowing with the fire of Christ, which lights up this powerful beacon.

The apocalyptic discourse on the Mount of Olives is the sequence to a struggle. The great challenge of the entry into Jerusalem and the purification of the Temple have preceded it. The disputes with his enemies, in which Jesus is interrogated about his authority and about the tribute money, and is then questioned by the Sadducees, have taken place. The three parables addressed to the enemies, the two sons in the vineyard, the wicked husbandmen and the marriage of the king's son, have been weapons in this spiritual contest. Ultimately, astonishing parallels and contrasts with the beginning of the Sermon on the Mount have formed themselves. The thunderstorm of *woes* breaking over scribes and Pharisees is an exact counterpart of the nine beatitudes. The lament over Jerusalem as a city doomed to destruction is the corresponding picture to the sympathy with which the Sermon on the Mount touches on the secret of the heavenly Jerusalem. 'A city set on a hill cannot be hid.'

But now Jesus leaves the field of battle, and climbs to the quiet summit of the Mount of Olives. The power of the word resolves into an apocalyptic vision of the future; and the self-bestowal of Christ breaks through into all his teaching. In stirring pictures the time in which the Second Coming of Christ will be accomplished is revealed to the disciples. Thus the Apocalypse on the Mount of Olives ends with the two parables of the Second Coming, the parables of the ten virgins and of the talents, and in the final vision of the separation of sheep and goats.

The correspondence with the Sermon on the Mount is recognizable even in the circumstances out of which it arises. Just as the Sermon on the Mount is prompted by the sight of the people left without a leader, so the Apocalypse on the Mount of Olives is prompted by the sight of the Temple doomed to destruction (Matt.24:1f). The whole future development of humanity will depend upon the building of a new temple in the midst of storm and stress. This Temple will be a new humanity, as the body of Christ himself.

The farewell discourses in the Gospel of John

The first three gospels lead from peace to struggle and finally to crisis. The single move from Galilee to Judea is the geographical background to this development. In John's Gospel, the scene of which has changed all the time from Galilee to Judea, the development is reversed. Here the peace of the words of farewell is at length born out of a spiritual battle which fills almost the whole of the first half of the gospel. The element of strife is easily overlooked because the picture of this continuous spiritual warfare is toned down by St John. But by far the greater number of Christ's sayings between Chapters 5 and 12 are addressed to his opponents. Even the first four *I am* sayings, the bread of life, the light of the world, the door, and the good shepherd, with all their heavenly quality, are flashes of the sunlit sword with which Christ fights his battle. Only at the end are we left with the peace of Christ, which we now know to have been potentially present throughout the whole struggle. Now one can see why the spiritual warfare of Christ is presented in such a subdued manner in John's Gospel. The element which up to Chapter 12 can be traced only indirectly, now clearly fills the words of farewell from the washing of the feet onwards. Christ gives himself with each word, manifesting his whole being when he says, 'I am at peace with the world; this peace I give unto you also.'

In the first three gospels the prophetic instruction of the disciples on the Mount of Olives issues directly from the spiritual fight. The apocalyptic revelation is a transformation of the continued thunder of the battle. But in the Gospel of John the farewell discourses breathe the inner quietness of the soul of Christ, after the immediacy of the battle has faded away. Out of this quietness arise also the last two *I am* sayings of 'the way' and 'the vine,' which are the only two out of the seven addressed intimately to the disciples.

The farewell discourses are a continuous communion. Previously, after the washing of the feet, Christ had given himself to the disciples in the elements of bread and wine; now he bestows himself upon them in the communion of words. It is solely Christ who speaks, no longer Jesus of Nazareth. The language of the Christ-being has reached a point where it no longer has need of the language of Jesus. The picture that St John gives of himself as he listens may well be the key to the relationship between the inner word and actual speech. The disciple whom Jesus loved leans on his breast. He perceives the Word in the heart of the Christ. The mature intuitive perception of St John is the source of the sacred stream of the farewell discourses. Perhaps the other disciples were able to divine only a little of what the Christ was really saying in the bestowal of his love, because only here and there was external speech added to the inner one. Christ's words already seem to sound from beyond the grave and to be the beginning of what the Risen One will say in the forty days after Easter, as he goes about in the circle of his disciples, teaching them the secrets of the kingdom.

Here the Word is no longer teaching, but entire self-bestowal. From the farewell discourses we can learn how much all the sayings of Jesus are filled with the substance of the Christ-being, and that they are therefore ways of formulating Christ's Word, 'Come unto Me.' They are keys to the nearness of Christ. This is the secret of the high priestly prayer in chapter 17 of John's Gospel; ultimately, indeed, it is the secret of all the sayings of Jesus throughout the four gospels, however varied their degree of transparency for the language of the Christ.

The Son of Man

There is in the gospels a formula which, wherever it occurs, points to a special harmony between the objective instruction of humanity and the essential self-bestowal of the Christ: this is the expression *Son of Man*. The formula *ho huios tou anthrôpou,* the Son of Man, is a glyph, a word of power connected with the ancient mysteries, the use of which turns every sentence where it is used into an enigma which is solved only by meditation. It is important to note that, with one single exception, this expression is to be found only in the mouth of Jesus himself. It contains the very heart of 'the doctrine of Jesus.'

Theologians have pored and puzzled over the meaning of this formula. One theory was that the *Son of Man* meant simply *man.* It was thought that the Greek expression was nothing else than a literal translation of the Hebrew *bar-enash* which was believed to be an ornate paraphrase for *man,* customary in many languages of the Near East. The other theory supposed, in accordance with the naive tradition of past centuries, that Jesus used the phrase simply as a name for himself.

There are in fact some *Son of Man* sayings which do seem to refer to the human being in general; for example, 'The Sabbath is there for the sake of Man, and not Man for the Sabbath. So is the Son of Man lord of the Sabbath.' (Mark 2:27f). On the other hand, the formula *Son of Man* seems very often to be an indubitable self-designation of Jesus. To this category belong sayings such as 'For the Son of Man also has not come to be served but to serve, and to give his life for the deliverance of many' (Mark 10:45); and, above all, the sayings about the Second Coming of Christ, which always use the formula *Son of Man.*

The alternatives with which theology seemed to be confronted do not, however, pose the right question, and this is why it could not arrive at a satisfactory solution to the problem. This was bound to happen, for there is really no bridge between these two opposite interpretations. Only if *Son of Man* is seen to designate *Man in a higher sense,* can it be both a mystical term of universal application and a self-designation of the Christ. By using this phrase for the Spirit Man who will one day be born out of natural Man, Christ uses it at the same time of himself.

The phrase *Son of Man* means the higher part of man which has to be developed, so that through it he may open his being to the spiritual world. By giving birth to this highest part of his soul, he overcomes his inner darkness and frustration and becomes the bearer of Spirit Man. Rudolf Steiner called the 'member' of the human soul to which the name *Son of Man* refers the *consciousness soul*, or *spirit soul*. In its unfolding it will receive the Spirit Self:

> In men who were living at the time of Christ Jesus the intellectual or mind-soul had developed in the perfectly normal way as their highest soul-principle; but although the intellectual or mind-soul was not able to receive into itself the Spirit-Self; there was to develop, as the child of the intellectual or mind-soul, the spiritual or consciousness-soul into which the Spirit-Self could descend.
>
> What was the expression used in the Mysteries when referring to this flower that was to unfold from man's own nature? ... Translated into our language the expression used was 'Son of Man.' The Greek *ho huios tou anthrôpou* has by no means the restricted meaning of our 'son,' as 'son of a father' but signifies the successor of a living being, an entity that evolves from a living being like the blossom or flower of the plant on which hitherto there have been leaves only. (*The Gospel of St Matthew*, p.188f)

An important passage in Rudolf Steiner's book *Theosophy* describes the character of this upper member of the soul:

> By letting what is intrinsically true and good come to life within us, we rise above the mere sentient soul. The eternal spirit shines into the sentient soul, kindling in it a light that will never go out. To the extent that our soul lives in this light, it takes part in something eternal, which it links to its own existence ... We will call this eternal element that lights up within the soul the consciousness soul. (p.45)

Such descriptions harmonize beautifully with the gospel. They enable us to understand a wonderful saying in John's Gospel, the only passage in which the name *Son of Man* is used by any other than Jesus himself. Jesus was speaking to the people of the *Son of Man*, and they asked him, 'Who is this Son of Man?' (John 12:34) Jesus' answer about the light is a complete answer to the question, something that had not hitherto been known. Thus we have a saying in which Christ himself describes the nature of the *Son of Man*. 'For a short time yet the light is in your midst. Tread your path while you have the light, so that the darkness does not overcome you. Whoever walks in darkness does not know where he is going. While you still have the light, open your hearts to the light, so that you may become sons of light.' (John 12:35f.)

The expression *Son of Man* also occurs once in the Epistles of Paul, but it has mostly been overlooked because the character of Paul's language as the language of the mysteries has not been recognized. In Ephesians, Paul writes, 'the mystery of Christ ... was not made known to the sons of men in other generations as it has now has been revealed to his holy apostles and prophets by the Spirit' (Eph.3:4f RSV). Obviously the term 'sons of men' is applied here to those outstanding men of ancient times who, as initiates, had evolved this higher faculty of the soul.

The sayings about the *Son of Man* in the gospels are part of a science of man which is at the same time true Christology, because through the Christ-being having become Man, the light of Spirit Man has been kindled in earthly man. This higher science of man, of which the New Testament is full, is never given in a didactic system, but is assumed throughout. Important elements of it can be traced in the Epistles of Paul, where he uses such familiar phrases as the old and the new man, the earthly and the heavenly man, the first and the second man (Adam and Christ).

Quite another aspect of the science of man is revealed in the *I am* sayings of the Gospel of John. The Pauline science of man is in terms of universal objective validity, with the Christ as the archetype of Man always in the background. The Johannine science of man reveals at first glance only the majesty of Christ's own testimony concerning himself; but it can also be applied to humanity, since it speaks of the secrets of the higher ego that can dwell in every man. The science of man that we learn in the *Son of Man* sayings from the mouth of Jesus himself takes its place between that of Paul and that of John. Here is a balance between the universal human and the self-testimony of the Christ. Nowadays, when the science of man borders on zoology, it is especially important to discover in the words of Jesus the prophetic science of the Spirit Man who will evolve through man's own inner effort.

The teaching implied in the formula *Son of Man* can be developed under three headings:

The trials of the Son of Man
The glory of the Son of Man
The *parousia* of the Son of Man

Under the first heading such passages would come as that in which someone approaches Jesus and says, 'Lord, I will follow Thee.' He receives the answer, 'Foxes have their holes and the birds of heaven have their nests, but the Son of Man has nowhere to lay his head' (Matt.8:20; Luke 9:58). By describing how simply he lives, Jesus is not trying to discourage the seeker. He means that the first stage on the way to the spirit is homelessness. Homelessness is the first of the trials on the path of the *Son of Man*. It is true of every person treading the inward path.

This theme of the first chapter is fully developed in the sayings of Jesus foretelling his Passion. They begin immediately after the transfiguration. He speaks to the disciples of *The Son of Man* already on the way down from the mountain: 'Do not speak to anyone of what you have seen, until the Son of Man is raised from the dead' (Matt.17:9). Christ does not abruptly order the disciples to be silent until after Easter. On the mountain they had been permitted to see the complete picture of Spirit Man. They will be justified in announcing what they have seen only when, having passed through all the stages of trial, the light of Spirit Man has become active as new life also within themselves.

From now on, in tireless repetition, Jesus places pictures before the disciples which show them the stages of trial and suffering they will have to undergo. In a conversation about the martyrdom of John the Baptist he says, 'The Son of Man will also have to suffer this from them' (Matt.17:12). A series of solemn warnings is included with the instruction of the disciples: 'The Son of Man will be delivered into the hands of men, and they will kill him and on the third day he will be raised' (Matt.17:22). 'See, we are gong up to Jerusalem. The Son of Man will be handed over to the power of the chief priests and scribes; he will be condemned to death and committed into the hands of the foreign peoples to be mocked and scourged and crucified. But on the third day he will be raised' (Matt.20:18). 'You know that it will be Passover festival in two days' time. The Son of Man will be betrayed and crucified' (Matt.26:2). 'The Son of Man must die, as the scriptures also say about him. But woe to that man by whom the Son of Man is betrayed!' (Matt.26:24). And finally in Gethsemane, 'See, the hour has come when the Son of Man is given into the hands of men alienated from God' (Matt.26:45). In these words Jesus is doing more than foretelling his own immediate future. He reveals the law of 'dying and becoming' to which everyone is subject who is bent on higher things. Spirit Man does not come to resurrection in man until the stages of suffering and death have been undergone in the soul.

The prophecies of the Passion disclose a teaching which until then had been cultivated only in secret places of initiation. In ancient times the law of dying and becoming was realized in the practice of initiation, when the candidate was led through prescribed trials and stages of suffering into the mystical death of the temple sleep, from which he returned to life after three days as one risen from the dead. The mystery words which Jesus spoke to his disciples were also able to forecast his own suffering and death, because through his crucifixion on Golgotha the law of death and resurrection of the *Son of Man* was to come out of the darkness of the temple on to the open stage of universal human history. In future the path of the spirit can be trodden in freedom by everyone who, as the Epistles of Paul say, suffers with Christ, dies with him and is raised with him from the dead. This inward correspondence with the drama of Golgotha represents the renewal of initiation on a Christian basis.

One of the most important statements about the trials of the *Son of Man* is made by Christ to Nicodemus, himself an initiate of the ancient world. 'No one has ascended into the world of spirit who has not also descended out of the world of spirit; that is the Son of Man' (John 3:13). Nicodemus is the representative of a spirituality which seeks to leave the earth behind in order to unite itself with the heights of heaven. Christ points out to him that the path of the *Son of Man* must first lead him right down to earth, before he can climb again to heaven. No resurrection and ascension are right unless they have been preceded by descent into the bitterness of earthly death.

The glory of the *Son of Man* is born from these trials. This glory is first referred to when Christ describes the *Son of Man* as lord of the Sabbath. The Spirit Man is above the law. These sayings of Jesus are seeds from which later there will grow Paul's doctrine of freedom; they will become clearer and clearer in the course of Christian history.

The inner nobility of the man who is the bearer of Spirit Man lies in the fact that he can submit himself to the law of the world in freedom. He is no longer a slave but a master of the law.

Spirit Man is the source from which higher forces flow to humanity. When Jesus says to the hostile bystanders at the healing of the man sick of the palsy that they should take the healing of the sick man as an indication that 'the Son of Man has the authority to forgive sins on earth' (Matt.9:6), he is not speaking so much of himself as revealing the secret of Spirit Man, which enables sickness and sin to be overcome from an inner source. Another saying about the healing force of Spirit Man is, 'The Son of Man has come to seek and to save what was lost' (Luke 19:10).

In the Gospel of John the *Son of Man* sayings assume a great solemnity. When the Christ says, 'I am the Bread of Life,' he suggests that the indwelling of his higher ego brings about in man the substance of a continuous communion. 'Do not put your efforts into acquiring the perishable nourishment, but the nourishment which endures and leads to imperishable life. The Son of Man will give it to you' (John 6:27). 'If you do not eat the earthly body of the Son of Man and drink his blood, you have no life in you' (John 6:53).

Lastly, St John, who does not describe the transfiguration, shows Jesus proclaiming the dawn of the glory of Spirit Man. 'The hour has come for the Son of Man to be revealed in his spirit-form' (John 12:23). Immediately after this comes the saying about the grain of wheat which can bear fruit only if it has previously died in the depth of the earth. In the events of Holy Week the light of the Resurrection already shines. When Judas has left the circle round the table of the Last Supper and gone out into the night, Jesus says, 'Now the Son of God is revealed; the divine in him has been revealed' (John 13:31). But the sun which now begins to rise is not only the dawn of the Resurrection of Christ. A light dawns into which all men can grow. Close to the sentence which announces the approaching glorification is another where, in response to a question concerning the nature of the Son of Man, Christ reveals the secret of the light of Spirit Man, and calls the people who bear this secret in them, 'Sons of Light' (John 12:35ff). The inner connection between the second *I am* saying, 'I am the Light of the World,' and the saying of Jesus to the disciples in the Sermon on the Mount, 'Ye are the light of the world,' becomes clear.

For the very first time the triumphal song of the glory of the Son of Man had been raised in Christ's words to Nathanael, immediately after the baptism: 'You will see heaven opened, and the angels of God ascending and descending above the Son of Man' (John 1:51).

Nathanael was granted sight of the glory of the Christ-being who had just entered incarnation. Now he was to understand that what he saw as immediately present was at the same time a picture of the future, now for the first time shown to man. One day it will be clearly revealed that Man is a member of the realm of the spirits. Above him, as the lowest hierarchy, will appear the heavenly ladder on which all the ranks of the choir of angels will ascend and descend.

When Christ speaks of the *parousia* and Second Coming, the formula *Son of Man* assumes apocalyptic power. It is of great significance that in all the books of the Bible which refer to the future manifestation of Christ which we are accustomed to call the Second Coming, invariably the *Son of Man* is spoken of. When the first coming was near men spoke of the *Son of God,* although the sacred event was to mean that the divine being would walk upon the earth *as man.* Thus the archangel, in announcing to Mary the birth of her son, said, 'The holy being to be born of you will be called Son of God' (Luke 1:35). It was the Son of God, because then the Christ-being was born out of the spiritual cosmos into the earth. The Second Coming of the Christ, always described primarily in the words of Jesus himself as the *parousia* of the Son of Man, indicates the fruition of Spirit Man, borne out of earthly humanity to the spiritual world. The Christ-event of the future will depend in great measure upon men themselves. At the turning-point of time, the Son of God was born from the heavens above. The new manifestation of the Christ has to be born from the spiritual element which will be developed in humanity itself through the inner power of sacrifice. The first time the Son of God came in human form. In future the Son of Man will manifest himself in divine form. The Second Coming of Christ means the achievement of the birth of Spirit Man. Actually the phrase 'Second Coming of Christ' has itself helped to obscure this secret, which is so clearly expressed in the books of the Bible. The Greek word *parousia* does not mean 'coming again' at all, it means *presence.* It is the dynamic emergence of the state of being present. The Christ does not need to come. Since he united himself with the earth and with humanity through the Mystery of Golgotha, he is always here. Similarly, the mystery of Spirit Man does not need to enter humanity from without. Through Christ's becoming man, its seed has been implanted in the soil of earthly humanity. The *parousia* of the Son of Man will be this, that for some of humanity their souls will at last be so filled with the substance of Christ that what has so far ripened in secret can announce itself directly to human feeling and perception. This will come about with the growing of the seed of Spirit Man on the soil of that part of humanity which unites itself with Christ. Spirit Man, together with Christ, will be visible to the new organ of spiritual perception which will develop in humanity. And thus the Second Coming of Christ will be the restoration of the lost image of Man. With the new manifestation of Christ the whole spiritual atmosphere will be lightened. 'For the spiritual coming of the Son of Man will be like the lightning which flashes up in the East and shines out as far as the West' (Matt.24:27). To his enemy Caiaphas, who asks about the *Son of Man,* Christ says, 'From now on you will see the Son of Man sitting at the right hand of power, coming in the ether-cloud realm of the heavens' (Matt.26:64). The last decisive events of human history will be connected with the *parousia.* 'The Son of Man will come in the light-revelation of the Father, the Ground of the World, accompanied by the angels who serve him. To each individual human being he will give the destiny which corresponds to his deeds' (Matt.16:27). 'When the Son of Man comes, illumined by the light of revelation, surrounded by all angels, then he will ascend the throne of the kingdom of his revelation. He will gather before his countenance all the peoples of the world, and he will cause a division among them, as a shepherd separates the sheep from the goats.' (Matt.25:31–33). Only through the birth-pangs of apocalyptic times of suffering will humanity give birth to Spirit Man, thus growing into the spiritual world with that inner core of the soul which has been spiritually developed. The light of faith in the heart is both the seed of Spirit Man, and at the same time the eye of vision with which the new manifestation of Christ will be perceived. Thus Christ confides to his disciples his concern for the future of humanity: 'But the Son of Man — when he comes, will he find the necessary inner strength in human beings living on the earth?' (Luke 18:8).

CHAPTER SIX

Christ the Healer

Redemption and healing

The name *Jesus* means 'the Healer.' The Hebrew word from which it is
derived corresponds to the Greek *soter,* and also to the German word
which exists in an archaic form, *der Heliand,* and has remained, with a
certain sentimental colouring, as *Heiland* (Saviour). It is not unimportant that the human name by which Jesus was called before he became
the bearer of the divine Christ points to the healing power which he
possessed. The name *Christ,* corresponding to the Hebrew *Messiah,*
means 'the Anointed,' 'the Messenger,' denoting the dedicated,
priestly being whom the divine realms have sent for the succour of
earthly humanity. From the outset, therefore, two different kinds of
healing activities have to be distinguished. The first kind proceeds
from the soul of Jesus, and plays its part in the foreground of the life
of Jesus. The healing activities of the second order proceed from the
Christ-being himself. In them lies the new meaning of earth and
humanity given by the great miracle of divinity taking upon itself the
nature of man. In these, then, the key can first be found to the higher
mysteries which are hidden in the stories of the New Testament healings.

The healings of disease in the gospels are not miracles, in the sense
of a breaking or circumventing of natural laws. They can and must be
understood naturally. Jesus exercises his healing power on the souls of
the sick, whence it radiates into the body. But the healing activity of
Jesus is only the transparent medium for the works of Christ. These
relate to the spiritual ego, the innermost kernel of a human being with
which man takes his way through death and rebirth. If the Christ had
worked directly upon the human soul and body, as is assumed by the

ordinary belief in miracles, no doubt the healings would have brought temporary relief, but in reality they would have meant an overpowering encroachment on human freedom. The effect of the Christ ego on the human ego is like the effect of fire upon fire. It does not work against freedom but with it, by providing sustenance for it. Even the indirect healing deeds of the man Jesus could easily have been prejudicial to freedom, for at that time the human ego was beginning to gain independence. That this did not come about was because the influence of the Christ was always present too, and the ego in man striving towards freedom was thereby strengthened. The works of Jesus, as phenomena accompanying the works of Christ, were simply an expression of the highest love and human sympathy.

The art of healing in ancient times

If the divine power of Christ had been the direct source of healing which worked upon the physical body of the sick, we should not have seen Jesus exercise such restraint after his baptism. Jesus began his healing activities only after the imprisonment of John the Baptist, that is, a good many months after the baptism. By that time the Christ-being was so far incarnated that his effect on people was no longer overpowering, and the harmony between the Christ and Jesus could show itself also in healing power.

The imprisonment of John the Baptist had left a void into which Jesus now entered; yet he did not continue to work in the way of John the Baptist, who had proclaimed the stern summons of divine wrath. From the very beginning the activity of Jesus is of a helping and healing kind, not that of a preacher of repentance. It is as if behind the flames of the wrath of God, the love of God becomes visible, subduing them.

In his endeavours to help man with his healing care, Jesus is linked less with John the Baptist than with certain traditions of the old popular practice of healing. At that time it was not so rare that men with healing powers travelled about, teaching and healing. It is only in the most recent centuries that the art of healing has assumed the academic character which it has today. Originally medicine originated in the temples and mystery centres. It has been developed in three great stages. The earliest period, in which healing was confined to the precincts of the temples and was exercised solely by the priests, can be studied in ancient Egypt. At that time people brought their sick into the temples. The patients were put into a hypnotic sleep, and the initiated priest-physician brought the healing process to bear on the souls thus freed from their bodies. Something resembling the mystic death, the temple sleep which was the culmination of the mystic's path of initiation, was thus employed for the curing of diseases.

In Greece, the art of healing assumed a form from which modern scientific medicine could eventually develop. The ancient temple practices lasted, it is true, far into Greek times especially in the temples dedicated to Aesculapius. But when in the time of Pericles the transformation of the mysteries into exoteric culture began, the ancient occult methods of healing were gradually replaced by external remedies.

Between the two main stages, the occult Egyptian and the exoteric form arising in Greece, there was the popular healing common at the outset of the Christian era, particularly in Asia Minor. It made use of the healing forces of the human soul and represented a transition from the occult methods of the past to the more external medicine of the future. The age of ego-development had already dawned, but the human body was still so plastic and receptive that it could be healed by natural human magnetism. This form of healing still played a great part at the time, and in the circles of early Christianity; and remnants of it continued into the Middle Ages. By these means, St Francis of Assisi is said to have cured numerous lepers. Like any other brother of an order, Francis was summoned to sick people in the neighbourhood. It was still usual in country places for healing to be practised by the religious orders rather than by a physician. There was no need for Francis to do more than lovingly tend the sick, passing his hand perhaps over the stricken limb. The fear of infection which has reached such a pitch in modern times was completely alien to such men as Francis of Assisi. With the human organism still very responsive to the healing influence of the soul, simple loving care without the use of any medicament would be capable of healing even serious complaints. Even today the nurse is often more important than the doctor in the recovery of a patient, and loving care more important than a well-stocked medicine chest.

Anachronistic survivals of both the hypnotic methods of the old temple physicians and of the later middle period of medicine continue in our day. These 'spiritual' or 'psychic' or 'magnetic' methods of healing need not necessarily be dangerous and harmful. It may well be that there are some healers who, through purity and goodness of heart, have the right and the capacity to help others through their own soul-forces without infringing on the freedom of the ego. The danger of charlatanism is nevertheless great: first, because the materialistic view of the world forbids a true knowledge of man, and secondly because the temptation to make money can easily distort the healing forces of the soul.

The share of Jesus in the gospel healings can best be understood in the light of the middle stage of medicine. But this was only the garment in which the cosmic healing will of Christ was clothed. As Christ Jesus passed through the land healing the sick, possibilities were created which can come to wider fulfilment only in the future. When Jesus laid his hand upon the sick, something more than the power of a kind and loving heart was at work; a spark from the cosmic ego of Christ flashed to the weaker ego of the sick person, anticipating a future when the ego-being of man will have matured and become so free that a force passing from man to man will work right into the bodily nature, driving out the demons of disease.

The healing forces of nature

People of old knew how to enlist the co-operation of nature. They recognized places with special etheric quality, where nature could contribute to the work of healing. The reputation of many modern spas rests on an earlier knowledge of the distinctive etheric character of their locality. It would never have occurred to earlier generations to attribute a curative effect solely to the chemical composition of the springs, or to any other material substance. In those places the etheric realm was seen to be filled with healing forces, and use was made of the waters of the spring chiefly because these forces were concentrated there in the most tangible way. It was known that at these places a special presence of the gods could be traced, and therefore the healing centres were at the same time the goal of devout pilgrimages. When, for instance, a pilgrimage was made to a famous sanctuary of the Virgin Mary, such as Loretto, Kevelaer or Odilienberg, in the firm faith that there the Mother of God would heal all who approached with true piety and the right offerings, it was only a continuation, often coloured by superstition, of customs stretching far back into pre-Christian ages. Originally, instead of the Mother of God people spoke of the goddess Natura, the dispenser of life-forces, who made the plants spring forth everywhere and whose presence and activity could be experienced in a special way in particular places. Worship of the Madonna is very largely a continuation of the cult of the goddess of fertility, the mother or virgin goddess of ancient times. It was, however, never thought possible to receive automatic benefits from the healing action of these sacred places. Only those who went there in true reverence could count upon healing. Without this, neither souls nor bodies would have been receptive enough to be healed.

At the height of Greek civilization, this visionary perception of the forces of nature brought into being Aesculapian sanctuaries with a rich culture of their own. An example of this is the *Hieron* of Epidaurus, near the east coast of Greece. There the substance and movement of the sea air combine with radiations from the earth to create an atmosphere which gives a wonderful natural foundation for harmonizing the human soul. It is especially striking that the ruins of the stadium and great amphitheatre are close to the remains of the buildings devoted to healing, and to the baths. The amphitheatre of Epidaurus, with its great open auditorium, is the largest and most beautiful of all surviving Greek theatres. Here, among the ruins of a rich civilization, every detail proves that the art of healing was understood. Use was made of the supersensory essence of natural forces; it was also known how to mobilize and exercise the forces of soul and body. The curative work was vitally helped by the fact that those who were taking a cure also followed, under the open sky and with hearts open to the gods, the tragedies of Aeschylus and Sophocles. When Aristotle evolved the theory that true drama calls forth a *catharsis* in man through pity and terror, he meant that art can affect man even in his bodily nature, purifying and healing it. The same applies to the ancient games, which were in no way comparable with modern sport. The exercises practised in the stadium of Epidaurus were able to reinforce the healing given by the gods, for they reckoned not only with the body, but with the whole man who through his soul and spirit is related to the divine. When, later, at Christian shrines the pilgrim was strictly forbidden to enter the sanctuary until he had knelt at the Stations of the Cross, and so had shared in the mystery-drama of Christ's Passion, the insight which had governed the ancient healing methods was expressing itself in a medieval form.

The effect of space and time

It is significant that Jesus' acts of healing began in Galilee, notably in the neighbourhood of the Lake of Genesaret. The power of the land of Galilee played its part. The spiritual forces of the sun, which can be felt in the atmosphere of Galilee even today, are like an echo from the paradisal infancy of the earth in spite of the dry, steppe-like character of the landscape. A few places round the Sea of Galilee may still be described as natural fountains of healing; and in the time of Jesus the etheric spirituality of the landscape was doubtless much stronger. Hence it came about that the Galilean healings were connected with the special mood of soul called forth by this 'heavenly' part of the earth. For nature never has a purely external influence, even when she is most richly endowed with elemental healing forces. Here in the neighbourhood of the Lake of Gennesaret, where it was natural for people to be less deeply embedded in the physical than elsewhere, they were the more able to retain something of the old visionary clairvoyance. And so a beautiful communion was possible between the spiritual sun-substance of the landscape and the soul of man, still sun-like and pure through natural piety and devotion.

The first three gospels tell of healings performed almost exclusively in Galilee. They place the healings of Jesus in the first half of the time between the baptism and the crucifixion, with Galilee as the background throughout. The Gospel of John is the first to leave the paradisal region of Galilee in recounting the works of healing. In accord with the other gospels, however, it places the first healing in Galilee. It relates the healing of the nobleman's son at Capernaum, and several times emphasizes that this healing was possible because 'he had come from Judea to Galilee' (John 4:47, 54).

John's Gospel describes the second healing as taking place in Judea. It is the healing of the sick man at the pool of Bethesda. But this is a place where, in spite of the deadness of nature in Judea, there were special hidden forces. The pool is at the northeastern edge of the city of Jerusalem; over it were built five porches where the sick people congregated. They waited for the bubbling up of the water in order to benefit from the curative power of the spring. Here is a world far removed from mechanical explanations of nature, according to which the pool of Bethesda would no doubt be called an 'intermittent spring.' It is a world where the divine-spiritual element is still instinctively accepted in the works of nature, and so the activity of the springs is attributed to an angel, descending from heaven to lend healing forces to the waves.

It is important that this first Judean healing is performed at a spot where the sick have formerly been freed of their infirmities through the healing forces of nature. But the man who has suffered for thirty-eight years is not now healed through the water stirred by the angel. He goes away cured without having gained any direct benefit from the power of the pool where he has so long hoped in vain to be healed. The force which springs from Jesus is similar to that of the waters and can therefore take its place. The Gospel of John, being throughout a revelation of the mystery of Christ, also allows us here a glimpse of Christ's contribution to the healing work of Jesus. If there were not an inner force in the sick man mature enough in its ego-substance to receive the impact of the ego-being of Christ, then the healing would not have been possible. This inner force is affirmed and strengthened to such a degree that a kind of self-healing results from within. Nevertheless, the healing forces of the pool of Bethesda have very likely played their part too. This elemental force is able to reach the sufferer because it harmonizes with the healing that comes from the soul of Jesus.

The only healing related after this in the Gospel of John is that of the man born blind. This, too, takes place in Jerusalem, in the landscape which seems to radiate not life but death. Hence the inner element in the healing process needs to be correspondingly strengthened. But here, too, the natural elements are brought in to support the work of healing. It is reported that Jesus mixed clay out of earth and spittle in order to anoint the eyes of the blind man, and further that the latter is told to go and bathe his eyes in the pool of Siloam. This is an ancient, sacred spring lying just below Jerusalem; in the early days of the city it had played a role resembling that of the Castalian spring near Delphi. Later on, all the pilgrims who journeyed to the holy Mount Zion had to purify themselves in the pool of Siloam before climbing the sacred steps to the temple sanctuary. Although John's Gospel is directed first and foremost to the power of Christ in the act of healing, it still mentions the contribution of nature at specific holy places.

Side by side with the geographical setting, the days and hours when sick people were healed are also significant. Mark's Gospel introduces the story of the first healings of Jesus with the words: 'It was already getting late, the sun was setting, and they brought to him all who were sick and possessed' (1:32). Such an indication is not just accidental. In southern countries such as Palestine, where the sun burns mercilessly down all day long most of the year, its rays have no healing quality. On the contrary, they must be avoided as dangerous. It is altogether erroneous to imagine that the physical rays of the sun alone have a healing character. In temperate zones the summer sunshine is always influenced by the atmosphere; otherwise sunbathing would long ago have had much worse results. In hot countries the situation is altogether different. Particularly near the equator an indescribable atmospheric miracle takes place at the hour of sunset. Almost daily for a short time a play of colour, which is not of this world, flames over the heavens, and at the same time all creation breathes a deep sigh of relief. The brilliance of the glaring sun dies away, and at a stroke the super-physical effects of the sun, with which the shade is mysteriously charged, make themselves felt.

I have seen incomparable sunset hours on the Nile. The air turned suddenly into an ocean of deep red, like blood. The moment the sun touched the horizon, a shiver ran through the whole of nature. The sweltering heat which had hung over the land all day rapidly faded. The concert of the birds and frogs struck up as if at a given signal, and since the people living there are still close to nature, a lively chattering of voices began at the same moment in the villages of the fellahin. In place of the glaring heat and the silence of the long day, the sound of human and animal voices rose on the softly coloured air. Etheric forces, which till the hour of sunset had lain under a spell, were at this moment set free, pouring out streams of life and waking all that has soul as if from deep slumber. I could readily understand why in the older civilizations of the southern Orient, the day was reckoned to begin at six o'clock in the evening, with the setting of the sun, and not at sunrise. In the East, life begins in the evening rather than in the morning. The sunset hour, six o'clock in the evening, is the hour of worship, both for the religion of the Old Testament and for Islam.

It is at this important moment of the day that Mark's Gospel places the first healings which Jesus performed by the Sea of Galilee. And just as the life-forces of Galilee contribute to these first works of healing, so do the life-forces of this sunset hour.

Healings on the Sabbath

A special problem arises in the fact that most of the healings performed by Jesus are on the Sabbath. This is emphasized by the vigorous protest from the guardians of tradition which follows each healing deed. For them, it is nothing less than a violation of the law of the Sabbath. On the Sabbath day no one may work, and equally on the Sabbath no one may heal. Clearly, those who witnessed Jesus' healing work regarded it as no different from that of the many wandering therapeutics who considered it part of their calling to give medical help to the sick.

The protests which the healings on the Sabbath aroused are not easy to understand in our time. The laws of the Sabbath have been applied without discrimination to the Christian Sunday, and this has helped to bring about a total loss of feeling for the actual Sabbath experience of the ancient Jews. Between Sabbath and Sunday a profound cosmic difference exists. In these two days Saturn and the sun confront each other. The peoples of the old Testament looked to the forces of Saturn for the sanctification of life whereas the New Testament turns to the forces of the sun. From Saturn issues the breath of an age-old world; all that has become old in the world stands under his sign. Chronos-Saturn is the primordial foundation of all existence, and to this extent there is represented in him the divine Father-principle. It was the Father-principle alone that could be reached through the Old Testament. Therefore to keep holy the Sabbath meant to contemplate things of the past, to meditate on death and the grave, and to refrain from all activity. The sun, on the other hand, is the cosmic image of the creative principle, and Sunday sounds the note of youthful force and action. Here rules not the Father of Worlds, but the Son, the creator of all that lives. And so the Christian festival mood is by rights a bright, happy, active one, rejoicing in life, while the Sabbath mood is sepulchral, and belongs to a world of old age.

When Jesus went from Galilee to Judea, and there performed his works of healing, he was no longer helped by the curative forces of nature. It was the same with the Sabbath healings, for the Sabbath day is not related to the healing forces from the cosmos. On this day the response to the healing purpose of Jesus had to come solely from within the people concerned. On the Sabbath their souls were suffused with a mood of devotion, even if grave and sombre. This played its part in the healings on the Sabbath day, particularly in those carried out in the synagogue while people were gathered for worship.

Since the help of nature played no part in the healings on the Sabbath, they cannot be understood in terms of the popular medicine of the time. They call on us to perceive, far more than the scenes on the shore of the lake, or at sunset, the victorious power of the Christ behind the actions of Jesus. The sun is about to challenge the sphere of Saturn. Under the rays of the sun a flower breaks through the hard saturnine shell, and at the same time a new light awakens that inner response which the healing presupposes in the sufferers.

The healing of the sick man at the pool of Bethesda is one of those which took place on the Sabbath. In fact, the Gospel of John points out that it was a special Sabbath festival, for the whole account is introduced with the sentence: 'It was near to a Jewish festival' (5:1). For thirty-eight years the man had suffered from his infirmity. With the popular modern idea that illness merely saps one's strength it is impossible to understand the inner side of this healing. Rightly understood, chronic diseases can bring about a wonderful maturing of our innermost nature. Prolonged illness can have its compensations in that it makes us more mature than those who are always well, who are perhaps so full of vitality that one could almost call them 'unhealthily healthy.' What comes into being through suffering rightly borne could even be described as an inner sun-element. Some such force of spiritual egohood must have been ripening in the sick man at the pool of Bethesda. When Jesus comes to him, the sick man not only feels the sacred mood of the Sabbath festival, but an inner sun is rising within him as the fruit of his long suffering. Christ appeals to this ego-force by asking, 'Have you the will to become whole?' Then the infirm man stands upright; the inner sun in him, awakened and sustained by the sun of the Christ-ego, breaks through the shell of Saturn, the hardening of the past.

The Gospel of Luke, in chapters 13 and 14, describes two healings on the Sabbath. The first takes place in the synagogue, the other in the house of one of the chief Pharisees, but the arrangement of the narrative shows that they are connected. The first is the healing of a woman who had been infirm for eighteen years, crippled and bowed. Jesus lays his hands on her and heals her, and she can freely stand upright. A fanatical protest is raised by those who cling to the Sabbath rest. Jesus answers with this picture, 'You hypocrites! Does not every one of you untie his ox or his ass from the manger on the Sabbath and lead it away to the water-trough?' (13:15.) The second Sabbath healing is recorded in the following chapter. Jesus is a guest in the house of one of the chief Pharisees, and there heals a man suffering from dropsy. And though this time the protest of the Jews is not expressed openly, Jesus answers it with a similar picture: 'If one of you has a child or an ox fall into the well, will you not pull it out at once, even on a Sabbath day?' (14:5)

The polarity between the two infirmities points to a deeper truth. Together with the healing forces which issue from Jesus, a force of balance comes into play where the Christ is active which affects the deeper level of karma and of eternal individuality. The shrivelling up and hardening from which the woman suffers is an extreme condition, and not only because it has endured for eighteen years. A woman's organism is softer by nature and more plastic than that of a man. Therefore the symptoms of the sickness are emphasized if they occur in a woman. The second scene shows the exactly opposite case. Dropsy is a surplus of fluid, and the character of the disease is intensified by the sick person being a man. The woman lacks the 'humours' of life; the man, the forces of form and strength. By healing both the excess and the deficiency Christ exercises his power as the one who balances connected destinies which have fallen apart into polar opposites. The dual story of the daughter of Jairus and the woman with the issue of blood (discussed in Chapter Seven), is the classic case of this balancing of lives and destinies. But in the two stories considered here, something is also implied which goes beyond the popular art of 'spiritual healing' of the time. The sun of Christ breaking through the constraint of Saturn, reaches the related egos of the two sick people, whose karma led them to these extreme forms of opposite illness. Through their suffering they have redeemed the weaknesses clinging to them from a past life. A seed of strength has formed itself within them. The rays of the sun of Christ, shining through Jesus, make this inner seed burst into life. And so by an inner effort they are able to throw off the burden of suffering. The 'golden mean' is active in Jesus, and the dark Sabbath is lit up by the dawn of the day of the sun.

From stage to stage

Specific healing acts are closely related to the stages which Christ reaches in his progressive incarnation into Jesus. The clearest example is the healing of the lunatic boy at the foot of the mount of the transfiguration. Raphael's famous painting illustrates this close connection most impressively. On the summit of Mount Tabor the three most trusted disciples have been permitted to see Christ's divine form shine through his earthly humanity. When they come down from the mountain, they find that the other nine disciples have tried in vain to heal a sick boy. After Jesus has healed him, the disciples ask the reason of their failure. They are told that this kind of healing is possible only as the fruit of prayer and strict soul-discipline. Thereby he gives a hint that the healing is connected with what has happened on the mountain. St Luke says specifically that the sun of transfiguration shone from Jesus *as he prayed*. It is indeed a direct result of this new stage in the life of Christ that the inner sun, beheld by the disciples on the mountain, triumphs over the moon-forces which are seeking to take possession of a human being. If the healing of the boy had been possible through the human healing forces of Jesus, then the nine disciples could also have accomplished it. But since it comes from the sun of the Christ, we are led to see it as an event that extends far beyond the mere healing of an individual. A new power is present on earth.

Just as the transfiguration was followed immediately by a healing act, so too are the other stages on Christ's way to becoming man. Thus after the nocturnal scene of Christ's walking on the waters, the Gospel of Matthew says: 'And when the people there recognized him, they made it known in all that region, and all who were sick were brought to him, and they asked him to be allowed only to touch the hem of his garment. And those who touched it were completely healed.' (15:34–36).

By linking event with event a better understanding can also be gained for the healing acts performed by Jesus in the dramatic last days of his earthly life, which consist of the healing of the blind in Jericho, and of the corresponding healing in Jerusalem of the man born blind.

These healings of the blind form a pattern. The first three gospels speak in two places of healings of blind people; a Galilean and a Judean scene are set over against one another. In Matthew, on both occasions, two blind men are healed; in Mark, each time it is only one. St Luke speaks only of the Judean healing, and again of only one blind man. In St Mark, the first blind man received his sight in direct connection with the feeding of the five thousand in Bethsaida on the shore of the Sea of Galilee. The healing progresses from stage to stage, and it is shown that the forces of the country strengthened it. Jesus takes the blind man who is brought to him and leads him out of the city to the shore of the lake, a place full of the tonic movement of the waters. Here he anoints the eyes of the blind man with saliva and lays his hands on him. In answer to the question if he sees anything, the blind man looks up and says: 'I see people as though they were walking trees.' Once more Jesus lays his hands on the eyes, and now the blind man's sight is fully restored (Mark 8:22–26). Particularly in the first stage of his recovery the special atmosphere of Galilee is noticeable. His eyes are not able at first to perceive physical things in hard outlines. Instead, the etheric world of growth and formative forces comes before the soul of the blind man. This effect of the natural forces of Galilee, however, is a superficial phenomenon. Hidden within it are the after-effects of the revelation of the Christ in the spiritual feeding of the five thousand. The disciples, it is true, were the chief partakers; but the event had its influence in the souls of those who lived nearby.

The second healing of the blind belongs to the final act of the drama when the last decision had been taken and Jesus began the journey to Jerusalem. Jesus had stayed in the neighbourhood of the Dead Sea, where John the Baptist had once baptized. The news had reached him of the deathly illness of Lazarus. He waited two more days and then set out to Jerusalem, a departure which signified the final act of resolve. The blind men of Jericho met Jesus on his way, just as he had left behind him the first stage of this chosen path. The power that now works with healing is the fiery sternness and the conquering will of Christ. It impels the blind men to go with him, though this could not happen had they not themselves possessed the germ of such a will.

Their own will, nourished and fortified by the Christ-will, breaks the bonds of blindness from within. The gospel makes it clear that this healing of the blind near Jericho is at the same time a final calling of disciples, for it says of the blind men, 'they followed him.' The Gospel of Mark speaks here, as in the Galilean scene, of only one blind man, and even gives his name — Bartimaeus — which is an indication that an apostolic mission had been kindled through the act of healing. Such men, although they do not belong to the twelve, still merit being recorded by name.

According to the Gospel of John, Jesus heals the man born blind in Jerusalem before he awakens Lazarus from the dead. This is the final climax in the series of healings of blind people. The same compelling power which was later revealed in the awakening of Lazarus lies behind this act of healing. After he has been healed, the man who was blind from birth is among those who are sent to join the missionary work of the disciples. The gospel makes this clear by emphasizing that the name of the pool of Siloam, with whose waters the blind man is to bathe his eyes, means 'the sent' or 'the pool of apostleship.'

Last of all, the gospel tells of the healing of Malchus in Gethsemane, whose ear has been struck off by Peter in a sudden impulse of resistance to destiny. Apart from the fact that the gospel brings two imaginative pictures into strong contrast, the destructive power of Peter's sword, and the reconstructing, healing power of Jesus, there is no question here of a healing work performed by Jesus for the benefit of an individual. The being of Christ is now directed solely and utterly towards the final consequences of his own resolve. A victory has already been won in Gethsemane, but only the death on the cross can set the seal upon it. The disciples cannot reach the height of his resolve. They want to hold back by their own will the events that must now take place. The wound inflicted by Peter is healed; this, in miniature, is a sign that the fight waged by Christ has for its goal nothing less than the healing of all humanity.

The demons

The healing of people possessed by evil spirits forms a large part of the healing activity of Jesus. In itself, the driving out of demons could be rather easily understood in the practice of the popular physicians and wandering therapeutics of the time. But in the background a dramatic meeting of Christ with the demon takes place which reaches quite different dimensions. At the time, almost an epidemic of *possessions* ravaged the civilized world. Luciferic demons of passion seemed to be on the point of gaining final mastery over man. The mania of the Caesars was typical. The twilight of the gods had come; the magical religions of the pre-Christian age were petering out and displayed all kinds of decadence. In the place of divine beings evil spirits visited the altars of worship, and the Luciferic fire flickered over the whole earth. The cosmic divinities of antiquity had withdrawn. As the time silently drew near when the Christ should take on human nature, humanity was in danger of falling prey to demons.

The first encounter of Christ with the demonic forces took place in the threefold temptation. Christ beheld the Adversary ascend from the depths of the body and soul of the human being into whom he had just entered. Lucifer and Ahriman,* intoxicated with their victory over humanity in general, now hoped that over this Man, too, they would gain mastery. They would have succeeded if Christ had used his divine power to become a miracle-worker. But when their insatiable appetite came up against an impassable barrier, they must have been seized with great terror. Christ had entered their territory in becoming man, but he came as lord and victor, not as their prey. They began to recognize that humanity, which they had thought safely in their power, was to escape them. In the very moment when they believed they had finally triumphed, *the* Man stood before them, free of all the distortions and weaknesses which they had grafted into men through the long stages of evolution.

The encounter was again and again renewed as Jesus went among the people, teaching and healing. Although the people might not recognize who it was that was passing amongst them, the demons knew him at once: 'You have come to destroy us. I know who you are, you are the Holy One of God.' (Mark 1:24 and Luke 4:34). The terror which went like a tempest through the kingdom of the Luciferic and Ahrimanic spirits speaks through the lips of the afflicted.

The diseases suffered through demonic influence penetrated to the inmost being of man. The ego was prevented from dwelling normally

---

*   *Lucifer* and *Ahriman* are the terms used in anthroposophy for the two powers of evil. Compare 'devil' and 'satan' in the New Testament.

in the sheath of soul and body, and the demons insinuated themselves
into the vacant realm. The healing of the possessed was at first an
activity of the soul of Jesus, producing a state of peace and harmony
through which man's estrangement from his own ego was removed.
At the same time, however, the activity of the Christ united with the
ego-nature of the sufferer; the fire of the Christ ego gave him strength
and led him to a firmer state of incarnation.

If the story of the temptation represents a prelude to this driving
out of demons, the drama continues with its cosmic significance in
what the early Christian traditions described as Christ's *descent into
hell*. When Christ died on the cross he entered into the realm of the
dead, over which the Luciferic and Ahrimanic spirits were on the point
of obtaining complete mastery. But in the hour of death, when on earth
the sun was darkened, the sun rose in the realm of the dead. The
power of the demons was broken. The medieval Easter Play from
Redentin makes the devils shriek out the question from the 24th
Psalm: *Quis est iste* — 'Who is this King in his Glory?' when the Christ
enters the sphere of the shades. They recognize him, but do not want
to believe it. The descent into hell is an overwhelming of demons on
the very greatest scale. Since that time a force exists by which the
human ego that has passed through the gate of death can be delivered
from darkness and self-estrangement.

The so-called Second Coming of Christ, which we expect in our
age, will lead to a new encounter on an intensified scale between
Christ and the demons. The Archangel Michael, who prepares the way
for the Christ, has gained a new victory over the dragon-powers in
spiritual realms (Rev.12). Thus the atmosphere 'above' is purified, but
the vanquished demons have been cast down to earth, and they strive
to regain there the mastery which was wrested from them two thousand years ago. For this reason the time for the return of Christ is also
the age of Antichrist. But the Christ sun has matured in power. Two
thousand years ago the Christ delivered first the living and then the
dead from the clutches of the demons. Now for the first time those of
the dead who are united with him share in his victorious light in the
purified air of spirit realms. Now on earth, too, the healing light must
break the spell of Antichrist and lift his heavy pressure from human
souls.

The consummation of a true ego-development in man will be the healing element in the age in which the coming Christ will renew the healing of demonic possession. Man must grasp directly the work of Christ which formerly shone only through the working of Jesus. The ego-nature of man must gain courage and strength to experience itself as fire, and to approach the greater fire of the Christ-ego in order to be nourished and fortified.

In the future the physician's art will likewise be incomplete unless man is warmed and inspired by a new inward fire. It will approach the strengthening Christ-forces and draw them into itself. One of the most fatal errors of materialistic thinking is to believe that one keeps healthy and well by sparing oneself. One whose destiny calls him to live in a sick and feeble body must of course husband his physical forces. But through such prudent economy the inner being must not become 'sicklied o'er.' The one thing which can keep man permanently healthy is the development of inner initiative and activity. If in order to spare himself a man reserves his strength he is really laying the foundation of weakness and ill-health. To throw oneself *all out* into whatever one is doing, to find courage to lead one's life out of the *whole* man, is the way to overcome hidden inferiority complexes and the roots of disease, and ultimately it contributes even to the healing of the physical body.

When the forces of heart and ego have become entirely selfless, there is present what the gospel calls *faith*. And Christ's own words show how much this inner attitude contributed to the works of healing related in the gospels. When time and again it was said to those who had been healed, 'Thy faith hath saved thee,' they could feel the words confirmed in the inmost kernel of their being. They became aware that they had actually been healed not from without, but through the higher self within. The human ego indwelt by the Christ ego was at that time no more than a bud; in the future, when it has come to full flower, it will become the staff of Aesculapius, before which both disease and demonic possession will be forced to yield.

CHAPTER SEVEN

Raising from the Dead in the Gospels

Initiation as a historic fact

The three sayings which Jesus uttered by the bed of the daughter of
Jairus, at the bier of the young man of Nain, and at the tomb of
Lazarus:

> 'Talitha cumi!'
>
> 'Young man, I say to you, stand up!'
>
> 'Lazarus, come forth!'

show the majesty of his spiritual power of command. The power of the
Christ-will breaks chains and bursts open tombs.

If we are contemplating these resurrection scenes as thinking men
of today we are deeply puzzled. It is no longer possible to conceive of
what happened at the gates of Nain in the naive uncritical manner of
centuries ago. Someone who had died was being carried to burial; the
sorrow of the mother arouses the compassion of Jesus, and he uses his
superhuman miraculous powers to call back to life the spirit which
had departed from the body. Even when we believe that Christ in his
divine power was really able to raise from the dead, we are beset with
doubts and queries. Why was it just *these* dead who were awakened?
Was not every other case equally deserving of pity? And in the end
Jairus' daughter, the youth at Nain, and Lazarus would all have to die
a second time. The mere extension for a short period of the earthly life
of these individuals could not surely have such a value as to induce the
Christ to transcend the limitations of his humanity in such a special
way. Or if it were a matter of showing that death did not have unlimited powers over the human being, why did Jesus not awaken many
more? He could thus have bestowed much blessing and consolation,
and a flood of human faith would have been released.

But, in fact, these raisings of the dead were not deeds of super-natural magic. In these events the principle of initiation comes into the gospels, which gave to the ancient world its divine guidance and the power of its temple worship.

At the beginning of the life of Jesus the three magi come as representatives of the ancient temple wisdom to do reverence to the new-born babe in Bethlehem. *Magi* signifies initiates. As initiates they could decipher the language of the stars and could read in the heavens that the Great One was to appear. Then there is a second type of event, which brings the mystery principle into the gospels in a more dramatic way. We meet with it in the three narratives of Jairus' daughter, the Son of the Widow, and Lazarus.

Wherever initiation appears in the background of the gospels, there are hints of the laws of destiny and repeated earth lives, of karma and reincarnation. The knowledge of these esoteric realities surviving in Palestine at the time of Christ was at best a mere echo, fragmentary and instinctive. The heyday of the ancient mysteries, which embraced a full understanding of karma and reincarnation, was long past. But the special destinies which came together at this turning-point of time were so significant that they appear repeatedly to break normal bounds. Indeed, these destinies can only be understood properly in the light of earlier lives on earth.

The law of karma was specially operative in the circle round Jesus, although this was not consciously recognized or fully comprehended by Christianity in its early days. Today, thanks to the methods of Rudolf Steiner's anthroposophy, we can penetrate these facts with fuller understanding.

In the Old Testament, where the lives of the prophets of Israel rise to their highest and most dramatic points, there are a number of parallels to the raisings from the dead in the gospels. In his lectures on St Mark's Gospel Rudolf Steiner gives important clues to an understanding of the lives of the prophets. He shows how the prophets whom destiny had produced in such numbers in a comparatively short period were not initiates in those lives. But in them individuals were incarnated who had received initiation in earlier earthly lives, and had acted as initiated leaders among peoples and civilizations of the most varied types. It was to the fruits of past initiation that they owed their powers and gifts of prophecy. During decisive earlier lives, in various parts of the world, they had passed through the temple mysteries. After many tests and trials these had culminated at last in the mystic death, the three days spent entombed in the death-like temple sleep. When at the end of the three days they were recalled to life by the hierophant, and raised up from the grave, their souls had won access to the spiritual worlds which are ordinarily entered only after death. They arose transformed beings, bearers of a new and widened consciousness. By living again through their initiation experiences the prophets could, from a certain moment of their lives, act from a higher inspiration and appear to humanity as interpreters inspired by God. In several dramatic scenes, foretelling the raisings from the dead in the New Testament, the books of the Old Testament describe the moments when the effects of a former initiation broke through in the souls of the prophets. Thus in the narratives of Elijah and Elisha we read how each of these two great prophets raised a boy from death; one of them, the boy recalled to life by Elijah, was actually the son of a widow. This event is also an imaginative picture of a particular crisis in the soul-life of the prophet. There is a similar occurrence, too, in the life of King Hezekiah, who must also be reckoned among the prophets. It is described in the Book of Isaiah, and brings out so clearly the mysteries of destiny that it needs no extra elaboration. Hezekiah falls victim to a severe illness just after Jerusalem has been saved, as though by a miracle, from a great danger. For three days he lies in a death-like condition, and then the prophet Isaiah calls him back to life. From that moment a mighty torch of prophecy is kindled in Hezekiah. This is a clear example of how, as by a great shock, not only the fruits of a former incarnation and initiation, but even the act of initiation itself can be re-enacted. The fate of the prophet Jonah is to be similarly understood. In times when the clues to such stories have been lost through lack of imaginative understanding, the story is bound to seem fantastic — a man is swallowed by a fish and after three days returns to land alive. The image of the three days spent by Jonah in the belly of the whale is simply a picture of the three days during which he once lay in the grave, and went to 'the roots of the mountains ... down to the land whose bars closed upon me for ever' (Jonah 2:6). This sudden resurgence of a past experience may have been brought about by a natural catastrophe, perhaps when the boat in which Jonah was crossing the sea was wrecked by a tempest and he had to fight the raging elements for three days. The transformation effected through a former initiation now reappears in a flash. This key to the lives and revelations of the prophets will help us also to solve the puzzles contained in the gospel accounts of the raisings of the dead.

The way to Capernaum

The polarity in landscape, which can be traced throughout the life of Jesus, governs also the raisings from the dead. The raising of Jairus' daughter and of the widow's son at Nain took place in Galilee. The town of Nain lies at the foot of Mount Tabor, that mountain of mountains which, by its very form, was predestined to be the stage for the transfiguration of Christ. The town of Capernaum, where the house of Jairus stood, lies on the shores of the Sea of Galilee, not far north of Bethsaida, the *Town of Fishes;* there is no other place where the wonderful life-giving atmosphere of Galilee is more strongly evident. The tossing waves of the lake of lakes are here at the height of their elemental activity.

The third awakening, that of Lazarus, has an exactly opposite setting. The stern country of Judea surrounds it. The little town of Bethany lies on the slopes of the Mount of Olives, on the side away from Jerusalem, leading down to the depths of the Dead Sea. Here the great Judean desert begins, and the name of the little town, *The House of Poverty,* expresses the quality that expands to cosmic dimensions in the whole landscape.

The event in the house of Jairus is not in the full sense a raising from the dead. The deep sleep in which the young girl was found had not yet become that of death. Jesus himself said: 'The girl is not dead but is sleeping.' What was accomplished in her case was rather an act of healing than an awakening from death. And yet the mystery played out here is similar to that of Nain and Bethany.

It occurred at a significant turning-point in the life of Jesus. He had made quite recently the decisive move from Nazareth to Capernaum. His whole youth had been spent in Nazareth, on the Galilean heights, where to the west there is the gleaming Mediterranean, and quite near inland the cobalt blue basin of the Sea of Galilee, and the rounded summit of Mount Tabor. After the imprisonment of John the Baptist, when Jesus felt impelled to go about and work among the people, he left the town of his childhood and youth. From then on the gospels speak of Capernaum as his town. Matthew states that: 'He went from Nazareth and chose for his dwelling-place Capernaum, a town by the sea in the territory of the tribes Zebulun and Naphtali. The word of the prophet Isaiah was to be fulfilled: Land of Zebulun, land of Naphtali, towards the sea, across the Jordan, Galilee, land of the peoples: The people who dwell in darkness see a great light. And for those who dwell in the realm of death and shadows the sun rises.' (Matt.4:13–16).

Despite the spaciousness of its surroundings, the town of Nazareth has a character of its own. Even today the bare rocks which surround it create the impression that here is an island of Judean aridity transferred into the garden of Galilee, just as Bethlehem is an oasis of life in the desert region of Judea. At the time of Jesus the life of the little town must have been harsh and narrow. It was not a free settlement, but a colony of ascetic Essenes, whose strict rule of life had to be observed in part by those of the local people who were in the service of the order. Through Capernaum, on the other hand, there moved not only the refreshing breath of the lake, but the life of the great world outside. Here the ancient *Via Maris*, mentioned in the gospel quotation from Isaiah, follows the sea shore as far as Bethesda. These ancient military and caravan routes connected the civilized countries of the old world, Babylon and Egypt. Along them Abraham journeyed when he left the land of his fathers in Mesopotamia and wandered towards Egypt, until at last he came to rest in the middle region between Babylon and Egypt. It was not to be long before Paul travelled from Jerusalem to Damascus by this road, and after his conversion returned by the same route.

When Jesus made his way from Nazareth to Capernaum, it meant a step to wider horizons. He left both the restricted circle of his family, and of the special religious traditions which had surrounded him in his town. Only now did he come to a place where he could address himself to all the peoples and spiritual streams of the world, to imbue them with a new breath of life. The step he now took was, in particular, the step from blood-relationship to the relationships of the spirit.

The Gospel of Luke uses two meetings in the synagogue to illustrate this transition. Jesus is gathered with the pious folk of his home town in the synagogue at Nazareth, devoutly observing the customs of his youth. It falls to him to read aloud from the roll of the scriptures. He recites from the Book of Isaiah the miraculous healings which will mark the coming of the Messiah. When he stops, all eyes are fixed on him expectantly. But instead of proceeding to the customary exposition of the text, he says: 'Today this word of scripture is fulfilled in your hearing' (Luke 4:21). At first it seems that his words may find a hearing, as if, even in his home town, there were devout people ready to recognize his unique mission. But as he goes on, he breaks through the bonds of blood and race and gives examples of how, even in the time of Elijah and the other great prophets, the greatest miracles of healing were done for the members of foreign communities. Now his boldness is met only with blind wrath. The people declare him mad and drive him out on to a rocky summit outside the town, from which they seek to cast him down. But, passing through the midst of them, he goes his way.

Immediately afterwards we find him in Capernaum, the town by the lake. Here, too, obedient to the law, he presents himself in the synagogue. And here he finds hearts open to receive his word, so that for the first time it can act like a force of nature. The evil spirits quickly recognize who he is. From a man among the throng, possessed by an evil spirit, come the same mysterious words spoken by Jesus to his mother at the Marriage at Cana, pointing to hidden forces operating between them: 'What is it that binds us to you?' Now it is the forces of healing and harmony coming wholly from Jesus which act; the possessed man is instantly healed and freed from his evil spirit, to the amazement of all in the synagogue. A mood of acceptance, stirred by the teaching and healing acts of Jesus, is felt by the whole district. Here is no longer the need to wage a bitter fight against the narrow exclusiveness of racial and religious groups.

Even today the two synagogues of Nazareth and Capernaum, although of course hardly anything of their original condition is preserved, symbolize the contrast which led to this decisive turning-point in the life of Jesus. The synagogue of Nazareth is a narrow, dark little hall, faithfully expressing the principle that ruled in the orthodox Jewish synagogues: the shutting out of sunlight and everything beautiful, the conscious exclusion of the gifts of art, the highest degree of sombre concentration on the inner world of man. As against this, the synagogue of Capernaum belongs to quite a different world. Coming upon its ruins, which are all that remain of the lakeside town, one might imagine a former Greek temple rather than any Jewish building. It stands in the midst of colonnades, open to the light and air. A wealth of statues shows the extent to which the builder drew on the products of human art. The capitals and architraves, now lying mostly in ruins, are carved not only with magical symbols, such as pentagrams and hexagrams, but also with symbols of the sun and moon; and near by, in examples of seven-branched candlesticks and in the tabernacle, we can trace the Dionysian motif of the vine. This delight in image and symbol led even to the choice of a heart-shape for the groundplan of the great corner pillars. The Old Testament prohibition of images, so strictly adhered to in the dark hall of Nazareth, seems here to be disregarded and thrust away. Instead, the Greek love of light is wedded with the severity of the ancient tradition, and gives an impression of sunlight almost suggesting a temple of Apollo. The stern and gloomy spirit of orthodox Jewry, concentrated on observance of the Law, is toned down into a freer and broader Greek Judaism which has combined with the spirit of Greek speech and art in order to sow the seed of the spirit in the soil of humanity, outside the restricted circle of the blood-tie.

Powers of the past and mysteries of the future

Jesus makes Capernaum his town because here he can quietly prepare the way from the principle of consanguinity to an all-embracing humanity. The gospel story shows how in Capernaum, owing to the broad views and openness of mind which prevail there, the circle of the disciples becomes a nucleus for a family of the spirit, which will spread far and wide and justify the discarding of the blood-tie. As though incidentally, too, there are several leading figures in the spiritual and cultural life of the town among those who respond intuitively. Two who stand out are the centurion of the Roman legions occupying the fortress near the town, and Jairus, the chief elder of the synagogue. Destiny has forged a living link between them, although they belong to different races and speak differing languages. This is shown when the leading members of the synagogue come to Jesus to beg his help for the centurion's son, who has fallen ill. In order to add weight to their intercession, the distinguished Jews of Capernaum, led by Jairus, praise the noble character of the centurion saying, as evidence of his good will, that although himself a gentile, he had built a synagogue for the Jews (Luke 7:5).

Although archaeologists are of the opinion that the ruins of this synagogue show by their style of architecture that it cannot have been built before the turn of the first and second centuries, tradition is surely right in holding that this is the building in which Jesus taught. It is no pious deception to imagine that on these stone benches, running the length of the inside walls, the people sat who listened to the words of Jesus. The evidence for this is that because of mourning for the destruction of Jerusalem and of the Temple in the year 70, almost no synagogues were built for a long time afterwards. Thus there is the remarkable fact that in the town where Jesus had gone to live, a Roman centurion had built a Jewish synagogue in the Greek tradition, without in the least realizing that he was thereby contributing a building stone for the all-embracing temple of Christianity.

Jairus, as a leader of the synagogue, can certainly not have met Jesus for the first time when he came to seek healing for his sick daughter. He must surely have been present on that first occasion when Jesus taught, read and healed in the synagogue. And in his own hour of distress he would recall the remarkable aid which had been given to the servant of the Roman centurion at his entreaty. Men like Jairus and the centurion were not necessarily members of the close community that was growing up round Jesus. Their common destiny may have been limited to a few meetings, and may have continued quite apart from earthly events. The essential truth is that their souls, by their unprejudiced and confident acceptance of the being who lived in Jesus of Nazareth, belonged to the human ground in which the seeds of the future could be sown.

The house of Jairus now presents a picture which reflects clearly the human stage to which the life of Jesus had attained. Jairus had come to beg for help for his dying daughter. Jesus and Jairus find the house already filled with the sound of mourning. Jesus takes with him only his three most trusted disciples, and dismisses the hysterical crowd of mourners. In the room are now a significant seven, as though the starry spheres were reflected in the quiet scene. Jesus stands in their midst, between two groups of three figures. On the one side, the father, mother and child represent the trinity of blood relationship. The three disciples stand in reverent silence representing the bond of the spirit, and fore-shadowing the new family which from this time onwards will be able to spring from the common ground of spiritual purpose. The girl is asleep; she has been lacking the forces necessary to pass the threshold of puberty. In the picture which arises there is a glimpse of the twilight which is falling on the blood-relationship out of which the life of humanity has hitherto been built up. And as Jesus, using the mantric form of the mysteries, utters the *talitha cumi*, 'Maiden, arise!' the light of a sphere quite different from that of physical birth begins to shine upon the dying world. A spiritual procreation takes place, as though the first rays of a new sun were quietly heralding the future.

The gospel itself suggests the key to this mystery by interweaving two apparently quite unconnected life-stories. As Jesus is on the way to the house, accompanied by his disciples and Jairus, he is approached from the crowded street by a woman who for twelve years had suffered from a severe illness, and is now full of faith that she needs only to touch the hem of his garment to be healed. She succeeds in her purpose, and Jesus does not fail to perceive it, in spite of the press of people. He says to the woman, who feels that her illness is already overcome, 'Daughter, the power of your faith has helped you,' and continues his way to the house of Jairus. The gospel would not have brought these two stories into such close connection if they had not had some common roots. It points to a deep karmic connection between the sick woman and the sleeping girl. The woman had suffered from an issue of blood for as many years as the girl had lived. When the girl was born, twelve years earlier, the sickness of the woman had started. As early as 1910, Rudolf Steiner drew attention repeatedly to the frequent way in which the gospels, through the very words they used, emphasize the links of destiny. The girl lacked those forces of the blood which were necessary for carrying her across the threshold of puberty. The woman, whose destiny ran parallel to the child's in such a remarkable way, suffered from a surplus of what was lacking in the other. She was organically unable to summon the formative forces necessary to restrain this surplus. Healing forces radiate from Jesus in both directions; they heal the 'too much' and the 'too little.' A golden mean reveals itself, bestowing its harmonizing power not only on individuals, but on a group of people united by destiny.

This is one of the places in the gospels where there is a puzzle which cannot be understood without the idea of repeated earth-lives. It is far from the purpose of the gospel to enunciate such ideas plainly. What the story does is to show a bond of union which could have arisen only through the working of karma from former earth-lives. The gospel waits patiently for the time when a knowledge of reincarnation will live again among men. Until then, the twofold aspect of the story of Jairus is left to make its mark on human feeling. But when that time comes it will be recognized that the original cause of the 'too much' in the woman as of the 'too little' in the sleeping girl lay in an earlier life. They had previously shared in some struggle with an obstacle placed in their path by destiny, and this difficulty reappeared in the guise of two opposite ailments. The eternal egos of the two beings brought about their bodily trials, so that by suffering them they might gain strength to make a fresh start. Should their lives come together again, it would behove them, in this or a later incarnation, to strive for a true balance of their soul-forces. Because destiny led them both to Jesus, their way was shortened. The harmony won by innocence and faith set them free from their bodily weaknesses; and even if they were not already known to each other, after this twofold healing they will probably have found themselves drawn together in the further course of their lives.

This is the first step towards solving the mystery of the raising of Jairus' daughter. Without taking into account the illness in past earth-lives, and healings in future ones, the events at Capernaum will appear merely as deeds of goodwill, from which two persons benefited more or less by chance, and in which others might just as well have shared. The roots of the illness lay far in the past; the fruits of the healing will ripen only in the future. We may at least suppose that the woman and the girl were individuals who in later lives will have tasks of great importance to fulfil. They were incarnated in the inconspicuous role of a delicate girl and a sick woman in order to meet the Christ-being in human form. The seed sown in them through Christ's healing deed was to come to fruition in future earth-lives. Widespread blessings for humanity may well spring from Christ's act of healing, and have great significance for the passage from physical to spiritual evolution.

If we thus penetrate the mysteries underlying this story we realize why Jesus allowed only three trusted disciples to witness the event. What was enacted in the house of Jairus was at the same time a part of the most intimate instruction of the disciples, given here not merely in words, but through deeds of destiny. There is a direct connection between the awakening of the girl and another scene which at first sight seems so very different, and in which again only the three disciples, Peter, James and John were present. This also was enacted in Galilee, on the summit of Mount Tabor. Here the Christ revealed himself to the three in his purest form as spirit. And in the vision of the pure etheric sun of the Christ, the disciples perceived to right and left two figures which they recognized as Moses and Elijah. In the house of Jairus they stood before a trinity of persons representing the ebb and flow of nature's life-forces. Within their own trinity, at that moment, they were the bearers of a seed of spiritual power, with a mission belonging to the future. Later, on the summit of the holy mount, a spiritual trinity appears before their souls. This time the Christ is not the seventh figure, the one between two trinities. He is himself the heart and centre of the trinity of spiritual humanity, in face of which the disciples represent humankind on earth.

In this vision, shared by the three disciples, past and present join hands. Moses and Elijah, great leading figures of the past, represent two polarities in the spiritual movements of former days. At this moment Peter, James and John might well have been struck with the thought that the higher egos of Moses and Elijah had lived through many lives in order always to bring new light to men. This dawning recognition may even have extended to the central figure, for the sunlike being of the Christ appeared to them through the translucent figure of Jesus. And the human individuality of Jesus of Nazareth, which had prepared the body for the incarnation of the Christ ego, belongs first and foremost with the great leaders who have illumined the path for humanity in all ages. But as they beheld this trinity, the disciples must have had a far stronger impression of it as a focus of mysteries yet to come. By means of the great central miracle of the Christ-become-Man, a force had entered humanity which would lead to a resurrection and transformation of all the great streams of spiritual endeavour of the past. At this moment the three trusted disciples must have experienced a spontaneous impulse to offer up their own human trinity for the service of the divine trinity. Faint memories of past lives, and willingly accepted premonitions of future ones, arose in their souls.

In the teaching given by Jesus to the three when he came down from the mount of transfiguration, he encouraged the growth of the seeds of knowledge which had been implanted in them in the house of Jairus. This was the occasion when for a moment there flashed into the minds of the disciples a conscious thought concerning the law of repeated earth-lives. They asked Jesus whether, according to the scriptures, Elijah would return before the Messiah came. Jesus answered that Elijah had already come. And the gospel again shows clearly the moment when light broke through into the souls of the disciples. 'Then the disciples understood that he was speaking to them of John the Baptist' (Matt.17:13). Doubtless the intimate teaching of karma which Jesus gave to the disciples after the experience on Mount Tabor went much further than appears from the gospel story which describes only faintly the sequence of events. It may be that in that hour the thought of repeated earth-lives turned back also to the mystery which the disciples had been allowed to witness in the house of Jairus. In this way powers would be granted them which would never again be lost in future lives. Thenceforward they would know that a man is not merely a child of his parents, but that he himself carries the essential core of his being from age to age, under the sheltering wing of the spirit. All that comes from inheritance can flower and pass away. In the human *I*, in the spiritual centre of man's being, creative and regenerative powers of the spirit are latent. The ego-being of man is the phoenix which ever and again passes through death and rebirth, rising to renewed life from its own ashes, to play its part in the forming of the future of humanity.

The son of the widow

The youth whose body was brought to Jesus outside the gates of Nain had died of no ordinary illness. In a former life he had experienced the mystic death in a mystery shrine. When he had now reached the critical stage of adolescence, that temple death rose from the depths of the past and struck him down. We owe to Rudolf Steiner some illuminating indications concerning the karmic path of the individual who was incarnated in the youth of Nain. The initiation death, once undergone, would not have been repeated in such tragic guise if, through it, the soul had been led all the way from darkness into light. The ego of this youth, however, after many incarnations as an initiate of ancient days, had finally gone through a time in Egypt when the ancient mysteries were dimmed and weakened. Isis, the divine mother, had been widowed by the death of Osiris, and those dedicated to serve her were called the *sons of the widow.* At that time the individuality of the youth, responding to the human tragedy of his age, had suffered a fate which gravely impeded his spiritual development. There is in fact a legend about a youth of Sais which throws light on this. It is related of a young mystic that, in the fervour of his zeal for knowledge, he ignored all warnings, and finally went so far as to tear the veil from the image of Isis, whereupon he fell dead. Through the legendary trappings of this story one can see the tragedy of a man who had resisted the gradual loss of the light which had previously illuminated Egyptian initiations. He had committed acts of such boldness and violence that his initiation was bound to suffer frustration. Instead of awakening from the temple sleep as an initiate, he had sunk into a real death.

This event, into which the universal darkening and impoverishment of the human spirit was concentrated, had made so deep an impression on the inner being of the young man that its shadow was cast into his incarnation in Nain as a contemporary of Jesus. At the threshold of a young man's coming of age the spiritual content of earlier lives rises up from the depths of his nature. The young man's soul was overpowered by this, and the Egyptian tragedy repeated itself. His vitality was checked, and from his inner life a death-like condition developed. The process was comparable to the mystic death, but so close to physical death that at any moment it was liable to turn into it. Then, by the wisdom and goodness of fate, Jesus appeared on the road along which the bier, followed by the sorrowing mother, was being carried to the burial place. Deep sympathy and compassion were aroused in the soul of Jesus at the sight of the weeping woman, but he did not act merely out of sympathy. In the gospel story the young man is described as the 'only son of a widow.' This phrase from the mysteries points to the hidden background of destiny. It may also indicate the flash of recognition which arises in Jesus at this moment. Through sympathy he sees the destiny of the soul whose youthful body lies before him on the bier. The fact that the initiates in Egypt had become

'sons of the widow' was one of the symptoms of that decline of the
spiritual life which it was his inmost concern to reverse. So he
approaches, stops the procession, and speaks the formula of awakening: 'Young man, I say to you, stand up!' (Luke 7:14).

Jesus acts just as the hierophant acted in the ancient mystery temples when, three days after the entombment of the candidate, he
approached the stone sarcophagus and uttered the words of awakening. Now an initiation ceremony takes place openly in the midst of
the people. The first acts of the drama are enacted by destiny itself.
Only at the final stage the role of the hierophant is taken over by
Christ. What happens at this moment is infinitely more than the pro-
longation of a young man's life. A deep wound in mankind is healed.
A process of decline is halted, and the way cleared for a re-ascent.
Out of the twilight of the gods the dawn of a new sunrise begins to
glow.

About the later life of the young man of Nain nothing is known. He
probably became one of the followers and disciples of Jesus, even if he
were not with him as constantly as the Twelve. But we do know that
the fruits of his awakening could not fully ripen at that time. The tribute for the tragedy of humanity, which was summarized in his own
destiny, had still to be paid. The seed of initiation sown in his soul by
the Christ himself could only bear fruit in a future incarnation. In the
third century, as we learn through Rudolf Steiner's lectures on the
Gospel of St Luke, the individuality of the youth appears again, charged
with a far-reaching mission of enlightenment for humanity. As Mani or
Manes, the founder of Manicheism, his task was to bring into the
development of Christianity the light of gnostic knowledge, thus giving it a form in which it could be accepted by Eastern peoples among
whom echoes of the old wisdom could still be found.

The western European fruit of Manichean Christianity was the
stream of the Holy Grail, which lived at the turning-point of the first
millennium as an esoteric undercurrent in western Christianity. Again,
as in ancient Egypt, the individuality of the young man of Nain
appears a legendary figure. He now goes through a reversal of his
Egyptian destiny. At that time he had been forbidden to ask questions,
and his attempt to lift the veil spelt death. Now, as the young knight
Parsifal, he is thrown back into the confusion of the world because, in
the presence of the suffering Amfortas, he was not awake to the ques-

tion that needed to be asked. Only when he was mature enough to ask the question, and had gained knowledge through sympathy, was he appointed guardian and king of the Grail.

The raising of Lazarus

In the raising of Lazarus the bond which connected Christ with the ancient mysteries comes to its fullest expression. From the earliest days legendary tradition saw it linked with the two similar events which preceded it. Fathers of the Church such as Ambrose asserted that the woman with the issue of blood, whom Jesus healed on the way to Jairus' house, was in fact Martha, the sister of Lazarus. This would indeed throw much light on the character of Martha. Her restless domestic activity could have been an echo of her former illness, until it was inwardly transformed into the meditative peace which Mary, the other sister of Lazarus, had already achieved. And if it were agreed that Martha was the sick woman, we could see an indirect link of destiny between Lazarus and Jairus' daughter.

Another legend connects the raising of Lazarus with that of the young man of Nain. Lazarus is said to have been a rich man, endowed with possessions on a princely scale. Then his destiny led him to a meeting with Jesus. He followed him, and took his words and deeds deeply to heart. So he was present when Jesus raised the son of the widow. This event affected him so profoundly that he broke with his former life and gave all he had to the poor. The legend leaves it open whether the shock of the experience might even help to explain his death. But through these legendary pictures shines an indubitable truth. The riches offered up by Lazarus under the influence of Christ were not purely material. They were the rich fruits brought from former earthly lives, in which he had been repeatedly ranked among the highest initiates. In the Christ-being there appeared to him something entirely new, in comparison with which the old dispensation seemed faded and worthless. In Christ he saw the fulfilment; all the rest had only been preparation and prophecy. Clearly, the hierophantic approach of Jesus to the bier of the young man of Nain must have had a specially disturbing influence on Lazarus' inner life. There are significant parallels between his destiny and that of the young man. With the young man a former initiation repeats itself and, having formerly brought about a tragic crisis, it is now directed to a good purpose through the Christ. With Lazarus, too, potent forces from former initiations are liberated, and he is no longer able to keep his soul, awakened to such overwhelming riches, bound to its bodily vehicle. In him, too, the temple sleep and mystic death of many former lives comes to expression once more. His two sisters, who had been at his side during his illness and death, evidently feel that all this has not come about merely through external causes. When Jesus first comes to Bethany, Martha and then Mary say to him: 'Lord, if you had been here, my brother would not have died.' The sisters know that the presence of Jesus would have helped their brother over the severe and dramatic crisis of his inner life.

As Jesus hears of the sickness of Lazarus, the far-reaching human background of it comes clearly before his soul, as had happened when he stood by the bier at Nain. He recognizes this crisis in the lives of those he loves as a stage on the way to a great revelation. So to those who brought him the news he could say: 'This illness does not lead to death but to the revelation of God; the creative might of the Son of God shall be revealed through it' (John 11:4). And when this seemed to be beyond the comprehension of the disciples, he stayed for two more days in the depths of the Jordan valley before going up to Bethany. He allows time for the crisis to develop.

What takes place in Bethany while Jesus and his disciples are absent is like an enormous heightening of the mysterious shocks and crises in the destinies of the Old Testament prophets. With them, only echoes and memories of an earlier initiation broke through into the present. With Lazarus, the dynamic power of fate is something greater. It drives him actually into death. But now there appears one who has prepared himself to be the master of fate, and so acts that not only an echo but a real initiation is attained, the *first Christian Initiation* in human history.

It has been said that the miraculous element in the events at Bethany, viewed as a real raising from the dead, is established by the gospel itself. Martha's reply particularly, when Jesus orders the opening of the grave, has been taken as proof that Lazarus was really dead and his body decomposed. But Martha's words, 'Lord, he has already begun to decompose,' merely show how far the sisters were from understanding what was happening. Martha speaks in this way before the grave is opened, out of discouragement and fear, not recognizing the kind of death which has overtaken her brother.

When the grave is opened, Christ utters the words: 'Lazarus, come out!' with the highest hierophantic power. Ancient Christian art in the catacombs could not do enough to represent this moment. With sure instinct it chose the episode through which the working of initiation could best be expressed. The body of Lazarus was depicted standing upright, in a grave to which a number of steps lead upward. The body is wrapped round with cloths, resembling the chrysalis from which the butterfly emerges to spread its wings. Jesus stands upright before the grave, and extends his hierophantic staff. (In the gospel, the formula which he utters is itself the hierophant's staff.)

In the mystery-drama of Bethany, as in that of Nain, that which led to death had been enacted through karma. But the final act, the Easter element in the old initiation, is fulfilled by the Christ himself. He does not hesitate to act as hierophant, although this unheard-of public enactment of an initiation drives his enemies to fury, and thus kindles the fire that is to light the way to his own sacrifice — the way of Golgotha, but also of the Resurrection.

The raising of Lazarus like that of the son of the widow is a preparation for the Christianity of the future. For after his initiation there is present among the disciples one who can implant the impulse for the Christianity of the future. Lazarus is he who wrote the Gospel of John and the Apocalypse; he is the great helper of Christianity on its way into the future. This is discreetly hinted at in the gospel itself. For the phrase 'whom Jesus loves,' is applied significantly both to Lazarus and later, after the events at Bethany, to John the 'beloved' disciple.*

The mystery of the raising of Lazarus is but partly understood if one sees in it only the renewed initiation of an individuality who had gone through many initiations in previous lives. The miracle of Bethany inaugurated in humanity the activity of a personal power, the genius of Christian brotherhood, which far outspans any individual destiny, even though the destiny of a pre-eminent individual is involved. This mystery is touched on in the thought that Lazarus, through his Christian initiation, became *John.* When he emerged from the grave, freed of his shroud, his illumined soul was not simply the

---

* See Rudolf Steiner, *Christianity as Mystical Fact.*

vehicle for an ego which had been raised into divine spheres. Through a mysterious process of grace his soul is also overshadowed and filled by an angel-like ego-being, whose priestly mission it is to bring together the human souls who are united with the Christ. Henceforth Lazarus is the disciple John, and he now becomes a special vessel for the ego-genius of John the Baptist.

After John the Baptist was beheaded in Herod's sinister fortress of Macherus, his spirit entered into a close union with all that was happening in the circle around Christ. It became the helper and protector of the Twelve, overshadowing and ensouling them, and empowering them to deeds of revelation. When Christ uttered the hierophantic call to Lazarus in Bethany, the genius of John entered into him and *Lazarus* became *John.* The genius which had overshadowed the whole group of disciples chose him as the seed-bearer of the future, as its central point of action.

'Die and become' as a Christian principle

In the temple of pre-Christian times, 'die and become' signified the path taken by individually pre-ordained souls in order that, as initiates, they might attain to union with the power and wisdom of the gods. At the centre point of time the Christ himself, by going through death and resurrection, placed this mystery on the open stage of ordinary human life. Since then, 'die and become' has been transformed into a law which holds good for the inner and outer destiny of every man, unless he refuses altogether to strive after higher things and gives himself over entirely to his animal nature. He who goes through 'death and becoming' with the power of Christ in his heart will find in his own being that a renewal of initiation on Christian ground has become a reality. In the Bible the transition from the old to the new principle of 'die and become' is wonderfully adumbrated in the destinies of the Old Testament prophets, and in the New Testament raisings from the dead.

Since the coming into action of the new 'die and become,' called by St Paul 'to die with Christ and rise again,' the help which Christ gave to three particular individuals for the strengthening of the ego-principle in the face of destiny, can now flow out from him into the lives and destinies of everyone. He quickens all that is stagnant, sets free all that is blocked up. Above all, he is the deliverer of the eternal being in humanity. In the realm of the souls who have gone through death and are preparing for a new incarnation he loosens the knots of destiny, and in the sunlight of his being brings to blossom whatever was frustrated by the spell of material life. Through his power of overcoming death, the path of the human ego through many deaths and births becomes a progressive resurrection for all who unite themselves with him.

CHAPTER EIGHT

Outstanding Personalities
on the Periphery

There are scenes in Christ's life in which figures are spotlighted who represented whole provinces of human life which would otherwise have remained dark. The historical concreteness of the Gospel of John again becomes apparent; it breaks right through the twilight, which in some measure still clouds the other gospels. Not only does it throw light upon the order of events in the three years, and upon the places in which they occur, but it reveals figures on the periphery — figures outside the circle of the twelve disciples — who are spiritual representatives of humankind at the midpoint and turning-point of its history. Two of these are Nathanael and Nicodemus.

Nathanael, the Galilean initiate

According to the Gospel of John, Nathanael is the last of the disciples to be called (John 1:45–51). The minute details of the description add emphasis to his personality, the call of Andrew, Peter and Philip being recorded in a few sentences (John 1:40–44). But between Jesus and Nathanael a conversation ensues which, puzzling at first, gains in significance as it goes on. In the end it appears as if all that happened between Jesus and the disciples of John as a result of their fateful meeting was fulfilled in the encounter between Jesus and Nathanael. Then Nathanael withdraws again into the background. He is not mentioned again during the whole of the three years. Only in the last chapter of St John, which in its different imaginative style is a kind of Easter supplement, does he emerge once more. He is one of the seven to whom the Risen One appears at the Lake of Gennesaret. Here, too, the town of his origin is named. He takes third place, after Peter and Thomas, as 'Nathanael from Cana in Galilee' (John 21:2).

The fact that Nathanael is never mentioned during the whole of Christ's active ministry presents an enigma. It has frequently been attempted to include him among the twelve disciples. It has been said that he was always present under another name. Thus legendary tradition has declared Bartholomew and Nathanael to be one and the same, and to this day a house in Cana carries an inscription describing it as the house of 'Bartholomew called Nathanael.'

There seems to be little doubt that Nathanael really did accompany Christ on his journeys during the three years. But the clearer the first conversation becomes, the more probable it seems that he was not one of the twelve, but the first of some special figures in a wider circle on whom the light of Christ was to fall. In the conversation with Nathanael a hint of the more inward content of the life of Christ is given, and of threads of destiny which the gospel otherwise passes over in silence.

The very composition of John's Gospel suggests from the first that Nathanael had a strong influence on the path of Jesus. When, after the conversation with Jesus, the scene of events moves from the Dead Sea straight to Cana in Galilee, Nathanael, who lived in Cana, can scarcely have failed to participate in these events. He was probably instrumental in bringing Jesus and the other men of Galilee as guests to the wedding feast, if he was not himself the host. Whatever the time that passed between the conversations with Nathanael and the marriage at Cana, the gospel, by making these two events succeed one another directly, gives the impression that Jesus followed into his own home country the man whom he greeted with such lofty words of recognition. Even if Nathanael did not take an active part in bringing about the festal gathering at Cana, he was still essentially connected with the miracle which took place there. To see the spring in his native land transfigured in such a way by the Christ must have made the deepest impression on him. His own being was thereby absorbed into the sunlike, transmuting glory of Christ.

When Philip, one of the disciples of John the Baptist, comes to Nathanael and in his enthusiasm tells him that he has found him whom Moses and the prophets had foretold, Nathanael shows at first the greatest reserve. He hears the name 'Jesus of Nazareth' and reacts with the objection, 'Can good come out of Nazareth?' Obviously he does not belong to the Essenes, who had a colony at Nazareth, and who observed strict ascetic principles. The sceptical remark about Nazareth also shows that Nathanael, true to the words of the prophets, expected their fulfilment to come from Bethlehem. But he follows Philip's call in spite of his doubts. As they come up to Jesus, the words with which he is greeted make him feel that his inmost being is recognized and approved. 'Behold, an Israelite indeed, in whom is no guile.' In the everyday meaning of these words, it must remain puzzling that Nathanael should ask with astonishment, 'From where do you know me?' Is it not in fact superfluous to call him an Israelite, and does it take so much depth of perception to recognize the candour of his nature?

The words with which Jesus greets Nathanael belong to the language of the mysteries. We misunderstand them if we take them in their everyday sense. Jesus recognizes at once that he who is coming to him has raised himself above the common human level. He need exercise no reserve towards him. He can speak to him quite openly in terms of the mysteries, and can name the rank he has attained in his path to the spirit. It is because Jesus addresses him as one who has reached the fifth stage along the sevenfold path of initiation that Nathanael feels himself to be recognized in his inmost being. He perceives that his destiny has led him to one who is far greater than himself.

We know from Rudolf Steiner something of the system of initiation of the ancient world, which remained alive in its last outposts right up to the time of the Mystery of Golgotha and into the first Christian centuries. His description is in complete agreement with the accounts which are to be found in the writings of the time, in spite of the secrecy surrounding the places of initiation. Thus even Jerome, the great Christian theologian and Church Father, speaks of seven stages of initiation in, for instance, the Mithraic mysteries. The four lowest grades were given symbolic names — the Raven, the Occultist, the Warrior, the Lion. The initiates of the fifth degree, because they had grown in their soul-development beyond the purely personal, and had attained the level of the guiding spirit of the nation, were given the name of the people to whom they belonged. Thus in the Mithraic mysteries the man who had attained the fifth grade was called a *Persian*. If he belonged to the Israelites he was called a *true Israelite*. Here is one of the descriptions which Rudolf Steiner has given of the fifth grade:

In the fifth degree he was ready for an extension of consciousness, giving him the power to become the spiritual guardian of
his people, whose name was therefore conferred upon him. An
initiate of the fifth degree in those times participated in a very
special way in the spiritual life

... we know that the people of the earth are led and guided
by those beings of the spiritual hierarchies known as the
Archangeloi, the Archangels. An initiate of the fifth degree was
lifted into the sphere where he participated in the life of the
Archangeloi. Such initiates ... were needed in the cosmos; that
is why, on the earth, there was an initiation into this fifth
degree. When such a personality had been initiated in the
Mysteries and had lived through the deep experiences and
acquired the enrichment of soul proper to the fifth degree, the
gaze of the Archangeloi was directed to this soul, reading in it
as we read in a book which tells us certain things we need to
know in order to perform some deed. In the soul of one who
had been initiated in the fifth degree the Archangeloi read
what was needful for this people. To enable the Archangeloi to
lead the people rightly, there must be initiates of the fifth
degree on earth. They are the intermediaries between the true
leaders of a people and the people itself. They bear upwards,
as it were, into the sphere of the Archangeloi, what is necessary for the right leadership of particular peoples.'*

Thus it is a high rank which the Christ recognizes in Nathanael at the first moment of their meeting. The sunny landscape of Galilee sends him not only the fishermen of the Sea of Galilee, but also an ini-tiate in whose soul the nature of the country is metamorphosed. Even the words with which Jesus answers Nathanael's astonished ques-tion, 'From where do you know me?' belong to the language of the mysteries. He is referring to no visible scene when he says 'Before Philip called you, when you were under the fig tree, I saw you.' 'Sitting under the fig tree' is an imaginative expression for the spiri-tual state into which a man enters through meditation. By meditating,

---

* *The Fifth Gospel*, p. 48f, lecture at Oslo, October 3, 1913.

the spiritual seeker in the ancient world freed himself from his physical body. His soul rose into a sphere where he felt himself to be
among the topmost branches of the Tree of Life. His own etheric body
opened itself to the cosmic ether. He was able to look into the spiritual
world, and the beings of the higher world read his soul; and their
reading was like a communication. On the walls of the gigantic temples in Thebes and Karnak, the ruins of which have been preserved
from ancient Egyptian times, one often finds a sculpture of a Pharaoh
sunk in meditation. He sits under the boughs of the sacred sycamore
and the divine messenger comes to him and writes with a stylus on
the leaves of the tree, in the shape of which appears the uplifted ether-
body of the meditator.

Thus what Jesus says to Nathanael in the hieroglyphic language of
the fig tree really means, 'I was with you when your soul dwelt in
prayer in a higher sphere. Before I looked upon you with earthly eyes,
I knew you already in another sphere.' Understood in this way, it is
obvious that full knowledge of who the Christ is lights up at once in
Nathanael's soul. 'You are the Son of God, you are the spiritual leader
of Israel.' This enthusiastic confession arises by no means merely from
the heightened self-esteem of a man who has been honoured with
recognition. By speaking of the fig tree Jesus kindles in Nathanael's
soul the light of seership, just as it had always flamed up in him when
he 'sat under the fig tree.' Here, at the beginning of his life on earth,
Christ shows full approval of the forces of the fig tree, which he will
denounce so sternly at the end of the three years. The meeting with the
pure soul of this man, a soul which has climbed to such a high level,
gives Christ the opportunity to reveal himself without reserve in his
cosmic sun-nature, shining through the *status nascendi* of his earthly
life. He speaks with such assurance, in a manner so far above earthly
speech, and words of such divine confidence follow those of recognition, that for a moment the veil is drawn back, not only from his being,
but also from the deepest mysteries of the future. 'You will see heaven
opened, and the angels of God ascending and descending above the
Son of Man.' Nathanael had spoken of the Son of God. Now Christ can
utter words which signify the highest title of nobility appertaining to
the Son of Man: the breach separating him from the hierarchies of the
heavens is healed. The Son of Man — man awakening to the spirit —
is the lowest member of the heavenly hierarchies. The ladder on which

the powers of heaven ascend and descend reaches down into his being. Christ is only expressing what Nathanael sees at that very moment before his eyes. The existence of this Galilean initiate, in whose soul the mystery of the Christ-being can be reflected, is the pledge that what is now entering into the human realm as a divine deed can one day become the common possession of humanity.

Nicodemus, the Jewish initiate

Nathanael, the representative initiate of Galilee, appears in the gospel as a link with the wedding-feast at Cana, which is celebrated in all the glories of a Galilean spring. In contrast to this, the initiate representing Judea emerges out of the darkness of night in the aftermath of the Passover scene in the Temple, which first reveals Christ's majesty in Jerusalem. The pendulum of his life swings right over from the spring in Galilee to the centre of Judea. Now the scenery no longer corresponds to the inner sun-being of Christ. It reflects the state into which human life has fallen. An aged humanity is gathered together to celebrate its oldest festival. People are meeting in a dead, moonlike world. They are flocking to the Temple, which has been the holiest place of the Old Testament for a thousand years. Here the water of new life should be able to flow upon the parched soil of their souls from the fountainhead of the divine presence, but the source has dried up. The holy place has become the centre of financial deals. Where the voice of prayer should dwell, the mercenary spirit of the ruling class has taken possession.

Christ walks among the crowd. In Galilee the glory of the divine being, just beginning to become man, had shone forth in harmony with the wonder of springtime. But here it works in terrifying majesty, exercising that power of the sun which brings unfailingly to light everything that is false and degenerate. The crowds of those buying and selling disperse, panic-stricken. It is not so much Christ's utterance as his whole being that pronounces judgment on the Temple which has lost its meaning. Not until two years later, at the third Passover festival of Christ's life, do the disciples understand that his words of judgment were at the same time an Easter prophecy: 'Destroy this Temple and in three days I will raise it up.' There is no longer any trace of the graciousness which showed itself at the Marriage of Cana.

In its place is the militant judgment of the sun, overcoming and expelling the forces of the moon.

A figure emerges from this crowd who, although he is one of the spiritual leaders of the Temple, is inwardly great enough to rise above its decline. From the aftermath of the dramatic scene in the Temple something leads him irresistibly to Jesus. It has already been said that the phrase *by night*, which the gospel repeats on every occasion that it mentions Nicodemus, means something more than just indication of the time. This man is connected with the mysteries. Hence not only the words of the actual conversation, but also the account in the gospel of the course of events is full of mystery terms. The meeting of Jesus with Nicodemus does not take place on the physical plane, as it does with Nathanael. It is a spiritual meeting, for Nicodemus can enter in full consciousness the realm where sleep normally spreads its veil of darkness. He, like Nathanael, had reached a high level on the path of the soul. In this sphere he is able to seek the Christ and to be accepted and approved by him. There is a meeting of Masters in the spirit, and a significant conversation ensues. Nicodemus thinks he has recognized a high initiate in Jesus, and addresses him as Master. Jesus acknowledges a similar rank in Nicodemus by saying, 'Thou art a Master in Israel.' Nicodemus comes to Jesus in more than his own name: he stands before him as the spokesman for initiates the whole world over — hence he uses the plural. 'Master, we know that you have come as a teacher from God; for no human being can do such signs of the spirit as you do, unless God himself works into his deeds' (John 3:2). And in answering Nicodemus Jesus also uses the 'we.' 'We speak of what we know and we testify to what we have seen.'

The description of the meeting with Nicodemus is not so plainly couched in mystery language as is that of the meeting with Nathanael. The brief formula, *by night*, which Rudolf Steiner explains as a mystery expression and thus the key to the whole, can very easily escape notice. But the style of the conversation itself impels a recognition of the plane of the scene, which is above ordinary human level. Nicodemus is described as one of the *archons* of the Jewish people. He is a member of the Sanhedrin, the college of seventy, whose task it is to guide the destiny of the people. He therefore holds in an external office the dignity which Nathanael, as a true Israelite, possesses inwardly. Further, the gospel reveals that he is a member of the order of the Pharisees. The whole future course of Christ's life will bear witness to the fact that the leaders of Judaism, particularly within the Pharisees, have become utterly degenerate. The spirituality of the Pharisees, which was at one time pure and holy, has become the ghost of its former self, and eventually even satanic. The Pharisees are the real opponents of Christ. Thus it is all the more significant that a leading Pharisee, one who is far advanced on the ancient path of initiation, should be received into the light of Christ's etheric life. Later on Christ will pronounce his *woes* to the Pharisees without pity. But at least one Pharisee was near to Christ, a disciple outside the ranks of the twelve in whom a spark of the still living Pharisaic initiation continued to burn.

The order of the Pharisees, founded towards the end of the Babylonian exile by the prophet Ezra, had been originally a true esoteric school. The discipline practised by the order was a last comprehensive expression of the spirituality of the Old Testament. The hereditary forces of the blood were made inward and spiritualized as the candidate, through a well-ordered series of stages of initiation, was led to the threshold of the spiritual world. The initiated Pharisee attained at last to ecstatic visions in which he beheld the future of humankind. The apocalyptic books associated with the name Ezra are a later deposit of Pharisaic eschatology in which souls who followed this path grew to seership. The Pharisees regarded man's physical body as a temple, because their spirituality was drawn wholly from the depths of the physical body. Thus the Temple on Mount Moriah was the central imaginative expression of their endeavours, although they left the priestly duties to others. But at the time of Jesus their order had long since fallen into decadence through lust for power. They terrified and enslaved souls by their eschatological visions of the Last Judgment which, according to their view, would precede the coming of the Messiah. The order had a fate similar to that which later befell the Jesuit order which has, indeed, a certain resemblance to it; after a short period of true spirituality at the time of its foundation, the Jesuit order quickly degenerated into a political force. The Pharisees ended by being in themselves the clearest proof that the spirituality derived only from physical corporeality and from the stream of heredity had arrived at a dead end.

That Nicodemus could be so shaken by the purification of the Temple, and that as a result of it his soul was so irresistibly drawn to

the Christ, shows that he was not far from realizing the spiritual collapse of Pharisaism. The answers which he receives from Christ signify
the complete rejection of a spiritual path bound up solely with earthly
birth, 'the birth from below.' Only the new impulse from above can
save the future of humanity. As a Pharisee, Nicodemus understands
only 'the birth from below.' Astonished he asks, 'How can a person be
born when he is already old? Can he return to his mother's womb to
be born again?' He receives the famous answer of the wind which
blows where it wills, the sound of which is heard, the origin and purpose of which are nevertheless hidden. Nicodemus has to recognize
that man is in fact a supersensory being. Birth and death are only the
beginning and end of man's body. It is not possible for man living on
the earth to see with earthly senses whence he comes and whither he
goes but, when his spirit stirs, he can hear from time to time the rushing of the wind from higher spheres.

Nicodemus, as a trained Pharisee, is quite familiar with the idea of
ascension; indeed he has practised the Pharisaic path of initiation to
the point where the soul lifts itself out of the body in an ecstasy of
vision. Christ shows Nicodemus the new path towards the spirit. 'No
one has ascended into the world of spirit who has not also descended
out of the world of spirit; that is the Son of Man' (John 3:13).

The secret of the Son of Man as explained in the preceding chapter
is familiar to Nicodemus. His spiritual school allows him to recognize
Spirit Man under the designation *Son of Man*, but only in so far as he
is born out of the forces of heredity. This old presentation of the Son of
Man is dying out. 'And as Moses lifted up the serpent in the wilderness, so must the Son of Man be lifted up' (John 3:14). In the time of
Moses the heathen clairvoyance, symbolized by the image of the
snake, had become decadent. By setting up the bronze snake wound
around the cross, Moses gave the sign of Aesculapius as medicine for
men's consciousness, and the sight of it healed the ecstasy which the
people had caught from the decadent heathen peoples around them.*
One day the Son of Man, crucified on a cross, was to be lifted up before
humanity as a sign that all the old forces which men had drawn on for
their life were given over to death. Here the end of the old path merges
into the grace-given beginnings of the new.

* See the author's *Moses*.

Nathanael could confess his belief in the Son of God out of the clear vision of his heart, which had grown under the sun of Galilee; and Christ answered him with the saying about the Son of Man's newly established future among the divine hierarchies. To Nicodemus Christ spoke first of the tragedy of the Son of Man, who strives towards the spirit from the earth. When the Son of Man, born from below, and the Son of God, born from above, meet and penetrate each other, then humanity overcomes its crisis of death. The saying about the Son of God, 'The Father showed his love for the world through this, that He offered up his only Son' (John 3:16), is only too often taken from its context for personal edification. The two statements about the Son of Man and the Son of God belong together in the sequence of the teaching which Christ, as a Master, imparted to the initiated Nicodemus. It is significant that both expressions were followed by identical words, 'From now on, no one shall perish who fills himself with his power; indeed, he shall win a share of the life that is beyond time' (John 3:15f). In the dark hour of Golgotha the true image of man will be placed anew before humankind. But since *Son of Man* and *Son of God* will therein be one, death will pass over into resurrection. And Nicodemus will be among those who stand beneath the cross.

The further destiny of Nicodemus

Three times Nicodemus appears on the stage of Christ's life in the Gospel of John. The second time, the glory of Christ's initial state had long since withdrawn into his advancing incarnation. The first signs of the decisive battle were already apparent. A year and a half after that first festival of the Passover, at the autumn feast of Tabernacles, Christ appeared, now here, now there, in the midst of the festive crowd and startled them with his powerful, burning words. It was as if the Archangel Michael were himself walking among men — Michael, into whose feast Christianity has in the course of time transformed this autumn festival. The enmity of Christ's opponents, which had been simmering for a long time, was provoked by his presence to an open outburst. Repeatedly they sent out their underlings to arrest him. But those who tried to lay hold of him were left with empty hands. The hatred of Christ's opponents then flared up all the more violently. They believed that the officers who were to have arrested him had themselves fallen under his spell. They cursed Jesus. Then Nicodemus, himself one of the leaders, opposed them. He said, 'Does our Law judge a man without first giving him a hearing and establishing his guilt?' (John 7:50f). But Nicodemus reaped nothing but scorn.

Although the gospel does not openly say so, this event suggests that Nicodemus had remained in contact with the followers of Christ. It does not matter whether he continued to draw near to Christ only *by night*, or whether, like the rest of the disciples, he came to him out-wardly. The advance from the first to the second scene with Nicodemus lies in the fact that the initiated Pharisee now intervened on behalf of Jesus. He passed on from the purely spiritual meeting and conversation to a socially significant deed. But Christ was not present in Jerusalem at the feast of Tabernacles in his physical body. He mani-fested himself among men through his inner force, while his body remained in Galilee. But the people could think only that he was walk-ing among them bodily. As a result of his nocturnal conversation, Nicodemus was perhaps among the very few who realized why those who sought to arrest him again and again found themselves, to their great annoyance, frustrated.

When Nicodemus steps for the third time out of the background, it is actually in the night. The cross is erected on Golgotha. Christ has drawn his last breath upon that cross. Joseph of Arimathea has obtained permission from Pilate to take down the body from the cross and to bury it in his own tomb. Then Nicodemus comes to help Joseph. He has brought with him myrrh and aloes, well-nigh a hundred pounds, with which to embalm the body of Jesus. Joseph of Arimathea and Nicodemus ease the body from the cross and bury it solemnly and silently (John 19:39–42).

Nicodemus is now drawn into the most intimate proximity with the Christ-being. He reveals his union with him and his love for him by taking the place of the disciples who have abandoned him. The tomb in the rock of Golgotha is the place of a new birth, as the stable in the rock of Bethlehem was previously the place of a new birth. On that earlier occasion three magi came as representatives of the ancient temple wisdom, and offered gold, frankincense and myrrh. Now at least one of the representatives of the mysteries is there. He offers myrrh, as formerly the third king did. Nicodemus follows Christ through the stages of his incarnation right down to the lowest level. At the first Easter festival he meets him in the sphere of the spirit. At the Michaelmas festival of the middle year he intervenes for him among men. Now, between Good Friday and Easter Sunday, he ministers to the one who unites himself with the earth, to be therein the seed of a new world. Through his deed the promise of redemption shines into the world from which he has come. After having received a glimpse into the future in that first conversation, and having interceded on behalf of Christ at the Feast of Tabernacles with a courage called forth by the immediate present, finally, through the ancient process of embalming, he pays his last tribute to the saturnine spirit of the primeval past which he has served as a spiritual leader of the Jews. He is thereby helping to break the spell cast over humanity by old age and death.

We do not meet Nathanael, the Galilean initiate, again, after his first meeting with Christ, until he appears as witness to the event of Easter. On the other hand, we see Nicodemus, the Jewish initiate, intimately involved in the happenings of Good Friday. Good Friday revealed the deepest meaning of Judea, while Christ's resurrection meant the fulfilment and renewal of the spirit of Galilee. To the disciples it was as if they were withdrawn into Galilee when they beheld the Risen One. Through Good Friday and Easter, Judea and Galilee exist as soul-spheres, in which we can at any time participate in Christ's destiny. Nicodemus and Nathanael can be our guides into this inner realm.

According to early Christian tradition, Nicodemus, although he remained true to his duties within Judaism, made the affairs of the first Christian communities entirely his own. Soon, of course, there was yet another Pharisee, Paul, who found the way to Christ. Nicodemus comes from the same circle from which Paul grew up into a traveller and missionary. It is said that Nicodemus was the nephew of Gamaliel, at whose feet the young Paul sat, and who intervened with the Sanhedrin for Paul in the same way that Nicodemus had done for Jesus (Acts 5:34ff). When Stephen was stoned by Jewish fanatics in the presence of the young Paul, legend says that Gamaliel and Nicodemus took his body and buried it in Gamaliel's field. By this act Nicodemus at last brought the hatred and scorn of the high priests and the Pharisees upon himself. He was deprived of his high office. All his property was taken from him, and he was beaten until there was scarcely a spark of life left in him. He died after a few days in Gamaliel's house, and was buried in the grave where Stephen already rested. According to tradition, his spirit was henceforth united with all that developed as esoteric life within Christianity, as was to happen also with Joseph of Arimathea.

Nothing throws more light on the high esteem with which Nicodemus was regarded in early Christian times than the fact that one of the most important apocryphal gospels has come down to posterity under his name. The Gospel of Nicodemus, also known as the Acts of Pilate, consists of two parts. The first part unfolds in detail the trial of Jesus, at which Nicodemus is among those who warmly testify for him. The second part describes Christ's descent into hell. Among the dead who rise from their graves awakened by the Easter earthquake, and show themselves in Jerusalem, are Carinus and Lucius, sons of the aged Simeon. In the presence of Nicodemus, Joseph of Arimathea and others, they tell how Christ entered the realm of the dead and with his light broke the chains of death and the spell of darkness. Here also a richly pictorial account is given of the part played by Nicodemus in the events of Good Friday. The Gospel of Nicodemus has provided the subject matter for many medieval miracle plays of the *Harrowing of Hell.*

Simon of Cyrene and Joseph of Arimathea

Nathanael and Nicodemus emerge from the morning mists of Christ's life after the baptism; in the twilight of Golgotha two other figures appear who are mentioned nowhere else in the gospels: Simon of Cyrene and Joseph of Arimathea. The part of Simon of Cyrene is recorded only in the first three gospels; Joseph of Arimathea is mentioned in all four. Both Simon and Joseph have a significant place in the dramatic events on Golgotha. One of them appears immediately before the crucifixion and death of Christ, the other directly after. When Jesus breaks down under the weight of the cross, the soldiers call Simon of Cyrene, and force him to carry it up the hill of Golgotha. After Christ has died upon the cross, Joseph of Arimathea asks for permission to take down the body and to bury it in his own tomb. The cross erected upon Golgotha stands just midway between the scenes in which we meet Simon and Joseph.

In order clearly to grasp the point at which these two stand, we will let the structure of the drama of Golgotha pass before us as stages of an inner path. According to Rudolf Steiner an esoteric Christian school existed in the medieval monasteries which practised a path of initiation in which the disciples moved through the seven stages of the Passion and Resurrection, contemplating each stage with profound feelings of devotion. These stages were:

> The washing of the feet
> The scourging
> The crowning with thorns
> The crucifixion
> The entombment
> The resurrection
> The ascension

The Gospel of Matthew describes very fully the middle five stages. The first and seventh are not specifically mentioned, but implied in the preceding and following events — the washing of the feet in the details of the Last Supper, and the Ascension in the appearance of the Risen One upon the mountain in Galilee. The Gospel of John describes clearly the first six stages; the stage of the Ascension is diffused, as it were, in the stories of the resurrection. The symmetry of the sevenfold drama, however, is clearly discernible throughout.

If these stages are taken as meditative imaginations, the first three and the last three group themselves into two symmetrical parts. In each group an ascent from below upwards takes place. In the first group the pictures move upwards from the feet (washing of the feet) to the breast (scourging) and to the head (crowning with thorns). In the second group there is a similar ascent. This time, however, in macrocosmic form. The tomb represents the feet of the world (the entombment); the etheric atmosphere surrounding the earth, the place of resurrection, is the cosmic breast (the resurrection); and the heavenly spheres, formed like the human head, constitute the cosmic head (the ascension).

The cross stands in the midst; in it lies the secret of the human form. It is perhaps significant that the spine is called the *cross* in German. All earthly destiny comes to people because they have a physical body. That is the cross which man has to learn to take up. But it is at the same time the gateway to the spirit. Man, who comes from the macrocosm, has first to learn to incarnate, to enter more and more deeply into the narrow microcosmic world of his physical body. Here he develops his personality through all the trials of loneliness. Only when he has taken full possession of his physical body can he free himself again from bondage to it, and either through self-development or through death, grow once more into the super-personal spheres of the macrocosm and the spirit.

The gospel sets the Cross as the dividing line between the three microcosmic and the three macrocosmic stages, which are illustrated in the two figures of Simon of Cyrene and Joseph of Arimathea. Simon of Cyrene, the cross-bearer, is the picture of the man who takes up his cross. The release from the cross leads into the three macrocosmic stages. Joseph of Arimathea, who frees the body of Christ from the cross, is the picture of the man who overcomes his bondage to the body and rises to the spirit.

The washing of the feet	Feet	
The Scourging	Breast	of the microcosm (man)
The Crowning with Thorns	Head	

Simon of Cyrene, who bears the Cross of Christ
Crucifixion: the transition from microcosmos to macrocosmos
Joseph of Arimathea, who takes Christ's body from the Cross

The Entombment	Feet	
The Resurrection	Breast	of the macrocosm (universe)
The Ascension	Head	

The first three of the seven stages, consisting of personal trials and purifications, are summed up in the bearing of the cross. Simon of Cyrene is, perhaps, the model of personal piety. Joseph of Arimathea appears as the patron saint of super-personal piety. Both in the stage of Simon of Cyrene and in that of Joseph of Arimathea, man is only loosely bound to the cross, but the first stage leads him in an opposite direction to that of the other. The bearing of the cross leads to a thorough moulding of the personality by identification with its earthly destiny. Through his release from the cross man becomes free of the body, and reaches super-personal existence.

There is no end to the religious value and significance of the two figures on either side of the cross. Simon does not bear his own cross. Joseph does not free his own body from the cross. Both are figures on the way to St Paul's goal of becoming crucified with Christ and rising again with him.

The three Simons

Great secrets of Christian development are hidden beneath the fact that it was not two of the twelve disciples who stood where Simon of Cyrene and Joseph of Arimathea stood. The disciples had fallen in the Garden of Gethsemane. Except the one who had himself already passed through death and resurrection, they all fail Christ when he carries the cross and dies upon it. At this significant moment an anonymous group of people sends two of its members as substitutes for the disciples. Because the two men who are now mentioned in the gospel for the first time do not come from among the twelve, but from the unseen group of nameless ones, they are no less important as types of human soul-development. Significant historic trends within the development of Christianity are to be traced to them.

Peter, who is himself later to undergo crucifixion, ought really to have been the cross-bearer on the road to Golgotha. It should have been his task to carry the personal experience of the first three stages to the altar of the centre. His consciousness dulled for the time being, he stopped short at the personal level. Simon of Cyrene took the place of Simon Peter. The similarity of the names here, where the invisible producer of the cosmic drama directs every detail with such wisdom, is by no means fortuitous or immaterial.

Golgotha is the scene of inexorable resolve. Here all weakness is exposed. Thus the bearing of the cross manifests the weakness of Peter's nature, and with it the weakness of the whole of Petrine Christianity. Peter fails at that point in the stations of the Passion where the step from the three stages of the personal to the fourth, the mystery of the midpoint, is involved. The Petrine nature is certain of itself only in the first three stages. When it comes to going beyond that, it is in danger of falling back. Hence the tendency of ecclesiastical Christianity to be halted at the third stage. It always falls back into the mood of purely personal redemption.

Who is Simon of Cyrene, who takes Simon Peter's place? His name is mentioned only at the one point. Even tradition is silent about him. Nevertheless he must have played an important part in the early phases of the establishment of a Christian community. This can be inferred from the fact that the Gospel of Mark says he was the father of Alexander and Rufus (Mark 15:21). At first this is also puzzling, for as little is known of the sons as of the father. But in the last chapter of Paul's Epistle to the Romans, Rufus is mentioned with his mother as among those whom Paul expressly greets (Rom.16:13). It has often been argued from this that Simon of Cyrene lived in Rome with his sons, and together with them took a leading part in the Christian community which was springing up there. This view finds support in the old and well-established tradition that Mark's Gospel was written in Rome. This would explain why this evangelist mentions Alexander and Rufus as well as Simon of Cyrene.

But Simon of Cyrene's significance for the beginnings of Roman Christianity is undoubtedly greater than can be admitted as a result of these theological speculations alone. Very likely we touch here on the very first beginnings of the Roman community, generally regarded as obscure.

The first Christian congregation in Rome was not founded by Peter. He found a community of some importance already in existence there. Quite different and much more concrete ideas can be formed about the spread of the Christian message in the very earliest times by taking into consideration the large group of Christ's unnamed followers who represented humankind in the drama on Golgotha, outside the actual circle of the disciples. Many personalities, especially from the orders of the Therapeutae and the Essenes, had come very early to a recognition of the Christ impulse through their capacity for inner experience. The influence of the order of the Essenes affected the culture of all the countries of the eastern Mediterranean. The groups who lived from the spiritual sources cultivated by the order, whether they were definitely among its initiated members, or whether they were lay members held together by some kind of semi-monastic rule, formed the basis of the original Christian communities to a far greater extent than has hitherto been recognized in the histories of early Christianity.

The Acts of the Apostles record that it was particularly a group of men from Cyprus and Cyrene who first carried the Christian message out into the world beyond the confines of Judaism. It is natural to suppose that these men of Cyprus and Cyrene were associated with the order of the Essenes. It may even be that the beginnings of the Roman community, which later became so important, goes back to them. One of these men was Barnabas, a native of Cyprus and St Mark's uncle, who with his nephew accompanied the early journeys of Paul. But Simon of Cyrene with his sons may also have played an important part in this group. As said above, a very special role in the foundation of the first community in Rome can perhaps be ascribed to him.

As long as the entire body of Christians, which soon spread to far distant lands, was directed from Jerusalem, it had special Judeo-Christian characteristics. James, the step-brother of Jesus, set its tone. When Paul began his activity, the consciously gentile Christian group was joined with it as its opposite pole. For a while this group had its centre in Antioch. Like Barnabas, the rest of the men from Cyprus and Cyrene appear to have gone at first with Paul. But when the paths of Paul and Barnabas had separated, a middle group from among the Essenes must have come into being, which soon made Rome its centre. For a long time Peter had wavered between the two extremes; but when he reached Rome he at once became the undisputed leader of this middle group, which gradually became the dominant one. In Rome then there is Mark, the nephew of Barnabas, as well as the family of Simon of Cyrene, at Peter's side.

Thus it seems that, just as Simon of Cyrene took Peter's place as cross-bearer on the way to Golgotha, he was also one of the most important of those who prepared his way in Rome. Perhaps, still earlier and more naturally than the *Prince of the Apostles,* he was the representative of the original Roman Christianity which lived in the catacombs, entirely detached from the world of the Caesars. It goes without saying that Peter, who was the driving force of Christian evangelism till his ripe old age, was also immune from the temptations of the imperial administration. Still, his life did not testify to the victory of his faithful heart without his soul being ravaged again and again by terrific storms. Yet another Simon appeared in Rome who, as Simon Peter's sombre double, reflected in advance the later aberrations of Petrine Christianity. This was Simon Magus who was always represented in medieval history as the prototype of the man who practised simony — that is to say of the man who mixed spiritual with worldly things and bartered spiritual values and forces for money and external power. Simon Peter, the great leader of Roman Christianity, stands between the silent figure of the Essene, Simon of Cyrene, and the demonic figure of Simon Magus.

The Holy Grail and its bearers

Joseph of Arimathea is described in the gospels as a counsellor, a 'good man and a just.' He, too, must have been connected with the Essenes. Even if not actually a member of the order, he must have been more deeply initiated into its mysteries than was Simon of Cyrene. On the Jerusalem group of Essenes, especially, he clearly had a decisive influence. Catherine Emmerich, the Belgian nun who bore the stigmata, and had many visions of the life and Passion of Christ, asserted that it was in the house of Joseph of Arimathea that Jesus celebrated the Passover with his disciples. In my previous book *Caesars and Apostles* I have tried to show that it was a room in the house belonging to the order of the Essenes which was placed at the disposal of Jesus and his disciples. This house was an important centre of the life of the growing Christian community until far into the history of early Christianity. Catherine of Emmerich's vision is a further pointer to the influential position held by Joseph of Arimathea between the Essene brethren and Christ.

A rich store of legends is woven round Joseph of Arimathea. They concern both the role he played on Golgotha, and the historic stream inaugurated by him. The spirituality of these legends is fundamentally different from that of the Roman Christianity of Peter; it is a spirituality which cannot seek to flow through any but hidden esoteric channels side by side with the broad exoteric current.

The very act which Joseph of Arimathea performed is a symbol. Joseph took down the body from the cross, and laid it in the tomb specially mentioned as his own property. Thus Joseph is the one who received the body of Christ in a quite special manner. The prototype of a special communion is formed beyond the sacramental communion in the upper room in which the disciples take part.

At this point extra-biblical tradition fills out the story. It tells us that Joseph was the owner of the chalice from which Christ in the upper room offered wine as his blood. In this chalice Joseph of Arimathea who, unlike the sleeping disciples in Gethsemane, was present at the foot of the cross, caught the blood that flowed from the wound in the side of the crucified Christ after the thrust of the spear. And when later, together with Nicodemus, he took down the body, embalmed it and laid it in the grave, he must have gathered into the cup whatever traces of Christ's blood were still to be found. Joseph of Arimathea receives not only the body but also the blood of Christ. The pictures of a sacrament of a special order are woven into his destiny. This confirms that he had already attained to the stage of the cross and the mystical death, on his path through the stations of trial, so that he was able to pass on to the super-personal macrocosmic stages.

The chalice in which Joseph of Arimathea received the blood of Christ is distinguished by legendary tradition as the wandering sign — a sign moving backwards and forwards through the centuries — of the highest mysteries of divine favour. The history of this chalice runs quietly through the whole history of humanity. It is said to have been made from a stone in Lucifer's crown; it moved from one mystery temple of ancient times to another. Thus, in the time of the builder Hiram, it was said to have been in the keeping of the city of Tyre. The Queen of Sheba brought it to Solomon, and finally it was brought from the treasury of the Temple at Jerusalem to the upper room on Mount Zion. Catherine Emmerich, in a glimpse of old imaginations, says that angels in white robes had at one time brought the chalice to Noah, and that the priest-king Melchizedek, whose sanctuary she places on the site of the upper room, later used it when he gave bread and wine to Abraham. Even more important than its previous history is the subsequent history of the chalice of the Last Supper. It is in fact the Holy Grail, in which esoteric Christianity of the Middle Ages saw its highest symbol. Thus Joseph of Arimathea plays an important part in all the traditions of the Grail. He had been in secret the first guardian and king of the Grail.

According to the Gospel of Nicodemus the Jews, angry with Joseph because of his burial of the crucified Christ, had immured him in a bricked-up room. In the night of the Resurrection, however, before Christ appeared to the women at the tomb and to the disciples in the upper room, he came to Joseph and fortified him from the chalice, and dried his tears. The whole room was filled with brilliant sunshine. Numerous traditions would then have us believe that Joseph remained many years in his prison cell, kept alive and nourished only by the cup of the Grail. It was not until the legions of Vespasian and Titus destroyed Jerusalem that the walls cutting Joseph off from the world were shattered, and he regained his freedom. There is a reference to the scene of his discovery and release in the Book of Yashar, a book of esoteric Judaism held especially sacred. Cedros, one of Titus's officers, discovered in one of the empty houses of Jerusalem a hidden, walled-up room. When he broke it open he found an old man in front of a pile of sacred writings. Together with this old man he established in Spain a training school in the sacred wisdom. Some light may be thrown on this description from the connection in which Joseph of Arimathea stood to the Essenes who, with and without books, cultivated the treasures of the ancient wisdom. The picture of the walled-up chamber is perhaps not to be taken quite literally. But in any case it expresses in an imaginative way Joseph's connection with ancient initiation.

Expressed in many ways, imaginative traditions point to Joseph as the bringer of a special Christian message to the countries of western Europe. It is he, more than any other, who sets in place of the ancient saying, *ex oriente lux,* the watchword of the Grail, *ex occidente lux,* which foretells that the light of the new and deeper Christian knowledge must rise in the west when the old eastern wisdom dies away. Joseph of Arimathea is considered to be among those who were the first to bring the gospel to England. Memories of his activity are centred on Glastonbury. Thus the *History of Glastonbury,* written in the twelfth century by William of Malmesbury, says: 'Now St Philip, as Freculfus tells us ... went to the land of the Franks to preach the gospel, and there he met many who accepted the Christian faith, and baptized them. In order to spread the gospel of Christ he chose twelve of his disciples and sent them to Britain to preach how Christ Jesus had become man and to proclaim the word of life according to the gospel. Over these twelve, as overseer as it were, he placed his greatest friend, Joseph of Arimathea, he who buried the Lord.'

Joseph of Arimathea is represented as the inaugurator of the Grail Stream in the poetic French romance of Robert de Boron, *The Holy Grail,* written about 1190. It says that when Christ appeared to Joseph in the night of the Resurrection, he charged him to administer the cup to three men only. Thereby the community to be established by Joseph is from the outset to be one for the elite, as an esoteric group. When Joseph is free from his prison his sister and her husband Hebron, or Bron, greet him. They are the parents of the race of the Grail. Joseph is to found a Round Table on the model of Christ's Table at the Last Supper. On this table Bron, the fisherman (as he is also described in the Grail romance of Chrétien de Troyes), lays the first fish. In the new circle of the Round Table the place of Judas is left vacant for the grandson of Bron, who is destined to be the Grail King. This early Parsifal figure, named Alein, grows up as the pupil of Joseph of Arimathea who thus, as teacher of the future Grail King, plays a part similar to that played in later Grail poems by the wise old men Trevrizent and Gurnemanz. Joseph is said to have carried out his mandate for the establishment of the Round Table in the Vale of Avalon, the scene of the Merlin Saga, which also shelters the grave of King Arthur. This is the place where later the town of Glastonbury was built.

One need not make too much of the local traditions laying claim to Joseph of Arimathea. The important points are that the pictorial fabric of tradition acknowledges Joseph as the source of the stream of Grail-Christianity, and that the mood of the mysteries and of initiation was carried far into the times which had long since received the external imprint of papal Christianity.

CHAPTER NINE

Pilate — the Trial of Jesus

Properly understood, the gospels contain archetypal drama. They are a piece of dramatic art of the highest possible rank. We stand before a unique tragedy which is at the same time historically true.

The drama of the gospels and the drama of ancient Greece are intimately related. When Aeschylus and Sophocles wrote their tragedies they made public, both consciously and unconsciously, part of the ancient mysteries. Aeschylus was accused of having actually betrayed the mysteries because he brought secrets on the stage which up to that time had been strictly preserved within the temple. The law of death and resurrection dominated the rites of initiation which were performed for selected individuals in the silent precincts of the mysteries. When the tragedies of Aeschylus began to be performed in the public theatres under the open sky of Greece, a reflection of the rites of initiation and with it a real share in that law reached the souls of all spectators. The intimate connection between Greek tragedy and the gospels lies in the fact that the Mystery of Golgotha represented the entire and final public revelation of the principle of the mysteries. Henceforth the archetypal drama has been in the very midst of humanity. It is above all other dramas, and it needs no specific performance. The inward perception of the life of Christ gives to every human being who is open for it a real share in the mystery of initiation. The tragedies of the great Greek dramatists are part of the preparation and prophecies leading to the Mystery of Golgotha. They were human acts of publicizing the mysteries. They preceded the divine act which made the mysteries public once and for all on Golgotha. Unfortunately, those who are looking for new dramatic themes today often turn their back on Christianity. But in truth there is no other setting for the rebirth of drama than the gospels themselves. The mystery drama of the future which will not only be a renewal of classical tragedy, but will represent a new stage beyond it, can and must be fertilized by the central archetypal drama of humanity which took place on Golgotha.

Caiaphas, Herod and Pilate

In the very last scenes of the life of Jesus, before the night of Golgotha is past, the dramatic character of events becomes so significant and precise that even the arrangement of space in which they occur becomes like that of a theatre. An archetypal stage is set. Even curtain and auditorium become real for a moment, when the trial of Jesus is carried out in front of the palace of Pilate. This scene is surrounded in a variety of ways by figures and events which again reveal dramatic archetypes. While theologians have never developed an adequate sense for these archetypal laws of the drama, from time to time a real poet has been able to grasp intuitively the dramatic reality of the Passion, and to give it poetic form. For instance, in *Christ* by August Strindberg, a scene occurs in which the triad of Caiaphas, Pilate and Herod appear in their archetypal quality. This triad is decisive among the personalities who act on the stage of Golgotha; it is they who play the leading parts on the threshold of Good Friday. It is only necessary to imagine, step by step, the events which occurred before and after the break of day, to realize how every single detail is transparent for a human mystery.

The night between Maundy Thursday and Good Friday is one of the most mysterious nights that have ever been. The silver light of the spring full moon shines over the country. It emphasizes the uncanny quiet which, at the moment of sunset, has replaced the turmoil of the vast multitude of pilgrims. The people assembled in the houses remember the night of terror in Egypt, in which the Angel of Death went from door to door. Nobody dares to leave the protected sphere of the home. Everybody is convinced that this very night the fear and dread of the original Passover night is repeated. In the small group which, contrary to strict Passover custom, has descended into the Kidron valley on their way to the Garden of Gethsemane, the sense of profound loneliness and isolation has reached a climax.

Towards morning cold winds begin to blow. They are due to a

strange atmospheric condition, which developed further on the morning of Good Friday, and which finally caused at noon a darkness of three hours. This darkness, of which the gospels speak, cannot, in the days of the full moon, have been due to an eclipse of the sun, since an eclipse of the sun can only occur at new moon. It can only have been the wind blowing from the desert, which often accompanies the beginning of spring in the Near East, and which is called *khamsin*. About a thousand feet high a storm rages through the country, carrying gigantic clouds of desert dust which form a thick curtain in front of the sun, threatening to asphyxiate every living creature. All life on earth is cut off from the heavens. Everyone gasps, and labours in the close heat which suddenly replaces the cool of the night.

When the soldiers, with the prisoner in their midst, climb the path up to the city from Gethsemane, it is still night, and the piercing cold is about to reach its climax. The glittering light of the full moon adds to the eeriness of the hour. The personalities into whose circle Jesus is led before sunrise appear like incarnations of dark and ghostly shadows of the night. Jesus is brought, to begin with, before two different authorities. This takes place inside the house which lies opposite the Cenacle. The ground plan of the primitive sacred buildings which David built on Mount Zion can still be traced in the juxtaposition of the house in which the events of the night of Maundy Thursday occurred. Where at the time of David a simple chapel sheltered the ark of the covenant, now the house of the Essene order stood, in the Cenacle in which Jesus celebrated the Passover meal with his disciples. To the north of the old palace of David the houses of the priests were built, in particular the house of the first high-priest Zadok, who was the ancestor of the clan of the Sadducees. In this place stood the palace of the high priest, into which Jesus was led by those who had arrested him in Gethsemane. The Gospel of John, which in this concluding act of the mystery drama is exceptionally precise in its biographical detail, shows that Jesus was not immediately placed before the Sanhedrin, which consisted of representatives of the Sadducees, Pharisees and scribes, but was confronted first with the family council of the Sadducees. At first the chair is taken, not by the actual holder of the high-priestly office, but by the old and shrivelled miser, Annas. The highest-placed Sadducees are the wire-pullers, not only of Jewish politics in general, but also in the drama which now draws to its conclusion. They have managed everything, making use of the eccentric Messianic expectation of Judas. In reality however, a greater, invisible producer is at work for whom these characters are nothing but puppets who have to act their part on the stage. They are in fact sub-human; ghosts of the night, flitting demons of darkness who hate the light and believe that they can sabotage the rising of the sun.

Under cover of night, Jesus is led to the second authority. The hosts of darkness are assembled round their captains. The seventy members of the Sanhedrin who are assembled under Caiaphas are like a body of demons of night. These fellows represent veritable caricatures of human thoughts which, separated from the powers of the heart, flit about like will-o'-the-wisps, and are incapable of grasping any real truth. Greed and hatred had dominated the house of Annas. Now lies and falsehood prevail. False witnesses shriek their lying testimonies. There is a ghastly harmony within and without, where the cutting wind still howls through the moonlit night. This is the world of Caiaphas.

By the time the session with Caiaphas has come to an end, and Jesus is dragged from the Mount of Zion through the whole city to the palace of Pilate, the sun is rising. Almost at once the heat becomes oppressive. The atmosphere is like glass, and the sun, just above the horizon, assumes an uncanny greenish colour. The way leads across the place of the Temple. A recapitulation of the whole of Old Testament history is concentrated into this moment; and when night finally gives way to morning, the most tragic day in the history of humanity has dawned.

Pilate steps out of his palace. He is obliged, however unwillingly, to concern himself with the charges which are put before him by these dark figures. The oppressive heat begins to affect people's brains. Probably the dignified Roman, in his white toga, must now and then have wiped the sweat from his forehead in the effort to retain his consciousness. Then the dramatic sequence of events begins which will be discussed below in greater detail.

But for the moment the scene shifts again. Pilate learns that the accused has come from Galilee, and heaves a sigh of relief. He is anxious to pass on this unpleasant and difficult business to someone else. He directs the accusers to Herod Antipas, who happens to be in Jerusalem at the time, and who is in charge of the province of Galilee.

So Jesus is taken before Herod. Before sunrise he stood in the circle of the nocturnal companions of Caiaphas. Now when the sun has already begun to become fierce he stands in front of a figure which harmonizes with the heat of the hour. It is not for nothing that in medieval nativity plays Herod is usually represented in a fiery red garment. He is a will-o'-the-wisp of the day, just as the people round Caiaphas are will-o'-the-wisps of the night. In the palace of the high priest Jesus was surrounded by the cold breath of hatred and lies. Now he is encircled by a sensuous Luciferic curiosity. Herod says to himself, 'I have always wanted to see such a clairvoyant and magician.' In fact, Caiaphas and Herod are opposites. They are a contrast of black darkness and red fire. And Pilate, in the white toga of the Roman, stands between the two.

The archetypal triad, however, is richly varied. Although Caiaphas is the official speaker for his circle, another stands behind him, Annas, nearly a hundred years old, wizened, bony and avaricious. More clearly than Caiaphas, he stands there like Ahriman incarnate. Hate, heartlessness and rapacious egotism have become flesh in him. But another figure hovers behind Herod too. It is Herodias, who inspires and urges Herod to all he does. She is the magician, the mistress of the dread castle of Macherus, who succeeded in having John the Baptist executed. As a female Lucifer Herodias lifted up the blood-stained vessel with the head of John the Baptist. As Lucifer become human, she is also present now as Jesus is taken before her husband. Perhaps it is she who orders Jesus to be clothed in a white garment in order to ridicule his insignificance, not realizing that thereby she enacts a visible prophecy of the luminous resurrection body of Christ.

The name of Pontius Pilate

The pendulum of events swings back to the centre. The formal trial of Jesus is conducted before Pontius Pilate. The significance of Pilate ought to be considered by every Christian, since there is hardly a Christian service held in which his name is not mentioned at an important point. In the creeds of all denominations it is said that Christ 'suffered under Pontius Pilate.' His name has been recited millions of times throughout the centuries. What is the mystery hidden in this fact?

When our activities in the newly-founded Christian Community began, and as we found our way into the marvellous gift of the new ritual, I came once upon an unexpected approach to this question. The privilege of having altars again allowed us to discover life and soul in the spatial dimensions of right and left, before and behind. We grew into a realization of a whole world of spiritual currents previously only dimly sensed, because certain parts of the holy act are celebrated at the left, others at the right side of the altar. I wondered whether the Roman Catholic clergy, who also practise the change of sides, had any conscious knowledge of the significance of right and left. Whenever I had a chance, I put the question to Catholic priests. 'What does it mean,' I asked, 'that during the mass you change from one side to the other, and back again?' The invariable response was, 'We have never been taught anything serious about it.' A few, however, added that the only explanation they had ever come across was the humorous phrase, that it meant 'going from Pontius to Pilate.' I have never met a single priest who was able to make sense of this, but I have come to the conclusion that, in a somewhat hieroglyphic manner, a fragment of ancient pictorial tradition must have survived in this phrase.

In this context, a curious remark became understandable to me with which Rudolf Steiner threw light on the puzzle of the name of Pontius Pilate. According to him, the name was no designation of a private individual, but a latinized description of a term used in the ancient mysteries. The name is derived from the Greek *pontos pyletos* which could be simply translated as *straits*. Literally it means 'the pillared sea,' the sea with doorposts, the sea into which a door with pillars leads. It may be remembered that the Straits of Gibraltar were known in the ancient world as the Pillars of Hercules. In those days the way out of the Mediterranean was experienced as a real door. It was felt as the frontier between the physical world and the threshold of the spiritual world into which the soul enters after death. Similar pictorial designations were current in the ancient world for the Bosphorus and the Straits of the Dardanelles which lead like gateways from the Mediterranean into the Black Sea. Used in the mysteries, the expression *pontos pyletos* does not, however, refer to a geographical location, but to a place in the soul-world. On the ocean of the soul-world the seeker arrives one day at the gate of the spiritual world. Here he must cross a crucial threshold. The fact that Pilate bears a name which is linked with the mysteries is not accidental, but is one of those pictorial realities which accumulate in the last act of the drama of Christ. The name underlines what could be read in the being and destiny of Pilate's personality. The figure of Pilate illustrates clearly what the human being has to face if his destiny brings him close to the threshold of the spiritual world. When the name of Pilate is spoken a secret password is pronounced which holds good for every human being, *Man at the Door*. In medieval legends, for instance in the 'Golden Legend: concerning the Passion of Our Lord,' strange interpretations of the name of Pilate are found which go back to imaginative descriptions of his youth. There are many links with legends about Judas. Events and experiences are described in the form of actual history which no doubt occurred only within the inward fields of the soul. The name Pontius is explained as acquired by the conquest of an island called Pontus on which the young Pilate is supposed to have tamed the wild natives. These hieroglyphic pictures may be remnants of a time in which the mysterious significance of the name was still understood. Perhaps they indicate that Pilate himself as a young man was in contact with some of the survivals of the ancient rites of initiation.

In the light of these mysterious overtones in the name of Pilate, it does not appear any longer quite so meaningless if the changing movement of the celebrating priest from one corner of the altar to the other is described as a 'walking from Pontius to Pilate.' Every altar on which a true ritual is celebrated is a door to the spiritual world. Earthly fact unites with heavenly, called down by prayer and devotion. The two ends of the altar are the pillars which form the gate at either side of the threshold which leads to another world. We shall see that the gospels describing the scenes in front of the palace of Pilate lead not only to the archetypal picture of a stage, but also to that of the altar. The occult form of the name of Pilate confirms that Pilate is 'the man of the centre,' between Caiaphas and Herod, that is, he is the typical human being.

Before we consider in detail the scenes around Pilate we may observe once more the dramatic variety of all the stages in the trial of Jesus. Jesus is placed before the three different authorities, Caiaphas, Herod and Pilate. Nothing can bring home so vividly the profound difference between these three worlds as the different attitude of Christ in each of them.

Still in the eerie darkness of the night he stands before Caiaphas.

Caiaphas says to him, 'I exhort you by the living God that you tell us whether you are the Christ, the Son of God.' Jesus does not refuse to answer, but his first two brief words carry a stern challenge. They are usually translated, 'You have said so.' In fact, great power is compressed into these three syllables. Their meaning is, 'That is for you to say.' The appearance of the divine Christ in Jesus, the Son of God among men, can be of value for humanity only when men recognize him and confess the truth of their recognition. However, Christ is not content with this brief challenge. He meets the question about the Son of God with one of the greatest sayings concerning the Son of Man, 'From now on you will see the Son of Man sitting at the right hand of power, coming in the ether-cloud realm of the heavens' (Matt.26:64). These words tear asunder the curtain which hides the future of humanity. Christ throws the radiant thought of a new epoch of the world into the face of his adversaries.

Christ's attitude towards Herod is very different. The Gospel of Luke describes vividly the curiosity with which Herod awaits the arrival of Jesus. 'When Herod saw Jesus, he was delighted, for he had wanted for a very long time to see him because of all that he had heard about him. He hoped to see him do some kind of magic feat. And so he asked him many questions.' (Luke 23:8). But Christ does not do him the honour of answering. He ignores all his questions. His silence is inexorable. He meets the Luciferic power with sublime dignity. That power has been greatest in the past, but basically it is already vanquished. The Ahrimanic power which speaks through Annas and Caiaphas is different. The spirit of icy cleverness will have its greatest triumphs in the future. Also its defeat will have to be achieved in times to come. The decisive encounter between Christ and the satanic power of Antichrist will occur in the times in which the coming of Christ, the revelation of the Son of Man in the clouds of heaven, will be fulfilled. Therefore Christ is not silent before the Ahrimanic adversaries. He fights for the future of humanity by summoning, in the dawn of Good Friday, the vision of that future conquest.

Before Pilate the attitude of Christ is again different. He is not silent, nor do his words pass above the heads of men like flashes of lightning. Before Pilate, Jesus is ready to answer. It is his nearest approach to speaking from man to man.

The stage of the drama

The scenes round Pilate demand, in a special degree, a comprehensive synoptic view. Comparatively full descriptions are found in all four gospels, each gospel contributing its own specific details. Since we have arrived in the progressive incarnation of Christ at the point where everything takes place entirely on the physical plane, there is no need to penetrate a veil of imaginative pictures in the first three gospels in order to realize the actual historic facts. At no other point can the synoptic view of the four gospels confine itself so entirely to a simple addition of the different stories. Thus in the end the events which occurred in the palace of Pilate appear before us in detail, hour by hour.

Very significantly, St John displays his biographical power in special measure. His contribution is incomparably richer and more exact than that of the first three gospels. The gospel which carries us to the highest spheres of spirit commands also the most profound insight into the factual events of the physical plane. John supplies the framework into which one can place every other detail contributed by the synoptics. The drama proceeds in three acts. In the Gospel of John the three acts are distinctly marked by Pilate's entering the house during the course of each act: twice in order to continue a conversation with Jesus in private, and once in order to prepare the climax of the trial. In each of the three acts outward scenes in the foreground surround an inward scene at the centre.

Imagine the picture of the stage — the façade of the palace of Pilate with a great terrace; above, the Procurator together with Jesus; down below, the shouting mob led by Caiaphas and other members of the Sanhedrin. It is as though we ourselves were among the people who look up to the two figures on the balcony above the stairs. The drama unfolds. The multitude below, although belonging to the actors, is at the same time the audience. Three times the curtain comes down when Pilate returns with Jesus into the house. But a comparison with the ordinary stage does not fully apply for the play continues behind the curtain. The people know this, and follow whatever may be happening inside the house with profound feelings of tension. The essential progress of the drama takes place *in camera*. An *arcanum* is placed into the midst of the theatre, for the events in the house are esoteric. One might even say that the original meaning of 'exoteric' and 'esoteric' is being specifically illustrated here. 'Outward' and 'inward' in Greek are *exo* and *eso*. Exoteric scenes surround esoteric ones.

In the middle scene inside the house, in the very centre of the Pilate-Christ drama, Pilate orders Jesus to be scourged, and the soldiers put on him the robe of purple, and press the crown of thorns upon his head. This is not done outside before the people but 'behind the curtain,' in a room of the Praetorium, an adjacent building used for the officers and sentries of the Roman guard. Previously, Herodias and Herod, in their mockery, have robed Jesus with a white garment. The Roman soldiers too are mocking Jesus, when they now carry out procedures which were customary as tests and symbolic actions in the mysteries of initiation, of which also the Roman army was cognizant. The soldiers are, however, not completely conscious of what they are doing: they are moved by a dim, uncertain feeling: Is this Jesus an initiate? If so, they had imagined something different.

All the same, the actions of both Herod and the Roman soldiers produce true pictures. The white garment and the purple robe are revelations of real secrets of Christ's being. In pictorial presentation the spiritualized life-body of Christ is shown to the unsuspecting people. The vision of this life-body was vouchsafed once to the most intimate disciples on Mount Tabor, and a few days later it will appear anew as the light-body of the Risen One in the midst of the disciples. The purple robe is the visible manifestation of the soul of Jesus, warmed through and through by the fire of love, in which there glows in royal majesty the will to sacrifice which transforms all.

When the internal central scene is followed by this next external scene, a point is reached which shakes the souls of the people to their depths. After the scourging, Jesus, robed in purple and crowned with thorns, is led out and shown to the people by Pilate. How moving is the change that has been wrought! The sight of Jesus must instil profound compassion in every heart capable of human feeling. At the same time, hidden secrets of the mysteries are made public. Now Pilate, acting as if he were the hierophant and stage-manager of this dramatic disclosure of the mysteries, utters the significant saying which is like a magic formula, *Ecce homo:* 'Behold the man!' This formula points not only to the sublimity of the Christ-being, but also to the universal human validity of the picture which is presented to humankind at this moment. In dramatic concentration, all the secrets of Man are revealed.

At the northern boundary of the old city of Jerusalem in the narrow, steep street which is known as Via Dolorosa, the place is still shown where Pilate spoke the words. An arch spans the road. It is known as the Ecce Homo arch. Unfortunately, nothing is really left at the place which would help us to imagine the scene of Good Friday morning. When I went there for the first time, I could not succeed in forming a picture of what the place may have been like at the time. The only possible link was the dark vaults in the Praetorium adjoining the palace of Pilate, which looked like dungeons. Here, it can easily be imagined how the soldiers scourged and mocked Jesus, at the same time adorning him with the symbols of initiation. But, to begin with, the narrow labyrinth of streets does not suggest the archetypal layout of stage, curtain and auditorium. On my second journey to Palestine, however, I gained a more vivid picture. I had the opportunity of being shown through the rooms of a convent which adjoins the Ecce Homo arch in the Via Dolorosa. It belongs to the highly cultured order of the Dames de Sion. In the basement of this building, approximately forty feet below the present street level, sections of the old street are visible. Great stone slabs, joined neatly together, lie there, forming the pavement of the ancient road. Chessboards, scratched into the stone by the Roman soldiers, are clearly distinguishable. It is profoundly moving to see so deep below the present street level the slabs upon which once the multitude crowded before the open staircase of Pilate's palace, and on which also the foot of Christ must have stepped.

There is a still greater surprise in the church of the convent itself. This possesses one of the most imposing high altars in the whole of the Roman Catholic world. Above the *mensa* considerable portions of the façade of the palace of Pilate are built into the wall. They show a Hellenistic building of a similar style and proportion as the great city gate of Miletum, which was once erected in the Pergamon Museum in Berlin. The wall consists of three sections, each of which contains a kind of arch resting on pillars. To the three times' withdrawal of Pilate with Jesus into the interior — it is undecided whether he went each time through another door — three doors correspond in the façade of the palace. These remnants of the palace of Pilate preserved in this church have not received anything like the attention which they deserve. They have therefore never exercised the power to unseal secrets in the life of Christ which they could have done. The portion of the staircase of Pilate which has been taken to Rome, and which now forms the steps of the altar of the church of Santa Scala on the Lateran, has played a far greater part in the history of Christianity, although it is rather misleading as a guide to the form of the palace of Pilate. Assuming that it is a genuine remnant at all, it can only have been a small part, put together rather arbitrarily, of the original wide staircase. To this day penitents go up and down the steps on their knees, and the great popularity of these stones witnesses to the lasting impression which the scene of Good Friday has made upon Christian souls.

The three gates in the façade which was both curtain and background of the mystery play of Good Friday, suggest the archetype of the altar almost more definitely and clearly than the archetype of the stage. The Eastern Churches, the Greek Orthodox as well as the Armenian and Coptic Church, have preserved a form of the altar which is basically different from that of the Roman Catholic Church, and is far more closely connected with the early Christian sacramental life. In an Eastern Church, the altar itself is hidden from view. It is concealed behind the *iconostasis*, the picture-screen. The iconostasis has the function of a curtain which gives the altar an esoteric character. That which is enacted on the altar is regarded as a *mystery* in the full and original meaning of the term. The Latin word *sacramentum* is, it is true, the exact translation of the Greek word *mysterion*, but the Roman Church has largely dispensed with the esoteric elements in its ritual. It has only preserved the altar rails which however no longer emphasize the difference between inside and outside, but rather that between the priests and the lay congregation. The iconostasis, a picture-screen of the Eastern Church, contains three doors. The central door is bigger than the others and is known as 'the Royal Gate.' Only part of the ritual is celebrated in front of the screen. In the Eastern Mass the dramatic element is enhanced by the fact that the priest not only moves at the altar from left to right and back, but that he proceeds repeatedly through the gates of the screen from the outside to the inside, and again from the inside to the outside. Also, on his way from one end of the altar to the other, he appears through one of the side entrances and returns through the other one. Among the parts which in the Eastern

Mass are celebrated behind the curtain is the Transubstantiation, the mysterious character of which is thereby dramatically preserved. The congregation does indeed know what is taking place, and unites itself with it in devotion, but it cannot actually see it. That the consecration of bread and wine is celebrated 'in a mystery,' enhances the devotional mood. In the Roman Catholic tradition only the ringing of the bell has remained, which indicates the moment of Transubstantiation, when the kneeling congregation cast down their eyes and make the sign of the cross. It is understood that one is now not to look at that which takes place at the altar.

The scene in front of the palace of Pilate is thus a sacramental ritual taking place openly in the world of external events. The Roman Procurator assumes the function of the celebrating priest. When he conducts Jesus, crowned with thorns and robed in purple, through the central gate and presents to the people archetypal Man, one is reminded of the moment in the Eastern eucharistic service when the priest, after the Transubstantiation, appears through the Royal Gate and lifts up the body and blood of Christ before the congregation. Three times the action is continued by Pilate behind the curtain. The tension and excitement of the people continues unabated. They feel instinctively the special significance of the process, just as the congregation grows more devout the more the sacred ritual is hidden behind the picture-screen. However, dark demonic sounds are mixed into that part which proceeds in front of the palace of Pilate. Like a perverted chant, the cry is raised, 'Crucify him, crucify him.'

The close link between stage and altar brings to mind an important principle in the spiritual history of humanity. Both the stage drama and the ritual have emerged from the mysteries. From times immemorial, on the stage and at the altar that part of the mystery has been placed before the people in exoteric form which was suitable to cultivate general human development. Sacrament and ritual are sisters of the drama. For this reason both stage and altar originally used a curtain which was a reminiscence of their common origin in the mysteries. The present attempt to revive and bring to a new birth the modern drama will only be successful if it goes with desire for a reconquest of the mysteries. The esoteric knowledge of the mysteries, however, must no longer be the special privilege of a few people; it must be accessible to everybody. It must prove its power and substance by inspiring artistic productions in the same way in which, in the ancient world, the dramatic and other arts were born from the mysteries. The same applies to the new altars which humanity needs in our time ever more urgently. They too can only be true sources of power if they are surrounded and cherished with a new and reverent knowledge of the esoteric mysteries. No external reconstruction of the screen is needed in front of the altar, but the inward sense of 'the mystery' must become alive again all the more vividly. This will be all the more possible when it is understood that on Golgotha the great disclosure of the mysteries took place which continues to flow through all genuine and valid acts on Christian altars. If we recognize in the scenes of Good Friday the mystery drama revealed and placed on the stage of human history by the great invisible producer, the divine services of Christianity will resume again their character as genuine sacrament, as a valid 'mystery.'

The first act of the drama

After the prelude in the house of Caiaphas the first act opens. Caiaphas and his people followed by the noisy crowd take Jesus to Pilate. It is in the first hours of the morning. The Gospel of Luke reports that, in the main, three charges were made against Jesus. He is accused of having incited the people, of having made propaganda against the Roman taxes, and of having said that he is Christ, a king.

Each accusation was a perversion of the truth. The first and the last were simple. It was easy to label Jesus as a rebel if the spiritual presence of Christ was falsified into a political challenge. The second accusation calls to mind the question concerning the tribute money, which had been put to Jesus as a trap.

This challenge is related to the worship of Caesar, which had taken on more and more of a demonic character. To refer to Caesar was no longer purely a political matter because the obedience to Caesar had been declared by the Caesar himself as a religious duty. The reply of Jesus 'Render unto Caesar what is Caesar's and unto God what is God's' showed his superior detachment. Although demonic power had got hold of the throne of Caesar, Jesus desired that the political power be given its due as if it had never been misused. The accusation now put forward that Jesus had indulged in anti-tax propaganda is a dastardly lie inspired by hate.

Pilate is surprised that Jesus does not reply. He fails in his efforts to make him defend himself. Jesus is adamant in his silence, so everything comes to a standstill. Pilate endeavours to evade responsibility, and asks the accusers to conduct a trial according to their own law. He is met with the reply that by the Jewish law Jesus is worthy of death, but that the political conditions deny the Jews the right of execution.

Now Pilate knows no other way out than to conduct Jesus into the interior of the house and to continue his talk with him there. This is the first scene in the interior. The Gospel of John describes it in detail. It gives a glimpse behind the curtain while the multitude remains outside in tense excitement. In this complete privacy Pilate addresses the question to Jesus, 'Are you the King of the Jews?' Jesus replies with the strange counter-question, 'Are you saying that out of yourself, or have others said it to you about me?' This answer points to the fact that Pilate is not entirely new to the case. No doubt Pilate had observed for some time the movement round Jesus. The question of Christ's personality must have puzzled him. Probably it met him in the form in which it lived in those who expected the Messiah to be the political liberator and leader of the Jews. Within the circle of the disciples it was chiefly Judas who could not shake off this spell of a political Messianic hope and who, in his impatience, tried to force the issue. Perhaps the kernel of truth in the legends which speak of Judas as a friend and servant of Pilate consists in this, that occasional meetings and conversations probably took place between Pilate and Judas.

Now Pilate recognized that he had allowed himself to be drawn more than is necessary into the internal affairs of the Jews. Perhaps he had a suspicion that at the back of the Jewish expectation of the Messiah there was more than a merely political faith. It is not impossible that as a detached observer he understood the principle of the coming of the Messiah better than the Jewish people. But now he wants to withdraw, and so he points out that he is not a Jew. But Christ does not respond to his evasions. He responds to what may have passed as a divination through the soul of Pilate, and so He says, 'My kingdom is not of this world.' It is significant that this is not said before the people. It is an esoteric saying. Pilate receives the privilege of a confidence. He is not insensitive to it, and does not seem incapable of conceiving the idea of a kingdom which is not of this world. Thus he continues, 'Are you a king then?' Christ answers in the affirmative. He allows it to be seen that he is a king in the kingdom of truth: 'I descended and was born into the earthly world to testify to the truth. Everyone who is of the world of truth hears my voice.' But now the natural limits of Pilate become apparent. Representing a civilization whose philosophic outlook has been reduced to a dignified scepticism, he coins the classic formula of spiritual resignation, 'What is truth?'

The dialogue of this first esoteric scene contains a number of significant overtones. The political and also super-political significance of the Messiah is very complicated. Since the Babylonian captivity the Jewish people had been deprived of their kings. The brief period of the Maccabean kings was not a continuation of the line of David. Even less so was the kingdom of the Herodians, who were Arab foreigners. The adherents of the political idea of the coming of the Messiah expected the restitution of the kingdom of David. Considering the exclusive significance of blood and race, the restitution and continuation of the kingdom of David was only thinkable through someone who was in the direct line of succession. It was a matter of course that the house and lineage of David was watched with the greatest interest and concern. The centre of this interest was always the eldest son in his generation who would have been king if his house had not been deposed by alien powers. When Pilate asked, 'Are you the King of the Jews?' he puts a very exact question. It means, 'Are you, according to your descent, the Pretender?' But the answers which he gets are beyond him. His sceptical remark, 'What is truth?' brings the first scene in the interior to an end.

(The profound secrets of the genealogy of Jesus, which are in the background to this scene, have been extensively dealt with in the author's *The Childhood of Jesus*.)

The second act

The second act of the drama is full of movement. It begins when Pilate and Jesus step out again on the balcony. Pilate says, 'I find no guilt in him.' Three times he attempts to set Jesus free. He learns now that Jesus comes from Galilee and is therefore under the authority of Herod. This seems to offer a way out. He commands Jesus to be conducted to Herod. This must cause a considerable interruption in the trial, particularly if Herod is in residence in the palace on Mount Zion, not far from the Cenacle and the palace of Caiaphas. On the other hand it is possible that Herod, who was only in Jerusalem for a short time, stayed in a house close to the palace of Pilate. The majority of historians hold the latter view. But I do not regard it as impossible that the meeting of Jesus with Herod and Herodias happened on Mount Zion. In that case Jesus would have been conducted the whole way, which he had already made when he was taken from Caiaphas to Pilate, once again there and back.

In his second attempt to release Jesus, Pilate offers to the crowd the reprieve of a prisoner, which was customary at the Passover. He gives them the choice between the murderer Barabbas, and Jesus. Three times he asks, 'Which of them shall I release?' Pilate thinks in human terms. He is not unaware of the fact that at certain moments the people can feel the greatness of Christ, and are even inclined to turn to him in great numbers. Was it not only last Sunday that the multitude had shouted its ecstatic *Hosanna* when Jesus entered the town, riding on the foal of an ass? Pilate cannot imagine but that the sympathy of the people for Jesus, which had been expressed so emphatically, must still be present and capable of being revived. But he is unaware of the spiritual battle which has been fought above the level of external events. Ever since Palm Sunday this spiritual warfare has been waged. An important factor was the cursing of the fig tree through which Jesus put an end to the old forces of ecstatic vision which had produced the cries of *Hosanna*. The crowds are now possessed by the hatred of the Ahrimanic spirits, whose exponents are Caiaphas and his followers. Now Pilate realizes his mistake. The people demand the release of Barabbas, and when he asks, 'What shall I do then with Jesus?' instead of *Hosanna* the cry goes up time and again, 'Crucify him, crucify him.' Pilate's well-intentioned threefold question eventually provokes only the demonic responses which fanatical humanity contributes to this Mass of death.

The Gospel of Matthew adds a scene which explains how in the middle of the central act the perplexity of Pilate reaches its height. Procla, his wife, sends a messenger to him with a warning. She has had a terrifying dream. She has dreamt of Christ, and has had a picture of his true being, which Pilate has only partly sensed. Now the symmetry of the actors is complete. Procla stands behind Pilate, as if to underline the *human* qualities of his character, just as Annas, *Ahrimanic* man, stands behind Caiphas, and the *Luciferic* figure of Herodias stands behind Herod.

Pilate makes a third attempt to set Jesus free. The third scene in the interior follows. The Procurator commands Jesus to be scourged, the soldiers clothe him with the purple robe and crown him with the crown of thorns. Pilate and the soldiers play at the symbols of initiation, the signs of the tests to be passed in the ancient mysteries. What they do becomes more and more irrational; less and less do they know what they do. Perhaps the oppressive heat of the *khamsin* has contributed not a little to the dimming out of consciousness. It may have still been a rational thought which made Pilate assume that the people might be open to compassion, even if their ecstatic enthusiasm for Jesus had evaporated. But what happens now surpasses all thought and reason. Pilate causes the most shattering picture in human history to be enacted. Only the view of the crucified Christ on Golgotha surpasses it, but then the darkening sun will spread a veil before it. When Pilate says 'Behold the Man,' he appeals to more than the sense of compassion. He is carried far beyond his own consciousness, and stirs the deepest power of divination which, however, still rests as an unawakened seed in the depths of the human soul. It will require the whole of human history to understand this saying. Alas this last attempt, with its stirring mystical presentation, is also doomed to failure. The only answer is the cry of hate demanding the death of Christ.

The third act: kingship and Messiahship

The third act opens with a scene in the exterior. In the sight of the people Pilate performs a symbolic act. He washes his hands: he is not going to be responsible for what follows. The symbolic significance is here again far-reaching. The sacred drama has reached the exact point where in the Roman Mass the priest also washes his hands. Every detail is a disclosure of the mysteries, the revealing of a spiritual order familiar to the temples of initiation in the ancient world, which in the future will be accessible to men when the essence of the mysteries will have flowed again into human life.

With demonic ecstasy the people reply, 'Let his blood be a burden upon us and our children.' They consent to the demand of Pilate that others must assume responsibility for the death of Jesus. Without knowing what they do the people call the most terrible curse upon their own heads. At this tense moment the high priests pronounce their spiritual accusation in addition to the political charges. They say, 'He has made himself a Son of God.' It is the first truth which they utter. Even the Ahrimanic adversary is compelled to pronounce the truth of Christ. Pilate is shaken to his depths. He can only understand the accusation by the high priestly clique in the sense that Jesus claims to be one of the highest initiates of humanity. But the Caesar in Rome also claims to be a Son of God. Pilate understands that this claim is made because of acts of initiation which the Caesars have forced. Strindberg may be very close to the historic truth when he says that Pilate was among those who, in their loyalty to the ancient Roman virtues, condemned the misuse of the Temple and the demonic decadence of the Caesars. Pilate was in an extremely difficult position. As a highly placed civil servant he was obliged to carry out the will of Caesar. As a human being, he was unable to accept without criticism the madness of Tiberius who ruled the world from the island of Capri, the legendary home of the Sirens.

Confronted with the redoubled charges of Caiaphas and his followers, Pilate sees no other way out but to retire again with Jesus into the interior and to continue the cross-examination there. Now the third esoteric scene begins. Pilate feels that he might really be face to face with a high initiate, with a man who is acting in accordance with a divine mission. This is implied in the question which he now directs to Jesus: *'Pothen ei su?'* The usual translation of this question, 'Whence art thou?' conceals its importance. Pilate no longer inquires after physical descent and origin. He inquires after Christ's spiritual mission. He desires to know whence Jesus has derived his charge. But he is confronted with the same inexorable silence as was Herod before him. For there is no answer to this question.

No being on earth could have commissioned Christ. His mission is not of this world. Pilate, in his perplexity, falls back on his own commission and authority. The plenipotentiary of the Caesar, too, is more than a political officer. He says, 'Do you not know that I have the power to release you and also to crucify you?' Once again Pilate is vouchsafed a unique confidence and privilege as he receives as an answer one of the greatest sayings of Christ, 'You would not have power over me unless it had been given you from on high.' Far beyond any human commission Christ points to the highest divine purposes which are worked out through all human intentions, but also through the clash and friction of human thought. Through this saying of Christ Pilate is received into that divine plan and texture of history to which the incarnation of Christ belongs. Something like an absolution is given him in advance. Then Pilate senses the true greatness of the being of Christ. He goes to the utmost limits of his authority. He leaves Jesus in the interior of the house and steps out before the people by himself. Once more he is determined to set Jesus free, but now Caiaphas and his gang play their highest trump. They identify themselves with the worship of Caesar, although it means death to their own Messianic faith. They shout, 'If you release him, you are no longer a friend of Caesar; for everyone who makes himself a king is against Caesar.' Pilate resolves to execute an ultimate decision. He speaks no longer in words, but through a solemn act of state. His action is so strange that hardly anyone has ever dared to take the implication of this act quite seriously. In order to pronounce formal judgment Pilate moves to the Judgment Seat situated at the place which is called Gabbatha, the 'Pavement.' He now speaks *ex cathedra* with the authority which is his as the representative of Caesar. In tremendous excitement all eyes turn to him. What will be his decision? With brief words he makes an incredible proclamation: 'See, this is your king!' This sentence implies a political act of tremendous consequence. Pilate takes it upon himself to reinstitute the Jewish monarchy. He confirms that kings are not incompatible with the imperial Roman crown, if the royal dignity has been conferred in the name of Caesar. Pilate is prepared to cede a part of his power and to establish a monarchy under the Roman protectorate.

It is impossible to understand this unheard-of decision of Pilate from purely human logic. There is something unreal in it. It could not have been carried out even if the fanatical hatred of the people had not been in the way, and apart from the unbridgeable gulf which existed between the political scheme of Pilate and the intention and mind of Christ. With this act Pilate is also one of those who do not know what they do. The perplexity in his soul which has grown to unmanageable proportions, and which is aggravated by the infernal heat, produces the strange phenomenon of a royal proclamation.

The cry of hate demanding the crucifixion of Jesus is again the only response. The satanic hosts of hell seem to join in the shouting. Exhausted, Pilate can only ask one more question, 'Shall I crucify your king?' The chief priests answer, 'We have no king but Caesar.' This is a fateful saying. It implies nothing less than the renunciation of the Messianic hope by the Jewish people. It is the spiritual suicide of Jewry.

This fact also has hitherto hardly been seen in its precise importance. The people were no longer in their right mind. Mediumistic somnambulism had taken hold of Pilate as well as of Caiaphas and his Sadducees. The consciousness of human souls was not equal to the magnitude of the historic moment. Even the disciples of Jesus, with the exception of the one who had already passed through death and resurrection, had fallen under the spell of sleep in Gethsemane, and had defaulted before the mystery drama at the palace of Pilate.

In a dramatic sketch by Hans Kunkel (*Caiaphas, a St John's Passion*) the consequences are drawn from the last reply which Pilate received from the Jews:

CAIAPHAS (*in great silence. The noise of the multitude has suddenly ceased*):
He calls himself Messiah. That is the secret king. The Messiah of the Jew is the enemy of Caesar. We have nothing to do with him, and renounce him.

PILATE: Is this true? You hand over your Messiah to Rome. You renounce him, and will never again demand liberation?

(*No reply. The spell of silence continues.*)

PILATE (*visibly reviving*): At last you offer your submission. You give up crying for the Messiah who will redeem you?

(*Pharisees and people move backward incapable of answering. Caiaphas alone remains facing Pilate. The general silence continues.*)

PILATE: You will hand over to me in future all who call for the Messiah? You admit at last that your Messiah is the enemy of Caesar? You will no longer cover up with your religious faith your treachery against the Empire?

Caiaphas confirms finally the repudiation of the Messiah with the sentence, 'We have no king but Caesar.'

Kunkel emphasizes, if in a one-sided manner, the point which in its consequence has nearly always been overlooked. What he does not consider is the breakdown of the human consciousness which becomes universal now the noon-hour of Good Friday approaches. Human thoughts and actions issue into a super-dimensional sphere. Whatever is said and done reveals much more than the purely individual content of souls. Great forces pass through human souls who do not know what they do. In fact, the whole of humanity is present and shares in the guilt when finally even Pilate is at his wits' end and delivers Jesus to his enemies to be crucified.

The end of Pilate

The further life of Pilate confirms the fact that the earthquake which shook the planet from Good Friday noon to Easter Sunday morning continued to be felt in the souls of men. In Pilate the dynamics of Easter laid hold even of the centre of the Roman Empire. After the crucifixion Pilate remained in office as Procurator in Jerusalem for another three years. Then he was called back by Tiberius. A great variety of reasons are given for his recall. The historic documents which ignore the figure of Christ and confine themselves to the purely external events of the time seem to suggest that Pilate became unpopular through a high-handed misuse of power, which provoked a series of insurrections among the Jews. The legends, however, whose pictorial language needs only translating into historic fact, always connect the recall of Pilate with his attitude in the trial of Christ. It is stated that he himself sent a report of the trial to Caesar Tiberius. Tiberius is said to have heard about Jesus previously and to have asked for him because he hoped he would heal his sickness. When Tiberius learned that Jesus had been crucified, his wrath is said to have turned against Pilate whom he recalls to Rome. The story continues to say that the anger of Caesar calmed down when Pilate appeared before him wearing the seamless robe of Jesus. But after Pilate had been compelled to appear before Caesar in his own clothes, the tempest of wrath broke over him. He was relieved of his office and fell into disgrace. Tiberius himself died in AD 37, insane and riddled with disease. Pilate survived him by two years. It is said that he was banished into the region of the Lake of Geneva, from which he was supposed to have come originally. Eventually, so tradition has it, he committed suicide. His corpse is said to have been thrown first into the Tiber at Rome, and then into the

Rhône. But everywhere the elements responded with such terrible commotion that in the end his body had to be dropped into the Lake of Lucerne, in which the summit of the mountain is mirrored which to this day is called *Pilatus*.

It is possible that in these legendary stories that meeting between Pilate and Tiberius is veiled to which Rudolf Steiner refers in his lectures published under the title *Building Stones for an Understanding of the Mystery of Golgotha*.* As a result of forced initiations and consequent attacks of mania, the first Caesars, in particular Tiberius, the contemporary and antithesis of Jesus, received hallucinatory impressions of the being of Christ. The demonized souls of the Caesars received flashes of cognition just as in the gospels the demons are said to have recognized Christ before he was recognized by men. Naturally the Caesars were incapable of drawing helpful consequences from such momentary impressions. But it occurred to them to incorporate Christ into the Roman pantheon alongside the gods of other conquered nations, and to control his power in the service of the worship of Caesar. Most significant perhaps is the legend 'Concerning St John before the Latin Gate.' It says, 'You must know that the Roman Emperors did not persecute the apostles because they preached Christ, for they rejected no God; but because Christ was declared God without a licence from the Senate, which was never permitted. Thus we read in the *Historia Ecclesiastica* that Pilate sent a letter to Tiberius concerning Christ, and that the Emperor was inclined to permit that the Romans should receive the Christian faith, but the Senate refused its consent because Christ called himself God without its approval.'†

The tragic circumstances in which the life of Pilate ends confirm the human character which he possessed. Obviously, the Mystery of Golgotha in which it was his lot to play such a decisive part had deeply affected him. Ultimately, every human being is Pontius Pilate, and like him is led to the threshold of decision. And if the legend lets the body of Pilate be carried from Rome via France to central Europe, it indicates the direction along which the centre of gravity of Christianity has moved in the course of history.

---

* Lecture 6.

† *Legenda Aurea*, 1.467.

CHAPTER TEN

The Events in Holy Week

Holy Week

The week before Easter is not only a significant and exceptional period in the Christian year, it is important also in the cycle of nature. In the Christian year, the whole drama of the Passion is enacted in this space of time, and its events form the grand conclusion of the gospel. In various regions of Christendom it is called not only Holy Week, but also the Great Week. Only those able to experience its greatness can fully participate in the festival of Easter.

In nature's year this week before Easter is important because the spring full moon occurs in it. The spell of winter is finally broken; by leaps and bounds the new life of the earth goes forward. In the equinoctial conflict of day with night day gains the victory, which is consolidated in the triumph of light on the first Sunday after the vernal full moon.

The events of Holy Week, as related in the gospel, do not harmonize at first with spring in nature. On the contrary, they stand in sharpest contrast to it. Only at the very end, when the Easter sun has risen, the festival of rejoicing harmonizes with the exultation of spring. The solemn drama of Holy Week is the preparation for this harmony. The springtime of nature comes about of itself. The inner spring of the Easter festival must be achieved by the path of pilgrimage which passes along the stations of Holy Week.

The seven days before Easter can be compared with the Twelve Holy Nights of Christmas. This period 'between the years' is the right preparation for the twelve months of the New Year for everyone who contemplates the inner meaning of midwinter. On those who inwardly participate in the mystery drama of the Passion the seven days of Holy Week bestow new forces for the whole of their future destiny.

The events which happened two thousand years ago were providential prototypes. Through them the seven days of each week have taken on new meaning. The names of the seven days of the week in the European languages show that they reflect the qualities of the seven planetary spheres. Thus we have the sun (Sunday), moon (Monday), Mars (Tuesday, French: *mardi*), Mercury (Wednesday, French: *mercredi*), Jupiter (Thursday, French: *jeudi*), Venus (Friday, French: *vendredi*), Saturn (Saturday). In that one week before Easter, at the end of the life of Jesus, each weekday was stamped anew with a Christian planetary aspect, over and above the cosmic differentiation.

Christendom at present has little understanding of the content of the days of Passion Week. Certainly, on Good Friday thoughts are turned to the cross on Golgotha, and in some parts of Christianity every Friday is marked as a fast day. But beyond this no striking picture has been attached to any day except Palm Sunday, which in some countries is celebrated with a display of palm branches. In reality, however, each of the seven days reveals a cosmic secret in human and historical form.

At the entry of the Christ into Jerusalem on Palm Sunday, the sun of the past, the old sun, stood again royally in the heavens. Nevertheless it was about to receive its dismissal, for the new sun, the Easter sun, was to rise on the following Sunday. When on the Monday Christ cursed the fig tree and cleansed the Temple in the holy city, his encounter was with the moon-forces of the ancient world which needed renewal. On the Tuesday, it was the Mars spirit which Christ bent to his purpose. For on the Tuesday of that week Christ was in conflict with his opponents, who came forward group after group in the hope of trapping him in his teaching. The Christ's weapon was the spirit-word; finally, in the echo of the conflict, he retired with the disciples to the Mount of Olives and revealed to them an apocalyptic view into the future. On the Wednesday, in the anointing at Bethany and in the betrayal of Judas, Mercury encountered the Christ-sun. And as on Maundy Thursday Christ washed the disciples' feet and administered the sacrament to them, there shone a Jupiter light, full of future promise, in the sorrow of their souls. On Good Friday all that has ever been granted to man by the goddess of love, Venus or Aphrodite, was most wonderfully transmuted and enhanced. A deed of love was done on that day greater than all other possible deeds of love. Love's sacrificial death on Golgotha was the transformation of the Venus-principle through the sun-principle of Christ. As the body of Christ rested in the grave, the Christ-sun met the Saturn-spirit in the universe; until finally Sunday brought the octave, and the sun itself rose in the heavens, the Christ-sun which had fought its way through all these stages.

The sacred drama of Holy Week is a complete artistic whole. Having grasped the value of stages in the life of Jesus, one can perceive in this drama the secret of its composition. For what takes place in the seven days before Easter is a concentration of Christ's life as a whole. The same archetypal laws, and the progress from stage to stage, which were manifested in the sacred biography of the three years, are repeated in dramatic brevity. In the light of Holy Week the three years of the complete life of Christ can be recognized as one great Passion.

Palm Sunday

Christ enters the holy city on the first day of Holy Week. It is at first an unpretentious sight. He rides through the gate of the city upon an ass, followed by his faithful believers. But suddenly, as though he were the god of spring himself, his entry creates a frenzy in the souls of the people. It is as though the crowd were seized with the ecstasy of a pagan spring festival. Primitive rites are revived when the people cast down palm branches from the trees. The palm has always ranked as the tree-symbol of the sun which shines in the spring sky with renewed strength. The crowd spread his path with the symbol of the sun. Is he in fact perhaps the friend and lord of the sun who has been promised to man as the great king of the light? Is the original spiritual significance of the city of Jerusalem to be released from enchantment, the city which sheltered on Mount Zion one of the oldest sun-sanctuaries of humanity, before it was overshadowed by Mount Moriah, the Mount of the moon, with the Temple of Solomon? Has the time of Melchizedek, the great sun-initiate, come back?

It would appear as though the Christ had now really found entrance into humanity. The high sun-spirit has already lived for three years in a human body and undergone earthly destiny. He held back and kept silence; and whenever he stepped forward he was met with hostility and lack of understanding. Is all this now to take a new direction? Is destiny to find a solution in an ecstatic jubilation?

No, this is the beginning of the most solemn week in human history. The same men who strew palms and break forth into fervid *Hosannas* will shriek with fanatical hatred a few days later: 'Crucify him! crucify him!' The cross on Golgotha, the symbol of death, will companion the palm branch, the symbol of life. It is Christ himself who brings about the sudden reversal of feeling. He passes through the ecstatic crowd in silence, with grave countenance. He sees through the acclamations; they are merely superficial, and he aims at deeper levels. His will is directed to something very different.

One might ask why Jesus did not stay in Galilee, in his home, especially at the time when the country round the Sea of Galilee blooms in all the miraculous colours of spring? Yes, if he had stayed in Galilee he would have remained alive. But one might just as well ask: Why did not Christ remain as a god in the heavenly worlds? His whole being found its meaning in making this renunciation. To make his entry into Jerusalem, knowing that in so doing he threw down the gauntlet to his enemies, was to complete his entry into the earthly world. The events of the first day of this solemn week corresponded, on another level, to those that had marked the inception of his earthly path. As at that time he forsook the heavens, so now he forsakes the glory of Galilee. It made no stir among men as Christ descended from the heavenly spheres to earth. Even John the Baptist, who played the role of priest at this entry into earth existence, scarcely noticed anything of what took place as Jesus of Nazareth became bearer and vessel of the Christ. But it was proclaimed in the spheres above humankind. The words rang out: 'This is my beloved Son in whom I am well pleased.' And on Palm Sunday, in this strange hour of ferment and exaltation, the event is acclaimed by men. The *Hosanna* of the ecstatic mob corresponds to the word which once sounded out of spiritual heights. Suddenly the people feel that he who comes riding on the ass's foal is not merely man. It is as though the folk-soul broke through and perceived the shining radiance, the sun-aura, that blazed forth from the figure of Jesus. For three years the divine nature of Christ had had to hold back, or it would have overwhelmed men with its power. But now this holding back bears its fruit. The divine element, which had sacrificed itself in humility to the human, is transformed into powerful resolution of the will. To begin with, the divine in him radiated through the human; but now the human nature is consumed in the fire of God. It is this scintillating fire of the will which scatters kindling sparks among the crowd. The people are seized with the presentiment of a revolutionary Passover feast, but they can only take it to mean a political springtide of the nation.

The Christ knows better. Into the holy city, that quintessence of the whole pre-Christian evolution of humanity, he bears something which is different from everything that earth can bring forth from herself. It is a seed which must change the world from the very foundations. The reaction may seem like a tremor of assent, but a few days more and it is plain that this superficial mood can curse as easily as bless. The earthly vessel into which Christ entered at the baptism can ultimately bring him only death. The city which cries *Hosanna* can at last only nail him to the cross.

The spark springs across, but the Christ goes calmly through the waves of enthusiasm and acclamation. He will make his entry on deeper levels. How wonderful is the sun when it rises in the morning and brings the day to birth. Yet this external sun with which man as a natural being is connected sets again each evening. When the height of summer has passed, it withdraws from the earth and its strength fades away. So it is with human life; at some moment of time each of us must die, no matter how vivacious we were in childhood and youth. Palm Sunday is the day of the old sun, the natural sun; Easter Sunday will be the day of the new sun, the spiritual sun. This spiritual sun does not set; it is steadfast and enduring. It can, moreover, be found more easily in times of difficulty, indeed, in sickness and death, than in happiness or in the carefree days of childhood. Christ enters the old Jerusalem on Palm Sunday, but he carries the new Jerusalem into the setting, dying world. Christ desires to kindle the new sun, which is steadfast, true and omnipresent deep within the earth and humankind. This is the way that leads from Palm Sunday to Easter Sunday, from the old sun to the new.

The story of the entry into Jerusalem shows how insufficient all ecstatic conditions are. It is certainly right that we should be joyful in the glory of spring, when we are among children and when we encounter youth and love. This natural enthusiasm assuredly must not be rejected.

But it is dangerous if it is mistaken for the reality of life. Purely natural enthusiasm springs from the body only; it touches the level of the spirit only for fleeting moments. True enthusiasm, one that does not rapidly pass from the *Hosanna* to the *crucify,* is not formed from below upwards, but from above downwards. True enthusiasm is born when the spiritual takes root in human nature; when the spark of the spirit comes to earthly realization and incarnation.

Monday in Holy Week

There is a certain quiet place which even today is shrouded in mystery. It is upon the road which every morning and every evening of Holy Week was traversed by Jesus and his disciples, whether leaving the city for Bethany in the evening or returning to Jerusalem in the morning. Crossing the summit of the Mount of Olives, coming from Jerusalem, and slowly descending the other side towards the valley, where from the depths of the Judean wilderness glitters the sub-earthly mirror of the Dead Sea, one comes to a spot surrounded by high walls. It lies halfway between the Mount of Olives and Bethany. Black cypresses rise above the walls and point heavenward like solemn beacons. In the time of Jesus there was a little settlement here, Bethphage, the *House of Figs.* This village was not like other villages. A group of persons led there a life in common, united by a special spiritual tie. The simple huts in which they probably dwelt were surrounded by a hedge of fig trees which gave the place its name. These fig trees, however, were not mere bearers of fruit; they were sacred to the people who lived there, visible symbols of their special training for the spirit. These were people who sought to preserve in their circle a spiritual mystery of the past, the same mystery which is hinted at in the story of Nathanael. The group at Bethphage cultivated a condition of supersensory sight which was called 'sitting under the fig tree.' It was attained by means of meditative exercises, supported partly by special postures of the body.

It was from Bethphage that in the early hours of Palm Sunday Jesus instructed Peter and John to fetch the ass and her colt. For just as there were trees there which were held as sacred, so too were these animals. The asses kept there were no beasts of burden; they, too, symbolized a mystery. The memory still lived of the magician Baalam who was called from Babylon to curse the Israelites and prevent them from entering the Land of Promise. Baalam was pictured in the Old Testament as riding on an ass. But it was known that the phrase had a hidden meaning: it referred to a definite state of soul. It was really a somnambulent withdrawal from consciousness in which formerly the Babylonian magician began to speak. Baalam spoke out of a kind of spiritual possession, not from his human consciousness, and without his knowing how it came about the magic curse which he was to utter became a blessing instead. The sacred animals harboured at Bethphage indicate that the supersensory vision cultivated there was somnambulistic and bound to the physical body. Right into modern times the ass often appears in fairy tales as the imaginative representative of the physical human body.

The ass's colt upon which Christ rode into the holy city on Palm Sunday belongs to the realm of memories associated with Bethphage. But as he rode boldly into the city on the sacred white beast, there was no repetition of the Baalam condition of 'riding on the ass;' it was the crowd who, beholding him, fell into the ecstatic withdrawal from ordinary consciousness. It was as though a language of Baalam gripped the people as they cried *Hosanna* to the one who rode upon the ass's colt.

When the day drew towards evening, Jesus went to Bethany with his disciples to rest, as also on the following days. In the night the echo of popular ecstasy with its *Hosannas* echoed in his soul. And when next morning they passed by Bethphage on the way to Jerusalem, neither he nor his disciples remained unchanged by what had taken place. There was something deeply earnest in the bearing of the Christ, something inexorable. Then comes the enigmatic approach to the fig tree. The disciples wondered why Jesus should expect to gather figs, when it is not their season. And they heard him speak the strangely harsh words: 'Never again shall fruit ripen on you in all ages.' Perhaps they dimly felt in this moment that something greater lay in the words than just a statement about the tree and its fruitfulness. But the scales did not fall from their eyes.

And now in Jerusalem the disciples pass a day with the Christ in which many dramatic scenes follow each other. As their Master sets foot on the threshold of the Temple precincts, chaos breaks out. Everywhere there is panic and terror; tables are overturned, money rolls across the ground. It is a reversal of the ecstatic jubilation of yesterday.

Then the night is again spent at Bethany, and the next morning Jesus and his disciples come by Bethphage at dawn. There the sight of the withered tree suddenly confronts them, and the disciples ask Jesus to explain it to them. It was no crude miracle, as though Jesus through his angry word of power had robbed a creature of its existence. How could he have destroyed a tree belonging to the people who had willingly placed at his disposal the ass and the ass's colt! No, it was a spiritual act, denoting an important moment in the mystery of Holy Week.

The signal for the decisive battle had already been given through the awakening of Lazarus. But it was on Palm Sunday that the full being of the Christ was revealed and it was this that stirred men's souls. But this moment had also its simple human meaning. Jesus, as other devout people, was going to the Temple for prayer and sacrifice in preparation for the Passover. But a foreboding of great decision had seized him. Things could no longer go on painlessly, as in the past. The Christ sees that mere enthusiasm is superficial and untrustworthy, but as yet he is not constrained to repulse it. That he cannot directly reprove the people is shown next day by a similar scene before the Temple. This time it is children who cry out *Hosanna*. When his enemies ask maliciously, 'Do you hear what they are saying?,' he replies, 'Yes, have you never read: By the mouth of children and newborn infants I am praised?' (Matt.21:16).

But now the night at Bethany has come between and there is a certain contrast with the mood of Palm Sunday. He approaches the fig tree at Bethphage and wishes to show the disciples how little value should be attached to the *Hosanna* of the previous day. All that it represented was the last fruits of the old visionary clairvoyance, given by nature, and bound to the body. The words he addresses to the fig tree are, as it were, a challenge to the whole realm of ancient ecstatic vision. Here a momentous decision is made in the history of humanity. Jesus rejects the *Hosannas* of the people, and himself brings about the transition to their cry, 'Crucify him.' He has the courage himself to summon the spiritual blindness through which the people will fanatically demand his death. Humanity must act out of a consciousness that leads to freedom, even if it means tragedy; even if men in their spiritual blindness nail him on the cross.

When the fig tree of Bethphage is seen again by the disciples on the morning of Tuesday, a wholesome disenchantment has come over them. They see the withered tree, just there on the spot which they have always treated with veneration. They receive teaching from Jesus which serves as a prelude to what they will hear from him in the evening hour on the Mount of Olives. Then they are led to realize that some day there will be a new *sight* for humankind, and that *faith* is to be the germ of this. Jesus says to his disciples: 'Yes, I say to you, if you have the power of faith without wavering, then you will not only bring forth the fruit of the fig tree, but you will be able to say to this mountain: Rise up and throw yourself into the sea, and it will be so.' There will be no barrier before you; the mountain of the sense world which bars your sight will disappear. Through the rocky stone of earthly existence you will see the true nature of things permeated by divine thought. The power of faith will bring to maturity in the human heart the eye of the new vision. The Sermon on the Mount speaks of this: 'Blessed are the pure in heart, for they shall see God.' But in between the old moon-vision, no longer serviceable, and the new sunlike vision of the heart, there lies a time of darkness, of blindness to the spirit. And in this stage of blindness Christ will be nailed on the cross.

On that Monday in Holy Week Christ rejects a temptation. Had he allied himself with the ancient clairvoyant forces, he might have found public recognition. Not only would people have cried *Hosanna*; they would have crowned him king. But a final pronouncement is made: Christ will form no link with the ancient forces. His sole aim is that humanity should find the way to awakening and freedom. It is no unloving curse that he utters on the fig trees of those who had lent him the ass and its colt. He acts purely from the nature of his own being. He is the sun, and when the sun rises, the moon perforce grows pale. So the moon-forces of the old vision fade away.

The Christ appears before the Temple. Many hundreds of pilgrims have assembled, and around the Temple buying and selling, trading and bargaining are being carried on. In the Temple itself a feverish activity prevails; sacrificial beasts are needed for the festival, the Passover lamb must be slaughtered. This is a source of business; for the animals have to be bought before they are sacrificed. Old Annas, the notorious miser of world history, knows how to make a profit. He has already made a vast fortune from this market. He has been the wire-puller in the political compromise with the Romans which is the basis of the Temple business. The pilgrims must change their local currency into the official currency which is valid in the Temple. This is Roman currency. Thus the Temple comprises also a Roman Exchange market. The Roman fiscal officers have been admitted to the Temple, although they were representatives of the cult of Caesar, because it was hoped by this compromise to keep them at least out of the Holy of Holies.

Now Christ comes on the scene. He is coming to fulfil the custom of the feast. But the fire of his burning will has its effect. There is no need for him to say much. The people are immediately seized with panic. Terror-stricken, they realize into what decadence they have fallen. Something similar had taken place at the feast of the Passover, three years before. At that time the terrifying effect came from the divine nature of the Christ, despite the conscious restraint which was still exercised by Jesus. But now the divinity is entirely transformed into humanity; it has become intensity of will. He has the right to tear down the mask of decadence of the Temple.

The sun of Christ shines, and the glimmer of the moon must fade away on the moon-hill of Mount Moriah. The spectres of the night flee from the sun. In place of a magnificent Temple appears a simple room on Mount Zion. There, in the Last Supper, the seed of a new ritual and worship, a sunlike sacrament, will be sown. The moon-religion of antiquity will be superseded on the evening of Maundy Thursday, when on the sun-hill of Mount Zion, Christ gives bread and wine to his disciples.

Tuesday in Holy Week

In the early morning Jesus enters the city with his disciples once more. The waves of acclamation and enthusiasm have long since died away. Jesus is already involved in the tension of his coming decision, but he will be obedient to the Law up to the last moment and fulfil the sacred customs of preparation for the Passover. There is the feeling that he himself is the sacrifice to be offered. The people's hatred is already surging up to him as flames that will consume the sacrifice. From day to day the powerful sense of his spiritual presence in the city has increased. The more silent the crowds, the more majestically his sovereign will shines in his countenance. Now the day of Mars has been reached and the conflict flares up in earnest. The crowd is silent; their leaders are full of anxiety; their fear produces the hatred which leads to the attack. Every hostile group sends out assailants. One after another they accost him with their crafty questions. What would otherwise be a blow in the face or a dagger-thrust takes on the guise of questioning.

First of all the members of the Jewish Sanhedrin approach: the high priests, scribes and elders. They ask Jesus what authority he has for his actions; He is required to legalize himself. Then come the others, the Pharisees and the Herodians, and put the insidious question: 'Is it lawful to give tribute unto Caesar?' The Sadducees follow. They ask Jesus' opinion concerning the resurrection of the dead. Finally, a single question, intending to expose him before all the people, asks which commandment he considers the most important of all.

These attacks, marking the outbreak of hostilities, are the best proof of how strongly the being of Christ was making itself felt. Just as dogs bark and bite only when they are afraid, so these ostensible questions, which are really arrows of hate, are the outcome of fear.

Jesus answers each of the four questions. He is not satisfied, however, with parrying the blows aimed at him; he accepts battle and fights back with weapons of the spirit. He uses powerful pictures. During the three previous years he has spoken to the people in poetic parables, and to the disciples in parables of deep mystery. To his opponents he now speaks parables of conflict. He tells the parable of the husbandmen to whom the vineyard has been entrusted; how they afterwards refuse to surrender the harvest, slay the owner's messengers, and finally even his son. The opponents realize that they themselves are meant. In fact, Jesus is telling his enemies that they will slay him. His parable is a last endeavour to reach the souls of his enemies. Perhaps it may yet bring them to an awakening; perhaps even now they may be shocked into self-knowledge.

The parable of the royal marriage feast follows. Guests are called to the marriage, and they all excuse themselves from attending. Then the invitation is passed on to strangers, to people who seem to have no occasion for coming. Because the duly licensed and established seekers after God have proved to be hypocrites, God finally summons people whom one would not credit with seeking the divine. This is a direct thrust at his opponents, who are the privileged religious people by ancient tradition. But when the fate of those wearing no wedding garment is described, a stern mirror is held up before the whole of humanity. The parable of the king's marriage feast is the strongest thrust dealt on the Mars day of Passion Week, directed ultimately to all people.

The Christ goes further; he now questions back. 'Whose son is the Messiah?' he asks. They answer: 'The son of David.' Christ cites the words of Psalm 110, well known to them, to show that David describes the Messiah as his Lord. He asks: 'How then can David, inspired by the Spirit, call him his Lord ... Since David calls him his Lord, how then can he be his son?' Christ exposes the superficial piety of his questioners; they are looking only at the earthly. The first step towards grasping the divine is to see that the Messiah is a Son of God and not a son of men. Christ is showing them at this moment what they should recognize in him, but they do not recognize it.

And so it comes to the fourth counterblow. This is the ninefold *woe*, the denunciation of the Pharisees which is followed by the lament over Jerusalem, as over a world doomed to destruction. At the beginning of his work, in the trusted circle of the disciples, Jesus once pronounced the nine beatitudes in the Sermon on the Mount, the ninefold ideal of Spirit Man. Now at the close of his earthly path he sets the ninefold shadow over against the ninefold light. The denunciations are a combative unmasking of those who are inimical to God, just as the beatitudes were a revelation of man's ninefold relation to God. In the lamentation over Jerusalem there is the reverse of the promise of the 'city set upon a hill,' which in the Sermon on the Mount calls up for the first time the picture of the heavenly Jerusalem.

As the day begins to decline, Jesus leaves the city with his disciples, as was his custom. He climbs the hill of Gethsemane beyond the vale of Kidron, and enters the garden which had been the scene of so much intimate teaching; but he does not continue towards Bethphage and Bethany. At the top of the Mount of Olives, where a wonderful peace surrounds them, he makes the disciples rest. Still imbued with the conflict which has been waged all day, he begins to speak to his disciples in the open air for the last time. And the words with which he instructs them are no less powerful than those he has spoken in the spiritual fight with his opponents. The courageous deeds which have been accomplished by the soul during the day call up an echo from the gods. The Christ can make revelations to his disciples as never before. What he gives on this evening, sometimes known as the Little Apocalypse, opens vast horizons of the future.

So it is always in life. If real deeds have ripened during the day, then evening and night call down a heavenly echo. The results of a day do not only lie in what has been directly achieved. When the activities of the day have knocked on the doors of the spiritual world, then with night descending the gates of another world can open. Genuine inner strength employed during the day is met by a spiritual response.

The present moment becomes translucent. All through the day the disciples have been with Christ near the Temple. He has shown them that it is all doomed to destruction. The destruction of Jerusalem and the Temple was a spiritual necessity and if it had not come to pass four decades later through the Roman army, it would have had to be brought about in some other way. As the vision of the downfall of the Temple rises before the disciples, a great cosmic catastrophe seems to shine through it. It is the downfall of a whole world that the Christ sets before their souls. The division, manifest all day between the hostile opponents and the little band striving for discipleship — this too becomes translucent. The history of the world will bring nothing less than a great dividing of humankind. Some strive towards the divine; others strive against it. And no matter how imposing what is accomplished on earth by the antagonists, it is only the outcome of a hidden fear. That which silently germinates in the little group seeking union with the divine will bear in itself the future of the world.

Jesus continues the apocalyptic discourse, and gives the disciples the most intimate parables that he can possibly give them, the two parables of the Second Coming. He had already spoken of the Son of Man coming in the clouds, while all around the universal storm is raging. He had pointed to a future where a new revelation of Christ must force a way for itself amidst hurricanes of destruction. Now, in the two parables of the ten virgins and the talents, he shows the disciples what people must do to prepare themselves for the return of the Christ. Some day the bridegroom of the soul will come; some day the one who entrusted the talents to his servants when he went away, will come again to claim the reckoning. Down below in the Temple the 'woe,' 'woe,' sounded as anti-beatitudes; now the day ends with another Sermon on the Mount, one even more sublime. With this final and most intimate teaching Christ arms the disciples with equipment of courage for millennia ahead. The parables of the Second Coming, and in particular the concluding vision of the division of humanity into sheep and goats, are to serve the disciples as provision on the road for many incarnations.

The words of the Tuesday in Holy Week, taken together, are wonderfully relevant to every battle of light with darkness, every struggle for Christian discipleship in conflict with Christ's enemies. Goethe's statement that world history is nothing but a continuous fight of belief against unbelief touches the truth that is given in all detail during the Tuesday of Holy Week. All opposition to Christ and hostility to the spirit has its root in unbelief, in deeply hidden weakness and fear. Discipleship of Christ means courage and strength. The battle is not necessarily fought by one group of men against another. It must be carried on within ourselves. In each human soul fear and courage, opposition to Christ and discipleship of Christ, are mingled.

The fighting parables directed against Christ's opponents make it clear that fear is always at the root of enmity to the spirit. The egotism of the husbandmen of the vineyard, who are unwilling to surrender the fruits of the harvest, is the offspring of inner weakness and fear — as is every egotism. When a man learns to leave and sacrifice all because he realizes that all he can ever possess is the property of God, the first seed of courage is born.

The denunciations uttered by Christ are an ever plainer unmasking of unbelief. They begin at once with words which tear away the mask not only of denial of the spirit, but of every kind of dragooning of human souls: 'Woe to you, scribes and Pharisees, you hypocrites! You shut the kingdom of the heavens against men. You cannot find entrance yourselves, and so you want to bar the entrance to those who can find it.' (Matt.23:13).

To work upon one's own soul demands the greatest courage. The wedding garment is the soul become radiant through purification and prayer. The oil in the lamps is a picture of the forces of the soul to be won by struggle. The talents increased by personal effort are the spiritual organs in man brought to further development.

In his answer concerning the tribute money Jesus shows that true courage attained through constant inner effort is able to hold the balance between earthly duties and spiritual ideals, and in so doing gains sovereignty over all earthly conditions. Even if, as at that time, a monster occupies the throne, he is able to say 'Render unto Caesar the things which are Caesar's and unto God the things which are God's.'

In the concluding vision of the dividing of humanity, the true quality of inner courage is described: 'Yes, I say to you, what you did for
the least of my brothers, that you did for me.' The true path to the
spirit shows itself in the power to love. Love is the opposite of fear. All
genuine inner development begins with inner courage and finds its
goal in love. True love of men is identical with love for Christ himself,
so his words of spiritual battle end in words of love.

Wednesday in Holy Week

The 'Still Week' — as Holy Week is called in some countries — is not
really still until the middle day is past. On Palm Sunday the city was
in a state of tremor; on Monday the tables of the vendors and money-
changers were overturned in the Temple; on Tuesday, sword-thrusts
were dealt in spiritual conflict between Christ and his opponents. It is
not until the last part of the week that stillness descends. Wednesday,
Mercury's day, is the turning point. The mercurial element of living
movement, represents the transition from the first unquiet days of the
'Still Week' to those in which the consummation of Christ's life moves
into ever deeper stillness.

Towards evening on Wednesday a scene stands out which,
although it has also occurred before, takes on a special significance on
this middle day of balance. Christ has turned from the tumult of the
city to the quiet country town of Bethany, beyond the Mount of Olives.
He stays in the circle of those with whom he is particularly united. A
meal has been prepared for him as on other evenings. But it is as
though a certain radiance fell upon the scene, shining in advance from
the meal which will be celebrated the next day. A presentiment of the
Last Supper hovers round the community at table. The country town
of Bethany, quiet as it is, has shortly before been the scene of the raising of Lazarus, the event which had given the signal for battle. Lazarus
is one of those gathered round the table; and it is he, as we know, who
is described by the gospel as resting on the heart of Jesus the next
evening. At the Last Supper it is he who is nearest to Christ, both outwardly and inwardly.

Two women also belong to the community at table, Martha and
Mary Magdalene, whom the Gospel of John states to be the sisters of
Lazarus. They have been led by the hand of providence into this circle,

which is more related by the spirit than by blood. In the life of each of these three persons there has been an event which brought a radical transformation. For Lazarus it was the awakening from the grave, the great release of the John-spirit for its flight to the heights. For Mary Magdalene the event lay somewhat farther back; it is called in the gospel a 'driving out of devils.' She had been healed of the tragedy of 'possession' and had experienced the freeing and purifying of her soul. For Martha there had also been a significant event; she is said in early Christian tradition to be the woman who was healed of the issue of blood. Destiny had decreed that she should bring with her into life a weakness through which her bodily organism was unable to hold its forces together. Through meeting with the one who could heal her, a staying power, a formative force, drew into her body, just as an inner peace had entered the soul of Mary Magdalene. The brother and sisters of Bethany became the intimate friends of Christ through healings of the spirit, the soul and the body.

As they all sit at table with the disciples, Mary is recorded as having anointed the feet of Christ with precious pure nard ointment and wiped them with her hair. John's Gospel says that the whole house was filled with the perfume. Mary Magdalene had performed a similar act a year and a half previously. She had experienced a freeing and redeeming through her meeting with the Christ, and in order to show her overflowing gratitude she had, as the Gospel of Luke describes, anointed the feet of Christ and dried them with her hair. John's Gospel, in the introductory words to the awakening of Lazarus, refers to this earlier scene (11:2). Mary Magdalene is described in St Luke's Gospel as the 'great sinner,' and it is possible, according to old traditions, that she was a prostitute, driven by demons, in the worldly spa town of Tiberias, near her home at Magdala. But what does her act of anointing signify now? It is the type and symbol of a sacramental act. Therefore, when others declare her deed extravagant and become indignant, Christ can accept what this woman does as a sacrament of death, as a fulfilment of the Last Anointing. On the occasion of the earlier anointing he had said, 'Her many sins are forgiven her, for she has shown much love.' And one can feel how Mary has since been able to deepen the natural forces of earthly love erring on false paths, and transmute them into religious devotion, and the capacity for sacrifice.

Then the solemn stillness is suddenly broken by a figure who forms a complete contrast to Mary Magdalene. It is one of the apostles, and as he sees the deed of Mary he loses all self-control. This is Judas. He says that the precious money which has just been squandered could have been given to the poor, and thus many social needs might have been relieved. John's Gospel, however, makes it plain that his real motives are not the ostensible ones. The gospel openly calls him a thief. It may well be that the anger which Judas felt at the deed of Mary Magdalene gave the final impetus to his act of betrayal. He had waited a long time in tense expectation that Jesus would come forward publicly: then a political miracle would inevitably follow. In his feverish impatience, it seems to him that Christ wastes his time; and finally at Bethany his patience can endure no more. In uncontrolled irritation he goes out to those who lie in wait for the Christ. The second crucial event of the Wednesday is the betrayal by Judas.

Both Judas and Mary Magdalene are typical Mercury people; they are active and temperamental. One of the virtues of their nature is that they are never tedious; something is always happening round them. Mary Magdalene, however, subdues her restlessness and transforms it into devotion, peace and the capacity for love. One can see from the gospel account that true devotion is the final achievement of an active soul, a soul for whom peace is not mere immobility, but mobility redeemed, made inward. Mary Magdalene has been storm-tossed; she has endured sinister experiences. But now an intense power of devotion grows from all that was formerly dark and disturbing. This intensity will later lift her above all other human beings; to her it is granted to be the first to meet and behold the Risen Christ.

Judas is the type of the restless man who must always be outwardly active. He pretends to want something for the poor. However good and commendable social activity may be, it is often only self-deception. The underlying motive is not always a genuine social impulse, but very often one's own inner restlessness. Many people would be most unhappy if they were obliged to do nothing for a time. It would then be seen that their social zeal is no true inner activity, but a yielding to an unacknowledged weakness. In Judas this kind of mercurial soul meets with a dark fate. His unrest springs from a deeply hidden fear, and it leads to his betrayal of Christ Jesus. Such a soul cannot show devotion; above all, it cannot love. A restless person is not capable of real love; for love is possible only where the soul has found peace. Thus in the two figures, Mary Magdalene and Judas, two roads separate, as at a crossroads. One leads to the realization of the nearness of Christ; the other into dark night, into the tragedy of suicide.

Martha, the other sister of Lazarus, is a transition, as it were, between Judas and Mary Magdalene. Luke's Gospel tells the story of Mary and Martha earlier on, and has a purpose in doing so. Martha is the constantly active one who cannot exist without undertaking some service. One cannot deny the genuine nature of her devotion, but one must not be blind to the fact that the unrest from which she was healed in the body has remained in her soul. Mary, who listens with devotion, is described as the one who has chosen the good part.

The figures taking part in these scenes on the Wednesday show us the crossroads which we must face before we may hope for admittance to the sphere of Maundy Thursday. The ways separate in face of the mystery of the sacrament. Judas is the man without ritual. He becomes restless and loses self-control when he comes into the sphere of true ceremonial worship. Mary Magdalene is the sacramental soul. On the following evening, when the circle of disciples will be united in the sacrament as under a great dome, it will be apparent who is nearer to Mary, and who to Judas.

Mercury, who for the Greco-Roman world was both the god of healing and also the god of merchants and of thieves, comes now into the orbit of the Christ-sun. The scene in the house of Lazarus and her sisters at Bethany shows how Mercury, the god of healing, can himself be healed by the sun of Christ.

Maundy Thursday

On Maundy Thursday evening a holy stillness descends, and all the clamour of the first half of the week passes into silence. By day the sounds of swarming streets, the bargaining and noisy talking of thousands of Passover pilgrims, have reached their peak. Then, shortly before the deep red sun has sunk in the west, faced by the silver disc of the rising full moon, the trumpets sound from the Temple and give the signal for the beginning of the day of preparation. On the eve of the Passover, the faithful of the old covenant are preparing for the Sabbath, which begins on the following evening. In every house people gather round the table to eat the Passover lamb in the circle of their blood-relations. The streets are suddenly emptied and an oppressive silence falls. It is the curfew of Passover night, when the destroying angel is abroad, as once long ago, in Egypt.

So Jesus and his disciples also withdraw to the room in which they are to celebrate the Passover. The stillness of this room is enhanced, for providence has brought them to no private dwelling, but to the house of the order of the Essenes. The Cenacle, which the Essene brotherhood has placed at the service of Jesus and his disciples for the eve of the Passover, stands on holy ground. Here, on Mount Zion, a sanctuary of humanity has existed from times immemorial. Immediately opposite, also on a traditional spot, stands the house of Caiaphas, the ancestral home of the Sadducean order. A circle has gathered there also to celebrate the Passover. They can scarcely give thought to the coming feast, for they are actively concerned with a plan of hatred and enmity. For a time the struggle must cease; the holy hour must first have passed. And so his enemies themselves give the order — 'Seek to arrest him, but not at the Feast.' In the room where Jesus is assembled with his disciples, the words of Psalm 23 are fulfilled: 'Thou preparest a table before me in the presence of my enemies.'

The Passover lamb on the table in the Cenacle assumes a new meaning. At the table is seated the one of whom John the Baptist could say: 'See, the Lamb of God, who takes the sin of the world upon himself' (John 1:29). Nowhere in that hour nor ever before nor since, has the Passover lamb been so near to the one for whom it was an image. For thousands of years the eating of the Passover lamb was a prophetic custom, and now the fulfilment of the prophecy is at hand. The apostle Paul will presently be able to say, 'Our passover lamb has been killed: that is Christ' (1Cor.5:7). In the Cenacle, prophecy and fulfilment meet each other. A heavy foreboding fills the room; separation and tragedy rest in the air. Christ's death of sacrifice throws its shadow before and the consciousness of the disciples has a heavy test to endure.

The ancient tradition of blood-sacrifice has its symbol in the Passover lamb upon the table. The magic of the blood, signified by all pre-Christian blood-sacrifices, has an active power. It was believed that the shedding of the blood of pure sacrificial animals was able to transport people's souls, formerly more loosely united with the body, into a state of ecstasy. Divine forces from the other world could then be reflected in human conditions. And now the ancient sacrifice loses its significance for ever in the Cenacle on Mount Zion. The divine being has now himself entered this world; therefore the old blood-sacrifice has become superfluous. The power which it was sought formerly to bring down from other worlds is now there, come to unite itself inseparably with this world. The Passover lamb has magical forces no longer, for in earth-existence itself a seed of heavenly forces is being formed. The lamb becomes the pure image of the sacrificial deed of divine love.

On the table of the holy meal, however, there is also bread and wine. And when the ancient custom of the Passover meal has been observed, Christ takes, to the astonishment of the disciples, these other representatives of food and drink and adds a new meal to that ordained by the Old Testament. It is a new and unexpected deed when Christ gives to his disciples bread and wine and says: 'Take, this is my body — this is my blood.' But these symbols are not on the table by accident. Something comes to light which has always existed. Externally blood-sacrifices were carried out in the Temple in the presence of the people, but in hidden sanctuaries esoteric sun-mysteries had always been preserved, where bread and wine were the symbols of the sun god. On the very spot where now the circle were gathered at the Last Supper, the sanctuary of Melchizedek had stood, whence he took forth bread and wine and carried them down to the valley of Kidron to dispense them to Abraham. Now bread and wine became more than symbols. The divine sun-spirit is present in Christ, and as he distributes the bread he can say: 'This is my body,' and in handing the disciples the chalice: 'This is my blood.' His soul surrenders itself and streams into the bread and wine. In the twilight of the room bread and wine are enveloped with a shining sun-aura. Inasmuch as they become body and blood of the Christ soul, they become body and blood of the sun-spirit himself. All the sun-mysteries of antiquity were but prophecy; at this moment they grow into fulfilment. In the transition from the blood offerings of the past to the bloodless offering of bread and wine, the whole idea of sacrifice changed. Ancient sacrifices were always material offerings. Now the sacrifice of the soul is founded, and there begins the true tradition of inner sacrifice. The lunar sacrifices of antiquity are at an end; the solar sacrifice of Christianity comes into being. Christianity, the true sun religion, dawns in this evening hour.

By performing significant acts before and after the meal, Christ brings about a fourfold whole, anticipating the four parts of the central Christian sacrament which thenceforward will be continually cele-brated. Before the meal he follows the custom observed in the order of the Essenes and washes the feet of each of the disciples, even of Judas. A deeply moving picture, unfathomable in its full significance: Christ utterly surrendering himself in loving devotion, on which his death will soon set the seal. After the meal another ceremonial act is observed by Christ, this time in accord with the custom followed by all the neighbouring households at this hour. When the Passover has been eaten, the head of the family begins to recite from the *Haggada,* the his-tory of the people from ancient times set down in legendary form. With Christ, too, the meal is followed by a discourse. This is recorded and gathered together by St John in the wonderful Farewell Discourse culminating in the High Priestly Prayer (John 14–17).

Four stages are passed through: the washing of the feet, the Passover lamb, the bread and wine, and the Farewell Discourse. The washing of the feet sums up in a pictorial act the essence of Christ's teaching: 'This is the task I put before you, that you love one another' (15:12). The washing of the feet is, as it were, the last of the parables, enacted, not merely spoken. It teaches love as the ultimate purpose of Christ's gospel. The eating of the Passover lamb corresponds in the structure of the communion service to the stage of the Offering, which follows the Reading of the Gospel. The image of the Offering emerges: Christ the Passover Lamb who on the next day dies for humanity on the cross.Then comes the third stage: Christ gives the disciples bread and wine. For the first time Transubstantiation is consummated, form-ing the third part of the sacrament, after the Reading of the Gospel and the Offering. Now the spiritual lights up in earthly substance. In the Farewell Discourse, the fourth stage, Christ imparts to the disciples the most intimate information about his own being. These words are body and blood of Christ in a still higher degree than the bread and wine. The soul of Christ gives itself to the souls of the disciples who are only able to receive them as yet as though in a dream. Only John, who lies at the breast of Jesus, and listens to the speaking heart of Christ, is able in his gospel to preserve for humanity a reflection of this moment.

Christ, from whom proceeds the stream of cosmic love, speaks at the same time as the spirit of wisdom. It is as though Jupiter, the god of wisdom, has appeared in new form among men.

The sacred Round Table breaks up dramatically. It is a strict regulation of the Passover that on this night no one may leave the protection of the house. If he does so, he meets the destroying angel. The streets remain empty of people. In spite of this, at a certain moment, someone does go out; he does not delay after he has received the bread from Jesus' hand. St John's Gospel adds: 'It was night.' It was also night within Judas; at this moment Satan entered into him. Judas goes to the house opposite, where Caiaphas and his circle are keeping the Passover. They are ready and eager for the business that Judas wants to transact.

The soul of Judas founders on the mystery of the sacrament. On the evening before, as the sacramental mood unfolded in the house at Bethany, he was already seized with the demon of unrest. In the Cenacle he has met the sacramental substance for the second time. Peace within himself would alone enable him to receive the blessing of peace through the sacrament, but this he does not possess. So that which could dispense peace to him serves to throw him into the final restlessness, into the Ahrimanic displacing of the ego, and possession.

Once more the Passover is broken. Jesus rises from the table and beckons to the astonished disciples. They follow him out into the night, where the light of the full moon had for some time been almost extinguished. It is passing through an eclipse. The frosty chills of winter giving place to spring begin to be felt as Jesus goes with his disciples to Gethsemane.

The two acts of going-out-into-the-night symbolize inner events. The going out of Judas shows that his true self has abandoned him; outside he meets the angel of death in reality. Ahrimanic spirits make him their pawn. The going-out of Christ is a picture of the free surrender of the soul which has been from the beginning the cosmic bearer of sacrifice. As Judas goes out, the gospel says, 'It was night' and the soul of Judas is also shrouded in night. As the Christ goes out, one could say, 'It was day.' A golden shimmer mingles with the chilly night as the Christ goes down with the disciples the same path into the valley that was trodden two thousand years before by Melchizedek, carrying down bread and wine.

The shining aura which people saw radiating from the being of Christ on Palm Sunday has now contracted into much deeper levels. No one perceives it, yet the world receives a new glory on this holy evening, which is more an Easter Eve than an eve of Good Friday. On that other Thursday, Ascension day six weeks later, the seed of light, whose growth began in the Cenacle, will have already spread over the whole earth with cosmic power.

Good Friday

As the *still* week really enters into stillness, the bearing of Jesus changes. His fiery fighting will is no longer evident. When between midnight and sunrise the band of soldiers lays hand upon him whom Judas has kissed, he does not oppose them. Rather, he opposes Peter who wants to fight for him. Then he is seized by rough hands and dragged through the city, from one end to the other. He is apparently delivered, helpless, to those who scourge him, press the crown of thorns on his brow, spit upon him and strike him in the face. The witnesses of the tragedy are overcome with anguish as he who has no physical strength left is forced to carry the heavy cross and is nailed upon it by the executioners with pitiless cruelty. What has become of the fighting power which blazed in him during the first days of the week? Has he abandoned the battle against the blindness and wickedness of men? No, the fight which was waged on the human level on the previous days is now carried on in a higher sphere, and so takes on still more powerful dimensions. Christ is not fighting against flesh and blood, but against the invisible demonic powers from whose tyranny he will deliver humanity. He fights against the Luciferic powers, the glittering beings of deceptive light, who want to estrange man from the earth and, likewise, against the Ahrimanic powers who want to harden and fetter man to dead matter. As Christ seems to lay down the weapons, he is really following the satanic powers into their hiding-places in order to overcome them there.

Ahriman displays his power over people most triumphantly when he approaches in the form of death. In humanity's evolution up to the 'turning-point of time,' death which had formerly been a friend of man had taken on more and more the features of Ahriman. The dark power knew how to use man's destiny of death to make it his sharpest weapon. The power of death is not only that we must die; it becomes really manifest only after death. When we have laid aside our earthly body it must then be proved whether we can still maintain a connection with what takes place on earth among those to whom we belong. Here lies death's actual power — that it can wrest us from earthly things and thrust us out into the unbridgeable exile of life on the other side. The Ahrimanic power of death uses the earth to mock at man. During earthly life it binds him to the world of matter; it makes all sorts of promises of earthly fulfilment, which are no longer kept after death. The more a man is attached to the things of 'this side' during life, the more inexorably he is affected by 'other-sidedness' after death. Only those people who have gained a firm foothold in the life of the spirit during life on earth can after death remain helpfully united with those who are still living on earth. After death we have only as much spiritual command over matter as we have gained upon earth.

When on Maundy Thursday Christ dispenses the Last Supper to the disciples in the peace of the Cenacle, there seems to be no conflict. And yet what a wonderful victory over the spirit of dead matter is shown when the Christ takes in his hand the earthly substances of bread and wine, and makes them luminous through the sun-force of his heart. He wrests the terrestrial creature from the powers of darkness and makes it the body and blood of his being of light. As he is able during his life to ensoul the earthly elements so that these become radiant, he will have all the more power to do so after death.

In Gethsemane the fight against the power of death enters a decisive phase. Here in the quiet grove of the Mount of Olives, where he has so often been with his disciples for intimate teaching, he must now withstand the most dangerous attack of the enemy in utmost loneliness.* The community which he has just established in the upper room for the future wellbeing of humanity does not bring help and benefit to himself. The consciousness of the disciples has not grown to the

---

* From the first to the fourth gospel the text contains an ever clearer revelation of the secret of Gethsemane. The first two gospels say only 'Jesus came with the disciples to a place called Gethsemane.' We assume that it was merely some unfamiliar spot. In Luke the text takes a new turn: 'And he left the house and went to the Mount of Olives as was his custom. And the disciples followed him.' It is not just any road, but one which leads to a spot where Jesus had often stayed. John's Gospel brings the full revelation: 'After these words Jesus left the house with his disciples and crossed over the Kidron brook. On the other side there was a garden which he and his disciples entered. This place was also known to Judas who betrayed him; for Jesus had often gathered his disciples around him there.' (18:1–2). Gethsemane is thus a place where esoteric instruction had been given to the disciples. The olive grove reached to the summit of the Mount of Olives. It was also the scene of the Little Apocalypse on the Tuesday evening of Passion week.

greatness of the moment. Judas has gone out into the night of betrayal, but the others, too, leave their Master in the lurch. They are absorbed in the twilight of their sleep in Gethsemane, out of which Peter will deny Christ.

It is not inner weakness and fear of death with which Christ has to wrestle in Gethsemane. One could not misunderstand more tragically the whole Passion of Christ than by thinking that Jesus prayed in Gethsemane that he might still be spared from death. Not fear of death, but death itself assails him. Death, already apprehensive of losing control over him, appears before him to lay hold of him. The destroying angel wants to possess him. The secret of the conflict in Gethsemane lies in the fact that death wants to outwit Jesus. It wants to wrest him away too soon, before he has ended his work and filled the last vestige of the earthly vessel with his spirit.

For three years the fire of divine egohood has burned in the body and soul of Jesus. The human vessel — from within outwards — has thus already been consumed almost to ashes. What still has to be suffered and completed demands so much strength from the earthly sheaths that there is a real danger of premature death. Ahriman lies in wait and hopes to make use of this moment. Luke, the physician, describes with precise words what happens, when he says 'And as he was in the throes of death he prayed with even greater intensity.' In the clinical sense of the term, the death-struggle had already come. When Luke adds, 'and his sweat became as drops of blood which fell to the earth,' he adds exact symptoms of the agony of death (Luke 22:44).

But Christ is victorious and death is repulsed. With the mightiest force of prayer ever known on earth he wrestles to remain in the body. It is an echo of this fight when he speaks on the cross the words that seem to betray a weakness: 'I thirst.' He still remains, even immediately before he breathes out his soul, true to the earth. It is not his will to pass into the spiritual world simply through dying. It is his will to remain united with the earth when he goes through death, and it is this that is to be his conquest over death. He wrestles to enter still more deeply into the earthly world of matter which he bears in himself through his physical body. There is still a last remnant to be ensouled. This, too, he will not abandon to the Prince of this World, who has begun to count on the material realm of the earthly as being in his possession once and for all.

The drama returns to human scenes and conditions. On the morning of Good Friday Christ confronts the whole of humanity, as represented by the three figures of Caiaphas, Pilate and Herod. Then the way leads up to Golgotha. Nails are driven by the soldiers into the hands and feet of the Christ, and it seems as though he allows everything to come about quite passively. In fact, through the medicine of bitter pain, his inmost being has gained the ultimate power of spirit over matter, so that death can no longer claim him. The Ahrimanic death-powers realize this, and appear for their last effort, furious that their might has been of no avail. When the sun is darkened during the sultry midday hours of Good Friday, it is as though the demon of the sun were straining to the utmost against the god of the sun. And when the earth is shaken by the earthquake, all the demons of the earth seem to storm forward in an endeavour to help the satanic death-power to victory. Antichrist moves the earthly elements and even the forces of the heavens. However, death can strip nothing from the sovereignty of Christ's spirit, from his authority over all earth existence. It is in accord with his own will that the cosmic powers rise up in the hour of Golgotha. He has said to the officers in Gethsemane, 'But this is your hour: Darkness rules' (Luke 22:53).

In the midst of the darkness a mystery was manifested on Golgotha which may be mentioned only with great reserve. The body which hung on the cross began to radiate light. In many country districts of Europe, in a field or at the roadside, one can find crucifixes with a gilded figure on a black wood cross. A momentous secret of Good Friday is living here in the naive wisdom of folklore. A mysterious brilliance broke through the dreadful noonday night. The sun of Christ revealed itself as the physical sun suffered eclipse. A ray of Easter already wove itself into the darkness of Good Friday.

The last of the Seven Words from the Cross, 'It is finished,' does not refer to the sufferings which have been surmounted, but to the complete conquest over the power of death which has been achieved. Whereas death casts into the banishment of 'the other side' the soul of a man whom it has mocked during his lifetime with the power of earthly matter, the Christ, in dying, goes directly to the earth. The blood streams from his wounds; his soul goes with it into the body of the earth. When blood streams out from a dying man, the blood and the soul go different ways; here the soul goes *with* the blood. Later, the body is lowered into the grave; the earth opens in an earthquake and takes into itself the body of Christ. When a human body given up by the soul is lowered into the grave, body and soul go different ways. Christ's soul goes the same way, to the earth. That is the great cosmic sacrifice of love which the Christ is able to accomplish for the whole of earth-existence, because death can no longer hinder him. The earth receives the body and blood of Christ, the great communion, and therewith the medicine for the spiritualizing of all material existence is incorporated into earth existence — 'the medicine that makes whole.'

Saturday in Holy Week

The body of the Christ has been laid in the tomb belonging to Joseph of Arimathea. Saturnine heaviness hangs in the air and the meaning of Saturn's day is fulfilled. It has always been the custom of the Sabbath, as Saturn's day, for the adherents of the Old Covenant to observe it as a strictly ordained day of death-like rest. Today is the Sabbath of all Sabbaths. It is as though a fighter had gone into a dark cavern to overcome a dragon. Will he return victoriously to the light of day?

In the dark midday hour of the previous day, when Christ on the cross bowed his head and expired, the veil of the Temple 'was torn in two.' Vistas were opened into the interior of the world. Archetypal pictures formed themselves in the saturnine twilight. Table and Cross summarize the events of the last two days. Now the Tomb is added as a third archetypal symbol.

From times immemorial tombs also served as altars; all divine worship proceeded originally from the worship of the dead. People went to the tombs when they wished to commune with the gods. The souls of the departed were intermediaries between men and the gods, for since the souls of the dead could appear at the tombs, other dwellers in the spiritual world could also be met there. This was so in far-distant ages, when death was still the brother of sleep and as yet had no terrifying power over humanity. Men were not so hopelessly bound to the substance of the earthly body during physical life. So after death they were not so separated from the plane of earth. The communion of the earthly world with the spiritual world still happened like breathing in and breathing out.

In the course of millennia man entered deeper and deeper into embodiment. The more he united with earthly substance, the less was it possible for him to remain in connection with the earth after death. The gap between 'here' and 'there' became increasingly difficult to bridge. Existence after death became, as is said in the First Epistle of Peter, a prison. Humanity was in danger of being deprived of immortality, of consciousness enduring beyond death. In the realm of the dead the souls were spellbound in a state of numbness. When the Egyptians mummified their dead and prayed before the embalmed bodies, they expressed their urgent desire to hold fast to the ancient conditions. It was an attempt, despite the ever-widening gulf, to unite the souls of men with the bodily remains of earthly life. But the downward trend of destiny could not be checked and, as the pre-Christian centuries advanced, dread of death took hold of humanity. The Greek world is filled with horror of the realm of the dead; in the Old Testament the idea of immortality fades away altogether. A great religious current arose without a certainty of immortal life, and the belief of living on in one's descendants took its place.

Yet in the pre-Christian centuries souls did not live nearly so heavily in the body as they do today. Hence those who were living on earth felt the tragic fate brought on by death as an oppressive burden. Though people still went to the tombs, the souls no longer came, and the gods were absent from the altars. The feeling of anxiety in pre-Christian times derived far less from external conditions than from distress of soul. The earth seemed a parched land that had had no rain for a long time. Death became a terrifying spectre. This feeling lay at the root of the expectation of the Messiah which inspired all the peoples of pre-Christian times.

It was now between Holy Saturday and Easter. The body had been taken from the cross and laid in the grave. Providence ordained that cross and grave should stand on a spot which thousands of years before had been experienced as the centre of the earth. Between the rocky hill of Golgotha, which is a continuation of the lunar Mount Moriah, and the grave with its surrounding garden on Mount Zion, there was formerly a primal fissure in the earth's surface.* Ancient humanity saw in this the grave of Adam: here for the first time humanity was overcome by death. And so from very ancient times this

---

* See the author's *Kings and Prophets* and *Caesars and Apostles*.

primeval gorge, which splits Jerusalem into two parts, was believed to
be the gate of the underworld. In this place the cross was erected and
there today the Church of the Holy Sepulchre stands.

When now we try once more to find the inner aspect of events, it is
as though the veil was rent before another sphere. The realm of the
shades opens. In the saturnine darkness of this sphere an unexpected
light is kindled. He who died upon the cross has entered the kingdom
of the dead. One has come who is not subject to the magic compulsion
of death, One who is free of all that dulls and deadens. He carries
through death the full glory of his genius; and while on earth the dark
Sabbath of the grave prevails, in the realm of the dead the sun rises.
This is the meaning of Christ's descent into hell. In the kingdom of the
departed a glimmer of hope lit up. The spell of death was loosened,
and the prospect opened towards a future victory of the human soul
over the spell of the underworld. While it was still Holy Saturday on
earth, it was already Easter in the kingdom of the dead.

At the moment of Christ's death on Good Friday the earthquake
began and it was still rumbling in the early hours of Easter morning. It
did not cease fully all through Holy Saturday, though the powers of
nature may have adapted themselves to the spell of the silence of the
grave which belongs to this day. Rudolf Steiner has imparted from his
spiritual investigations a certain fact which may be hard to accept, but
which could be verified from a knowledge of the geological secrets
which lie in the soil of Jerusalem. As a cosmic climax to the Mystery of
Golgotha, the earthquake tore open again the original fissure which
had been filled in the time of Solomon. And thus the whole earth
became the grave of the Christ. The earth took deep into herself the
Host that was administered to her. When with the words of the creed
as it is used in the Christian Community, we express the event of Holy
Saturday, 'He was lowered into the grave of the earth,' we touch upon
the cosmic aspect of the Mystery of Golgotha. It was the physical body
and the physical blood of the human being, Jesus of Nazareth, which
was the medicine received by the earth. The sacramental stream which
has gone through humanity henceforward is linked to Easter.

It has been a right and valid principle that in all parts of the
Christian Church altars have always been formed in the likeness of a
tomb. Also the altars of the renewed sacrament in the Christian
Community have the form of a tomb. And when the members of the

congregation are assembled round them, the principle of Holy Saturday is always present. We are the ones waiting round the sacred sepulchre, and at the table and tomb of the Lord our dead can also draw near again. Those who have inwardly united themselves in life with the renewed sacrament can assuredly after death find their way to this tomb more easily than to their own graves. Souls no longer have any intensive relation to the cast-off body. But when we are assembled round the altar, they can be in our midst, and thereby strengthen our relationship to the spiritual world. The new altars are surrounded with the same play of archetypal pictures as was once the grave in the precincts of the garden on Mount Zion. The gulf is closed between this world and the other. The Easter garden begins to bloom in which our soul, like Mary Magdalene, can behold the Risen One as the gardener of a new world. The darkness of Saturn is lit up from within by the sun of Easter.

Contemporary parallels

The planetary stages of the drama of Holy Week have a significance that transcends time, and the drama is re-enacted in every detail at decisive turning-points of human history. This applies to the apocalyptic upheavals of the present day — we are passing through a Passion Week in no small measure. The turmoils and convulsions that are racking the nations today, whether expressed externally in warfare or only experienced inwardly, are not of a physical origin; it is an illusion to see their cause on the physical plane. They are brought about by the powerful entry of supersensory forces and beings into earthly existence. The new Coming of Christ represents the entry into Jerusalem on a cosmic scale. The tempestuous approach of the world of spirit is experienced dimly in humanity, and in the present clamour of war and peace, *Hosanna* and *Crucify him* are intermingled. But the cry of hatred far outweighs the song of praise.

The character of the Monday in Passion Week is plainly being manifested now. Traditional spiritual life has reached a crisis. Does not much that lately seemed to bloom, and was highly prized, suddenly seem to stand there like a withered tree? Many temples are crumbling, and only that which is really genuine can endure.

The powers of Mars kindle the torches of the Apocalypse, and anyone who is able to see through the happenings recognizes that spiritual conflicts are being waged behind the outer warfare. Light is fighting with darkness above our heads, while on earth there is the greater danger that some are fighting on the side of darkness who would fight for the light if their consciousness were sufficiently awake. In spite of this, however, a tiny group devoted to the service of the spiritual sun can win the victory. Just as once the apocalyptic vision was given to the disciples on the Mount of Olives, so there will be given to this little group an insight into the future by which they can recognize the meaning of their suffering.

People are being called upon more and more to make clear inner decisions. They either find their way to a devotional life and the sacrament, or they are thrust into the darkness by the curse of neurotic restlessness. They must choose between Mary Magdalene and Judas. In these days many must have felt, if only for moments, the light of hope which proceeds from Maundy Thursday. The question is one of consciousness. Does the soul awake, like that of John; or does it sink into the sleep of Gethsemane, like that of Peter who denied the Lord, or fall into the grip of the demons, like that of Judas who betrayed him?

The Christ is now here again among humanity; that is the real secret of our time. The Christian churches may be persecuted, Christianity rooted out; but Christ himself can at most be scourged anew, crowned with thorns and nailed on the cross. And this is done by Christians, too. No wonder that the wrath of God fills the world with its avenging tempests. Nevertheless, the inmost heart of all is the divine and infinite love. The Christ-being who is cosmic love himself dies anew in our world; dies for the salvation of those who persecute and crucify him.

Actually the whole of humanity stands waiting and hoping before a grave: Holy Saturday is here. Christ, and with him the true image of man, is held in a tomb. All that has hardened in human nature is a stony sepulchre. Are we standing on the eve of an Easter morning, or have all the sufferings and trials been endured in vain? It might seem that in the catastrophes which humanity has brought upon itself it stands further than ever from the mystery of the Resurrection. But at that time the earthquake lasted right up to Easter morning, and so we may dare to hope that even amid the upheavals taking place in our day, the angel of the Lord is there who will roll away the stone.

The motif of going forth on the night of Maundy Thursday

The moment in which Jesus leaves the Cenacle with the disciples on the night of Maundy Thursday and goes to Gethsemane is by no means depicted in a uniform manner in the four gospels. We have here another example how the language of the contradictions in the gospels can reveal important mysteries even where such contradictions refer to apparently insignificant details.

Matthew and Mark give more or less the same description of the course of the Last Supper. After Jesus has sat down at table with the disciples, the announcement of the betrayal is reported first, with the subsequent to and fro of questions and answers. This dialogue is the testing zone and once it has been passed through the sacramental mystery can be fulfilled: bread and wine are blessed and shared out. Then we have the mysterious words of Jesus about not drinking the fruit of the vine until he will drink it again in the kingdom of God. Then all those gathered for the Last Supper sing a hymn and Jesus leaves the house with the disciples and walks towards the Mount of Olives. Now it is important that in the first two gospels the conversation in the Cenacle is continued in a certain sense. If the betrayal was heralded in the Cenacle, this is now followed by the proclamation of Peter's denial. This is preceded by Jesus saying to the disciples: 'In this night you will all lose your faith in me' (Matt.26:31). In addition the harsh phrase of 'scattering abroad,' derived in Greek from the name of the scorpion, is spoken. Nevertheless, this phrase is immediately followed by the promise of Easter. Jesus tells the disciples that after his resurrection he will go ahead of them to Galilee. But Peter denies that he will lose faith in Christ, even though Jesus tells him that he will deny him thrice before the cock crows. This proclamation is denied even more by Peter through the most sacred protestations. Then the Gethsemane scene happens.

These conversations, only briefly indicated, have a different meaning if they are spoken before or after leaving the house. The process of leaving itself must have led to a kind of dissociation in the souls of the shocked disciples. The phrase about being scattered abroad increases this dissociation. An understanding of this provides a key for the mysterious phrase about Galilee: this phrase is spoken into a dissociated state of soul and also refers to a dissociated state in terms of its content.

However, the landscape of the soul into which the momentary and the later state of dissociation at Easter leads is a fundamentally different one. And that precisely is reflected in the mysterious appearance of the Galilee motif which is not meant externally but internally. The heralding of the denial is therefore both spoken into a state of dissociation and related to a future state of dissociation. The first instance is a thoroughly nocturnal dissociation whose main instrument will be Peter. Perhaps the mysterious hint which can already be perceived in the phrase about the vine is a first indication that all happenings and words of this night will lead into a dissociation which is initially tragic but then leads to salvation through the death of Christ.

In the Gospel of Luke the conversation at the Last Supper become more detailed. A transition begins to form to the great farewell address of the Gospel of John. The important thing is that Luke does not divide the words reported by him into two groups in that he reports them partly before and partly after the departure from the house. In Luke, the conversations on the way to Gethsemane in Matthew and Mark are already held in the Cenacle. It is particularly conspicuous that the pronouncement of the denial takes place before the departure from the Cenacle. The motif of departure is followed without any break by the Gethsemane scene. However, all the words spoken in Luke in connection with the Last Supper are of a mysteriousness which only becomes clearer when we understand them as spoken into the dissociated souls of the disciples. Even the strange dispute among the disciples as to who is the greatest, which is particularly strange after having received the communion, and which then flows into the words of Christ (representing the parallel in Luke to the washing of the feet in John), must in all likelihood be understood as a symptom of the state of dissociation overcoming the disciples. The phrase about the two swords with the questions and answers which it concludes must be understood as words of dissociation even more so. Inwardly the departure has already taken place both in Jesus and the disciples although Luke only reports the actual leaving of the Cenacle later. Only in this way can the apparently minor, yet very revealing, contradiction be resolved, that Luke does not have the announcement of the denial spoken outside like the first two gospels, but inside. The statement about the departure comes later in Luke than in Matthew or Mark because Luke sets out in his account the inner process of leaving with greater clarity.

In John the metamorphosis started in Luke is continued at an escalated level. John does not report about the bread and wine but the pronouncement of the betrayal and denial are woven into the account of the washing of the feet and the Passover meal, emphasized in great detail here but not mentioned in the other three gospels. Before the outer leaving of the room and the walk to Gethsemane are reported, the Gospel of John leads us for four whole chapters through the so-called farewell discourses, ending in the farewell prayer. In this way the pronouncement of the denial of Peter, which took place on the way to Gethsemane in Matthew and Mark, and which moved into the Cenacle with Luke, moves another step further into the interior of the room. The Gospel of John is the one which least indicates the shift in consciousness level caused by the dissociation. The physical course of events is most clearly evident here. But that means that the words and events which provoked the dissociation in the other disciples and the three first evangelists are grasped here with wakeful, conscious understanding.

It is all the more moving, then, how the motif of going forth appears once more in a highly significant way in the Gospel of John. Before it says at the start of Chapter 18: 'When Jesus had spoken these words, he went forth with his disciples ...' it already says in the middle of the farewell discourses at the end of Chapter 14: 'Arise, let us go hence,' or as a translation by Rudolf Steiner puts it: 'If you are ready, too, then we can leave this place.' If we takes these words of Jesus at the end of Chapter 14 as more than a meaningless phrase or as something which is forgotten as Jesus continues to talk, these words give the impression as if the last three chapters of the farewell discourses in John were spoken after Jesus had already risen from the table with the disciples and was preparing to leave the house. The majority of the farewell discourses would then have been spoken in passing on the threshold. There can be no clearer description of the inner departure before the outer leaving of the room than we find at the end of Chapter 14 in the Gospel of John. The farewell discourses are spoken from the soul of Christ who has already started to separate from his body; and in the souls of the disciples who have passed into a dissociated state of soul through shock and fear, this is only experienced as a distant lightning flash which still comes to expression in Luke to a certain extent, and which in Matthew and Mark has been completed subsumed into the short, apparently purely external account. Only the soul of John, at home in both worlds since Lazarus was awakened a short while before, is able to keep a balance between the dissociation of Christ and the dissociation of the disciples. He watches and understands the Christ soul being revealed in the process of separation without being torn into the dark, scorpion-like dissociation of the other disciples, and is thus able to grasp the sacred words of teaching at the Last Supper.

The vision of Christ

The Gospel of John is the only gospel to reflect the sphere of inspiration, in contrast to the other three which remain in the imaginative realm. Whereas the spirituality of the others culminates in the image, the element of the Gospel of John is the word as such. Thus it contains turns of phrase which in themselves remain inconspicuous but which nevertheless brightly accentuate intimate highlights from the life of Christ. The repeated return of particular formulations in John creates muted shapes which reveal important inner developments and stages.

Among these phrases, one of the most intimate is the one usually translated as 'Jesus lifted up his eyes,' *(eparas tous opthalmous)*. It occurs in three places:

> Before the feeding of the five thousand (6:5)
> Before the awakening of Lazarus (11:41)
> Before the farewell prayer (17:1)

Before the story of the feeding of the five thousand, this only designates a perceptual content: Jesus sees that a large mass of people is streaming towards him. Before the awakening of Lazarus and the last solemn section of the farewell discourses these words introduce words of prayer as if the lifting of the eyes contains a particular orientation towards the Father, who is then addressed: 'Father, I thank thee ...' 'Father, the hour is come ...' As long as we assume that Jesus looking at the crowd in need of nourishment is an outer sensory perception, a gap arises between the first and the latter two occurrences. But this is refuted by the fact that it does not say he *looks at* but he *sees* the large crowd *(theasamenos)*.

In all three occurrences this formulation is an expression for the entry of the Christ-being into a state of supersensory vision. The precise translation, as Rudolf Steiner once formulated it for John 17:1, is: 'Jesus put himself in a state of spiritual vision...' In this context it is important to note that this state leads not just to perceptions but also to contact with the seen realities and higher forces: on each occasion particular effects arise from such vision which is truly more than the pious raising of the eyes.

The three occurrences have a kind of prelude in Chapter 4 where Jesus calls on the disciples to raise their eyes *(eparate tous ophthalmous)* 'lift up the eyes of your souls! You will see the fields, shining white already and ripe for harvesting.' (4:35). Jesus opens the inner vision of the disciples so they can see the condition of humankind.

The first of the three occurrences directly connects to this: the crowd which sees Christ approaching is not physically present; it is the humankind of the future which appears in the spirit. The feeding is more in the nature of giving the disciples the strength for their apostolic mission than momentarily satisfying the hunger of people who are present. In the other two occurrences it can be clearly recognized that the vision of Christ is closely connected to the state of prayer of his soul and that in general praying and seeing are linked in a close causal relationship.

The three occurrences are not completely similar. They increase in power in terms of the sphere which is perceived and whose power is called upon:

1. *eparas tous ophthalmous*
2. *êren tous ophthalmous anô* (upwards)
3. *eparas tous ophthalmous eis ton ouranon* (to heaven)

The fruit of the vision of Christ is not as tangible as in the feeding of the five thousand and the awakening of Lazarus. But it is no less important: it is the whole of the sanctified future destiny of the disciples.

CHAPTER ELEVEN

The Sphere of the Risen Christ

Easter joy

The Easter message is the heart and fountainhead of the Christian faith. The saying of Paul: 'If Christ did not rise again, then ... the power of our faith in your hearts is an illusion' (1Cor.15:14) justifies a description of Christianity simply as the religion of the Risen Christ. Christian devotion has ultimately no other purpose than this: to cherish community with the Risen Christ. Christ is not to be sought either in the past or in the future, but in the immediate present. His sphere is not a 'beyond;' he is near to us in this world in which we live.

Where is the sphere into which we must enter in order to feel and experience the nearness of the Risen Christ? Every year, during the Easter season, the hymnlike texts spoken at the altars of the Christian Community point to this sphere, and suggest at once its tremendous magnitude. A jubilant breath pervades the prayers of Easter, expressing itself twice, as with inward necessity, in the word 'rejoice.' Who rejoices? Who is made to rejoice by the Easter mysteries? In the first place the text says, 'the airy regions of the earth rejoice exceedingly,' and soon after, 'Christ has invaded man's rejoicing pulse of life.' First, the breathing soul-sphere of the whole planet rejoices, that renewed cosmic sphere of sunlit clouds, air and wind into which the earth grows in spring; then, the inward life of man, touched by the Risen Christ, rejoices too. We recognize the wide span of the soul at Easter; it comprises the outward and the inward world, macrocosm and microcosm.

The fourfold Easter gospel

The artistic fourfoldness of the gospels meets us nowhere so vividly as in the Easter stories; here, the gospels are more differentiated in their special quality and colouring than anywhere else. They become four separate books, each with its individual character; and the synoptic harmony of the four, with all their differences and apparent contradictions, makes the universal totality of 'the gospel in the four gospels' appear with greatest clarity.

The composition of the Easter story in the Gospel of Matthew has a special grandeur. The first gospel completely surpasses the others in poetic design. A double drama, full of tension, frames the Easter scenes themselves. The cosmic drama of the earthquake prepares and attunes our soul from the beginning for the power and magnitude of the event. Only Matthew's Gospel mentions the shocks of the earthquake which, beginning with the afternoon of Good Friday, tore open the ground of the earth, and continued reverberating until the morning of Easter Sunday. The cosmic drama at the beginning is followed by a human drama at the end, the deception of the priests at the sepulchre of Joseph of Arimathea. The high priests have posted watchers because they are afraid of fraud; but now they themselves attempt a fraud, by inducing the watchers through bribes to make false statements. Then the story proceeds in terse and dramatic stages. The Easter scenes themselves begin at the tomb. This forms a prelude, which is also contained in the other three gospels. Afterwards, we are taken at once to the summit of a high mountain. The angel at the tomb has asked the women to tell the disciples that the Risen Christ will go before them into Galilee; and now we also are immediately in Galilee. Together with the disciples we are transported to a height from which the world can be surveyed as if we were on the summit of that marvellous mountain where once the three most intimate disciples saw the Christ in his transfigured glory: on the summit of Tabor, the mountain of mountains, which rises in the sunny landscape of Galilee. Here, the Risen One speaks to his disciples: 'Now all creative power in heaven and on the earth has been given me;' and he sends his disciples as apostles into all the kingdoms of the world.

In Mark, the framework of the external dramatic events is missing; an inward dramatic quality takes its place. After the meeting with the angel at the tomb, we see the women return to the room where the disciples are united. It is the Cenacle, the room of the washing of the feet and the Last Supper; the sacred, time-honoured place on Mount Zion; the centre of the spiritual history of humanity from times immemorial. In this room the events of Easter continue. Here the Risen One enters the circle of the disciples and, speaking to them, conquers their hardened hearts. Having been at first without understanding for the Easter message, and even for the words of the Risen Christ, they can now become bearers of the cosmic impulse which has come into the world through the Resurrection. And now they experience how the Christ is raised before their eyes into heavenly heights, although they remain in the house; a first glimpse of the Ascension moves them within the four walls of the room.

Now we begin to see the deeper symbolism in the Easter stories, which belong together: Matthew leads to the top of the mountain, Mark leads into the house. In contrast to the dramatic study of Matthew, a great and wonderful inwardness lives in the Gospel of Luke. The transition from outside to inside which takes place in passing from the first to the second gospel is further deepened. This transition dominates the story of the two disciples who walk to Emmaus, which follows the scene at the tomb. For these disciples, too, the real meeting with the Risen One, by which they recognize him, occurs only at the moment when they have entered the house at the end of the way and have sat down at the table at twilight, in the stillness of the house. The theme of the transition from outside to inside is continued here; at a quick pace we return with the two disciples on the same evening to Jerusalem, and enter with them into the Cenacle, where the other disciples are assembled; and we are made witnesses of the Risen One appearing suddenly in the midst of the disciples and taking food and drink before their eyes, in order to unite himself with them in the sacred meal. In Luke, as in Mark, the interior of the house is the scene of the real Easter meeting, following the prelude at the tomb; but the scenes of the inward drama in Luke have more soul and are more richly differentiated.

John presents us with a very great wealth of Easter scenes. Even the prelude at the tomb develops into a whole drama. Mary Magdalene comes to the tomb; no angel is there to mitigate the shock which she feels at the sight of the empty tomb. She walks back all the way to find the disciples. Two of the disciples, seized with great anxiety, run through the whole city until they come to the tomb, but they also find it empty; no spiritual figure appears to them; they have to leave, taking with them an apparently insoluble riddle; in silence they return to the Cenacle. Mary Magdalene is left alone at the tomb. Only now, when she stands at the tomb for the second time, her soul is opened up for the presence of spiritual beings who are there; and the first meeting with the angels grows into the first meeting with the Risen One himself who appears to her as the gardener. And once more, but now charged with increasing content, the transition from outside to inside takes place. We find ourselves again within the room of the Last Supper, and share in the experience of how the Risen One manifests himself to the disciples. The following scenes develop with such rich detail that we begin to recognize how the Easter fellowship of the disciples with the Risen One extends beyond Easter Sunday, and fills the whole season. One week after, Thomas, the doubter, is permitted to convince himself through physical touch of the fact of the bodily resurrection. But the sequence in John is not yet at an end; the steps which have led us from outside to inside are reversed. The gospel leads us again outward. The interior scenes are followed by a series of scenes which take place under the open sky of Galilee. All of a sudden, the disciples are transported to the Sea of Galilee. During the night, they draw in the miraculous draught of fishes; and in the cool of the morning, on the shores of the blue lake, the radiant figure of the Risen One appears to them. A holy meal unites them with him. Then he addresses three times his earnest quesion to Peter; eventually he gives to the disciples their apostolic charge, pointing into the far distant future with mysterious words.

We can now discern an important aspect in the wonderful composition of the gospels as a whole. In the scenes which follow the prelude at the tomb, we are led, in the sequence of Matthew to John, through three archetypal settings: on the mountain, in the house and on the sea. Apparently physical landscape is described, but in fact we are shown regions of the soul which we have to traverse in order to meet the Risen One. The Gospel, taken in its entirety in the four gospels, has given the first pictorial hint of his sphere.

The angels at the tomb

Most Bible readers take it that the Easter stories in all four gospels agree in describing first the meeting with the angels at the tomb. But this is not so.

The Gospel of Matthew says that the women come to the grave and in the early light of dawn receive a severe shock, for the earthquake, which seemed to have subsided for a whole day, breaks out afresh. They have to make their way among trembling rocks. Then a flash of lightning tears away the curtain, as it were, from the world of the senses. When they reach the grave, a spirit-form shines before them in overwhelming brilliance. 'When the Sabbath was over, in the early morning light of the first day of the week, Mary of Magdala and the other Mary came to see to the tomb. And see, there was a great earthquake, the angel of the Lord descended from heaven, came and rolled the stone away and sat upon it. His appearance was like lightning, and his garment was shining white like snow.' (Matt.28:1). When the lightning has struck the watchers to the ground, the angel speaks to the women. The first premonition of Easter is given them, and they receive a message enjoining the disciples to go to Galilee.

In the light of the supersensory conception of the world which is the basis of the gospels, the earthquake is described, not as a natural process, but as the activity of supersensory powers and beings. Through the souls of the women we, too, see a powerful being from the angelic hierarchies taking part. An angel who resembles the powers of lightning and of snow descends from heaven to roll away the stone. It is important to note that the women perceive the angel while they are still outside the tomb. The vision that overtakes them is mingled with the physical perception that the entry to the tomb is exposed by the rolling away of the stone which has covered it. The supersensory experiences which the gospels recount are never arbitrary, but have a firm psychological basis. Even in the gospels people do not have supersensory experiences without some cause. In every case a specific emotion is active in the soul which releases the vision. According to the description in the Gospel of Matthew an overwhelming shock brought it about that suddenly, as the rock split, not only the outer event but also the supersensory being, the angel of the earthquake, was perceived.

In the Gospel of Mark the account of the meeting of the women with the angel is different, both in its inner aspect, and in the circumstances of its place and time. On their way to the tomb the women are full of anxiety as to how they will be able to get into the closed sepulchre. But as they reach the end of their journey they are greatly surprised to find that the stone has been rolled away, and that the entrance to the tomb is open. The problem that has worried them has been solved, but such a solution must prepare them for still further and perhaps greater surprises. Mark's comment, 'for the stone was very large,' makes us share in the women's breathless astonishment. They go inside the tomb, and there a bright light streams towards them out of the darkness. On their right they see an angelic form in a long white garment. The angel, who is described as a young man, speaks to them of the Resurrection, and gives them the message for the disciples about Galilee.

This experience of the angel does not occur as in the Gospel of Matthew, before they enter the tomb, but inside it, and it happens also at a somewhat later point of time. While Matthew describes the angelic being as 'the angel of the Lord,' which in Hebrew would read 'the angel of Yahweh,' Mark speaks of the 'young man' who sits to the right of the tomb. This is an entirely different situation and it is also a different condition which releases the vision. This time it is not fear but astonishment. Here is a first apparent contradiction between the two gospels.

In the Gospel of Luke things progress still further before the experience occurs that leads out of the sphere of sense-perception into the supersensory. The description of the external situation is carried to the point to which it had been taken by St Mark. The women come to the grave; they find the stone rolled away from the entrance and go inside. They search for the dead body of Jesus. And the longer they search, the more anxious and disturbed they become because they cannot find him. Only when their anxiety has reached its climax are their eyes opened to the spiritual beings who are there. 'And while they stood there, completely at a loss, suddenly two men were standing before them in raiment which shone like continuous lightning. They were overcome by terror and they bowed their faces to the ground.' (Luke 24:4f).

In this case the women have penetrated many paces deeper into the tomb than in the account given by Mark, and have already been there for some time. Now it is not fear of the earthquake, nor astonishment over the open tomb, but their anxiety over the empty grave which releases the vision. The feeling which goes beyond sense-perception is quite different and belongs to a more advanced consciousness. This time, surprisingly, it is two angel beings who reveal themselves to the women, and instead of being called 'angel of the Lord' or 'young man,' they are now called 'two men in white raiment.'

By this time it is obvious that there is nothing haphazard in these discrepancies between the several gospels, but that the advance from one gospel to the next follows a specific law. The meetings with the angels undergo such an orderly transformation, a metamorphosis so significant, that the differences in the gospels, taken as a whole, draw attention to a special secret.

This becomes specially clear when we come to the Gospel of John. Here, Mary Magdalene comes alone to the tomb. She enters and finds it empty. Thus the external course of events is once more taken up at the point reached in the preceding gospel. The feelings that had been stirred in the soul of Mary Magdalene by the earthquake, the open tomb and the empty grave are not described. The Fourth Gospel is concerned with experiences which take place later. Mary Magdalene leaves the tomb without having met with an angel. She goes all the way back through the city to the disciples. Now Peter and John run to the tomb, and with her they peer into the empty grave. Although there is no direct mention of this in the gospel, it is in accordance with the spirit of the Gospel of John to suppose that the disciples saw something of the cosmic aspect of the empty grave. On the site of the tomb the earthquake had reopened a deep cleft which formed part of the ancient chasm in the ground of Jerusalem which had been levelled by Solomon.* Thus the disciples not only look into the empty grave, they look into a gloomy chasm. They have a unique experience of the mystical stage called 'standing before the abyss.' Bewildered, they go away again, and Mary Magdalene remains there alone. Some time elapses. Then Mary Magdalene weeps. The tears that she now sheds are due neither to fright, nor to astonishment or anxiety. She weeps because she is wholly absorbed in love for him who has been torn

---

* See *Caesars and Apostles.*

away from her. Much more has happened than that Jesus has died. All the miraculous and inexplicable events since midday on Good Friday awaken dreamlike perceptions, whereby the greatness of him who has passed through death stands before the soul of Mary Magdalene as never before. The more she feels his greatness, the greater is her love. This love opens the eyes of her soul. While her physical sight is blinded with tears, her weeping awakens spiritual sight, and she perceives two figures. But these are not the same as those described by Luke. She sees two angels in white garments, one at the head and one at the foot of the place where the body of Jesus had been laid. Although there is still no trace of the beloved body, yet now, through her spiritual experience, she is conscious of the exact spot where he had lain. The two angels say to her, 'Woman, why are you weeping?' In that moment, as she collects herself to answer them, the experience moves forward to a new stage. She turns round, and there, in Joseph of Arimathea's garden, she sees a figure facing the tomb. She does not recognize him as Jesus. He who stands outside appears to her in the form of a gardener. And her first impulse is to ask him if he can tell her whither the body of Jesus has vanished. Then Jesus speaks to her in the very same words which earlier the angels had used, 'Woman, why are you weeping?'

We should not think that either the angel or the Risen One speaks in human language. What is heard inwardly by the soul is reproduced by the gospel in human words. It is only by silencing the human words that we can hope to enter into the inner hearing from which they come. In the Gospel of John it is out of the inner hearing of the question put by the angels that the new spiritual meeting arises whereby Mary Magdalene becomes the first bearer of the real Easter perception. The figure out there facing the tomb takes, as it were, the words from the angels' mouths.

Again, the figure that Mary Magdalene sees as a continuation of her perception of the angels is clearly that of a man. When the gospel says that she thought it was the gardener, this does not mean that she was deceived. Jesus does appear to her as a gardener. The medieval painters, by representing the Risen Christ as a gardener, have adequately reproduced the imagination which passed before Mary Magdalene's soul. The Risen One is really the gardener of a new garden, the planter and cultivator of a new life on earth.

The sight of the gardener brings new hope to her loving soul. Perhaps he who appears before her can restore to her the lost one. Only a few moments ago, love of Christ had caused her tears to flow. Now that same love lights up her soul. At that moment she feels herself called by name, and at last understands that it is Christ who stands before her in the Easter garden. She has really found again him who had been wrested from her. She puts out her hands to embrace him. But the stern warning meets her 'Do not touch me!' The Easter mystery is not yet consummated. What happens at the tomb takes place only in the forecourt. The complete manifestation of the Risen One in his spirit-body is first experienced only when the outdoor scenes have come to an end, and the indoor scenes within the circle of the disciples have begun.

The Gospel of John carries further the metamorphosis of the Easter prelude at the tomb. The significant transformations and amplifications in the meetings with the angels of the first three gospels here reach their climax. After the terror of the earthquake, the amazement at the open tomb, the anxiety over the empty grave, it is now tears of love which open the eye of Mary Magdalene's soul for the angels. Then the meeting with the gardener forms the transition from the angelic forecourt to the actual temple of Easter.

Concerning the celestial hierarchies

Each of the evangelists describes the angelic beings at the tomb in a characteristically different manner. It must not be supposed that the angel of the Lord mentioned by Matthew, the young man by Mark, the two men by Luke and the two angels by John refer to the same super-sensory fact, variously expressed according to the dictate of fancy. The evangelists remain true to themselves even in the matter of the names they give to the angel at the tomb. The young man in the Gospel of Mark appears on another, earlier occasion before the Easter story. Luke also mentions the two men in white garments again, after the conclusion of the actual Easter scenes. The same young man who later appears to the women at the tomb becomes for a moment visible in Mark's description of Christ's capture in Gethsemane. 'And there was a youth there who followed him. He was clad only in a white linen cloth next to the skin. They tried to seize him, but he left the linen cloth behind and fled naked.' It is not surprising that this scene is usually understood in purely physical terms. But to anyone who views the gospel as a whole with a lively sense for metamorphosis it will readily suggest itself as a supersensory event. The same figure of the 'young man in a white garment' appears on the night of Maundy Thursday and on the Easter morning, though on each occasion in an entirely different mood and setting.

The second appearance of the two men in white garments mentioned by Luke is in the Acts of the Apostles, at the Ascension. When the divine sun of the Risen Christ vanishes in a cloud from the sight of the disciples, there are the two men who say, 'You men from Galille, why do you stand there looking up to heaven?' The 'two men' appeared to the women in the dawn which preceded the sunrise of the Resurrection. They appear to the disciples when this sun is no longer visible.

The metamorphosis of the scenes at the tomb from the first to the fourth gospel shows a clearly traceable path from the sphere of the earthquake outside it to a scene in the interior. A similar succession of stages marks the description of the angels. According to the Gospel of Matthew, the women experienced a supersensory form who revealed himself to them in the realm of nature, in the agitation of the elements. This represents a stage of supersensory experience that once before played an important part in the religious history of humanity: in the revelation on Mount Sinai. God spoke to Moses on Mount Sinai in the earthquake, in fire and smoke, in thunder and lightning. The angel of the Lord who met the women on Easter morning came from the same sphere.

Then, passing directly to the description of John, Mary Magdalene becomes aware of the forms of two angels at the head and at the foot of the place where the body had lain but, in the metamorphoses of her soul's experience, a second spirit-encounter follows at once. The pair of angels is replaced by the human form of the gardener. In the first gospel the powers were of the higher hierarchies; now there are angels and, at last, man himself. In fact, the descriptions which the four gospels give of the scenes at the tomb lead down through the stages of specific hierarchies to the archetypal picture of man.

In the gradations of beings which continue upwards beyond stones, plants, animals and men, the stage above man is that of the

Angels. Their task is to guide the destiny of the individual. Each man has his own angel. He can open himself to the divine guidance which would work into his destiny through the angel. But he can also estrange himself from his angel, and so go astray. The next sphere above the angels is that of the Archangels. They guide the nations, of which they are the real 'folk-spirits.' Each nation has its own individual archangel, who tries to give a purpose to its destiny. The next hierarchical stage is that of the Primal Forces, or Archai. They are spiritual powers who guide whole ages of time. It is their task to communicate a new impulse to evolution in each age. They are revolutionary beings, instilling new activity and tendencies into the flow of human history. When a new age dawns it announces itself through the activity of a new Time Spirit, a new force of Primal Beginning, which supersedes its predecessor. The Archai are rejuvenating beings, beings of will, who introduce something fresh and unspent into the world. Above the level of the Primal Beginnings there are the Exousiai, the Spirits of Creation whom the Old Testament calls the Elohim. They are the spiritual powers who work creatively and give form to nature. The beginning of Genesis speaks of them because through their creative activity our planet earth entered upon its present physical existence. The most powerful of the Elohim is Yahweh, the God of the Old Testament, who manifested himself to Moses in the thunder and lightning of Mount Sinai.

The fourfold Easter Gospel leads through the spheres of the Exousiai, of the Archai, of the Archangels and of the Angels down to the figure of Man. The sphere of the Elohim appears in the form of the angel of the earthquake whom the gospel describes as a flash of lightning and calls the angel of the Lord. In the form of the young man who appears to the women in the Gospel of Mark the sphere of the Archai is disclosed who introduce new impulses and new beginnings into the destiny of humanity.

In the two men in white garments of whom Luke speaks, the sphere of the Archangels appears. The three 'men' who once visited Abraham on the plains of Mamre as bearers of a divine message were, according to tradition, the Archangels Michael, Gabriel and Raphael. And lastly, in the two angels of the Gospel of John there is the sphere of the angelic beings next to man. Eventually the Gospel of John comes down from the level of the hierarchies to man.

As we draw near to the grave we have to pass through concentric circles. In the centre the archetype of man appears before the soul, and forms the transition between the preliminary angelic experiences and the actual meeting with the Risen One himself. The next concentric spheres are those of the Angels, the Archangels and the Archai. The outer sphere which is first to be crossed is that of the Exousiai with their hosts. Christ's hierarchical beings are gathered around the grave in their ranks. The tomb is not guarded only by watchmen who fall to the ground; it is also guarded by the angelic spheres. Just as the angelic hosts gathered round the crib at Bethlehem, perceptible to the hearts of the simple shepherds, so now they press around the grave on Golgotha, and are seen by the deeply stirred souls of the women. But the homely scene of Christmas has given way to a dramatic conflict which is fought out in the cosmos. The gates of hell are forced open. Death is overcome. A victorious force unites itself with the earth and makes its influence felt from the cosmic horizon right into the inmost being of Man.

The Risen One and the angels at the tomb

Through the medium of different angels it is, however, always the Christ-being who is perceived. Whether it is the angel of the earthquake, or the young man in white raiment, or the two men in white garments, or the two angels at the head and at the foot of the grave, it is nevertheless the Risen One who shows himself to the women. Even the gardener is an image, of which the reality behind it has gradually to be perceived. Mary Magdalene is able to do this at the moment when she hears herself addressed by name. From then on the Risen One shows himself in his very own form. But it is important to feel him already, as the women did, behind the manifestations of the angelic forms. That the Angel of the Lord shows himself in the earthquake enables one to understand that the Risen One is preparing to become the new spirit of the earth, the power which moves the new creation. When, in the same gospel which records the women's experiences with the angel of the earthquake, the Risen One says, 'To me is given all power [*exousia* in Greek] in heaven and upon earth,' he discloses that it is he himself who appeared to the women through the angel of the Lord, a being from the realm of the Exousiai. The Christ-being is also the young man. Through his Resurrection the most powerful impulse of rejuvenation enters the dying world of creation. And in the angelic manifestations of the gospels of Luke and John yet more secret aspects of Christ are revealed.

There is an illustration of this in the history of painting. Up to the end of the Middle Ages, illustrations of the Easter story show, almost exclusively, the Risen One bursting open the grave and rising victoriously towards heaven out of the depths. Without casting the slightest reflection on the beauty and the religious value of these pictures, it must yet be said that something more than this is needed. Christ rising from the ground with the Easter banner gives only Matthew's aspect of the Resurrection. It contains an element of unthinking dogmatism, which hinders the full understanding of Easter. For the power of the Risen Christ is not directed from below to above, away from the earth, but towards the earth, from above to below. Very few pictures of the Resurrection have been painted in the spirit of Luke or John. Among these is Rembrandt's pictures of the scene at Emmaus, in which Christ, sitting at table with the two disciples, appears like a flash of lightning. Most beautiful is Raphael's well-known picture of the Easter scene on the shore of the Sea of Galilee, drawn originally as a cartoon for a tapestry in the Vatican, and now in London in the Victoria and Albert Museum. It would help very much to deepen the conception of Easter if there were more such paintings. St John's aspect especially ought to inspire modern pictures of Easter, because it leads on from the appearance of the gardener to the human form divine re-established in and through Christ.

The sphere of enlightened remembrance

The two men in white garments say to the women inside the sepulchre these words: 'Remember the words that he spoke while he was still in Galilee.' This is an extension of the commission about Galilee which they receive in the first two gospels. Instead of being directed by the angels to Galilee, which might be taken as meaning the geographical Galilee, they are now reminded of the sphere of memory, and are told to walk once more in recollection over the roads of Galilee which they had walked with Jesus, and to reflect once more on the words he had spoken to them there. As the vision of the angel fades, it is said of the

women, 'And they remembered his words and returned home from
the tomb.' At first the meaning seems to be that it now suddenly
occurs to the women, stirred by the words of the angel, that Christ had
in fact prophesied all that had since happened. But a more intimate
secret is hidden here. In the supersensory experience of Easter morning an appeal is made to the force of remembrance as an organ of the
soul. The sphere of memory is touched by the spirit.

That we possess the gift of memory, and bear in us a treasure-
chamber out of which we can recall the past, is a far greater miracle
than we realize. Today we often damage this treasure. Through our
insistence on training the brain to memorize, the deeper-rooted, more
comprehensive force of recollection is pushed into the background.

The power of memory plays a significant part in our being and destiny. As people get older, and suffer perhaps already from weakness of
memory in daily affairs, they have a great revival of remembrance, and
are able to recall things of their childhood far more vividly than they
could in middle age. The nearer we get to death, and the more we
escape from the spell of the physical, the more is remembrance set free.
This can give an indication of what is experienced after death. In the
days immediately following death, one is surrounded by a panorama
of the sum-total of all one's memories. The eye of memory is fully
released. From this we can gauge anew what an inexpressibly great
miracle our faculty of memory is.

In the faculty of memory an inner power of vision is at work. As it
exists today, this faculty is the remnant of a past clairvoyance. If we
cultivate it we can become seers. This will one day become important
for our life with the dead. Anyone who mourns a beloved friend lives
in the memories they had in common. If this experience is made a conscious exercise, faithfully practised, we shall find that memory
acquires a strength which may lead to an unhoped-for immediacy of
meeting, which may even be lasting.

This is the key to the momentous Easter experiences of the disciples during the forty days. While they were gathered together in the
upper room, living in the great memories of the last three years, again
and again they became aware of certain words and actions of their
Master, as fresh and as overwhelming as if they were now being spoken or enacted before them for the first time. While the events were
actually taking place they had for the most part been living as in a

dream; now each memory was an awakening that flashed through their souls. This caused their eyes to be opened for the Risen One. The force of true recollection had called him into their midst. It was he who spoke to them in enhanced light the words they remembered, and who carried out in their presence the actions they recollected. Through him their memories, only now really becoming their own, grew into a whole world of revelation. Thus, in the story of Emmaus a special fact belonging to the sphere of enlightened recollection is contained. The two disciples feel someone walking by their side. This sense of being accompanied by a form from a spiritual realm will one day be of universal significance.

We can have two kinds of 'double.' A familiar example of one kind is given in Goethe's *Faust*. Mephistopheles, the dark double, causes men to lose themselves in the maze of life. But people who have a relationship to the divine can feel the presence of an illuminated double, as if their own angel were walking beside them. There is a famous example of the angelic experience of the double in the apocryphal story of Tobias. The young Tobias is able to go his way comforted by the presence at his side of the Archangel Raphael.

In the future the shining form who walks by man's side will become translucent for the form of the Risen Christ himself. In the beautiful old church of St Apollinaris Nuova in Ravenna, high up on the walls of the middle aisle of the nave, a series of mosaics represent stories from the gospels. In most of these scenes Jesus is represented with another who stands near him, a little behind, clad in a white garment. There Jesus is already accompanied by the angel who will appear to the women at the grave on Easter morning.

Lastly, the secret of the Easter double is touched on also in the words spoken to Peter on the shore of the sea of Galilee. 'When you were young you tied your own belt and followed aims you had set yourself; but when you reach maturity of age you will stretch out your hands, and someone else will gird you and lead you to aims you do not set yourself' (John 21:18.)

The interplay of the forces of remembrance will, if faithfully cultivated in the soul, undergo a deepening: this will enable organs for the spiritual to develop, and they will speak either for people's immediate guidance, or for their future. With the development of the faculty of recollection the voice of conscience will form itself anew. While the earlier instinctive conscience focused on the past, and recalled past errors, the new conscience will be an organ for the helping and counselling being who walks by man's side. Through conscience awakened to the spirit, man will be able to cultivate a lasting relationship with the angel of Easter morning and through him with the Risen One himself. The Risen Christ will manifest himself as the true Lord of human destiny, and the 'other' who walks beside man, and guides him, will be felt as the hand of Christ. Thus man will acquire the strength and security to bear, and to win through, even the hardest fate. The permanent relationship to the fact of Easter is the real source of consolation. The Risen One is near to us as 'the Comforter of our earth existence.'

But memory is not simply a part of our being over which we ourselves have sole control. It is a projection of divine forces into human nature. It still surrounds us for a while even after death, in order to mirror the divine verdict on the life through which we have just passed. Even during life our memory is in fact under continuous control of the archangels. The beings related to the 'two men in white garments' control the sphere in which we enter through the power of memory. So it comes about that by transforming our remembrance into devotion, and by the practice of recalling backwards the day's experiences, we acquire the power to call angels to our help, and with their help gradually to become clairvoyant for the Risen Christ.

St Luke, as a pupil of St Paul, is especially fitted to show just this intimate way to the revelation of the etheric Christ. One of the main threads in the Christology of Luke and Paul, who agree in their description of the institution of the Lord's Supper, are in these words mentioned by both of them: 'This do in remembrance of me,' — words which are not mentioned in any other gospel. They do not refer to the superficial faculty of memory, bound up with the brain. The Greek word *anamnêsis* touches the secrets of supersensory man more deeply. A better rendering would say 'And always when you do this, make my Being come alive within you.' The *anamnêsis* of Christ has to be practised, and the sacrifice of bread and wine is the act in which this exercise can be successful. Why should remembrance of the Christ be practised? Because it enables him to draw very near to men. He who observes the injunction of the words of the Lord's Supper remembers the Risen One. Actually, all reading of the gospel ought to take place 'in remembrance of him': that is, it ought to bring him truly into the present. He who does this is not alone. But sacramental life, above all, makes it possible to feel the Risen One near, as guide and comforter.

Bodily resurrection

The disciples experience the Risen Christ not only as a soul-being, as countless people experienced their dead in those times. Resurrection is more than immortality. If the essential meaning of the three years lay in the incarnation, in the being of God really becoming flesh, then Christ's Resurrection was his victory over death, over 'the flesh,' over the material body which had been his habitation. How can one form an idea of the 'resurrection of the body'?

For every human being, differentiated mysteries of excarnation are involved in the process of death. Death is more than the laying aside of the physical body. Of course, in drawing his last breath man does put off the garment of the corruptible material body. But in the forms of life and destiny into which man now enters, a shadow follows him like the after-effect of the relationship in which he stood towards his body in earthly life. According to how much he clung to what is earthly and material, separation from which now causes him to suffer, the shadow of this bodily sphere darkens the world into which he is gradually growing. But in the measure in which he has, during life, made himself the master of matter, and of the instincts due to matter, he possesses even after death a flowing force of light which banishes the shadow and fills the darkness. The spiritual power over matter which man has attained during life is not lost. But if before death he has lost himself to the perishable world of 'this side,' he is now banished into a powerless beyond; he lacks the force of light to cross the dark abyss, and to participate with those still living on earth in the fight of light against darkness. But the more strength he has gained during life to wrest the spirit from matter, the imperishable from the perishable, the less will the abyss terrify him and cut him off. Thus souls are distinguished after death by the extent to which they have developed mastery over matter. The Easter miracle, the victory of Christ over death, was that a being crossed the threshold from whom death was unable to wrest anything at all. For three years the ego of Christ, by penetrating further and further the earthly body, had proved himself the lord and victor over matter. Transmutation of dead matter through unremitting permeation by the spirit — this was the result of the three years. It is this which throughout the Passion gave to Jesus the majestic fire of humanity raised to the divine. The same imperious greatness with which he approached the grave of Lazarus, and with which he entered into Jerusalem and purified the Temple, remained with him on Golgotha and beyond. By sharing in the human destiny of death he had brought his earthly body as a sacrifice to the cross, yet when he revealed himself to his disciples the elemental power of his spirit over matter was so great that they could not but believe that they were perceiving him with their physical senses. The body which appeared before them was not palpable to earthly sense; but they clearly felt the effect of the fiery power with which the super-sensory form of the Risen Christ was active in the sphere of earthly matter. The intensity of the victory over death was so great that the border-zone in which the spiritual is able to create matter out of itself was laid open to them.

The unique mystery of the resurrection body of Christ may become more accessible to our understanding if we consider the general stages of waxing and waning which, according to the descriptions of anthro-posophy, every human being has to undergo immediately after death. When the physical body is cast off, an enveloping, supersensory frame or 'sheath' remains for a short time which, placed as it is between body and soul, forms a bridge between the state of incarnation and the period of soul-existence which will continue for a long time. This sheath is the ether-body, the body of formative forces, which has given life and form to the physical body. This etheric body, man's lowest supersensory member, is the bearer of memory. Into this etheric body the pictures of our earthly experiences are woven, and so long as the physical body still absorbs and conceals the etheric body, these mem-ories emerge into consciousness only in fragments. In the moment of death, when the dense earthly covering is laid aside, the sum total of our memory expands. The soul sees the close network of pictures con-centrated in the etheric body as an overwhelmingly bright sphere. For three days the vast tableau lasts, embracing in backward order every detail of the past life, until this second vehicle of life, the ether body, is also laid aside and, expanding, merges with the cosmic ether.

The entrance after three days into the world of soul and spirit presents a severe trial for the human being. It is only at this point that the threshold is fully crossed. Uncovered, the soul is exposed to the eye of cosmic judgment. Strength to make the crossing comes to the soul only in so far as it has gained, during life, inner force through union with God. No light shines in the darkness unless an inner light has been acquired through goodness and an inclination towards the spirit. Only he maintains his ground here who can in very truth stand on his own feet. Only he has light at his disposal who himself radiates light. He whose only link was with the earth sinks, powerless, into unconsciousness. He is in danger of the 'second death,' the death of the soul. The hideous power of death over the human being is fully seen for the first time only at the moment when the soul throws off its second garment.

The complete power of the spirit over matter which holds good even after death shows itself when a quintessence of the two sheaths which the soul has discarded, the physical body and the etheric body, is left to it. Human beings vary in this respect after they have crossed the threshold. The draught of Lethe which man swallows when he reaches the far shore of his flowing ether body, and exchanges the sum of his memories for the great oblivion, can be a miserable drop which is consumed by the fires of the zone of trial. But it can also resemble a shining crystal, which draws to itself a permanent spiritual component, not only from the etheric forces of the cosmos but also from the creative plane of corporeal potentiality which lies between the etheric and the physical. Christ's power over matter and death was so great that he was able to wrest from death the whole of the etheric body in which he had dwelt for three years. After three days of spiritual struggle, the victory of Easter morning lay in the fact that the Christ, instead of being banished by death into another world, remained on earth in his etheric body, which had become entirely a crystal of light. And the body in which the Risen One manifests himself to his disciples was at the same time far, far more than an ordinary etheric body. It would not have been able to overcome its innate centrifugal tendency to unite itself with the cosmic ether had it not become saturated by the quintessence of the physical body and thus made capable of retaining form. Here we come upon the original meaning of the word *quintessence*. The *quinta essentia* is a mysterious supersensory fifth element, beyond the four elements which, according to ancient tradition, made up the physical world of matter. The *quinta essentia* is a principle of form which holds the four elements together. Thus the etheric body of Christ, which had been wrested from death, was in its uniqueness richly imbued with nascent life-forces and creative power. It was not a physical body, but in terms of force and form it stood in the closest possible relationship to the plane on which the disciples lived, as creatures of flesh and blood. The spiritual body of the Risen One could be described either as an etheric body which had at its disposal the form and earthly faculties of a physical body, or as a physical body raised out of its mortality to the plane of an etheric body. We can only grope helplessly for human words to describe the greatest miracle that has ever happened in the existence of the earth. But if here we succeed in finding at least a beginning of a living understanding — and the knowledge won by Rudolf Steiner has made this possible — we shall grasp the Archimedean point which our entire thinking and understanding can use as purchase for a new ascent.

The encounters of the disciples with the Risen Christ in the Easter days in the upper room in Jerusalem were miraculous, and yet they are not miracles that can be accepted only by a sacrifice of reason. They were supersensory experiences, but experiences which tended so powerfully towards the physical plane that the disciples could believe that they were perceiving the Risen One with their senses. When Thomas sought to touch his hands and his side, the faculties of perception in his own etheric body were so highly enhanced by entering into relation with the life-body of Christ that the powerful tendency of this body to take on form and substance revealed itself to him as something verging on the physical. When the disciples experience how the Risen One sat with them at table and took food and drink, there was a resumption on the higher Easter level of the events of Maundy Thursday. Then the power of the Christ over earthly matter had manifested itself to their dimly apprehending souls as the power of transformation, as the faculty of transubstantiation; bread and wine were illumined and filled with his life forces and his soul forces, and so became his body and his blood. Now in their midst the Risen One assimilated into himself food and drink. Under the stimulus of spiritualized memory the etheric forces of the disciples became clairvoyant for the etheric light-form of Christ, and they perceived the miracle of transubstantiation as the eating and drinking of the Risen One, in that they saw the gifts on the table received into the glory of light of the corporeality wrested from death.

Lastly, they felt themselves transported into the scenery of a new cosmic springtime. In the midst of the dying earth existence they walked in the garden of a new earth. They called the world of their Easter 'Galilee,' because the scenery around the Sea of Galilee and round the holy mount of the transfiguration, still filled with the ether of the Old Sun, became a prophetic transparency for the earth which will one day be raised to the new sun-ether, the paradise regained, springing from the seed sown on Golgotha. In the sphere of Easter communion the dimensions of a new cosmos open out. The miracle of bodily resurrection bridges the gulf between what is within and what is without, between microcosm and macrocosm. Man's inmost pulse of life rejoices exceedingly, and with him rejoice the airy regions of the earth.

CHAPTER TWELVE

The Teaching of the Risen Christ

The Eastern Churches have a strong tradition that the Christ gave his greatest teaching after Easter. During the forty days between his Resurrection and his Ascension he is said to have imparted to his disciples the most intimate secrets of the spiritual life and the word of the spirit. The New Testament itself is very reserved in speaking about this. Only one terse sentence in the Acts of the Apostles refers to it. 'By many manifestations of his being he had shown himself as the victor over death after his passion. For forty days he revealed himself to their seeing souls and spoke to them of the mysteries of the Kingdom of God.' (Acts 1:3).

Among Eastern Christians it would be felt as not only unnecessary but unnatural to doubt the reality of this statement. Christianity in the East regards it as completely self-evident that the Risen One conversed with his disciples, and that in every age, for those who are devout enough, it is possible to see him and hear him as the disciples did. Notwithstanding all the cultural decline that has come upon the Eastern peoples, there is the unquestioned conviction among Greek, Armenian, Coptic and Ethiopian Christians of the nearness and attainable reality of the Risen Christ.

Gnostic documents

To this very day the East lives in the echo of the ancient clairvoyant consciousness which in the West was lost much earlier and more completely. In the first centuries of Christian development the light of this ancient consciousness was still burning brightly. We tend to forget that once this ancient eastern faculty brought forth a voluminous and lofty gospel literature, which had as its main subject just these very conversations between the Risen One and his disciples, and which was penetrated with the light of the continuous Easter meeting. This was the gnostic literature. It was concerned with the secret of the forty days. It is a great loss to the spiritual history of mankind that this literature has fallen victim to the persecutions which were directed by the Church against the gnostic influence. How much recent discoveries will add to our knowledge of it remains to be seen.*

However, one single continuous script of greater length, called *Pistis Sophia,* had previously been saved from destruction by a fortunate chance. How this came about we do not know. The manuscript was found at the end of the eighteenth century among the effects of a much-travelled London doctor, from whence it came into the possession of the British Museum.

The glimpse that the *Pistis Sophia* and the other Coptic fragments of gnosticism give of the spiritual atmosphere of those forty days is extremely startling. It is a literature which indeed cannot be understood by the customary thinking of the West. From the point of view of form and connected thought it seems fantastic and extravagant. Western thought has acquired its clarity and strict logic by modelling itself upon the hard forms and outlines of the sense-perceptible world and from the sense of efficiency and purpose which action in this external world demands. The gnostic writings, on the other hand, are influenced by a spirituality which does not take the world of perceptible things into consideration, does not care about that world — a spirituality which looks exclusively towards the supersensory. The logic of ordinary thought is laid aside. At first it gives us westerners the feeling that we have lost the ground from under our feet. It is as though we had before us a late product of the original Christian 'speaking with tongues' which, when it occurred in the earlier communities, could not be understood by the person who spoke it, but needed to be specially translated into the usual language of thought. But even if we do not approach these writings only with the customary thinking of the West, but try to understand them in the light of the new spiritual knowledge which we can acquire nowadays, we cannot help feeling that this literature is one-sided. That it was regarded as dangerous by

* These words were written prior to the publication of the gnostic texts discovered at Nag Hammadi in 1945 (Editor).

the leaders of the early Church and was rejected by them, seems quite understandable; although it does not excuse the great wrong of simply destroying it.

When we have recovered from the effect of our first contact with the *Pistis Sophia,* and try to find out what it can tell us about the Easter mystery, we still have to come to terms with its verbosity and apparently fantastic extravagance. Right at the beginning we are startled by a truly Luciferic unconcern with earthly relationships of time and place. We are told that the Risen Christ had remained among his disciples, teaching them, for eleven years. 'It came to pass, when Jesus had risen from the dead, that he passed eleven years speaking with his disciples and instructing them about the places and the spheres.' The fullness beyond all understanding of what took place during those forty days is felt so strongly that a date is given which cannot be accepted in a material sense. Even the space of eleven years does not seem enough to grasp the fullness of the event of Easter, for it is only after this lapse of time that the unending stream of conversations and instructions which are recorded here begins.

It is described how the disciples thought that the Risen One had already revealed to them the ultimate and highest mystery. Now the Christ makes clear to them that they stand only at the very beginning of the path. The 'Place of the mystery' into which they have been led is the lowest of twenty-four spheres. Only when they have risen through all these spheres, learning all the time, will their initiation be complete. 'And Jesus said to his disciples, "I have come from that first mystery, which is the last, the twenty-fourth mystery".'

The disciples are dismayed to learn that their instruction must continue beyond the first stage even to the highest:

> It came to pass that the disciples were sitting together on the
> Mount of Olives, and they said to one another in great joy,
> 'Blessed are we above all men on earth because the Saviour has
> revealed this to us, for we have received the *pleroma* [the full-
> ness] and the entire consummation [initiation].' They spoke
> thus while Jesus sat a little way from them. Then it came to
> pass on a day of the full moon, as the sun came forth on its
> course, that a mighty stream of light unfolded itself behind the
> sun, shining exceedingly. There was no measure to the light
> that issued forth from it, for it came from the light of lights ...

This stream of light descended upon Jesus and enveloped him completely, while he was sitting apart from his disciples. And he was greatly shining, so that there was no measure to the light that streamed out from him. The disciples did not see Jesus because of the great light that surrounded him; their eyes were dazzled by the strong light. Thus they only saw the light and the bright rays emanating from it. The light reached from the earth right up to heaven. The sight of it stirred the disciples and made them afraid. And it came to pass as the power of light descended upon Jesus and little by little enveloped him completely, that he rose into the heights, shining in immeasurable light.

Silently the disciples gaze at the cloud of light ascending into heaven. After three hours all the forces of heaven are stirred into movement. The earth, too, begins to tremble. The disciples think that the moment has come when earthly creation will be rolled up like a scroll. This goes on until the ninth hour of the following day. Then the heaven opens and the disciples, trembling with fear, see Jesus descending again from heaven. He shines in a still more radiant and powerful light than on the day before. A threefold sheath surrounds him, each sheath being different in its radiations. When he becomes aware of the fear dominating his disciples, he speaks to them the same words which once he spoke in the night when he walked on the sea, 'Be of good cheer. It is I. Be not afraid.' This restores the power of speech to the disciples. They ask Christ to shade them from the excess of light which dazzles them. Then Jesus withdraws into himself the brilliance of his light. The disciples approach him, fall down before him and beg him to explain to them what has taken place in this terrifying hour. The Risen One answers, 'Rejoice and be glad from this hour, for I have risen to the places whence I came. From this day forth I shall speak openly with you face to face, without parable, from the beginning of the truth up to its highest fulfilment. I shall no more conceal anything from you.'

The Risen One begins to describe the spheres of the spiritual world through which he has just risen. He explains to them why he is only now able to give them the unlimited stream of his teaching. By his Ascension into the heights he had entered into the space of the upper mysteries, where on descending to earth he had left behind the garment of light. The threefold light-sheath, upon which the names of all the beings in heaven and upon earth are inscribed, gives him the full power to pour out without reserve the all-embracing wisdom of light.

> Lo, I have put on my vesture and all power is given to me through the uppermost mystery. It will not be long before I shall impart to you the mysteries of the pleroma and of the pleroma of the *pleroma*. Henceforth I will conceal nothing from you. But in perfection will I perfect you, in the whole pleroma, in every initiation and in every mystery, which is the initiation of all initiations, the pleroma of all pleromas, and the gnosis of all gnoses. All these are contained in my vesture. I will explain to you all mysteries, from the outermost to the inmost.

In the unending stream of spiritual conversation which now develops, the Risen Christ describes his passage through all the spheres and all the hierarchies which he encounters during the breathing in and breathing out of light. The disciples are instructed about the strata, provinces and positions in space of the supersensory spheres. The world of sense lies far below them. The spiritual world is described quite naturally, just as one describes the districts, streets and single houses of a city. But the picture is not clear all at once. Now, any way of checking this outpouring of spirit by earthly reason seems quite impossible. But it is unreasonable to expect systematic structure in a literature which presupposes the old clairvoyance, or at least the last echoes of it. The text is not meant for readers who have not yet taken the first steps towards acquaintance with the separate spheres of force and the separate forms of the supersensory plane. It does not address itself to the reason, which was formed in man only after the supersensory world had already been forgotten. It speaks rather to spiritual vision, and tells of the manifold beings, orders, and forms of the spiritual world as of something still known at least instinctively.

The whole description is entirely dominated by the theme of light. Again and again the great 'Treasure of Light' is mentioned as lying at the heart of the realms of spirit. From there, as from a sun-centre resembling a temple or citadel, the light streams out on all sides and forms pictures, and also forces and beings which become denser and

denser as they get lower and lower. The Treasure of Light is surrounded by gates guarded by powerful watchers. Twelve radiant figures form a circle round the holy source of light. Moving outwards
from this highest Holy of Holies, sphere by sphere, passing for example through the *Heirarmene*, the region of destiny, and through the
twelve aeons, towards our earthly world, passing through the stages
of the twenty-four mysteries, we are all the time surrounded by a rich
world of figures in precise ranks and with clearly defined boundaries.
A thousand strange names sound around us. We meet, too, several
specially privileged heralds of light, as for example, Melchizedek, the
'Plenipotentiary of the Treasure of Light,' Jeu, the 'Bishop of the
Treasure of Light;' and, against them and the good hierarchies, the
dark, cruel army of the opposing powers. Out of the group among the
Archai which has become hardened in tyranny come such figures as
Adamas and Authades. The figures change at every moment, as in a
giant kaleidoscope.

Christ describes his passage through the manifold pleroma of the
light-world. Both the spirit hosts who serve the light, as well as those
fighting it, are deeply stirred by the Ascension of Christ and his re-
descent. All the beings of the pleroma are given new functions in the
working out of Easter. A third of their power is taken away from the
counter-powers. They can no longer darken and confuse human destinies without restraint, as they had done hitherto. The Risen One,
with his own angel-beings, makes himself the Lord of Destiny. During
the three years of his earthly life he had already introduced the reflection of the highest figures of light into the life of earthly man. Thus he
describes how he took a force from each of the twelve healers who
form the shining circle around the Treasure of Light, and sank it into
the individuality of each of the apostles. Endless secrets arise before
us; like dreams, they are often unintelligible, yet we recognize in them
sparks of truth — as, for example, the secret of the Elijah-John being,
or of the two Jesus boys.*

Often the thousand names form a series for meditation. Thus one
of the Coptic fragments, akin to the *Pistis Sophia,* speaks of the twelve
Deeps into which the divine pleroma is divided:

* See *The Childhood of Jesus.*

The first Deep is the All-Source, out of which all sources come.

The second Deep is the All-Wise, out of which all wise things proceed.

The third Deep is the All-mystery, out of which all mysteries proceed.

The Fourth Deep is the All-Knowledge, out of which all knowledge flows.

The fifth Deep is the All-Holy, from which everything holy springs.

The sixth Deep is Silence, out of which all silence comes.

The seventh Deep is the Beingless gate from which all beings come.

The eighth Deep is the Forefather from whom all forefathers are descended.

But the ninth Deep is an All-Father-Self-Father, in whom are all fathers in so far as they are fathers of themselves.

The tenth Deep is the All-Force, from which all forces proceed.

But the eleventh Deep is the one in which the Uppermost Invisible is found, from whom all things invisible proceed.

The twelfth Deep is the Truth from which all truth flows.

The last Order we divine through the veil behind which the great King of the Light-realm sits enthroned.

Much of the *Pistis Sophia* is interwoven with significant myth. On his way through the spheres, Christ meets with a female form sunk in deep sorrow. It is she who bears the name Pistis Sophia. In her, who from now on is the chief person in the drama, we recognize the human soul. Once she formed part of the highest Aeon of Light. But a long time ago, through the hostile power of Authades, she fell from her high place into the black depths of imprisonment, suffering and loneliness. When she sees the Risen One in his threefold shining aura of light and recognizes her own name upon his garment, a sense of approaching salvation comes to her. She rises and sings the hymn of praise to the light, which has been silent on her lips for so long.

From now on, the questions and answers between the disciples, Mary, and Mary Magdalene on the one side, and the Risen One on the other, are accompanied by the prayers of Pistis Sophia and by the encouraging words which the Risen One addresses to her. Christ teaches the human soul prayers which can again reach the summit she had lost. And Pistis Sophia recites one after the other a series of penitential psalms which really belong to the Old Testament, but now, in the flowing realms of spirit, they take on the distinctive character of prayers belonging to stages of initiation. Thus the deepest mysteries of the Fall and of Redemption become subjects of converse with the Risen One.

'Apparent' body and resurrection body

While the gnosis draws on veritable floods of supersensory wisdom, its vision is unable to penetrate the darker and tragic regions of the physical plane and thus, although it was able to develop its rich half-visionary, half-reflective knowledge about the being of Christ, it has fatally missed his essential deed of salvation. The solemnity and the full import of the becoming flesh of the cosmic Word remained a sealed book to the gnosis. It led to the conception that Christ walked upon earth only in an 'apparent' body, a *phantasm,* a doctrine known as Docetism.

This source of error in the *Pistis Sophia* must not be overlooked. The relationship of gnostic spirituality to the light is well fitted for bringing to full manifestation the divine being of light. But an adequate grasp of the Resurrection eluded the gnostics, because it requires the death on Golgotha to be taken absolutely seriously. Had the Christ-being not really penetrated into the very lowest depths of human incarnation, the analogy between his death and the death that is the lot of all human beings would not have been true.

By speaking of the threefold fullness of light which the Risen Christ bears around him, and from which he derives the doctrine that he passes on to his disciples, the *Pistis Sophia* imparts an important truth. Nevertheless, it is just here that the fundamental error of gnosticism comes out. From its descriptions it would seem as if the threefold garment of light belonged to the Christ-being before, and quite apart from, his incarnation. It describes how, when the Christ came down to earth to become man, he left this garment of light behind him in a particular sphere of the supersensory world. The *Pistis Sophia* goes on to describe how after his death and Resurrection he has to make a special journey to heaven in order to reclothe himself in the supersensory light-sheath which he had left behind. In truth, however, the teaching of the Risen One in every single detail was possible only because of his having passed through Good Friday and Easter: that is to say, because of an incarnation which tasted things earthly to the dregs, and of which the death on Golgotha was the very essence. Every word that the Risen One says to the disciples is wrested from the powers of earthly matter and of death. The wisdom out of which he speaks is something quite newly established. Never before had it been attainable, not even in the highest divine realms.

The gnosis describes Christ in the way that the ancient peoples, of whom the Greeks were the last, conceived of the gods as coming down from heaven to hold converse with men. When Jupiter or Athene approached a mortal in some human form, as for instance Homer describes it in the story of Odysseus, a quite real event was taking place. Yet at the same time one cannot help feeling that here a supersensory being intervened only temporarily in human affairs, and was making use of earthly forms and earthly words to reveal himself. It is precisely here that Christ is different from all the gods of antiquity: He has entered into earthly incarnation not transitorily or as a means of manifesting himself, but in actual fact uniting himself permanently with it. And Christ differs from the ancient gods especially in his resurrected state. Now while it might seem that he is once more clothed in a celestial body of light like the other leaders of supersensory spheres, he is actually clothed in a spirit-body woven of light, which does not come from above but from below, because it is wrested from the plane of matter and of death.

Once we have grasped the one-sidedness of gnostic spirituality on this concrete point, we can gauge the character of the *Pistis Sophia* document as a whole. There is something magnificent in the central role played by light in this work. But the fullness of light also has in it something dazzling, which alienates us from the life that we have to live here on earth. Because this theme of light is so one-sidedly prominent it ceases to be 'glory,' *(doxa)*, which is always tinged golden with warmth as a ground-tone. It takes on a Luciferic brilliance. We learn a great deal if we turn from the gnostic texts to the Gospel of John. A thread of most important sayings about the light runs through this gospel. But the impressive words in which St John speaks of the light are spoken with reserve. 'And the light shines in the darkness; and the darkness has not accepted it' (John 1:5). 'I AM the Light of the World' (John 8:12). 'While you still have the light, open your hearts to the light, so that you may become sons of light' (John 12:36). In the farewell discourses in John which anticipate the teaching of the Risen Christ, the theme of light only gleams through the words of the high-priestly prayer in which Christ speaks of his transfiguration (*gloria* in Latin, *doxa* in Greek). Gnostic spirituality must be measured by the standard of the spirituality of the Gospel of John. He, too, is a bearer of the gnosis of Light, but since he understands the profundities of the mystery that the Word was made flesh, he remains all the time in the state of balance between heaven and earth. This is what the gnosis lacks. In the *Pistis Sophia* the Risen One assumes almost Luciferic features when he appears in the garment of light which dazzles the disciples; he has to subdue its brilliance before he can bestow on them the wisdom of the light.

Nevertheless in our own day when the Easter mystery, as indeed the Christian mysteries in general, are in danger of being completely forgotten, these ancient books of wisdom can furnish valuable help. Naturally, in reading such imaginative discourses we must learn to see them in their right perspective. And the more we have lived in the spiritual knowledge proper to our own time, the better shall we be able to do this.

At its very outset the *Pistis Sophia* itself comes near to a truth capable of surmounting the fundamental errors of gnosticism. When the Christ says that it is the very lowest stratum, the one nearest to earth, from which he has come, they take for granted that in his endless wanderings through the cosmos on his way down to earth, he has already passed through all the spheres above the twenty-fourth, right up to the first, the mystery nearest to the Treasure of Light. But now it is most emphatically stressed that in coming down to earth he left not a far-distant beyond, but the layer of the spiritual world which borders directly upon the earthly. From this point it is only a step to the knowledge (to which the gnosis never really penetrates) that the Christ-being, not only apparently, but actually entered physical incarnation.

The mystery of incarnation is fully contained in the mystery of Easter, because the Resurrection is not only a return into the divine-spiritual being of Christ which had existed previously, but it signifies a conquest over death, and a foothold for the divine in the realm of death. That the Christ passed through death had a meaning not only for men and for the earth, but also for the gods and for heaven. The gods in heaven, despite their sublime light-wisdom, did not know the mystery of death. Even before the Mystery of Golgotha, mortal men had really no reason to be envious of the immortal gods, for through their imprisonment in death they were acquainted with an important mystery in advance of the gods. Because they had to undergo death, which in fact runs through the whole of earthly life and at the drawing of the last breath only assumes its most extreme and concentrated force, people are experiencing something that the gods do not have. Only since the death of Christ have the gods had any share in this experience. To understand this truth has been one of the most important tasks of knowledge since the entry of Christianity into the world. For this reason Rudolf Steiner was never tired of fostering this insight from every new aspect.

The materialist thinks that man gets nothing from death; that it means simply a loss and an end. But in fact, we get far more from death than from life. It is through the process of death, permeating his whole life, that the human being encounters those experiences which bring him forward on his cosmic course. Without death he could not attain to any real progress in his evolution. But death also asks what degree of preparation and ripeness we have reached by the life we have led. Up to the turning-point of time people passed through birth and death without the help of the gods, because the gods themselves were without the experience of death. So it came about that death gained increasing power over humanity. At some time, therefore, something had to happen whereby divine help should be available to man in his passage through death. This happened with the death of Christ.

What was the difference between the Easter meeting of Christ with the disciples in the forty days and the appearances of the gods in ancient times? The fundamentally new thing was that the Christ was present among the disciples and spoke to them with all the experiences and consequences of his earthly bodily life and his earthly human death. He showed himself to them as a spirit-form which was interwoven with the effects of death in a way that had never before been possible to a divine being. The Risen One bore in himself an achievement of which hitherto the spiritual world itself was ignorant. He was more than a manifestation of spirit; he bore not, it is true, a corruptible body, but a body nevertheless. The light-sheath in which he appeared radiantly before the disciples was at the same time woven

out of all his victories over what was earthly, and out of the consequences of his triumphant passage through death. Manifesting a life
that was not merely identical with that of the divine heights, but which
represented at the same time an advance and an octave of death, the
Risen One could reveal to the disciples deeper secrets than were ever
before imparted to men by their gods. In the words which he spoke to
the disciples there was not only the highest divine wisdom, but the
sum of all the possibilities of knowledge which Christ had won from
the depths of the defeated powers of death.

The understanding of the Easter mystery will lead to a revaluation
of the fact that we have to live and die in earthly bodies. If we go
through birth and death accompanied by the force of the Risen Christ,
we take part in the founding and creating of a spirituality that is not
attuned merely to an abstract beyond, but is capable of rooting itself in
the facts of earthly existence. We grow into that power of the spirit
over matter which announces itself in archetypal form in the story of
Easter, when the Risen One takes food and drink in the midst of his
disciples and offers his hand and his side to the doubting Thomas that
he may touch him.

Remembrance and the meeting with the spirit

What was the language in which the Christ spoke to the disciples during the forty days? Obviously, he did not speak in ordinary human language, any more than did the angels of whom the gospel speaks.
Speech and hearing were experienced more within the soul than
through the intermediary of mouth and ear. But the inner speech and
hearing were of such intensity that in the consciousness of the disciples they resembled external speech and hearing.

An important clue to the soul-sphere is given in the *Pistis Sophia*
by the scene of these conversations. Why is it that the quotations
from scripture occupy a very large place? It is the same principle
which we have observed in St Luke's account of Easter. It is of such
importance that at the risk of repetition we must examine it in detail
once more.

The two disciples who are on their way to Emmaus do not know
what to make of the impressions of the last days. But their intense
effort to get their memory clear leads them to the experience that one

walks beside them and speaks to them. This third one takes them through the books of Moses and of the prophets, calling up into their memories a series of writings which suddenly appear to them in a new light. Thus on Easter Sunday a supersensory instruction takes place, the structure of which is determined by words from the Old Testament. Out of these familiar texts a light falls suddenly upon the event which their souls have been struggling to understand.

This is a process of soul similar to the one released in the women when the two men in white garments say to them, 'Remember how he spoke to you when you were still with him in Galilee.' The angel quotes a saying of Jesus, a text of scripture. Thus the women in the morning go through an experience somewhat like that of the disciples in the evening on the road to Emmaus; in recollecting words that had been spoken earlier and suddenly understanding them anew, they begin at the same time to understand the enigmatic event that has burst upon them. In these scenes, too, nothing is said outwardly. The words arise within them, although they cannot on that account be discounted as merely subjective. This inner hearing has at least the same objectivity as outer hearing with the physical ear. The first result of this supersensory language is that words from the holy scripture occur to the women and the disciples, or words that Jesus had once spoken. Memory speaks in the soul, and Christ and the angels make use of memory's language to speak in this way to the souls of men.

From this the experiences of the disciples during the forty days can be understood. The sound of Christ's voice was still in the ears of those who had been near to him. By recalling the sound of his words in memory, they felt him once more in their midst, as if he were speaking to them. The recollection of Jesus' words became to them an ear for the present speech of the Risen One. And even when at first the words which came to their consciousness were the same words which the Lord had then spoken to them, they were still something quite new. All that previously had only lived between the lines now expanded into a glorious teaching. The saying was fulfilled, 'The Comforter, the Holy Spirit, will teach you all things, and bring all things to your remembrance that I have said unto you.' In the instruction which the Risen One gives to the disciples the Holy Spirit also speaks.

The origin of the gospels

If the disciples had possessed nothing more than their ordinary recollection of the past three years, the four gospels would not exist. It is a mistake to suppose that the gospels originated as ordinary reports of external events. Their source is in the inspired, heightened memory of the forty days, when everything became once more really present. Everything, especially the words of Jesus, resounded on the background of cosmic perspectives which we can recapture today through a meditative penetration into the gospels. The mystery of recollection has its counterpart in the mystery of forgetting. What wretched creatures men would be if they could not forget! If we could not forget, we would soon end up in an asylum. The power to forget is a blessing indeed.

It is interesting to observe how we forget some things more easily than others. Thoughts relating to the supersensory and to the divine are usually forgotten very quickly, because they will not accommodate themselves to intellectual memory. It is common experience that books which impart knowledge of the spiritual world have to be gone through over and over again, and yet each occasion seems like the first.

What is forgotten is not lost, however. It has sunk into a deeper, unconscious layer of our being. When one says that something has got into our very bones, this points to the positive side of forgetting. Everything of value received by our consciousness must at some time pass into the deeper regions of our being, just as food and drink does. What we properly forget is changed into a force in the sphere of our will.

Think how we have forgotten what we experienced in the first three years of our lives. Why has it been forgotten? Because children under three are not yet completely upon the earth, and still reach into the heavens with the most important part of their souls. We have also forgotten what we experienced before our birth, when we passed through the aeons and spheres of the spiritual world. So too we forget everything that we experience in the night while we are asleep, apart from a few fleeting dreams. What a blessing it is for us that each night we are allowed to plunge into a world which we will not remember until after death! The world before birth, the world of early childhood, the world of sleep, all these we forget, because it is the spiritual part of our being with which we lived, and live, there. Even those who deny the spiritual world have dwelt in it before their birth, and dwell in it every night; only they have forgotten it. All of us before we came down to earth lived with angels and beings of other spheres. The memory of it has sunk deep into the depths of our being. Even for materialists the spiritual world has passed over into flesh and blood. Our present intellectual thinking has little to do with the real spirit. We take part in the spiritual all the more through that part of our being which retains what is forgotten. Psychoanalysts have discovered that certain experiences and sensations of early life have been forgotten, and as 'complexes' have become causes of illness. They attempt to cure these illnesses by drawing up the complex into consciousness. But for the most part the content that the psychoanalyst seeks to wrest from oblivion is so earth-bound that it is questionable whether the process will do more harm than good. Would it not be a far better method of healing to summon from the depths of man's being, not those forgotten realms which make him ill, but those which make him well, the real spiritual worlds?

All true art and religion owes its existence to such remembrance. All beauty and enlightened devotion rises from instinctive spirit-memory. Art and religion spring from that delicate awakening and recollection which are experienced when on emerging from sleep certain dreams are remembered, or when suddenly whole scenes from childhood are conjured up by some scent or other impression. On such occasions the memory seems to come from a completely different sphere, and this experience gives a hint of that part of our being into which we continually 'forget' the spiritual world. To this sphere belongs also the well-known experience of feeling that this is not the first encounter with a certain landscape or person, although we know quite well that in our present life it must be so.

Natural religion rests on the rising up of memories of our pre-earthly time in the spiritual world, bestowed upon us as a grace. It is not for nothing that the religious man calls heaven his home. Where a religious community gathers around an altar, in and above the common life of a group of people memory of the spiritual world breaks through. It is the nature of a true, spiritually valid ritual that it reflects on earth the angelic activities which we witnessed before birth.

Sacramental communion, seen from this angle awakens — apart from the sensation of becoming one with the divine — distant memories of the way in which we were nourished before we were born on earth.

When the disciples sat at table in the upper room, where on Maundy Thursday they had shared the meal with Christ, and now broke bread among themselves, the glory of Christ was in their midst and their memories held them spellbound. The eating of the sacred meal was memory in action. And thus the presence of the Risen One among the disciples was a real fulfilment of his command: 'This do in remembrance of me, that my being may really be present.' This saying was acted upon during the whole of the forty days. Out of the most wonderful experience that could ever happen to them, the disciples knew with absolute certainty, 'When we eat bread and drink wine in his name, then he is in our midst.' Out of these experiences the gospels came into being.

And one can see why Eastern Christianity to this day holds as the most certain and self-evident foundation of Christian life that the Risen Christ instituted the sacrament of the altar in the time between Easter and Ascension. If the *gospels* are the first fruit of the teaching of the Risen One, then the second fruit is the *sacrament*. The *light* of the forty days is collected in the gospels. The *warmth* of the conversations with the Risen One is perpetuated in the sacrament. The name Pistis Sophia, given to the human soul in the Coptic gnostic writings, embraces these two poles of Christian life. The disciples participated in rich measure in *Sophia*, wisdom, through the illumination imparted by the Risen Christ. Through their communion with him, *Pistis*, faith, the divine force of the heart filled with warmth, lived in them; and from that source, in the room of the Easter meetings, it has kindled a flame throughout the world. This faith is within us as an organ for the remembrance of heaven, and thus also an organ with which in our own time we can perceive the Risen One, and receive light and warmth from his being.

CHAPTER THIRTEEN

The Stages of the Risen Christ

Metamorphoses

The Christ-being never stands still. He is engaged in a continuous, never-ending transformation of himself for the benefit of humanity. The stages of transformation of the Christ-being extend not only over the Christian, but also over the pre-Christian epochs of the history of humanity. The progressions of the Christ-being through the cosmic spheres beyond the earth can be summarized as the *metamorphoses of pre-existence*. They represent the first stage. Pre-Christian religions are full of the light that shines from the successive stages reached by the Christ as he moves from sphere to sphere towards the earth. The second stage is that of *becoming man*. This is introduced by the baptism in the Jordan, when the divine ego of Christ enters earthly incarnation. *Death and resurrection* represent the third stage. They are a further step along the same way that led to earth from the cosmic heights. Through the events of Good Friday and Easter Day the Christ-being begins to unite himself with the whole earth. *Ascension,* as the fourth stage, although in apparent contradiction to the usual conception, sets the seal upon Christ's union with the earth; it is a complete outpouring of himself into the whole earth sphere. *Whitsun* is the fifth metamorphosis. The subsequent stage is announced for the first time in that midday hour at *Damascus* when the Risen Christ appears to Paul, who was at that time still his enemy. The seventh stage is still to come. This future metamorphosis, of which we are experiencing the beginning in our own day, is what we are accustomed to call the *Second Coming of Christ.*

In the preceding chapters material has been presented for a contemplative study of the first three stages. For an understanding of

Ascension as the fourth stage, it is illuminating to compare the forty days between Easter and Ascension with the forty days in the wilderness. When Christ faced the temptation, he underwent a transformation of his own being without which he would not have been able to work among people in the way he wished to do. After the divine ego of Christ had entered with all its cosmic power the narrow dwelling of a human body and soul, the cosmic content still surged above and around the earthly vessel. Had the Christ gone about among the people immediately after the baptism, overwhelming magical activities would have emanated from him. He had to feel it as a temptation of the devil that he should thus exercise the irresistible compulsion of his divine power. But his will was to be a brother to man, becoming one like all others. And so he withdrew into solitude for forty days, not only out of modesty, but in order that his being should attain the desired balance between divine and human. The forty days of the temptation signify the transmutation of a special condition of his being which occurred only once. At the end of the forty days Christ is really able to begin his life and work as a man among human beings.

And so the forty days between Easter and Ascension also represent the transmutation of a special condition of his being which occurred only once. In the victory over death at Easter the light and fire of Christ's will broke through with overwhelming power. When the disciples saw the form of the Risen One the very first stages of the gathering of this overwhelming spiritual force into a spirit-body had just been attained. But the irresistible force with which the Christ-will was directed towards the earthly body remained so great that the disciples' experience of the Risen One extended right into their sense-perceptions, although he was not present in a physical form. So powerfully did the spiritual will of the Risen One press towards the sphere of earthly visibility that he became perceptible to physical faculties. Had Christ remained in this special condition, he could have made himself miraculously manifest everywhere to people who acknowledged him. People would have had to believe that he was in their midst in a physical body, and would not have perceived that his form was a spiritual one.

Once again, a continuance of this special condition could not lie in the will of Christ. It was never his purpose to overpower the soul and spirit of the earth, but always to permeate it. And so, as he goes on to the further stages of his self-transformation, this special condition comes to an end. Christ's sudden disappearance from the eyes of the disciples on Ascension day marked the end of this stage and at the same time his entry into a new stage of becoming, which does not lead him away from the earth, but nearer to it. Christ enters thereby a state which brings him near to everyone in the same way. It is the state of earthly omnipresence. He lives and breathes henceforth with the soul of the whole earth. He sacrifices for the benefit of humanity the special condition through which he first had to pass. In place of the unique Easter *event*, the Easter *sphere* is permanently present in the entire earth.

The apostolic mission

The Gospel of John, which does not mention in so many words either Christ's Ascension or the event of Pentecost, nevertheless makes an important contribution to the understanding of the Christ's stages of transformation after the Resurrection. In his Easter stories, St John anticipates Ascension and Pentecost. When Mary Magdalene recognizes the Christ in the form of the gardener and would embrace him, he says to her, 'Do not touch me, for I have not yet ascended to the Father. Now go to my brothers and say to them: I ascend to the Father who gives existence to me and to you and who lives as a divine power in me and also in you.' And when on that same Easter evening the Risen One appears to the disciples in the upper room, he says to them, 'As the Father has sent me, so I send you.' And the gospel goes on, 'And when he had said this, he breathed on them and said, "Receive Holy Spirit".'

Mary Magdalene is made aware of the Ascension as of something to come. The outpouring of the holy spirit, on the other hand, seems from John's description to be already beginning. By implication the gospel seems nevertheless to convey that the Ascension also is a process which has begun directly after Easter. The fact that Christ says 'Do not touch me, for I have *not yet* ascended to the Father' must remain quite incomprehensible if one thinks of the Ascension in the usual way, as the withdrawing of Christ from the earth into a sphere beyond. If Mary Magdalene may not touch the Risen One now as he stands before her, how is she to touch him when he has ascended into heaven?

We come to realize that the Gospel of John is intent on introducing us into the secret of the Ascension. For after a week has passed, the Risen One says to Thomas the very opposite of what he had said to Mary Magdalene. He invites Thomas to touch him. Does his saying, 'I have not yet ascended to the Father,' no longer hold good? Obviously, the Gospel of John envisages the Ascension as a mysterious growth and an intensified manifestation of the spirit-body of Christ here, on 'this side.' Because the Ascension, as an outpouring of himself into the whole earthly sphere, has already begun, even while he is still passing through a special stage, Thomas can touch his body with his hands. The Resurrection is like a bud which will blossom into the subsequent transformations of the Christ.

The first two gospels contain an exact parallel to the passage in John. According to Matthew and Mark, the angel at the grave says to the women, 'Go quickly to his disciples and say to them: He has risen from the dead and will lead you to Galilee where you will behold him.' Here the disciples are to be told that Christ is on his way to Galilee; in St John, that he is ascending into heaven. The exact correspondence of these two sayings shows that they both refer to the same process of self-transformation. The women are given the task of conveying to the disciples that Christ is now advancing further in the course of the great offering of himself.

Now light falls upon the Galilee scenes in the Easter story. There can be no question of the disciples having actually returned to Galilee between Easter and Whitsun. They remained in Jerusalem, as according to the Gospel of Luke Christ had commanded them to do. The two Easter scenes in Galilee given by Matthew and John, on the mountain and by the lakeside respectively, have to be understood imaginatively. In each of them Galilee represents a landscape of the soul into which the disciples are withdrawn when they meet the Risen One. Christ pursues his own course of transformation and carries the souls of his disciples with him. The important synoptic parallels containing the angelic injunctions to the women show that Galilee is a stage in Christ's path of Ascension. The Christ-being who has overcome the power of death, which would retain him in the other world, pours himself out and grows into the atmosphere of the earth, so founding a heaven upon earth. The souls of the disciples are drawn into this marvellous flowering. Although their bodies remain in Jerusalem, they themselves are withdrawn from their bodies into Galilee, into its sunny landscape on the mountain and by the lake. This spiritual journey means that they are taking part in the first stage of the Ascension of Christ. Gathered together in the quiet upper room, they receive in advance, in the soul-landscape brought about by the nearness of the Risen One, something of the experience that will be theirs forty days after Easter, when Christ will surprise them by appearing under the open sky on the summit of the Mount of Olives. On Ascension day the process of growth, which had already expanded the room in which they were assembled into a wonderful Galilee of the soul, reaches a definitive stage. No wonder that the quiet park on the Mount of Olives, an extension of the Garden of Gethsemane at a higher level, seemed to them henceforth like Galilee transported into Judea. The wood on the quiet northern slope of the summit of the mountain is called 'Little Galilee' to this day.

In this significant springtime of the year 33 there lights up for the disciples an inner scene of spring on the very spot which looks out on an impressive view of the barren Judean desert. A potential sun is formed in the realm of the dying earth. This is the result of the Ascension of Christ, through which heaven receives earthly fruit, and the earth heavenly.

Galilee means 'the country of nations.' The growth of the Risen One beyond himself is a great gift of himself to humanity. Abandoning the special state in which he could only draw near to a few individuals in a supernatural way, Christ poured himself out into the sphere of the forces of the earth so that henceforth he is near to everyone. If in this process he seems to pass through earthly localities, it is because the different landscapes of the Holy Land are at the same time archetypes of the regions of the soul which surround the earth. The road from Judea to Galilee, representing the transition from confinement within one's own race and nation to a life in common with the people of all the world, is now followed in the spirit.

From this standpoint a new understanding can be gained of the mandate which the Risen One gives to his disciples. Matthew makes him say on the mountain in Galilee, 'Go forth and be the teachers of all peoples.' John writes that on the shore of the lake he directed his call particularly to Peter. But according to John, the Risen One also spoke to the disciples of their mission the first time he stood in their midst. And in doing so he breathed into them the breath of the holy spirit. In this scene Whitsun is foreshadowed at Easter time. 'As the Father has sent me, so I send you.'

None of these sayings was spoken with human words. The whole being of Christ speaks to the disciples through the movement and processes of growth in which he is engaged. The process of Christ's earthly Ascension constitutes in itself the sending forth of the disciples. It is by allowing their souls to be drawn into this process that the disciples realize that they must go into the world as apostles.

To make visible through word and sacrament the universal presence of the Risen Christ which was established by his Ascension — that is the meaning of the Christian apostolate and priesthood. That it is possible, by preaching the Christian message and by celebrating the sacred act to bring to all peoples the experience of the direct presence of Christ in different parts of the earth at the same time, is the result of the process of growth into which the disciples were caught up on the day of Ascension and beyond it. Since that time there exists upon earth an omnipresent Galilee of everlasting springtime.

Whitsun

On Whitsun morning, at sunrise in the upper room, the fire of holy enthusiasm comes over the assembled disciples. This is the culmination of all the Easter experiences during the forty days — those 'in the house' as well as those 'on the mountain' and 'by the lakeside.' Since the night of Gethsemane the disciples had found themselves in a strange state. They were not fully masters of their consciousness. Deeply moved as they were by the wondrous pictures and sayings that accompanied their meetings with the Risen One during the forty days, these had passed through their souls only like potent dreams. Even the experiences referring to their apostolic mandate came to their consciousness only as a dim vision. Their souls were far withdrawn, especially in the ten days between the Ascension and Whitsun, when the meetings with the Risen One had ceased and they were in danger of sinking into the abyss of a cosmic loneliness and sorrow.

Suddenly on Whitsun morning they were again in possession of themselves. The rushing wind and the flames of fire were the accompaniments to a mighty awakening. Just as when we wake from sleep in the morning we bring with us the fruits of our nocturnal journey through the heavens, so now it was not only the human egos of the disciples which returned to them. In each of those egos glowed the fruits of their Easter and Ascension withdrawal. The Christ-ego in the egos of the disciples, the Christ-spark which the souls of the disciples had brought back from their participation in the Ascension of the Risen One — this is what constituted the 'fiery tongues' which blazed forth from their heads.

The souls of the disciples were the bearers of something akin to what is in the soul of nature in spring. The enchantment of the springtime flowering usually culminates round about Ascension tide. By Whitsuntide, most of the blossoms have already fallen to the earth. It seems as if the climax of beauty is now over. But it lives on invisibly in the formation of the fruit. Now we see how the miracle of Ascension is tangibly embodied in the earth. Fruits are the gift that the soul of the earth collects during its ascension. A clairvoyant perception of nature at Whitsuntide would see the seed-cases of the plants aglow with tiny flames. So it was with the souls of the disciples when on Whitsun morning the great Christ-awakening came to them.

The ecstasy of Easter gives way to the indwelling of Whitsun. The fire of Christ pouring itself out even more freely into the circumference of the earth, now begins to be born as fiery sparks also in the souls of men. The Risen One lives on as seed in the souls of his own, who are thereby enveloped in spiritual flames. Human beings are the firstfruits of the new creation. The 'Christ in us' is the beginning of the fruitful indwelling of the Christ in all that is earthly.

To the disciples the spiritual fire dwelling within them came to consciousness as courage and force for the realization of their mission. While previously the ascending Christ had carried them along with him in his process of becoming and had shown them from a higher level and in pictures the range of their apostolate, now the indwelling of the Christ-ego bestows upon them the courage to go forth into all lands and to confront all the demons of the world with the sword of the Word of Christ.

Damascus

When several years later Paul meets on the road to Damascus him whom he believed he had a duty to oppose, this marks a new stage in the process of Christ's becoming. Paul's vision at Damascus does not arise only from within himself. Natural conditions play an important part in the experience. Even today, looking down on the city of Damascus from the neighbouring heights, one can still recognize the oasis which from ancient times has made it famous as an earthly paradise. Situated in the midst of desert landscape stretching far and wide under the burning sun, Damascus is situated in a green girdle of fruitful vegetation. At the turn of the seasons the character of Damascus as an oasis, its contrast with the burning desert surrounding it, may be still more clearly seen. If we can imagine that midday hour when the veil of the sense-world is torn from Paul's soul, the locality must seem predestined. As he crosses from the scorching glare of the desert into the cool shade of the oasis, suddenly the light of the Risen One shines overpoweringly on his awakening soul. The mysterious symbolism of the shadow is fulfilled: where the dazzling light of the rays of the sun recedes, the might of the spiritual sun is revealed. So does the sun-spirit, who has become the Spirit of the earth, announce his presence in the earthly realm to the dawning vision of Paul's soul.

This stage in Christ's metamorphoses, of which Paul is the first witness at Damascus, is given with precision in the words of the Act of Consecration of Man, the communion service of The Christian Community: 'Christ's Passion and Death, His Resurrection, *His Revelation.*' The redeeming self-transformation and sacrificial deed of Christ does not end with death and resurrection. As the Risen Christ progresses, he begins to appear to humanity in that continuation of his self-bestowal which is expressed in the word 'Revelation.' The hour of Damascus represents the beginning, the first manifestation of this all-embracing stage of existence, where we too must seek the Risen Christ today.

As the form seen by Paul at Damascus is a further development of the light-form of the Resurrection, so the consciousness that awoke in Paul at that hour points to the stage of consciousness to which man must rise if he is to find Christ at the stage of Revelation. To describe Paul as the first Christian theologian is a mistake. Were he no more than that, his Epistles would not form part of the New Testament. He is the first interpreter of 'Christ's Revelation.' His Epistles are not merely inspired in a general sense. In them the Risen One speaks at the Damascus stage. When in the eleventh chapter of the First Epistle to the Corinthians Paul says, 'I received these words, as I handed them on to you, from the Lord himself,' he is drawing attention to a specific level, a quite particular kind of spiritual life, which is the source of his teaching. Paul's outlook on life is inspired by Easter. Not for nothing does he describe himself as the last witness of the Resurrection just as he is the first witness of the 'Revelation' (1Cor.15).

The impulse behind Paul's journeys comes from a mighty urge to press outwards, which is characteristic of the Christ-being himself at his new stage. He who pours himself out into the earthly sphere and forms therein an ever-present Damascus, has become Paul's Master. The journeys of Paul bear witness to the growth of the sphere of Easter even more significantly than do the travels of the other apostles. It is very striking that the range of these travels coincides with the regions in which the olive tree grows. As early as 1913 Rudolf Steiner pointed this out in a cycle of lectures given in Leipzig with the title, *Christ and the Spiritual World;* and it has also been mentioned by Adolf Deissman in his book *Paulus.* The field of Paul's activity could be described as an extended Mount of Olives and Gethsemane. The role which the olive trees of Gethsemane play in the Mystery of Golgotha, as representatives of created life, is taken over by the olive tree for the whole sphere of Christ's activity represented by the journeys of Paul. The Epistles of Paul are influenced by the new atmosphere of the earth, the ever-present Damascus event. The new Spirit of the earth speaks in them through the words of the apostle.

In the accounts in the New Testament of the event at Damascus an apparent contradiction occurs which, however, may help to throw light on the path which can lead everyone to the sphere of Damascus. In one passage it says that many of Paul's companions see nothing, but hear voices, whilst other accounts describe how some are aware of the bright light, but hear nothing of what is said. The approach to the sphere of Damascus is to be found in a variety of ways. The development of some souls will lead them gradually to perceive the light-form of the Christ who is revealing himself. But many will have first to learn to hear the voice of Christ. The Epistles of Paul are a help to the attainment of this inward hearing. But the Paulinism of the present day must no longer be limited to a theology of his Epistles, but should be a permeation by the spirit of all our thinking and all our knowledge, not excluding the provinces of science; and a sense for the light of revelation in the events of life and destiny. An all-embracing open-mindedness leads to the hearing of Christ's voice as at Damascus, and to the seeing of the revelation of Christ.

The Second Coming of Christ

When the experience of Damascus becomes general, the mystery of Christ's Second Coming as a further stage in the revelation of his being will be realized. In our age the Second Coming of Christ should cease to be treated only as a future possibility. We are close to the point at which a synthesis of the Whitsun and Damascus experience can and must be found. Both the indwelling of Christ in the human soul, as well as his increasing permeation of the earth-sphere, can now come to maturity. On Whitsun morning the inward Second Coming began with the indwelling of Christ in the souls of the apostles, as the seed of the cosmic Second Coming. And when on Ascension day the Christ-being began to pour himself out into the whole earth, the seed was sown of his renewed cosmic existence, which one day is to grow through the Damascus stage into the stage of Second Coming. The image of the clouds, contained both in Luke's account of the Ascension and in all the sayings of Christ concerning his Second Coming, gives a helpful clue. When the atmosphere of the earth is saturated with moisture, clouds are formed. When the saturation is increased beyond a certain point, the clouds condense into rain. This simile can be applied to the mystery of Christ's Second Coming. When the sphere of the earth is completely saturated with the process of growth that has begun at Easter, when Christ has become quite close to the sphere of humanity, the light and the strength of Christ's Revelation will sink into souls opened to meet it as rain streams down to earth from the clouds.

In this sense, it may be said that Christ will come *like* the clouds of heaven. But this is even more than a simile. The clouds indicate a specific supersensory sphere. The moisture of the earth, which evaporates and is borne upwards in the air, becomes etherized in the heights before becoming physical again and condensing into cloud. The cloud does not arise simply out of the physical atmosphere. It is borne into the atmosphere out of the cosmic ether. Behind and beyond the cloud work the forces of the etheric sphere, whose physical revelation it is. This etheric sphere received the Risen One into itself, when forty days after Easter the clouds received him. Out of this sphere — the sphere from which the clouds of heaven are formed — he will come forth for those whose souls are ready for the experience of his Second Coming. That is why the gospel says, 'He comes on the clouds.'

In Luke's version of the parable of the ten pounds, the secret of the Second Coming is expressed in significant terms: 'There was once a man of noble birth; he went to a distant country to win the royal crown and then return home' (Luke 19:12). This picture describes the Christ who at his Second Coming will demand of people an account of how they have developed the seed of the spirit planted in their souls. Christ is like a king who sets out to acquire a new kingdom, for he pours himself out into the whole etheric circumference of the earth. But when he has quite filled this sphere, it will bring him close to humanity again. And this new nearness will lead to a testing and division of spirits.

The mystery of the Second Coming is fulfilled at the point where it becomes possible for the Risen One to be present at the same time without and within — when Damascus and Whitsun meet. Those who come to participate in the mystery will see the Christ in the circumference and at the same time feel him as a potent force within them, and at their side as a quite personal comforter and guide. Thus they will be equal to the bitterest trials of destiny.

The metamorphoses of the Risen Christ which follow upon Easter culminate finally into a unity:

The Ascension gives strength to uplift the soul, and with that comes the true *Christian joy.*

The event of Whitsun yields inner fruitfulness by kindling the spark of the ego in the soul. In response to its offering the soul receives the spirit. This is at the same time the true *Christian freedom.*

The experience of Damascus gives the profound insight which recognizes the spiritual in nature and reads revelation in all existence. There can no longer be any other source of *true wisdom.*

The Second Coming of Christ establishes the new divine friendship from which flows *cosmic consolation.*

Heaven and Ascension

The atmosphere after Easter is full of colour, warmth and light, the scent of flowers, the flight and song of the birds. In the heavens, too, the clouds sing their songs of praise, and rival the earth in the joy of 'becoming.' At no season of the year is the character of heaven and the heavenly forces so manifest, but still the important question arises: 'What is heaven?'

Modern science rightly defends itself against the belief in a 'beyond' which tears the universe into two; and a conception of the world that acknowledges the spiritual and supersensory in the cosmos must also reject this dualism. Where, then, lies the frontier between the earthly 'this side' and the 'beyond'?

Heaven is not in the distant 'beyond;' it is all around us; it fills us, and with us the entire existence of 'this side.' Materialistic thought combats dualism by extending 'this side' to infinity, thus suppressing the 'beyond.' In a spiritual picture of the world which takes into account the spiritual world, everything on 'this side' is permeated a thousandfold with the forces and the life of the heavenly 'beyond.'

However, closely as heaven and earth are bound together, their relationship is not always the same. Herein lies the miracle of the seasons — that the earth, through the breathing-in and breathing-out of its soul, is for a period wholly united with the heavens. The dualistic conception of the world is most nearly justified in winter time, when the heavens seem to retreat and leave the earth without the warm breath of life. Summer, however, is the annual refutation of dualism. The earth has then breathed itself fully out. Its soul is poured out into the heavens, is wedded to the heavenly heights, filled with light and warmth.

At midsummer and in midwinter, at St John's Tide and at Christmas, the soul of the earth holds its breath. It goes through exalted stages of rest — rest of complete penetration by the heavens, and the rest of the greatest degree of enclosure within itself. In between these two pauses are stages of intense metamorphosis. In springtime, at Easter and in the weeks that follow, the soul of the earth strives powerfully heavenwards, and in autumn, at Michaelmas, celebrates its farewell to the cosmic heights and prepares to plunge again into the depths of earth.

The time between Easter and Whitsun is the period when the

interplay between the soul of the earth and the heavenly forces is most obvious. When before and around Easter the plants begin to sprout, the earth at the same time bursts the grave which has held it prisoner through the winter ... A wonderful mood of growth, of joyful ascent and expansion, pervades the earth and its atmosphere in those weeks after Easter. At the time when our Christian festival of the Ascension falls, nature celebrates the ascension of the soul of the earth.

It was not by chance that the forty days during which the disciples experienced at Jerusalem the blessing of their great destiny — the destiny which enables them to communicate with the Risen One — coincide with the season of the year in which the soul of the earth seeks the heavens once more, and, filled with heavenly forces, draws new life from the soil.

That was the astounding miracle, the miracle that the disciples could not understand, but could only dimly divine, and that Christendom as a whole will only come gradually to understand — that Christ revealed himself in a new bodily condition; that through his Resurrection he established for earthly physical existence — indeed for the earth itself — the first beginning of a new becoming and a new life.

When a person dies, a tyrannical power wrests his supersensory being out of its earthly vehicle, and so out of 'this side' altogether. Our true being is immortal, but since death has power over us and tries to grasp complete power over everything earthly, the scene of our immortality is a sphere 'beyond,' completely separated from everything earthly. He who passed through death on Golgotha was more than man. And he conquered death. The dark power was not able to banish him to a 'beyond.' Resurrection is more than immortality; its scene is therefore the earth, and not a world beyond. The highest power of the spirit over earthly matter was at the disposal of the Risen One, and so he was able, through the new, incorruptible spiritual-physical condition in which he revealed himself to the disciples between Easter and Ascension, to found the first germinal beginning of a new earth. The direction of the activity of his being was not away from the earth, but towards it. This was brought home to the disciples when the Risen One in their midst asked, 'Have you nothing to eat?' and when he said to Thomas, 'Stretch out your finger and see my hands, and stretch out your hand and place it in my side.'

No idea is more mistaken than that the Risen One at his Ascension returned into the 'beyond' from which he once descended. He was not untrue to the earth when the cloud which enveloped him 'took him away' from the disciples' sight. He united himself with the earth in a more inward way. Neither is the soul of the earth unfaithful to the earth when between springtime and summer it celebrates its ascension. Just as the ascension of the soul of the earth in the natural course of the seasons brings abundant heavenly forces to the benefit of the earth, so too it is only Christ's Ascension that bestows upon the earth and embodies within it the divine forces of heaven in the fullness of their sun-nature. The disciples beheld the Risen One in the midst of a wonderful atmosphere of spring. They saw him rising and growing outwards with the rising and expanding soul of the earth. And he disappeared from their sight only because their souls were not strong enough to follow him. It was at that time that he became 'Lord of the heavenly forces upon earth.' Pouring himself out into the whole of the earth-sphere, he brought it about that the earth began to be a Heaven. A highest divine 'beyond' became inseparably interwoven and united with the earthly 'this side,' filling and ensouling it gradually more and more.

The feast of the Ascension, rightly celebrated and experienced, will one day contribute most of all towards dispelling the error that Christianity is an 'other-worldly religion.' No other festival in the Christian calendar can more clearly show that a rightly understood and rightly experienced Christianity is just what is needed to satisfy the hunger of our own age for a new religion of nature and of 'this side.' Every year, when the earth breathes out in springtime, the being and the force of the Risen Christ breathe out with it. At every ascension of the soul of the earth, the mystery of the Ascension of Christ, who is the Spirit of the earth, is renewed. When the capacity for perception is great enough, the experience of the Second Coming will be born in a special way out of the experience of the Ascension. In the clouds that took him away, the ascending one will reveal himself to spiritual vision as the Son of Man.

Meanwhile at Ascension time our hearts can learn to recognize the signs of the heavenly forces upon earth, to love and to cherish them. The flowers in their splendour, especially the roses, which shine in their most luminous crimson round about Whitsun and St John's day, are among the most beautiful images of the soul of the earth ascending. And the true images of Christ breathing himself out together with the soul of the earth are the fiery flames of the pentecostal spirit in the souls of men.

Descent into hell and ascent into heaven

When, after the wonderful forty days of Easter had come to an end, the disciples gazed helplessly up at him who was vanishing from their sight, and when the two men in white garments said to them, 'This Jesus, who has been taken up before you into heaven, will come again,' were they being referred for consolation to a far-distant future which they themselves would probably not experience? When Christ was still living in an earthly body he had once said to them, 'Among those who are standing here there are some who before they taste death, will see the Son of Man as he comes in his kingdom' (Matt.16:28). This was not holding out an indefinite future as a consolation to them. The gospel scene which directly follows shows the beginning of the fulfilment of that promise; on the mount of the transfiguration the three chosen disciples experience the commencement of the coming of the Son of Man in his kingdom. Nor was the Ascension-promise, which connected the secret of the Ascension with that of the Second Coming, a reference to the future. A seed of fulfilment was already contained in the event which the disciples witnessed without understanding it. And ten days later the event of Whitsun morning put the seal on that experience.

Of course, the first effect of the Ascension on the disciples was the bewildering sensation of great loss. Nevertheless, when every springtime the festival of the Ascension comes round again as a festival of inward gain and peaceful blessing, some truth must be hidden behind it. For those who live with the sacramental life of the Christian Community, the secret joy that this festival holds, lights up more and more. The Easter Act of Consecration of Man has been celebrated for forty days. Upon the bright red of the altar and the vestments, the green of the symbols has spoken of the new life of nature and of the soul. When Ascension day comes the Easter red remains, but gold takes the place of the green. We are led gently from the foreground of the world of the senses, with the riches of springtime, to the hidden, creative background of all things. Now we begin to perceive that all things rest upon a secret background of gold, from which they originate. The golden heaven that slumbers in all things would reveal itself in earthly things. The sphere of seeds and origins, which lies supersensibly behind all that is perceptible to the senses, opens, and enables us to recognize the heaven into which the Risen One entered at his Ascension.

As the experience of the Ascension lies between Easter and Whitsun, so between Good Friday and Easter lies the event which ancient Christian tradition called the descent into hell. According to the usual idea, Christ disappeared into a 'beyond,' both at his Ascension and on his descent into hell. One thinks of heaven as the upper beyond, and of hell — which in reality is all too definitely 'this side' — as the nether beyond.

What was in truth the way taken by the Christ after he had passed through the Mystery of Golgotha? Since he made himself a sharer in the destiny to which all men are subject, he entered the sphere of the souls of the dead. The direction taken by the dead is one which leads away from the earth. By rising into spheres beyond the earth, the dead free themselves from their attachment to 'this side,' and become citizens of the 'beyond.' If the soul frees itself easily, the process of dying can be easy. Souls which find it difficult to free themselves, because they have united themselves too fully with the untransmuted earthly, may remain for a long time chained as shadows in the neighbourhood of the earth, lacking the freedom of flight which would bear them forth into true immortality.

Before Christ came upon the earth as man, human souls were in danger of losing their power of flight, and thereby their true immortality. The ancient spiritual forces were exhausted, and the hardening earth gained an ever increasing power over souls. The dark mystery of the 'second death' came upon humanity. To the death of the body was added the still more terrifying death of the soul, that rendered a man incapable of raising himself to the true 'beyond.' The sphere of death then became Hades, the kingdom of the shades, and, as the New Testament puts it, a prison. But when Christ died on the cross, one entered into the sphere of the souls of the dead who was in possession of true immortality. He tore away the chains of darkness, and carried the free breath of light into the kingdom of the shades. Hence the first

Epistle of Peter thus describes the descent into hell: 'In the realm of earthly matter he suffered death; in the realm of the Spirit he won through to new life. And in the Spirit he also went and brought the proclamation to the spirits in prison, who once closed themselves off from the will of God ... That is why the Gospel has also been proclaimed to the dead.' (1Peter 3:18–19; 4:6).

The dead celebrated Easter before men on earth could do so. By his death Christ opened up again the paths of their destiny into higher spheres; through him they received strength to cut themselves free and to soar aloft. Thus in the sacramental rite that the Christian Community celebrates at the graveside, it says that Christ, through his death, has overcome the death of the human soul. And where the older creeds say 'descended into hell,' today we can say, 'In death he became the helper of the souls of the dead who had lost their divine nature.' Through Christ's descent into hell the 'beyond,' as the true source of immortality, was given back to humanity. The descent into hell rescued the 'beyond' for man; the Ascension rescued 'this side' for the divine.

To perceive aright the secret of the Ascension prepares men for Whitsun, the festival of fulfilment of the soul. An ascension of the striving human soul can unite itself with the ascension of the soul of the earth. As in springtime the earth is larger than it seems, so too man, if he strives towards the spirit, is greater than he seems, because he then grows beyond himself. Michael Bauer once said, 'Every glance upwards means the stirring of the forces of the will for the ascent; he who no longer looks up, no longer climbs.' By growing beyond itself the earth does not lose itself, but finds itself again in an enhanced sense. Neither does man lose himself when he climbs in a right way to the spirit. In fact, it is only then that he really does find himself in his higher self. When we look up to the form of Christ with the thought of the Ascension, we stand before a being who seizes hold of our own being, transforming it, and who wills to kindle in us the flame of the higher self.

If we practise the 'looking up to him,' of which the Act of Consecration of Man speaks at Ascensiontide, we shall be aware of a perpetual coming which announces itself within us, ever anew, through the fiery sign of the higher self. The festival of the Ascension is a special opportunity for entering into the secret of the Second

Coming of Christ. When it was said to the disciples, 'This Jesus, who has been taken up before you into heaven, will come again, revealed in the same kind of way as you have now seen him pass into the heavenly sphere,' (Acts 1:11), and when it says that Christ will come again on the clouds of heaven as at that time he was taken up into the clouds, it means that the Ascension of Christ was the seed of his Second Coming, and that his Second Coming is the fulfilment of the Ascension.

The Second Coming of Christ enhances and perfects the descent into hell, as well as the Ascension. He who dies in Christ dies in the pure, fresh dew of heaven which gives him courage for the 'beyond.' Therefore the dead who are united with Christ perceive his Second Coming, as Paul says in his Epistle to the Thessalonians, sooner than men on earth. *Christ gives to humanity the new Beyond.* And he who lives his life on earth in Christ is ever more able to receive the Christ on the clouds of heaven as a force of spiritualization and transmutation. *Christ gives to humanity the new 'this side.'* This is what makes the lines of Novalis a true prayer of the Ascension and the Second Coming:

> In heavy clouds let Him be drawn
> And so let Him be downward borne.
> In cooling streams let Him be sent,
> In flames of fire blaze His descent,
> In air and essence, sound and dew
> To permeate our whole earth through.

> *In schweren Wolken sammle ihn*
> *Und lass ihn so herniederziehen.*
> *In kühlen Strömen send' ihn her,*
> *In Feuerflammen lodre er,*
> *In Luft und Öl, in Klang und Tau*
> *Durchdring' er unsrer Erde Bau.*

(*Spiritual Songs*, 11)

Index of Biblical References

Psalms

2:7	43
23	253
110	246

Jonah

2:6	173

Matthew

4:11	114
4:12	80
4:17	57
5:1f	142
8:20	149
8:28f	142
9:6	151
15:34–36	166
16:4	118
16:16	120
16:17	120
16:18	121
16:27	117, 139, 153
16:28	322
17:9	149
17:12	149
17:13	182
17:22	149
18:11–14	140
20:18	149
21:16	242
23:13	248
24:1f	144
24:27	153
24:30	117
25:31	117, 153
25:31–33	140
25:40, 45	141

26:2	149
26:24	150
26:31	266
26:45	150
26:53	116
26:64	153, 219

Mark

1:13	114
1:14	80
1:15	57
1:24	168
1:32	161
2:27f	146
4:21f	135
8:22–26	166
10:37	108
10:45	146
15:21	206

Luke

1:35	152
2:49	63
3:21	131
4:21	176
4:34	62, 168
5:2f	74
5:9–11	75
5:16	131
6:12	131
7:5	178
7:14	184
9:18	131
9:28	131
9:58	149
11:1	131
11:8	131

Index

clairvoyance 73
Coliseum 30
Commodus 33
Coptic fragments 293
crown of thorns 221, 229
Crucifixion 107
Cyprus 23

Damascus 315–18
—, Paul at 308, 315
Damis 21
Deeps 297, 298
Dio Cassius 29
Diocletian 34
Dominus vobiscum 50
Domitian, Emperor 24, 30–32
Dostoevsky 40, 42
Dead Sea 78
death 300, 302f
Deissman, Adolf 316
Demetrius 23, 29
demons 167
Docetism 299
drama 212
draught of fish 74, 77

Easter 114, 319
Eastern Churches 292
Eleusinian mysteries 23
Elijah 173, 181, 182
Elisha 173
Emmaus, way to 303
Emmerich, Catherine von 91, 208f
Ephesus 23–26, 35
Epidaurus 158
Essenes 54f, 206, 208
Ethiopia 24
Euphrates (member of the Stoics) 30
Eusebius 18
Ezra 197

fakir, fakirism 55f
farewell discourses 144, 145
feeding of the five thousand 56, 106, 111, 119
fiery tongues 314

fig tree 110, 193f, 240–42
forty days in the wilderness 51
Francis of Assisi, St 156
Frederick the Great 16

Gabbatha 231
Galba 28
Galilee 95–97, 238, 311
Galilee, Little 312
—, Sea of 69–73, 78, 174
Gamaliel 201
Gennesareth, Lake of *see* Galilee, Sea of
Gethsemane 115, 256
Glastonbury 210, 211
gnosticism 292f, 301
gospels 307
Grail, the 184, 209
Gurnemanz 211
Gymnosophists 24

healing 89, 154, 156
— at the pool of Bethesda 119
— of the blind 166
— of the lunatic boy 165
— of Peter's mother-in-law 75
— of the man born blind 120, 160, 167
— of the man with palsy 119
— of the nobleman's son 119, 159
— of the woman with haemorrage 179, 180, 185
heaven 319, 322
Heliand (Heiland, saviour) 154
hell 322
—, descent into 169, 323f
Herod Antipas 57, 215–19, 227–29
Herodias 57, 216, 229
Hezekiah 173
Hierocles 18, 19
Hiram 209
Holy Grail 184, 209

'I am' sayings 134
incarnation 46, 102, 103, 107, 301
iconostasis 223

Emil Bock

Saint Paul

Describing the environment into which Saul was born, his education, his conversion before Damascus and his subsequent journeys, Bock's study gives a spiritual dimension to Paul's background, providing a deeper understanding of this great Christian figure and his teaching.

Above all Emil Bock shows that Paul was the apostle who carried Christianity beyond the Jewish communities to humanity at large. As a zealous Jew, Paul was convinced he was serving the coming Messiah in his persecution of the followers of Jesus. When the light suddenly came to him before Damascus his inmost being was opened. Here Paul shows that the time of the Law of Moses had run its course and conscience as 'inner jurisdiction' was now to replace the rules and laws imposed from without.

Floris Books

Emil Bock

Apocalypse

Bock interprets John's rich pictorial language, often found harsh and mysterious, and we understand that John is dealing with the universal problems of spiritual development. This is not just a detailed commentary on the Apocalypse. It is a profound and encouraging examination of human needs in today's world, and shows how we can read Revelation to understand Christ's position as leader through danger in the present and the future.

Floris Books